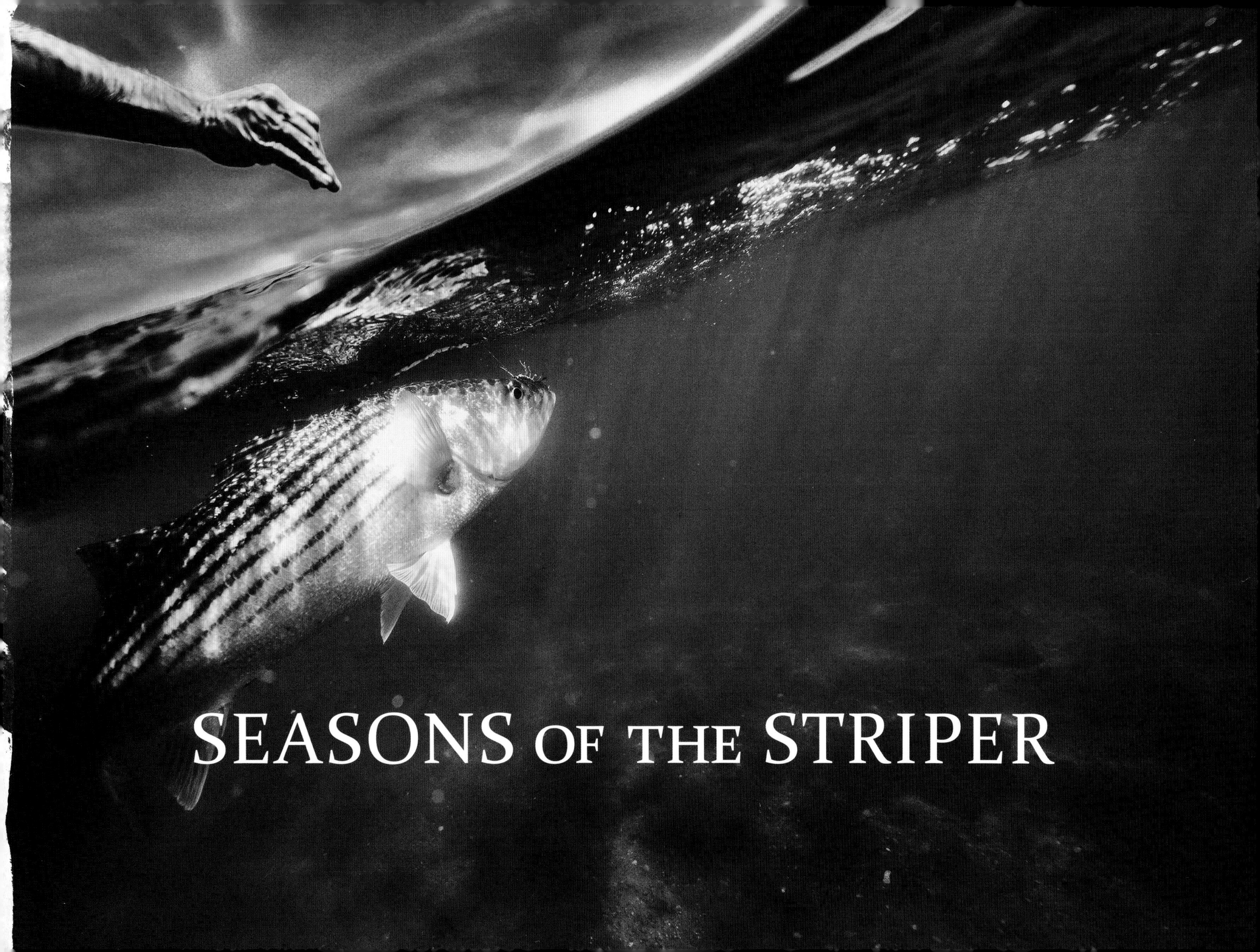

SEASONS OF THE STRIPER

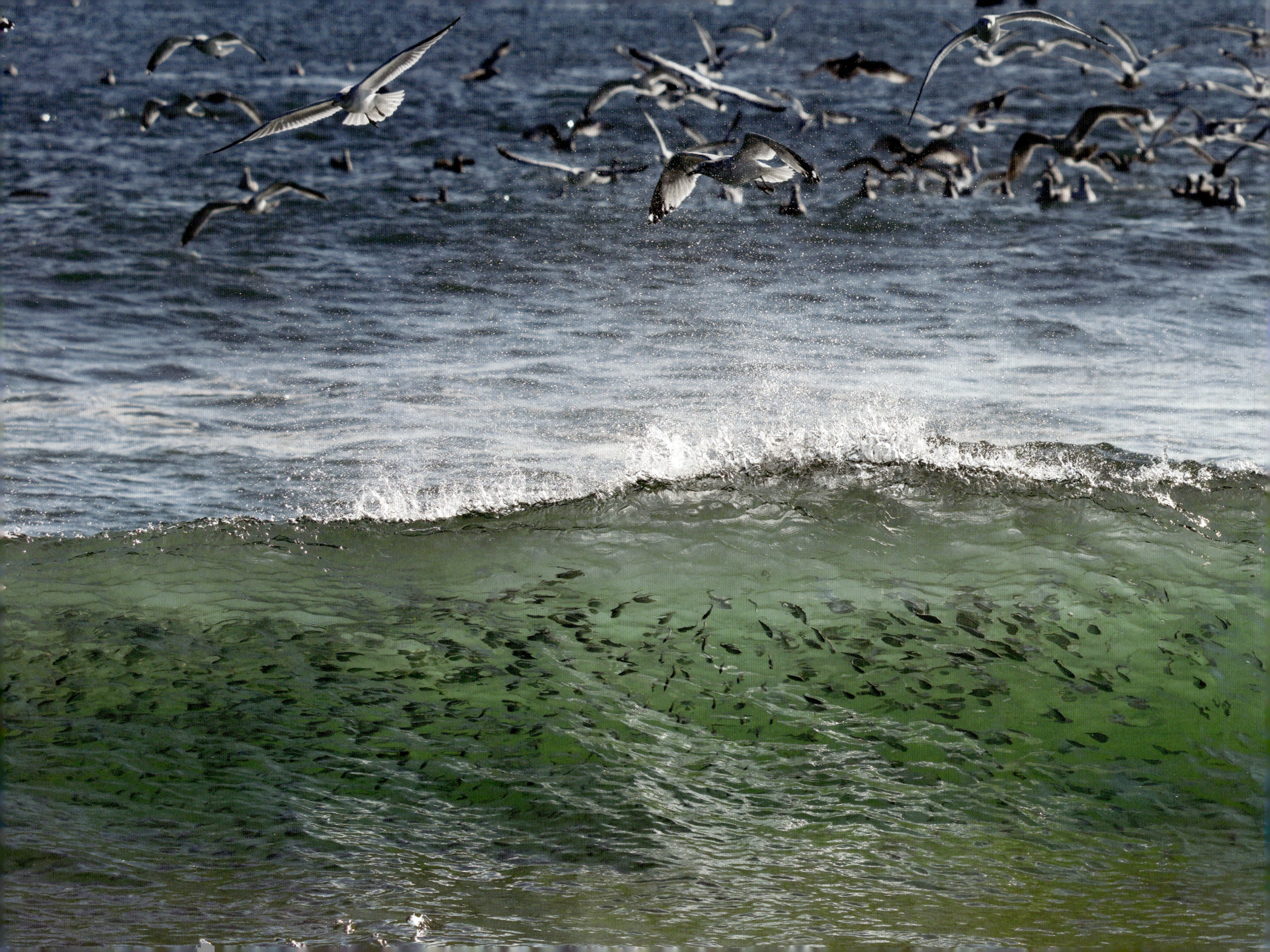

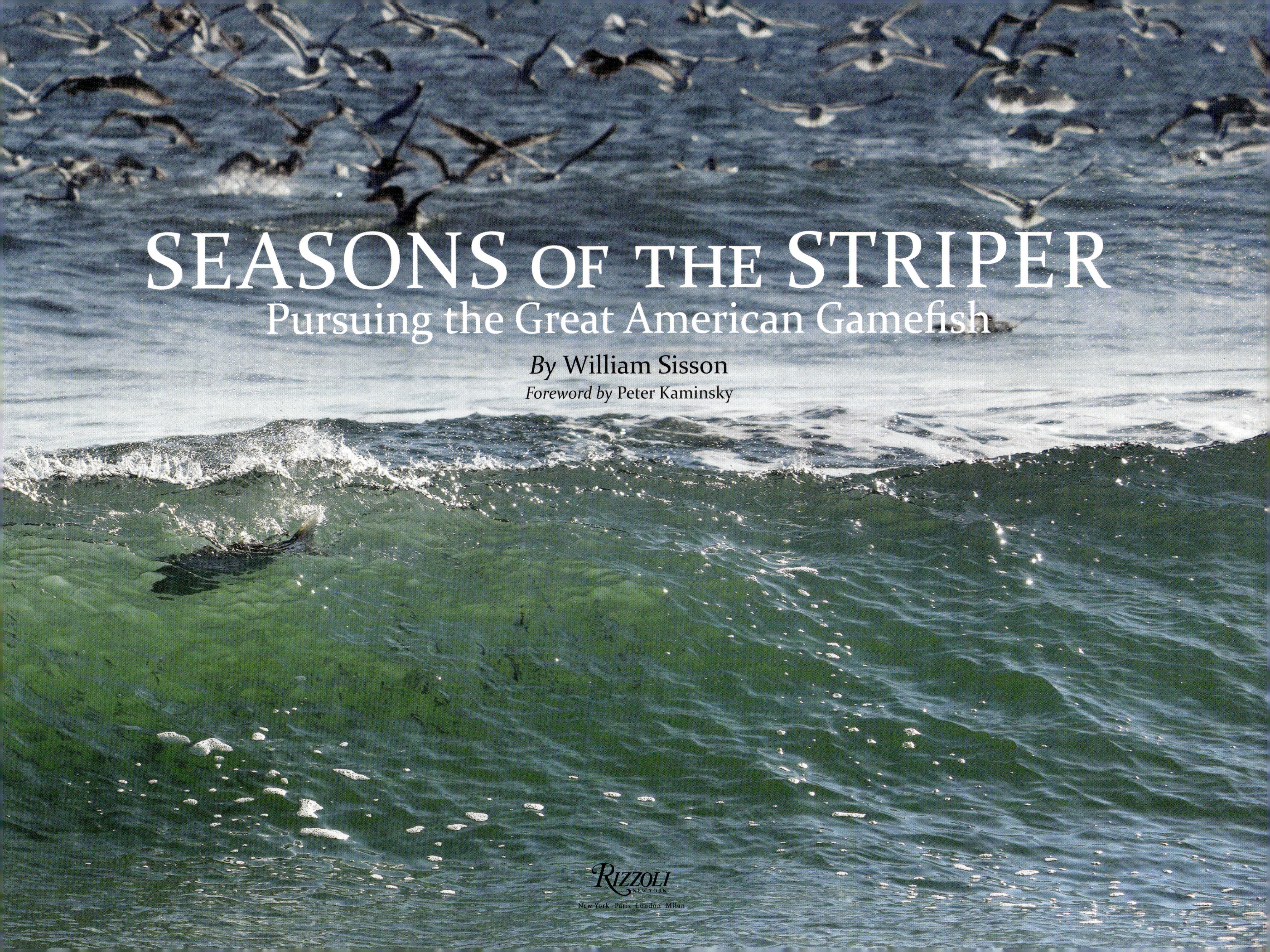

SEASONS OF THE STRIPER

Pursuing the Great American Gamefish

By William Sisson

Foreword by Peter Kaminsky

RIZZOLI
NEW YORK
New York Paris London Milan

ACKNOWLEDGMENTS

This book is dedicated to my wife, Patty, an outdoor girl and my creative partner, for her editing and unwavering support. Many thanks to my longtime collaborator Erin Kenney for her layouts and designs; to my friend Henry Hughes for his thoughtful suggestions; to Jim Muschett and Rizzoli International Publications for believing in the project; to my weekend readers, Michael LaBella and Carly Sisson; to *Anglers Journal,* where some of this content first took shape; to all the photographers who contributed, especially Tom Lynch, who was in it from the start; and to my mother and father, who introduced me to poetry and the sea, and indulged a boy's fascination with fishing.

First published in the United States of America in 2022 by
Rizzoli International Publications, Inc.
300 Park Avenue South
New York, NY 10010
www.rizzoliusa.com

Publisher: Charles Miers
Associate Publisher: James Muschett
Managing Editor: Lynn Scrabis
Editor: Candice Fehrman
Design: Erin Kenney

Printed in China

2022 2023 2024 2025 / 10 9 8 7 6 5 4 3 2 1

ISBN: 978-0-8478-7230-5

Library of Congress Control Number: 2022933562

Visit us online:
Facebook.com/RizzoliNewYork
Twitter: @Rizzoli_Books
Instagram.com/RizzoliBooks
Pinterest.com/RizzoliBooks
Youtube.com/user/RizzoliNY
Issuu.com/Rizzoli

Page 1: Photo by James Manning.
Previous spread: Photo by Tom Lynch.
Right: Photo by Don Schroder.
Following spread: Illustration by Nick Mayer.

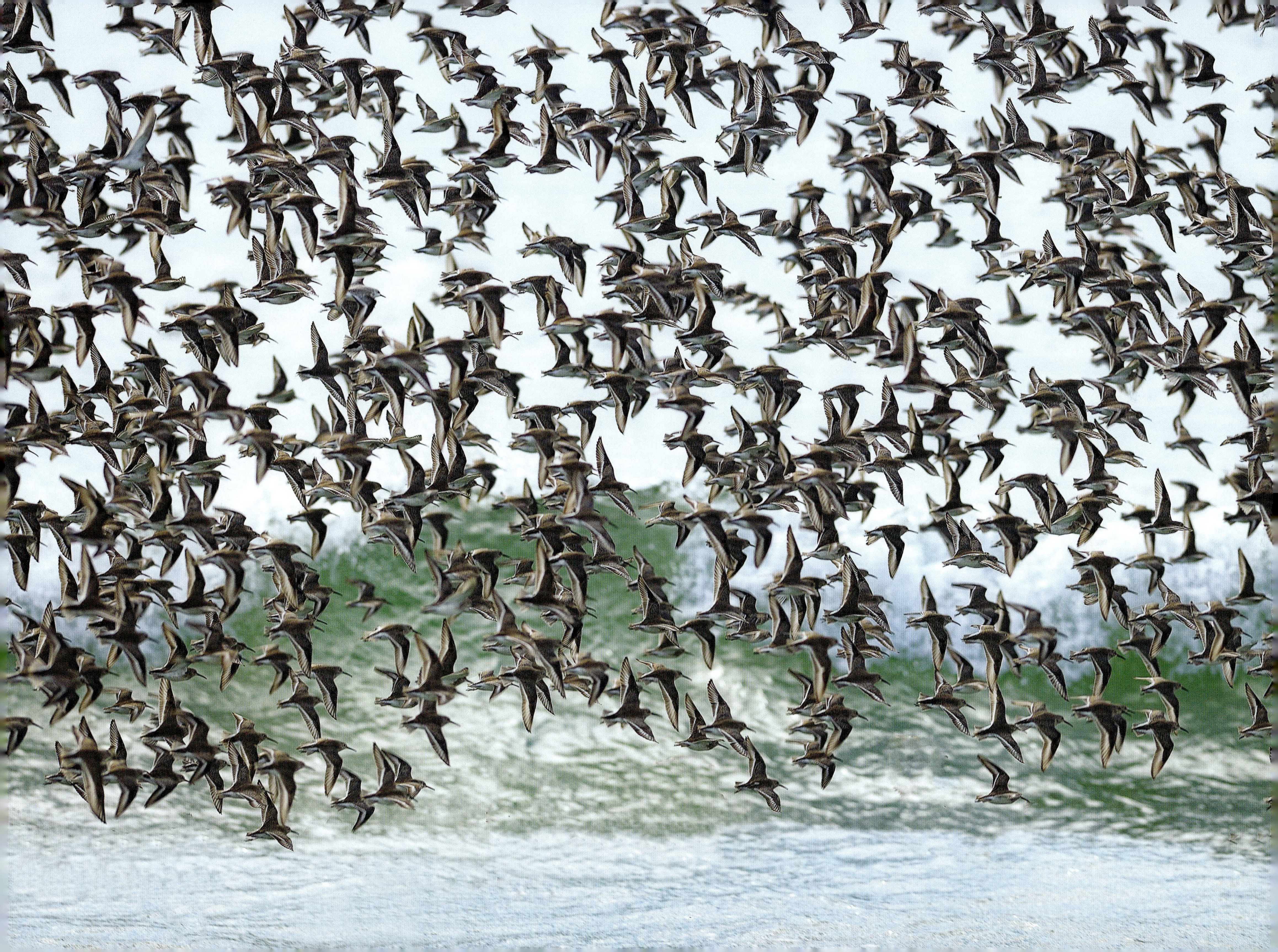

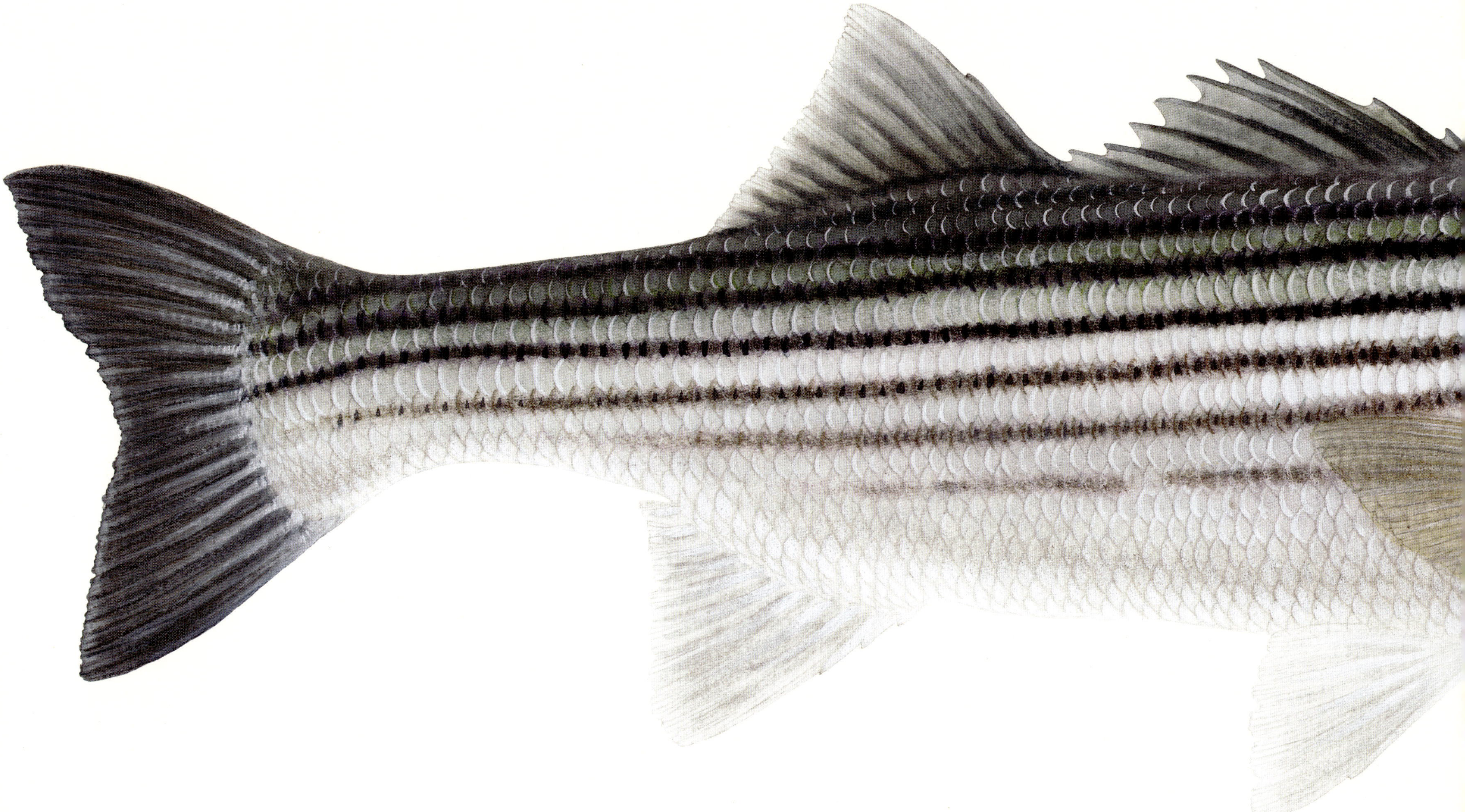

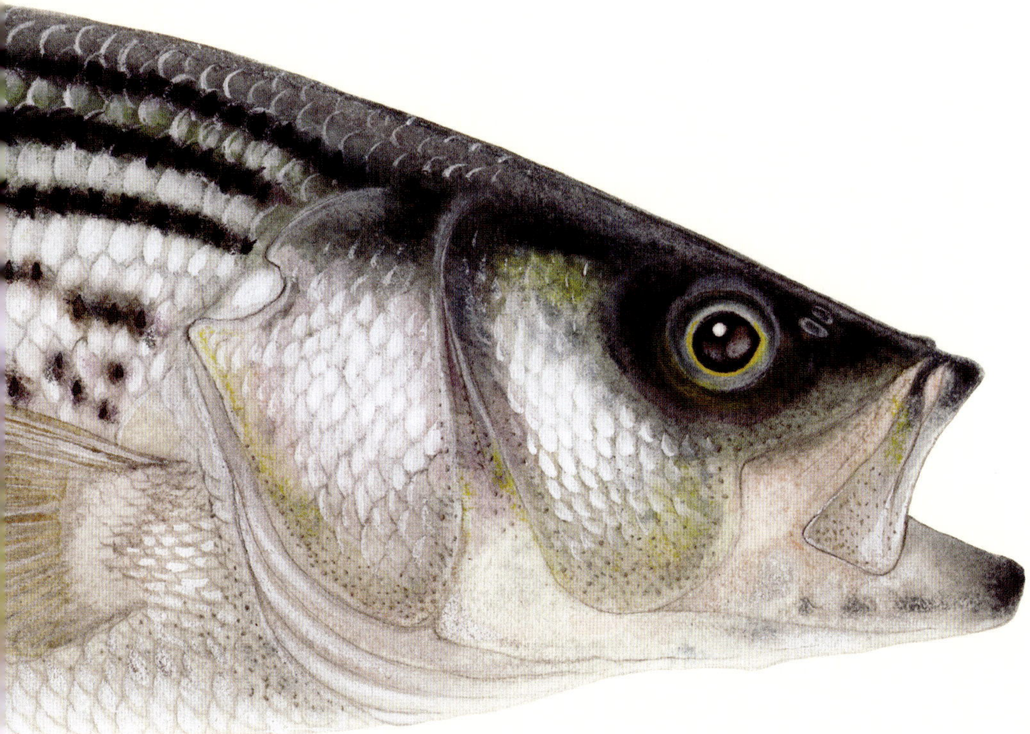

CONTENTS

FOREWORD

BY PETER KAMINSKY

"He will be exposed to the sea-breeze, or it may be the storm wind at early day-light, and the spray from the salt waves, and wet and cold will be his portion; but he will forget these trivial evils, when he strikes the bass of forty, fifty, or sixty pounds, the fish that he has been living for, and when he lands him safely on the slippery rocks."

—*Robert Barnwell Roosevelt,*
Superior Fishing, *1865*

For most of the time that we humans have been on this Earth, we have followed wild creatures through the cycle of seasons. We fed ourselves on their flesh and clothed ourselves with their hides. In the spring, we knew when the bison would graze their way north across prairies as wide as the ocean. We knew when passenger pigeons—six billion of them—would fly south in the autumn, darkening the skies like approaching thunderheads. We knew when salmon would fill the length of the Connecticut River from bank to bank.

It is only in recent times—the blink of a geologic eye—that people have lost this connection to the rhythms of nature. But if you are lucky enough to be a striper fisherman, you know what it's like to encounter the magic of wild creatures in a massive migration that once was the rule all over our green-and-blue planet.

Each spring, striped bass pour from their winter retreats in the Hudson River and Chesapeake Bay, streaming northward as the lengthening days warm the waters along the coast. The bass move in boisterous battalions, and we anglers are jolted from our winter doldrums, intoxicated with the pulse-quickening action. As the seasons progress, they spread out along white, sandy flats, rocky coves, and brackish bays. Spring's brawling wolf packs give way to fish in small groups, silver phantoms over white sand. Like bonefish cruising the flats, summer stripers are catchable, but equally as easy to spook. And then comes blessed fall! It's the season when all creation seems to riot and pulse with life on the move. Uncountable millions of living things head south: baitfish, blues, albies, and stripers, mile-long convoys of waterfowl, whales, dolphins, the whole panorama bejeweled with the passage of monarch butterflies.

I have fished for striped bass in New York City waters for more than 40 years. The discovery that I could catch them a short walk from my home near the Brooklyn waterfront rescued me from enjoyable, but not very successful, attempts to hunt grouse and woodcock in the Catskills. Instead, I could keep on fishing, some years until Christmas. Fly rod in hand, I have cast to stripers from the shores of Jamaica Bay, the piers of the Williamsburg neighborhood in Brooklyn, and the churning tides of Hell Gate.

Bill Sisson was born in the beating heart of striper country, in South County, Rhode Island. Of his earliest days, he wrote, "I was barely out of boyhood the first time I saw a striper race up the back of a big green breaker, chasing bait a moment before the wave toppled in a roar of foam and spray."

From that day until this, nearly half a century, Bill has haunted the beaches, coves, backwaters, and headlands of the Northeast in pursuit of striped bass. In these pages, he has fullheartedly distilled the wisdom of generations of striper-holics. He speaks to the inner angler of every fisherman who prizes the fish that looks, for all the world, like the rippling light of the moon on midnight waters.

Photo by Rex Messing.

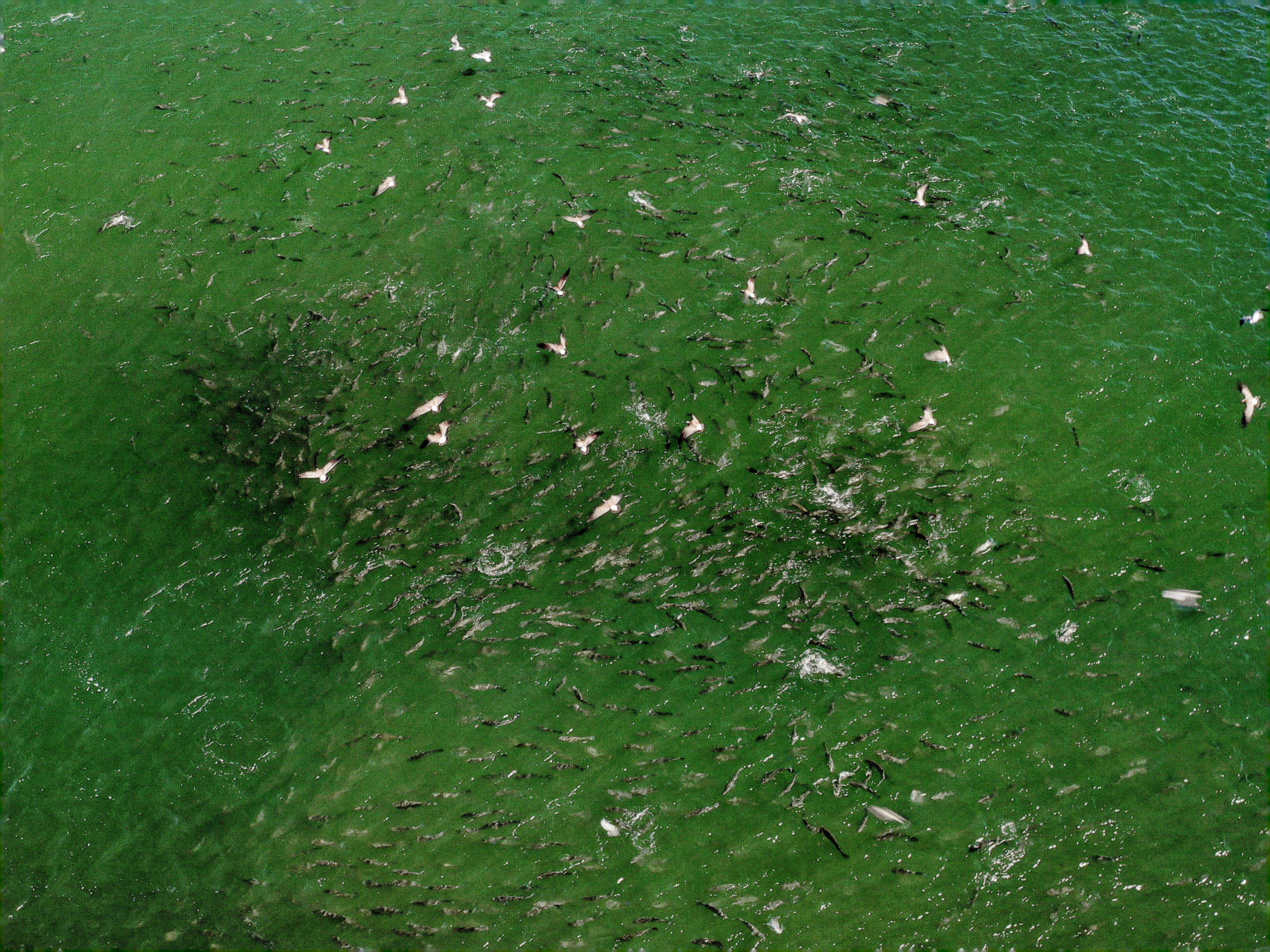

EDUCATION OF A BASS BUM

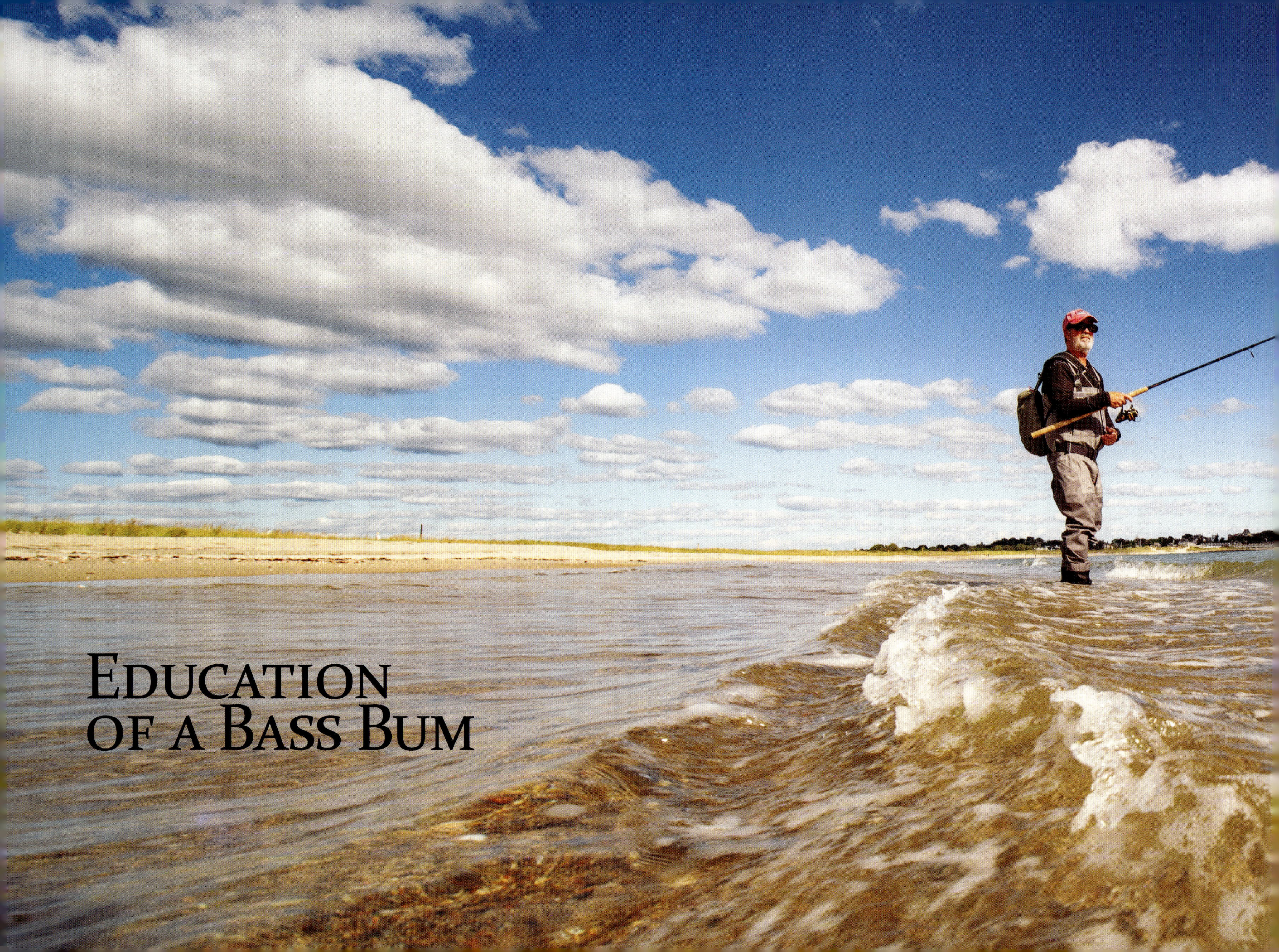

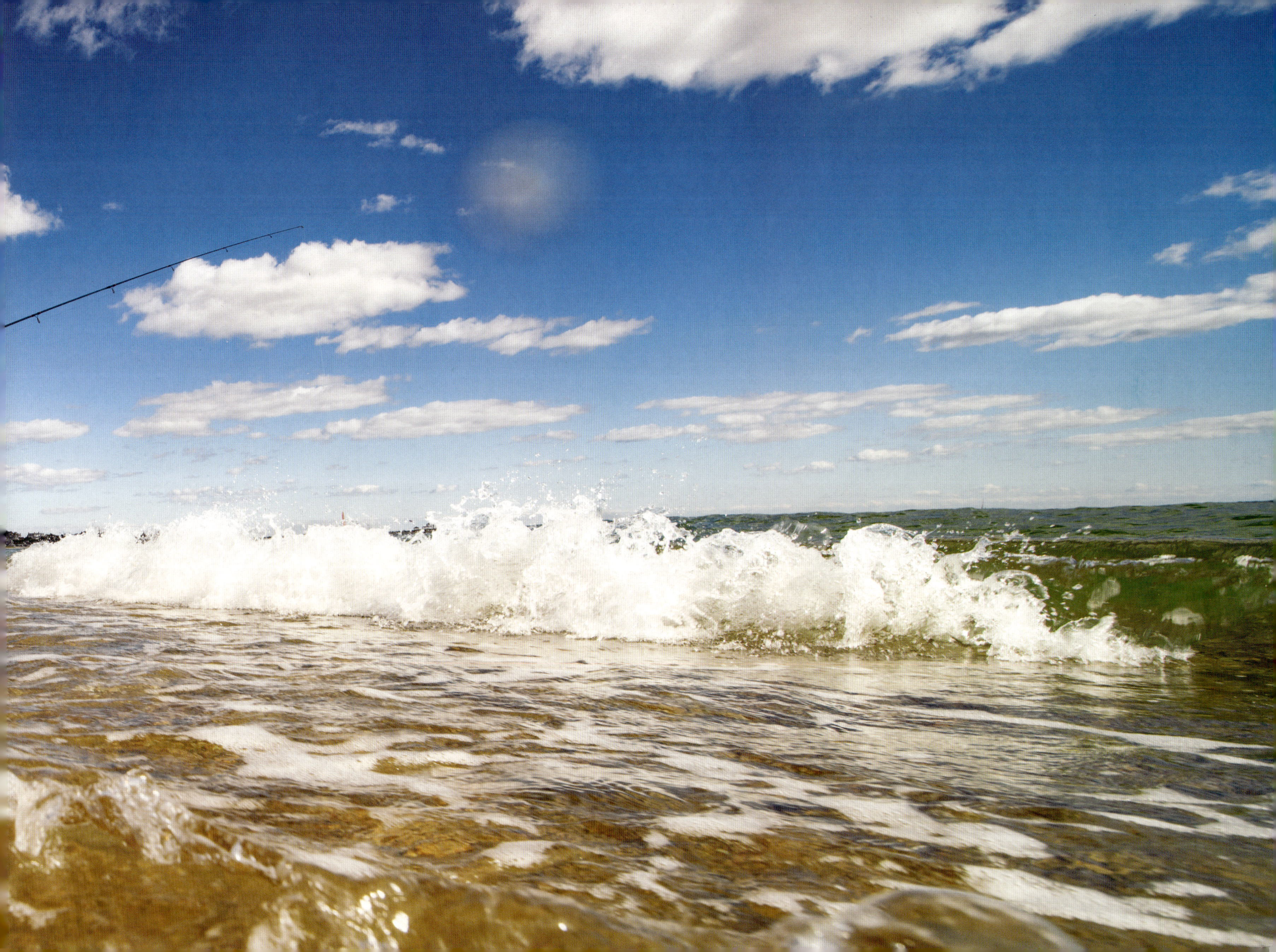

I was eight years old when I first stepped onto the running board of my uncle Kid's faded green pickup and pulled myself aboard. It felt like climbing into a tree fort. Already smitten by fishing, I was giddy to head off with this tall, rangy outdoorsman to fish the beaches of South County, Rhode Island, for striped bass.

When I grew up along the salt in Rhode Island, striped bass was *the* fish. The adults who had standing in the fishing community were striper guys. Their ability to catch them regularly—large ones, especially—defined what it meant to be a fisherman and, to a boy, what it meant to be a man.

Uncle Kid set me up with one of his old fly rods, to which he attached a small spinning reel and a little Atom popper; I'm guessing it struck the World War II veteran from the hills of Campbell County, Tennessee, as prudent to start me with what he had on hand. *Let's see if this surf-fishing thing sticks with the kid before we spend real money on it.* Children of the Great Depression—my father and mother, aunts and uncles—were unapologetically frugal. I may have later let them all down in other ways, but I was a good bet when it came to my fervor for fishing.

Sixty years is a long time to do any one thing, including chasing after a fish. And except for a few years in the 1970s when I roamed the West, I have been a faithful parishioner in the church of striped bass, following them from the Bay of Fundy to the Chesapeake. For decades, and sometimes at the expense of family and work, striped bass have been the focus of my time, energy, and passion. I have felt most like a kid when plotting fishing strategies, tinkering with boats and gear, and embarking into new waters. The fish has been a constant and worthy object of my obsession, curiosity, and dreams.

Previous spread: Author Bill Sisson on a Rhode Island beach. Photo by Tom Lynch.
Right: Heading out and a bent rear treble. Photo by Tom Lynch.

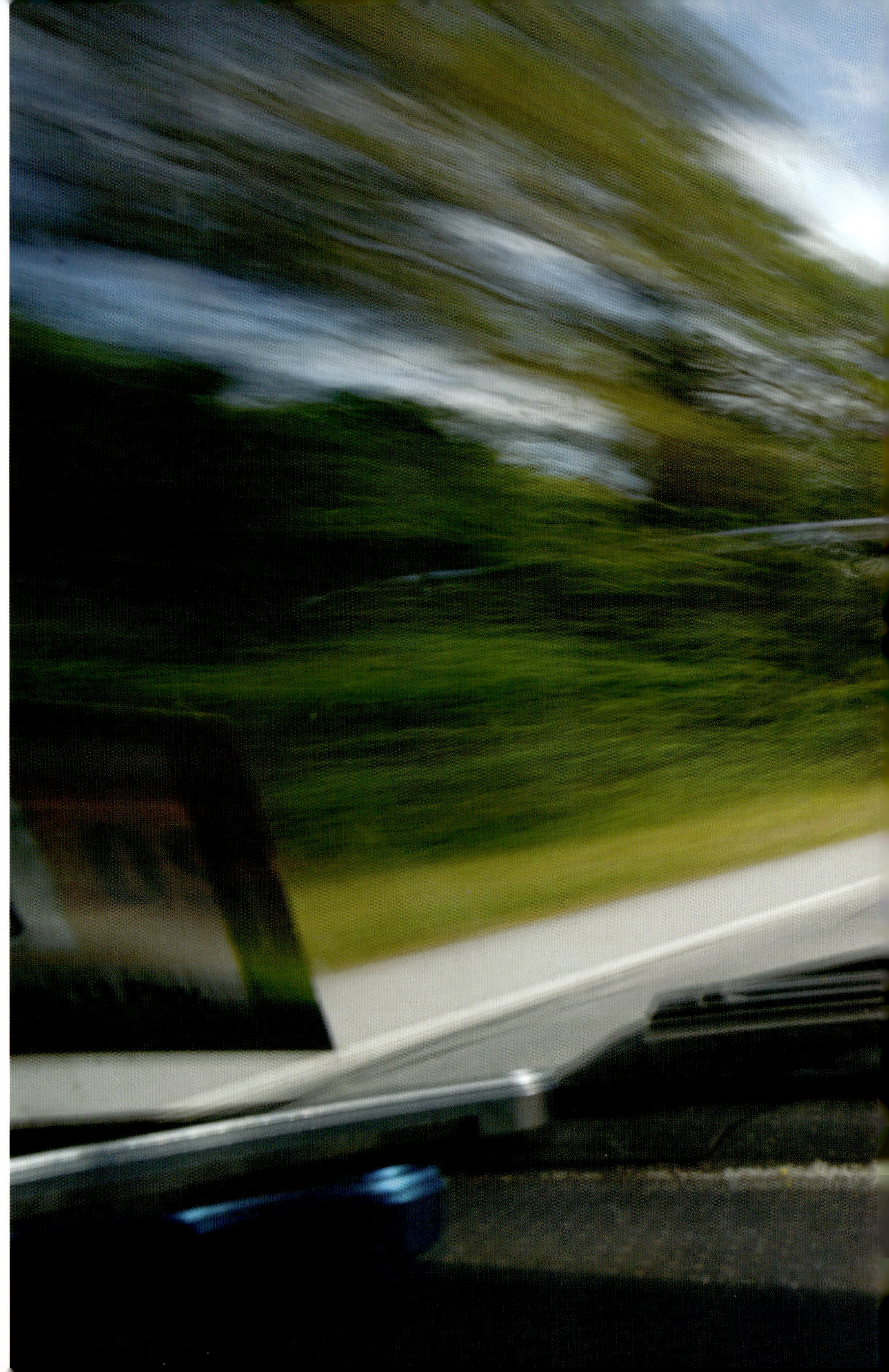

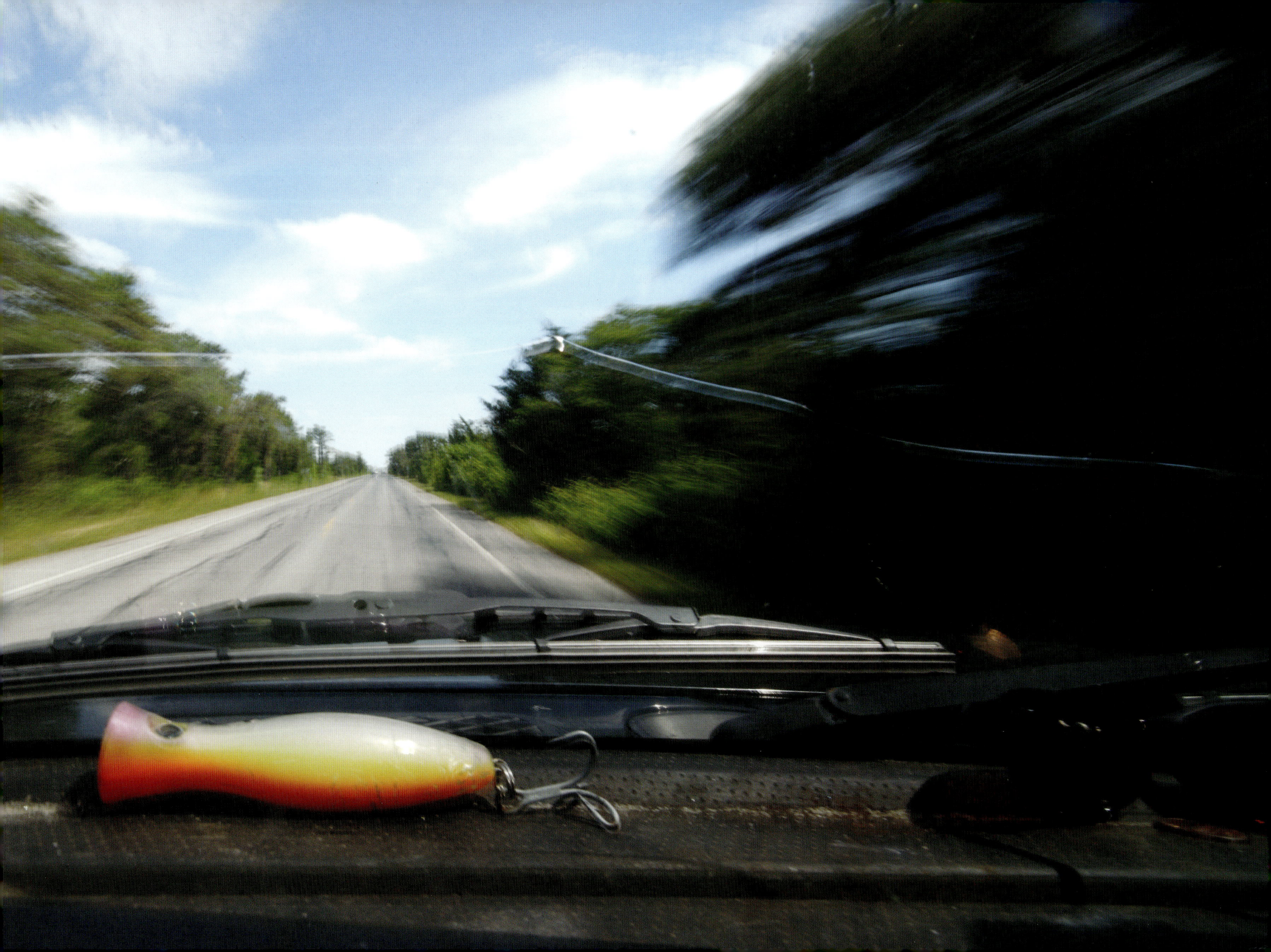

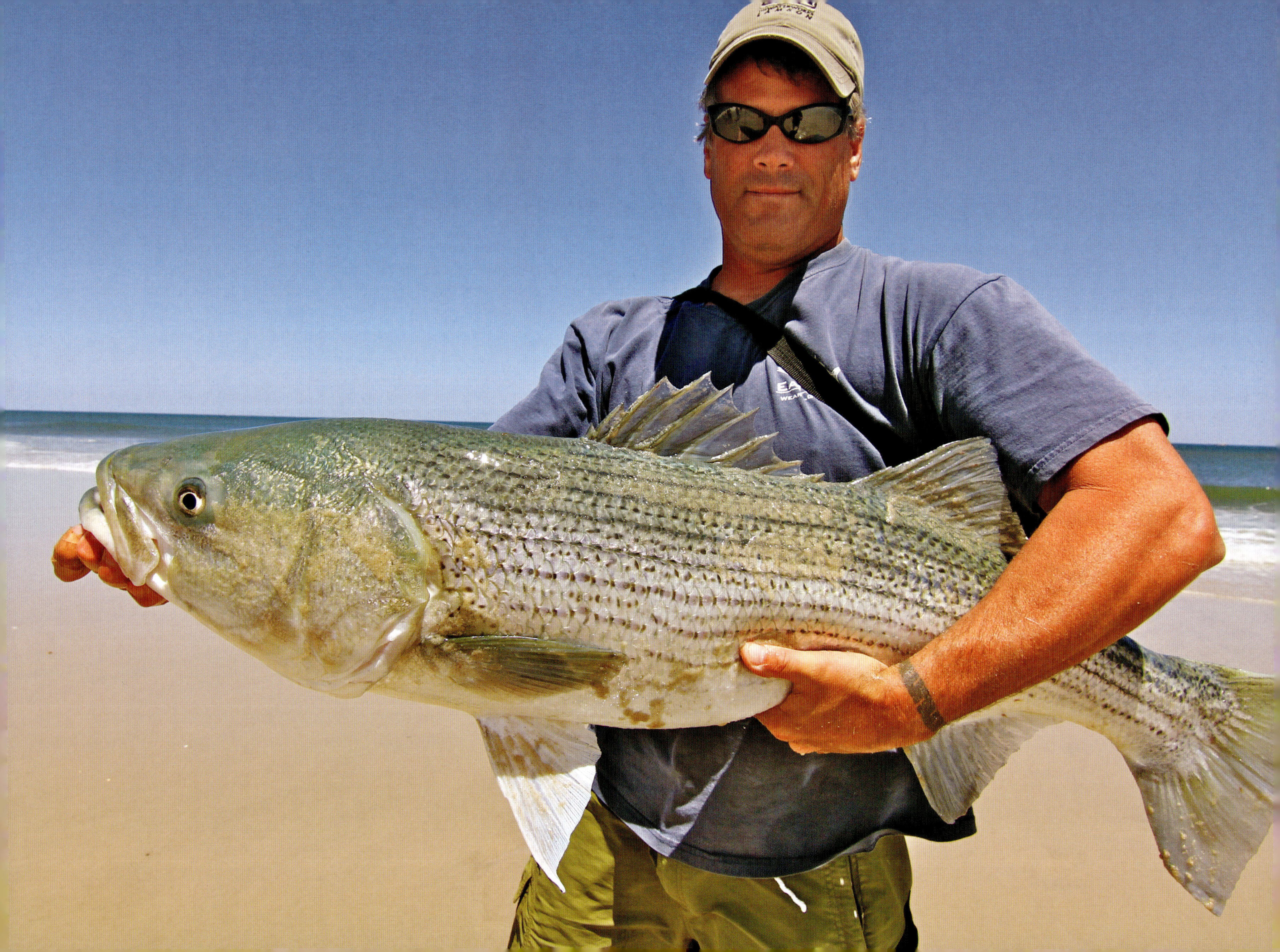

Even after all these years, stripers still put a spring in my step. They still draw me out of a warm home in late fall to cast into a southeast gale or drift a boat through roiled waters on a new-moon tide. Big stripers always quicken my pulse. I feel most at home casting on an empty, windy, end-of-season beach at night, the shore break thumping, the cold air numbing my hands and making my face ruddy, a bright Milky Way overhead, and a dozen sanderlings racing the waves as they feed through the night preparing for their long migration.

STRIPED BASS HAVE ALWAYS MOVED ME MORE THAN MONEY. When I am catching well, I carry the "high" through the next day—I wear the feeling like armor under my clothes, shielding me from the banality of our consumer-focused world. I wrote an essay 18 years ago titled "50 and Broke." I never intended to publish it. Instead, the writing helped me take stock of where I was at one of those cultural touchstones that I tend to blow past. Here is a snippet:

I can't say I like being broke, but then I've never really given two hoots about making a ton of money either. Nor did my wife. When I think about it, I shake my head and tell friends that if I put as much effort into making money as I have into catching striped bass, I'd be a wealthy man today. But if I could go back and do things differently, that's one thing I wouldn't change.

I've been happy for decades working as a reporter and magazine editor by day and living a striper bum's life by night. I found my people in the wind and salt spray, as well as in the newsroom where I have worked for 40 years. I am as comfortable with a reporter's notebook in my back pocket and knocking out a story in front of a keyboard as I am in a wet suit hauling myself onto a submerged rock at midnight. Two very different lives lived at the same time. Twice lucky.

Photographer Tom Lynch with a fish he released. Photo by Ray Kerico.

I gave myself to the briny world of striped bass—waves and beaches, late nights on fishy islands, rips, flats, salt ponds, and hundreds of waypoints in between. All the while, I filled dozens of notebooks and journals with reporting and impressions, sometimes resorting to scraps of paper and envelopes. Although I caught my share of fish, I didn't catch the most or the largest fish on the striper coast. But I was a careful observer with a good eye and ear and an obsession for writing down what I saw, heard, and experienced. I scribbled phone numbers on candy wrappers and inside matchbooks. I scrawled in the margins of beat-up paperbacks I found under piles of damp fishing clothes on the floor of my truck. If I had nothing else, I wrote on my hand.

I jotted descriptions of outings, seasons, the people I fished with, and others I encountered in the middle of the night: sharpies and newcomers, young bucks and old-timers, and those who mostly grunted. I noted snippets of conversation; observations on tides, winds, waves, fog, and moon phases; lure types, sizes, and colors; the pursuit of live bait; plenty of gospel on fishing eels; and whatever else happened to be in the zeitgeist that season.

I recorded conversations I had with both the living and the dead. My notebooks include the long-dead voices of three haul seiners, a couple of lobstermen, a trio of old-school charter skippers, the captain of a lightship, and a powder monkey who sailed with Admiral Perry. I continue to speak regularly with the departed who traipse over the dunes to visit me when the fishing slows. Some appear in the pages of this book.

I NEVER HAD A SINGLE STRIPED BASS TAKE A SWIPE at my little popper during the dozen afternoons I fished with Uncle Kid. It wasn't his fault. Likely, the fish that had fed close to his boots the previous couple of seasons had found easier pickings elsewhere. Who knows? I was

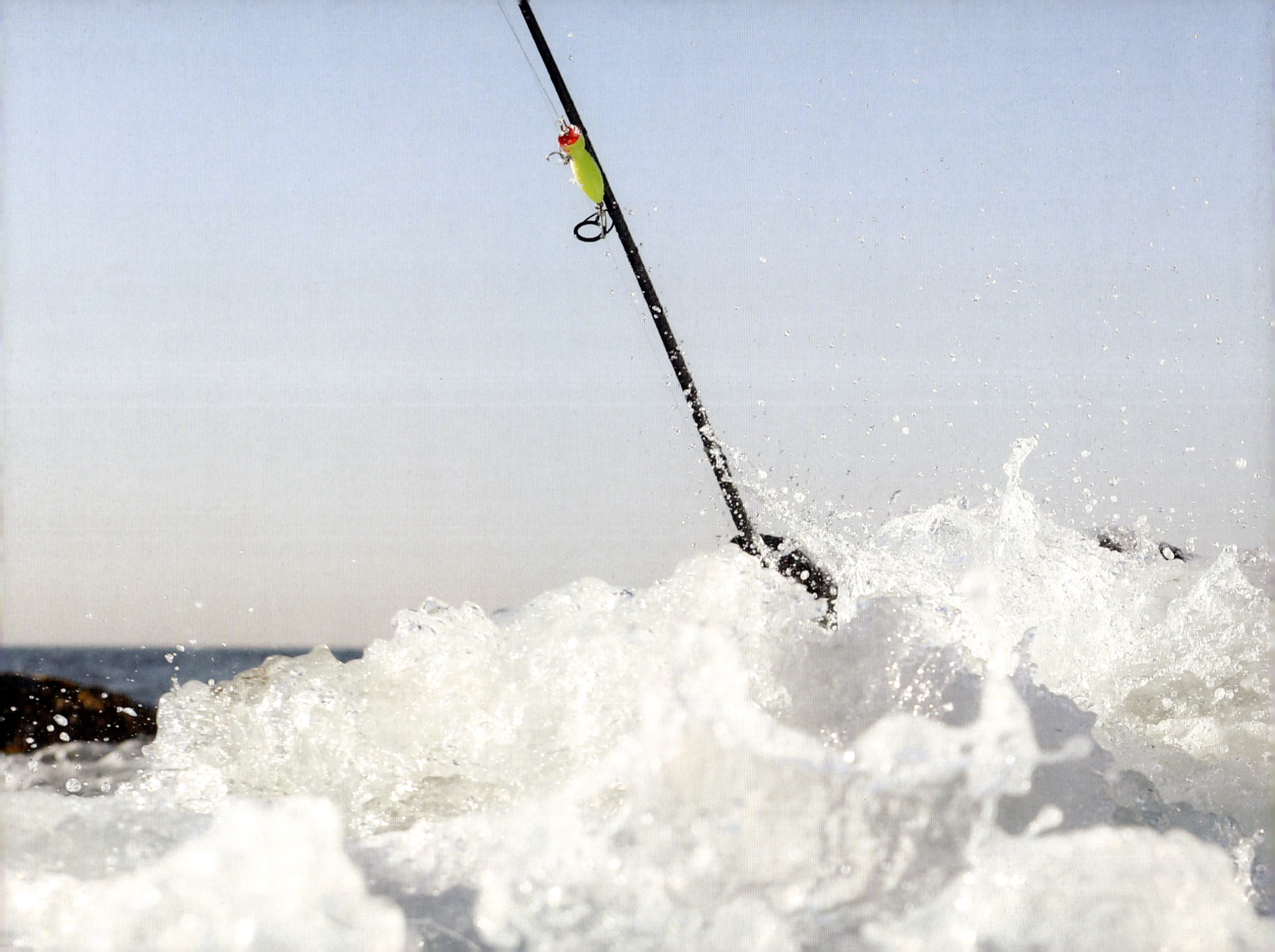

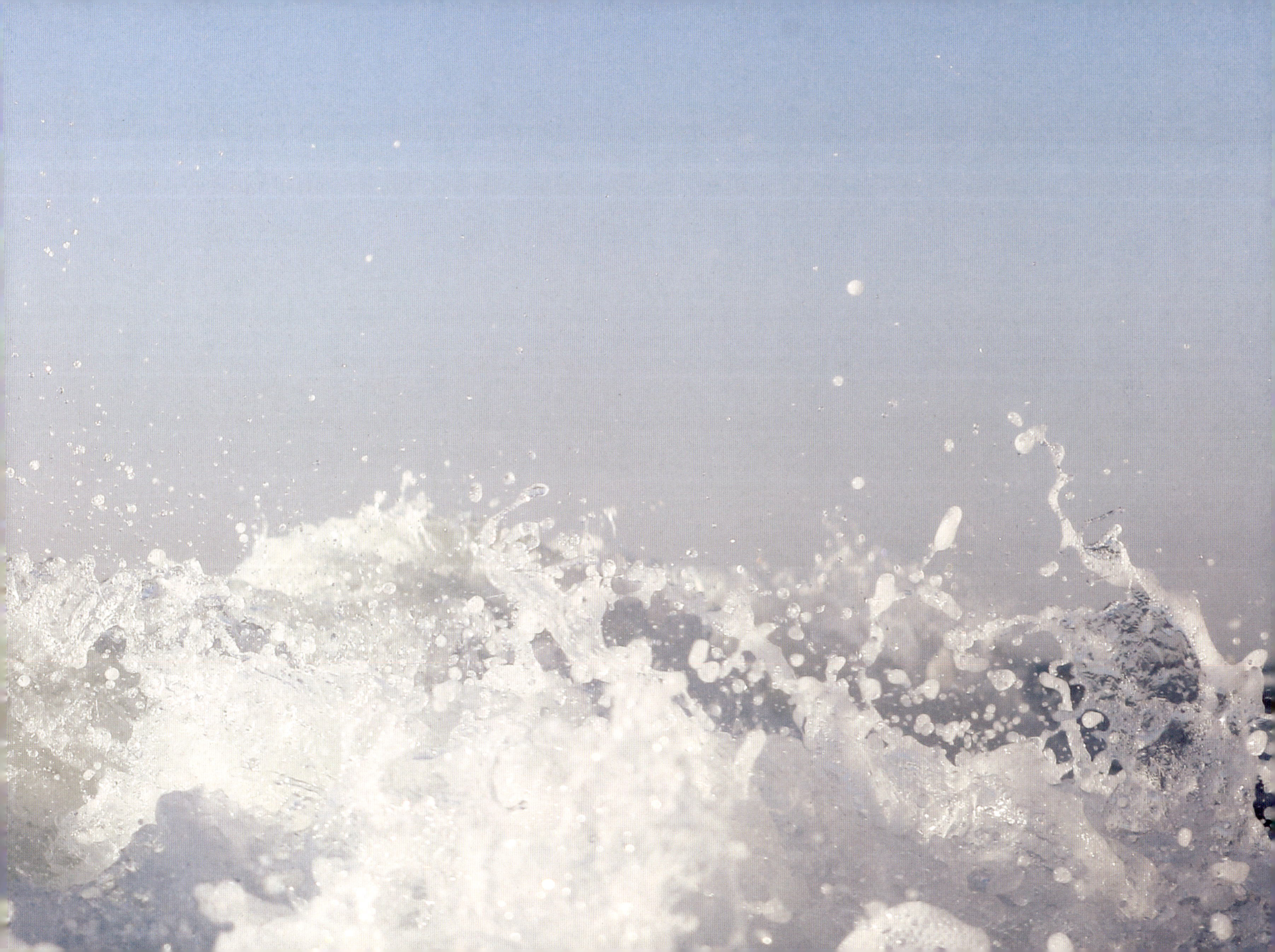

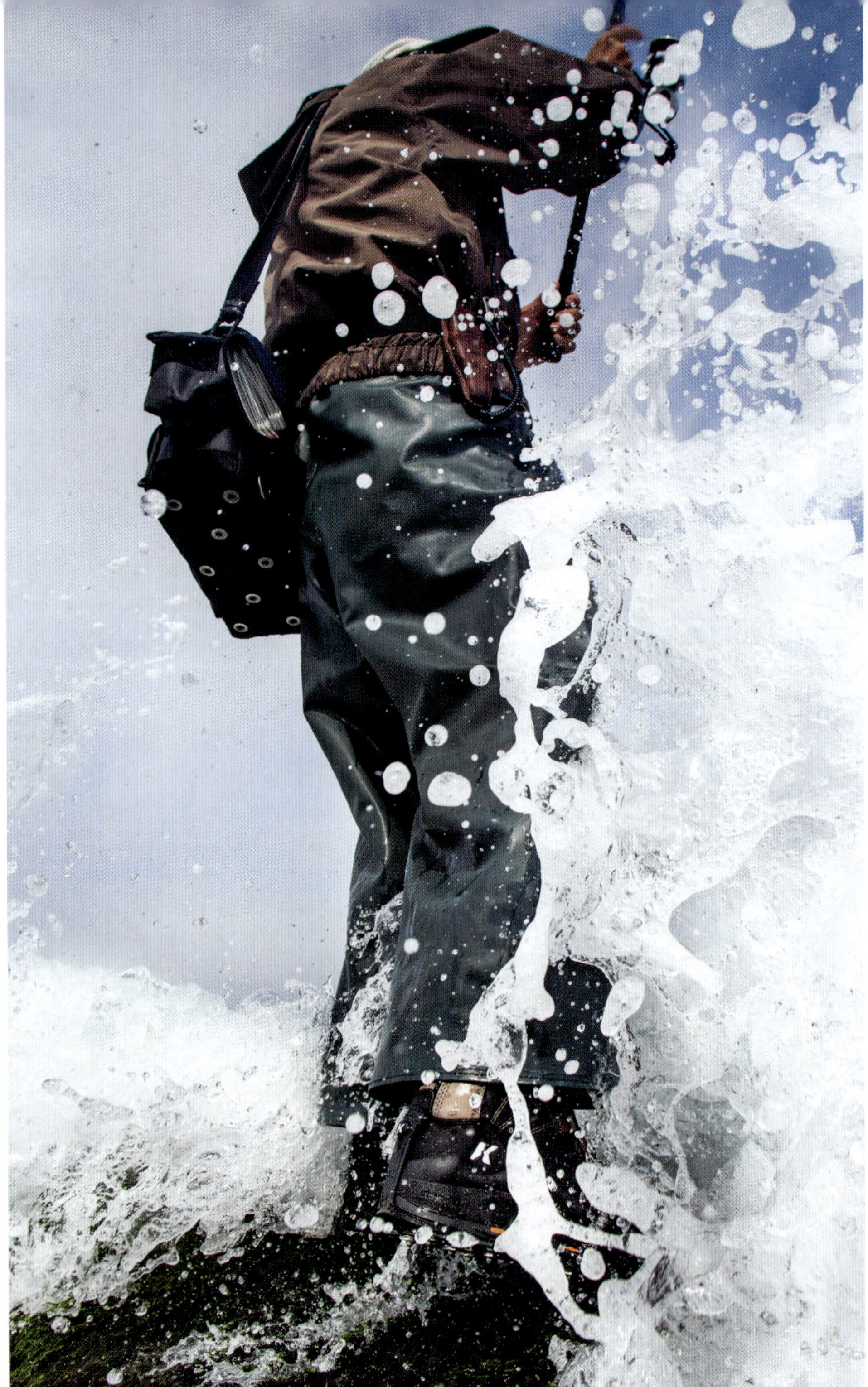

just a kid along for the ride. My eyes and ears were wide open, but I also was living in that perpetual daydream between childhood and puberty. I worked my feet back and forth so my boots would sink into the sand. I skipped stones. I watched Kid lob his big plugs into the blue, following their trajectory until they scuffed the surface of Block Island Sound. Most important, I learned that this fish was not like the cunners, tinker mackerel, and snapper blues I caught off the town dock. Stripers were never going to be easy to find or fool. I learned the meaning of the phrase "paying your dues."

My sharpest recollections were from those outings when my uncle pulled into our driveway with his fishing partner. I sat between the two of them, feeling as safe as a kid could feel, a fingerling among lunkers. I enjoyed their camaraderie and banter. I appreciated their closeness. I sensed I was on the periphery of a secret fraternity and wanted in, even though I didn't know what it was about. They laughed, told ribald jokes, and smoked cigarettes. I didn't understand any of the humor—not the meaning of the words, not the context, none of the nuance or innuendos.

"Now don't go telling your mother," said Kid, who was part of the Normandy Invasion, D-Day Plus 2. Tell her what? It was as if they were speaking in tongues. They passed a bottle. The scent of the whiskey mixed with that of rubber waders and tobacco to fill the warm truck cab. As fall came on strong, I bounced down a rutted beach road in the company of men. My journey had begun.

I WORKED SUMMERS in my father's store in Watch Hill, Rhode Island. It was a combination pharmacy, hardware store, and gift shop, with a big candy counter, two long shelves of magazines and comics, cigars, cigarettes, sunglasses, and sunblock. We sold thumbtacks, light bulbs, hammers, handlines, Kastmasters, pocket watches, and postcards. I swept the sidewalks, squeegeed

Previous spread: Buried by a wave. Photo by Tom Lynch.
Left: Dressed in the proper uniform. Photo by Tom Lynch.
Right: Fighting to the beach. Photo by Tom Lynch.

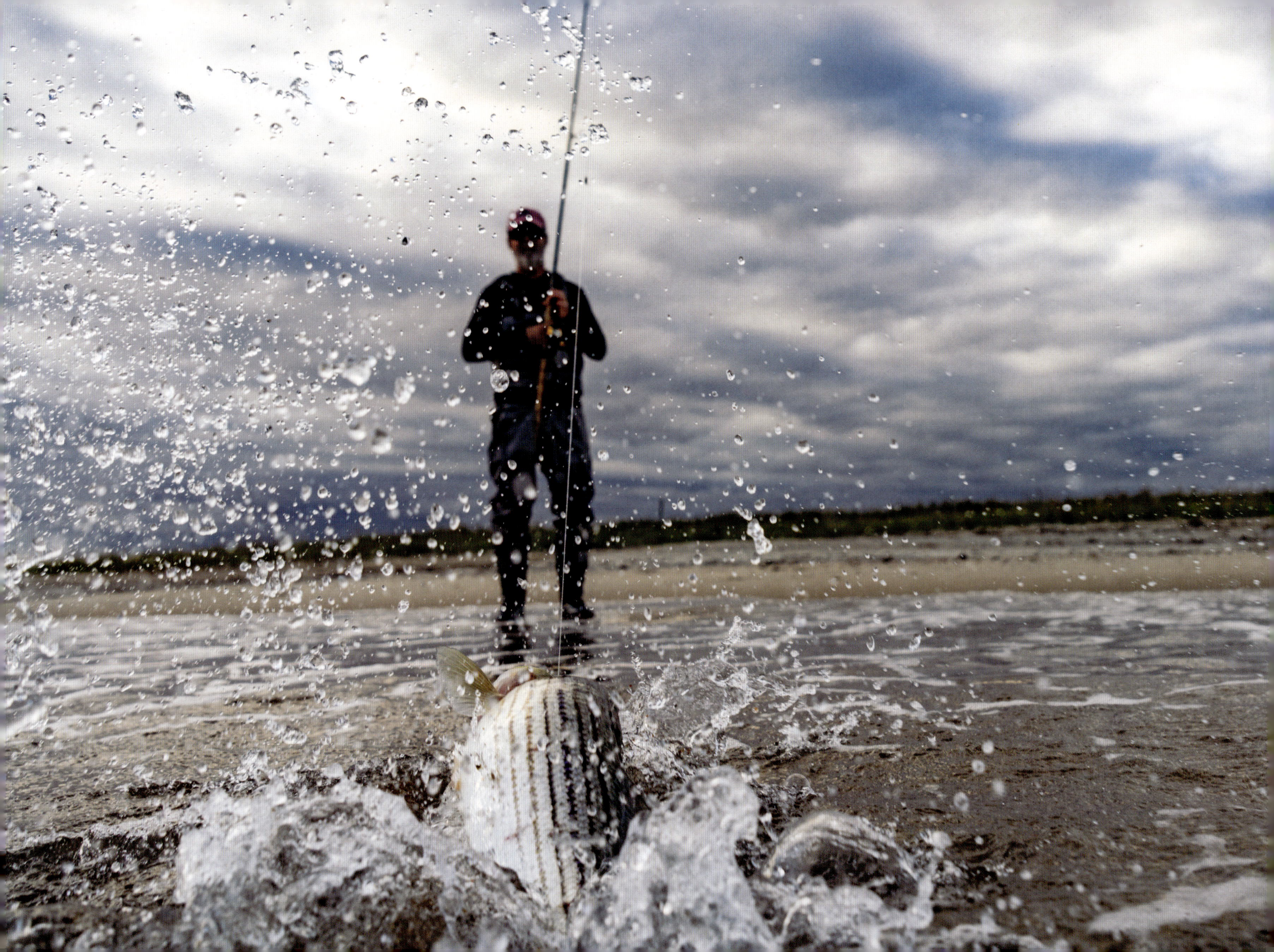

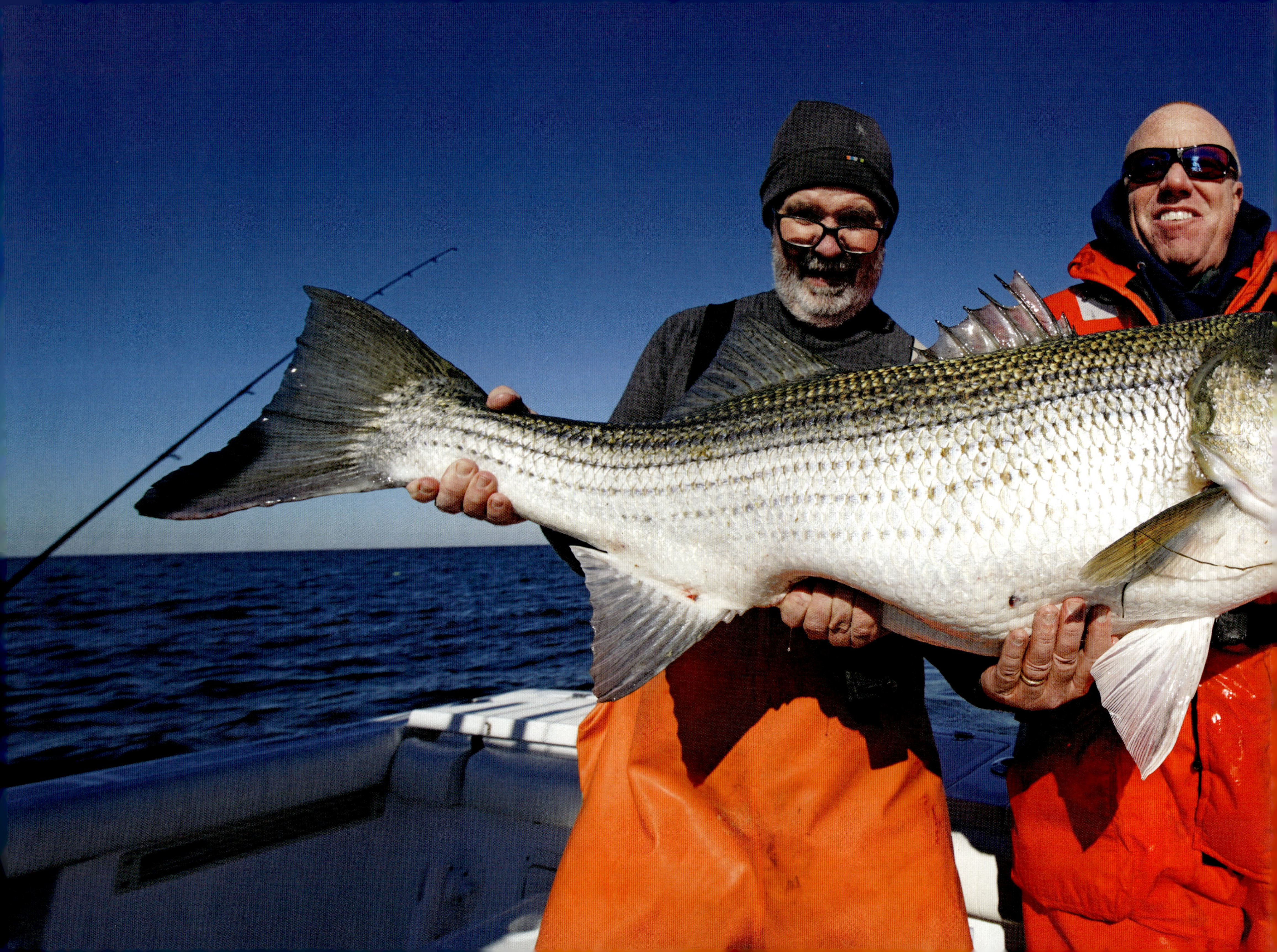

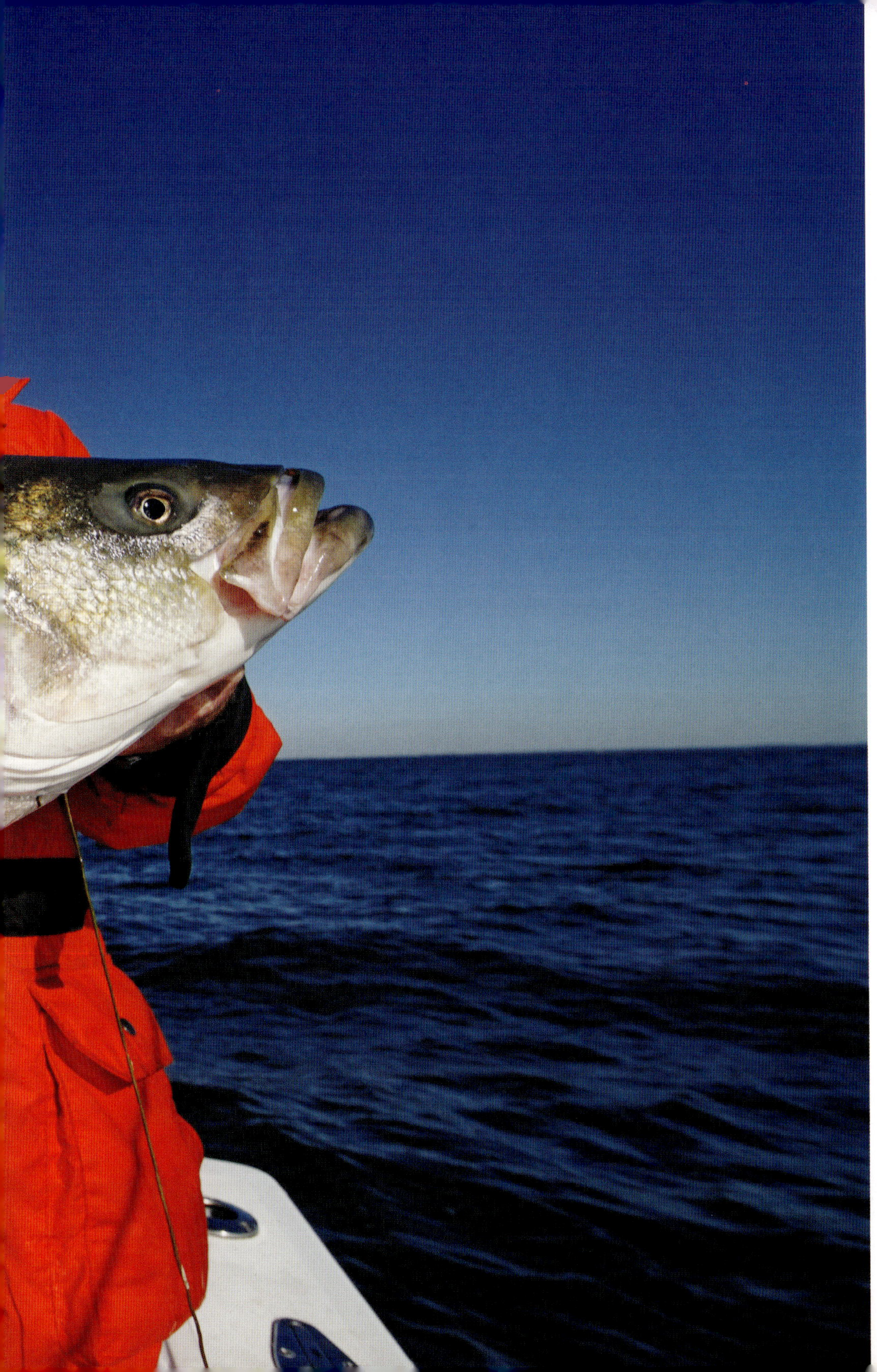

the windows, stocked shelves, worked the registers, and raised and lowered the awnings and canvas curtains that kept the window stock from fading.

The arrangement with my father was like a company store. He kept track of my hours and held my wages. I pestered him to let me use my earnings to purchase a proper surf rod. Finally, he drove me to the Weekapaug Tackle Shop, watched while I received a quick casting lesson in the breachway, then brought me back to work with a nine-foot rod and a black Penn 710 reel. It was an important moment in my young fishing life. With this proper surf outfit, I could at last fish the beaches and rocks with the adults.

MY FIRST SURF STRIPER DIDN'T COME EASILY. Atlantic salmon are sometimes called a "fish of ten thousand casts." I'm certain I made that many tosses for stripers from the beach and the rocks at the lighthouse with my new rod and reel. The difficulty only raised my esteem for the fish. Striped bass seemed a kind of ghost fish—difficult, remote, and special. One that surely must be worth this effort.

Back then, casting the hours away felt a bit like sitting beside my parents in St. Clare Church, murmuring prayers. Plenty of rote and repetition without anything ever happening. Both prayers and casts seemed to sail off on a one-way trip to nowhere. Was anything actually out there?

One September afternoon after school, a message finally came screaming back from the ether and cracked open my world. That's when a striper walloped my green cedar popper. I fished alone, lost in my daydreams, and hadn't been paying attention. I never saw the strike, but suddenly my rod was throbbing and the spool was spinning madly. I knew immediately that

Bill Sisson, left, and Chuck Many, right, with a 53-pound fish Sisson caught and released in Chesapeake Bay aboard Many's boat. Photo by Tom Lynch.

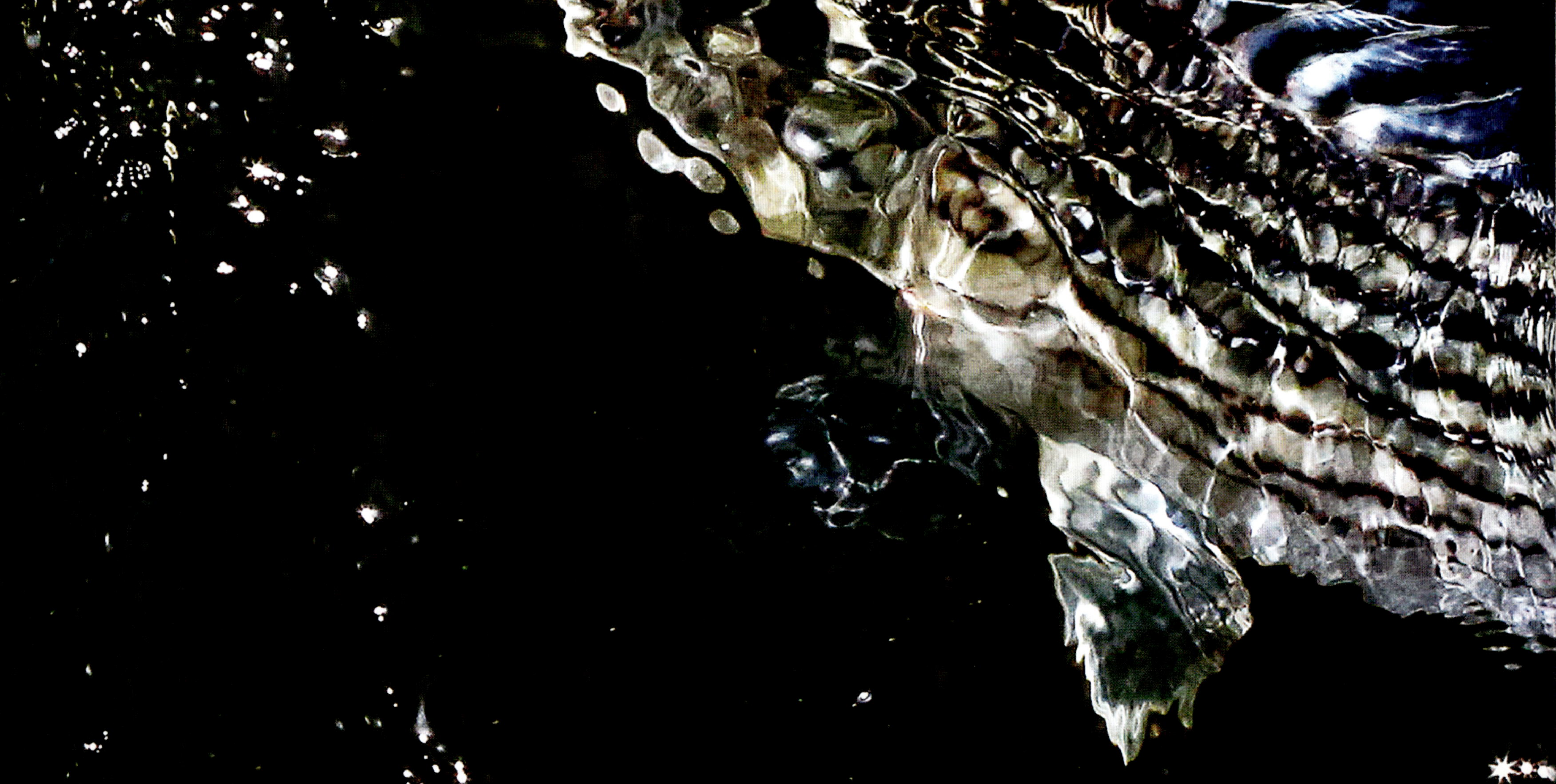

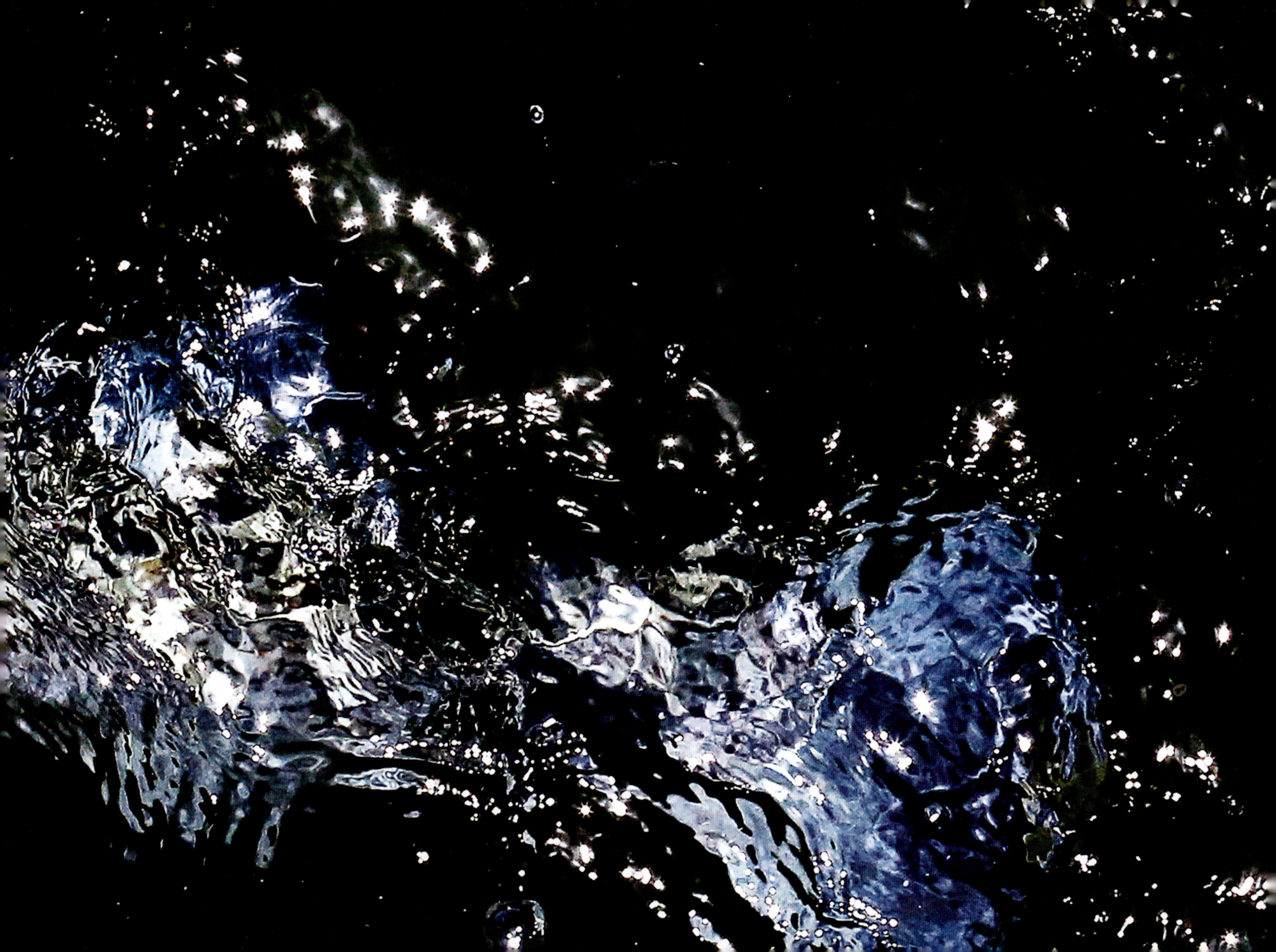

I had tapped into something larger and wilder than I'd imagined. I landed a tired, gorgeous striped bass, and there, at long last, was a fish to be proud of. It weighed eight pounds. I hugged it and dragged it back to the store to show my parents, brothers, the other shopkeepers, and a half-dozen neighbors.

Here, too, was a definitive answer—not to the mysteries of the universe, but to something far more tangible to a young angler. This puzzling world of tides, currents, and beautiful fish just might be the thing after all. I don't recall the second bass I caught that fall, but having broken the striper schneid, I was revved up and running.

FAST-FORWARD 25 YEARS. The stripers arrived late that spring, and I changed my hat several times in hopes of changing my luck, but it didn't change a damn thing. I still wound up sleeping on the couches of friends as my first wife and I separated and divorced. My lobster skiff sat on a trailer through spring and summer looking like a least tern with a broken wing. I didn't fish much that season as we sorted things out, though I did follow plenty of small bass with a mask and snorkel as my kids played on a beach.

It was early October when I pulled to the side of a dead-end road at a spot once called Bishops Beach. I reached in the back of my pickup and grabbed my prized old Lamiglas surf rod, the one wound by Joe Castagnaro of Cove Edge Tackle Shop. As a teen, I'd long admired a similar rod in his shop before I saved enough money to have him build me one just like it. Shouldering the 11-footer, I headed down the sandy tire tracks to the surf. The moment I cleared the dunes, I spotted gulls diving and fish breaking 100 yards to the east. There was a tightness in my chest—the good kind—as my adrenaline kicked in and a long-dormant part of me suddenly woke.

Previous spread: Beauty below the surface. Photo by Tom Lynch.
Right: Released with a swish of its tail. Photo by James Manning.

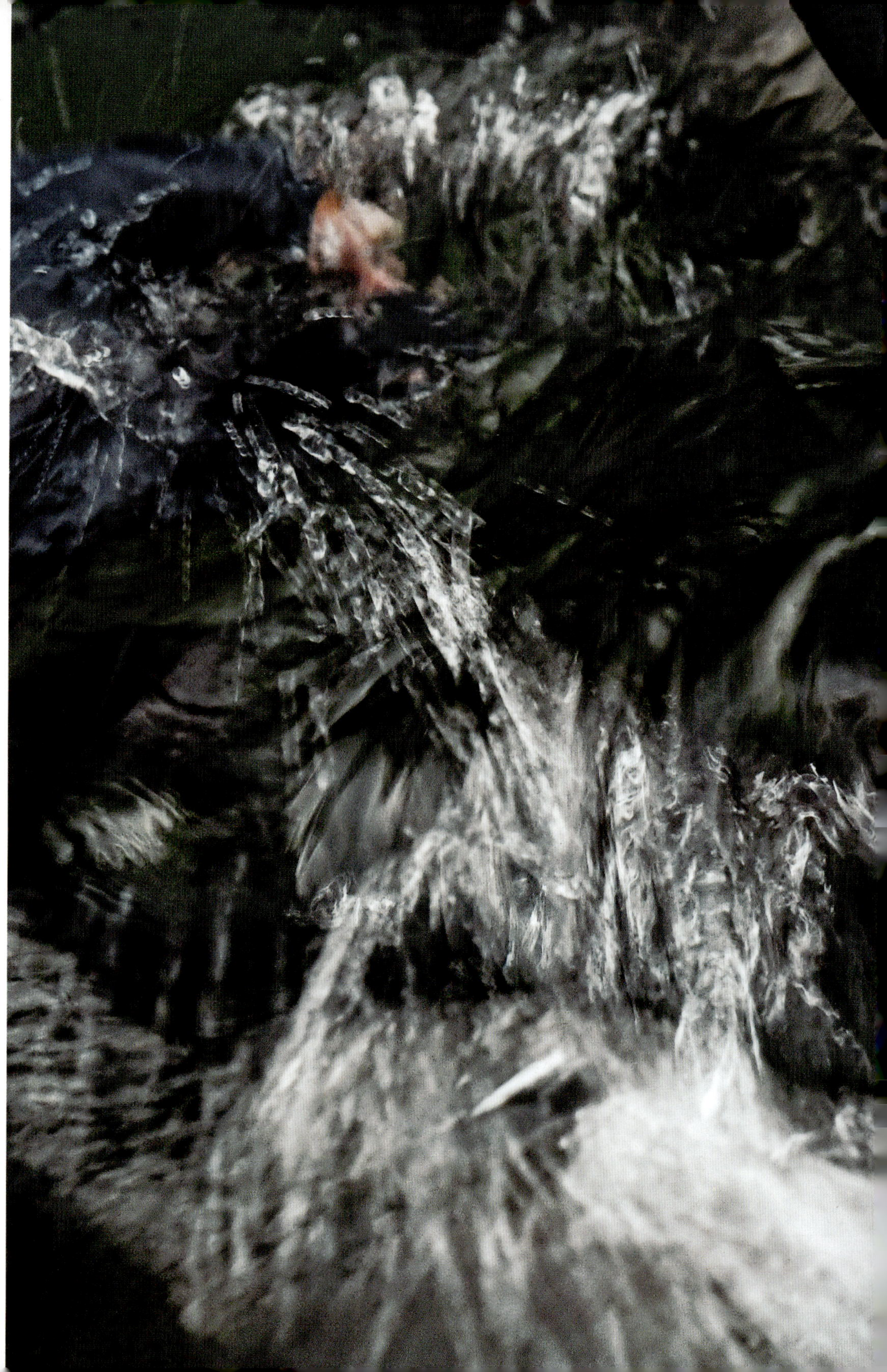

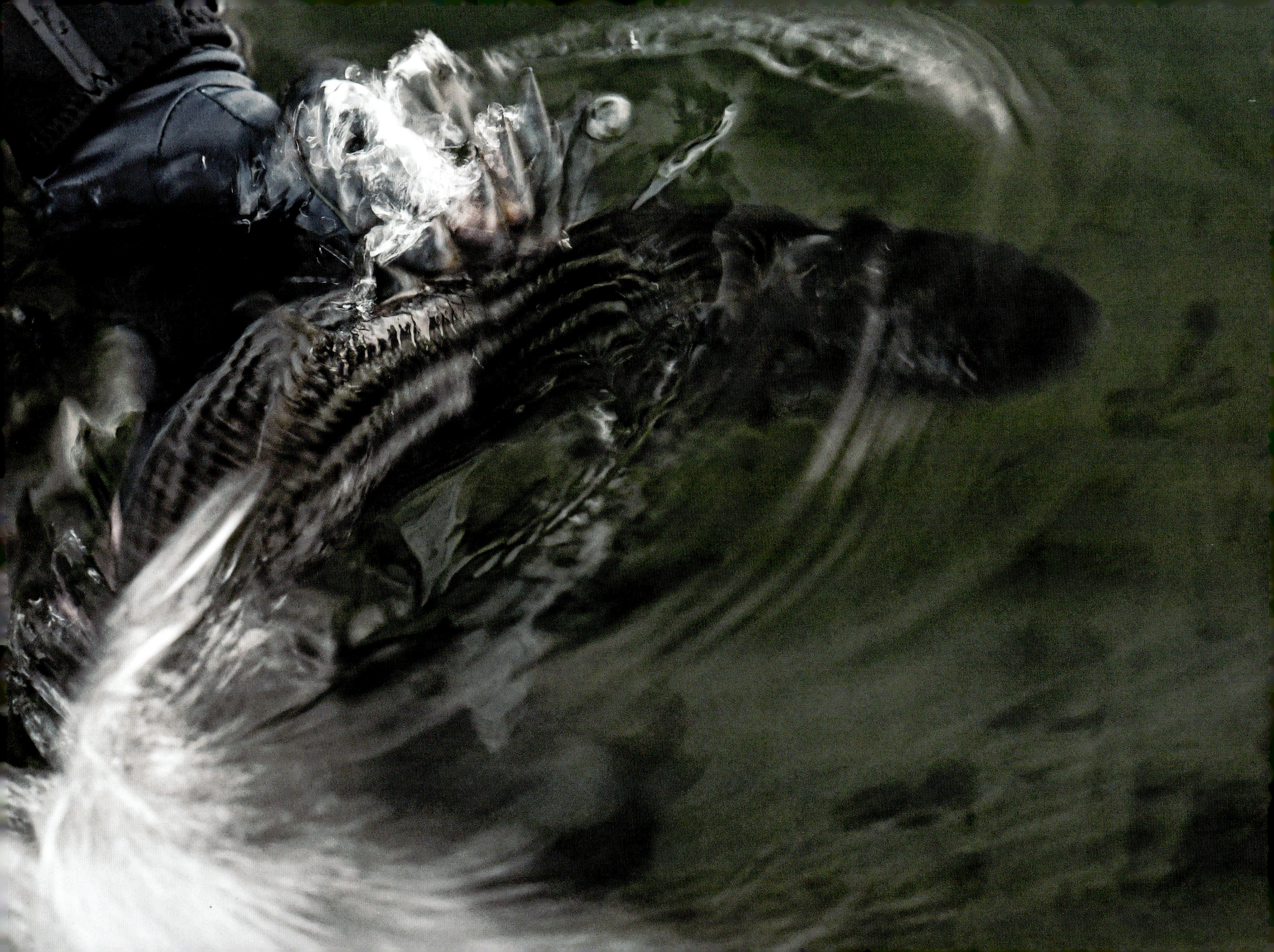

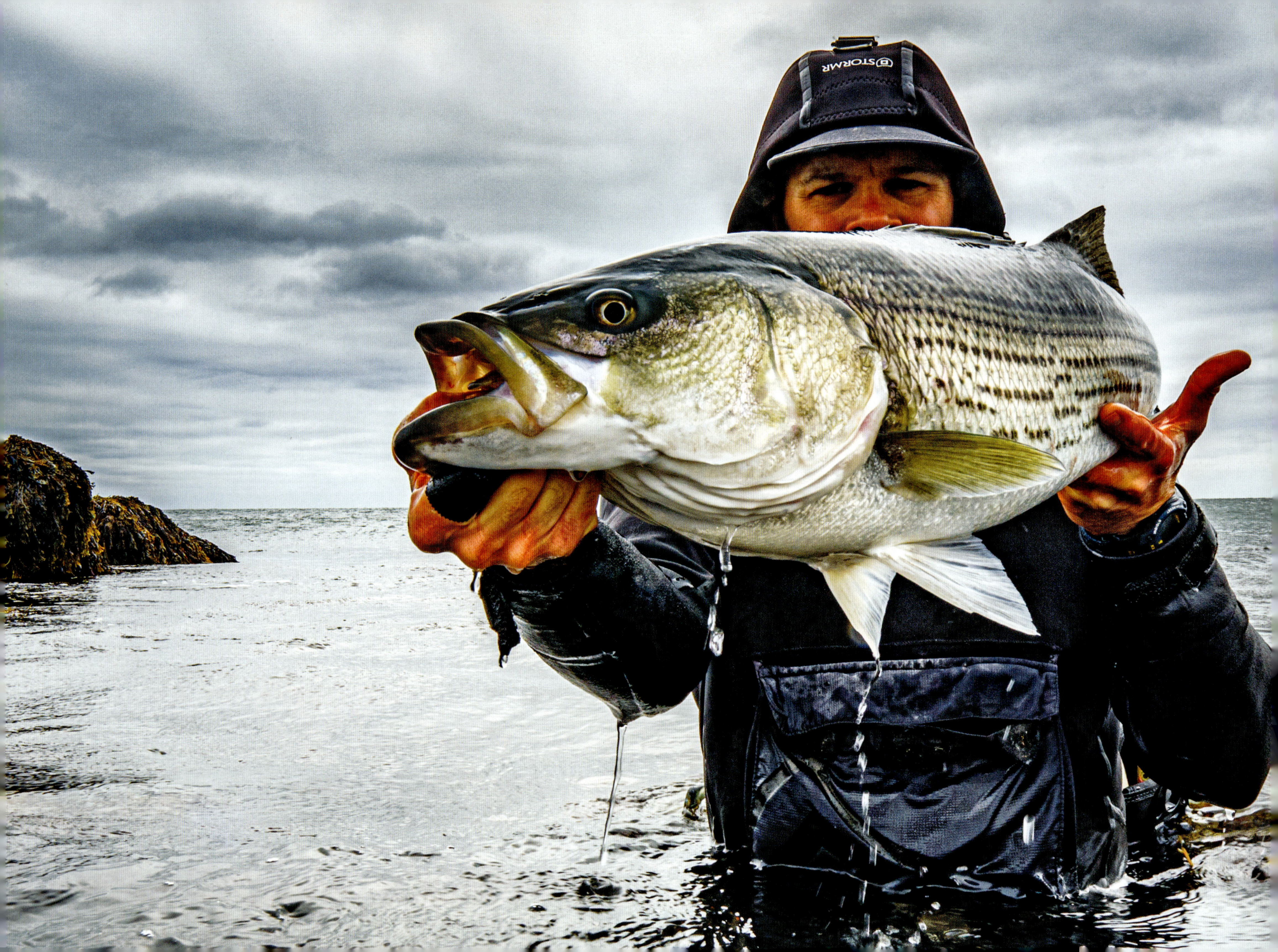
STORMR

I sprinted toward the melee and suddenly gained a surprise realization: *Everything's going to be OK. You're chasing fish.* It was a sure sign. As an adolescent, I ran over the rocks at a lighthouse toward busting fish, easily beating the lumbering adults. That's how you bested the panting grown-ups by a cast or two before they perched on your shoulders and cast for the horizon while trying to exert their seniority.

FOOT RACING FOR FISH HAS REMAINED A GOOD INDICATOR of my mental and physical health. It was fall, and photographer Tom Lynch and I were scouting a barrier beach. Early afternoon was warm and slow, but as evening approached, gulls, bait, and breaking fish began to pop. I released a schoolie I'd hooked from a pod that erupted in front of us and quickly vanished. We continued walking and searching, staring intently in the western glare as the sun inched lower.

"There they are!" Tom said. It's easy to underestimate how quickly fish travel when the fall run is on. The birds hovered 150 yards away, and we both saw splashes.

"You know, if we were 14," I said, "we'd both be running now."

"We're not 14," he replied, reminding me that he had 35 pounds of camera gear in his backpack, not to mention that both of us were dressed in waders.

"Well, I think I'm going to run," I replied, breaking into a jog. A good sport, Tom toiled along behind me. By the time I reached the edge of the moving fracas, I was out of breath. I cast and hooked another fish. Tom juggled shooting and fishing. The circus moved yet again, and I became the old plow horse that suddenly catches a whiff of hay and discovers more left in its tank. *Clunk, clunk, clunk . . .*

A Cuttyhunk striper. Photo by Jerry Audet.

IN A HOST OF WAYS, STRIPERS HAVE DEFINED ME. They provide purpose and vigor to my after-work life. Stripers guided me to fishing partners who became lifelong friends, and determined when and where I took vacations, how I spent my money, and when I'd be home. They shaped my ideas of loyalty, secrecy, toughness, and endurance—not turning in early, never saying, *Not tonight, I'm too tired.* And catching them is just plain fun.

The old-timers taught me to keep my ears open, my mouth closed, and my bragging muzzled. The important stuff—the when, where, and how of catching—was shared among a small circle of like-minded bass bums.

Striped bass continue to lure me into the loveliest waters in New England: salt ponds, bays and breaking surf, sand flats and shoals, ocean reefs, rocky shores, mussel bars, and the bony waters beneath island bluffs. Current, fog, wind, and darkness. The landscape has shaped the fish and molded me.

Artist Nick Mayer grew up in East Providence, Rhode Island, on Narragansett Bay. He caught his first striped bass when he was 12, about the same age I was. "There was a time when all I thought about was striped bass," said Nick, who is 51 and now lives in Vermont. "When I was really obsessed, I'd go out at midnight or 1:00 a.m. and fish to daybreak. For me, it's the fish that represents home."

It symbolizes home for me as well. The fish binds you to the waters, sandbars, and glacial rock piles.

I SIT ON A BEACH LOG IN EARLY OCTOBER and listen to a conversation the southwest breeze is having with the young flood. The small swells answer, and terns carry the tune a little farther with their dips and dives and cries.

Windy light sweeps the bluffs, beach grass, and waves, and my small corner of the world catches its breath and comes alive. It's as if I waved a wand. All the players—from the wind and tide to predators and prey to myself—are held together like the atoms in a chemical bond, possibly unbreakable and without any reason to disconnect.

I work my way west. Ribbons of bait slide nervously inside and outside the breakers. I fish a series of small bars in a cove by a lighthouse. The bluefish are just beyond the outside bar, and the bass feed on the inside. The surf is waist-high and breaks with a good snap. I cast a lead head with a plastic tail the size and color of the peanut bunker, which attracts everything from cormorants to albies to blue crabs. Over a span of 90 minutes, I catch and release six fish—three bass and three blues—by casting steadily, even though nothing is showing. This is the time of day and time of year to stop looking and waiting and talking. It's time to fish.

Twilight rises from the east and finds me momentarily seated on the same rock wall where I fished so many years ago. Looking back, I scarcely recognize the boy whom I have pulled from memory. As I see him casting from the wall, I suddenly realize that I miss him. I'm surprised. I don't think about the boy at this age very often. He is young and eager and lonely. Where did he go? I wonder what happened to his dreams. Have things turned out the way he hoped?

Then the fish begin to explode in front of me. I drop my notebook into my backpack, pick up my rod, and wade out into the gray light. It's probably a good thing. I need to visit with the boy again, but first I need to tango with the fish that brought both of us here.

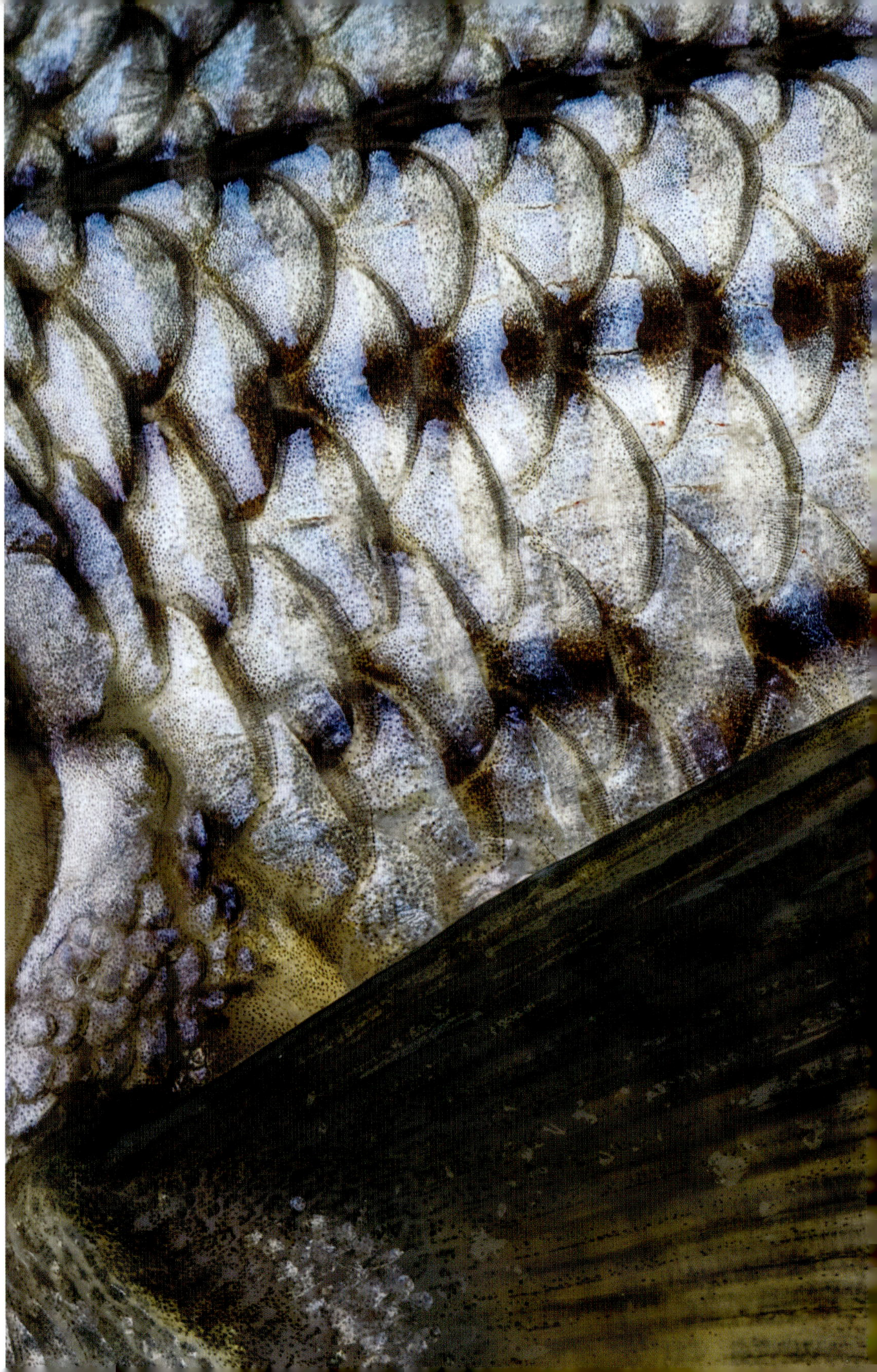

Pectoral fin and scales. Photo by Jay Fleming.

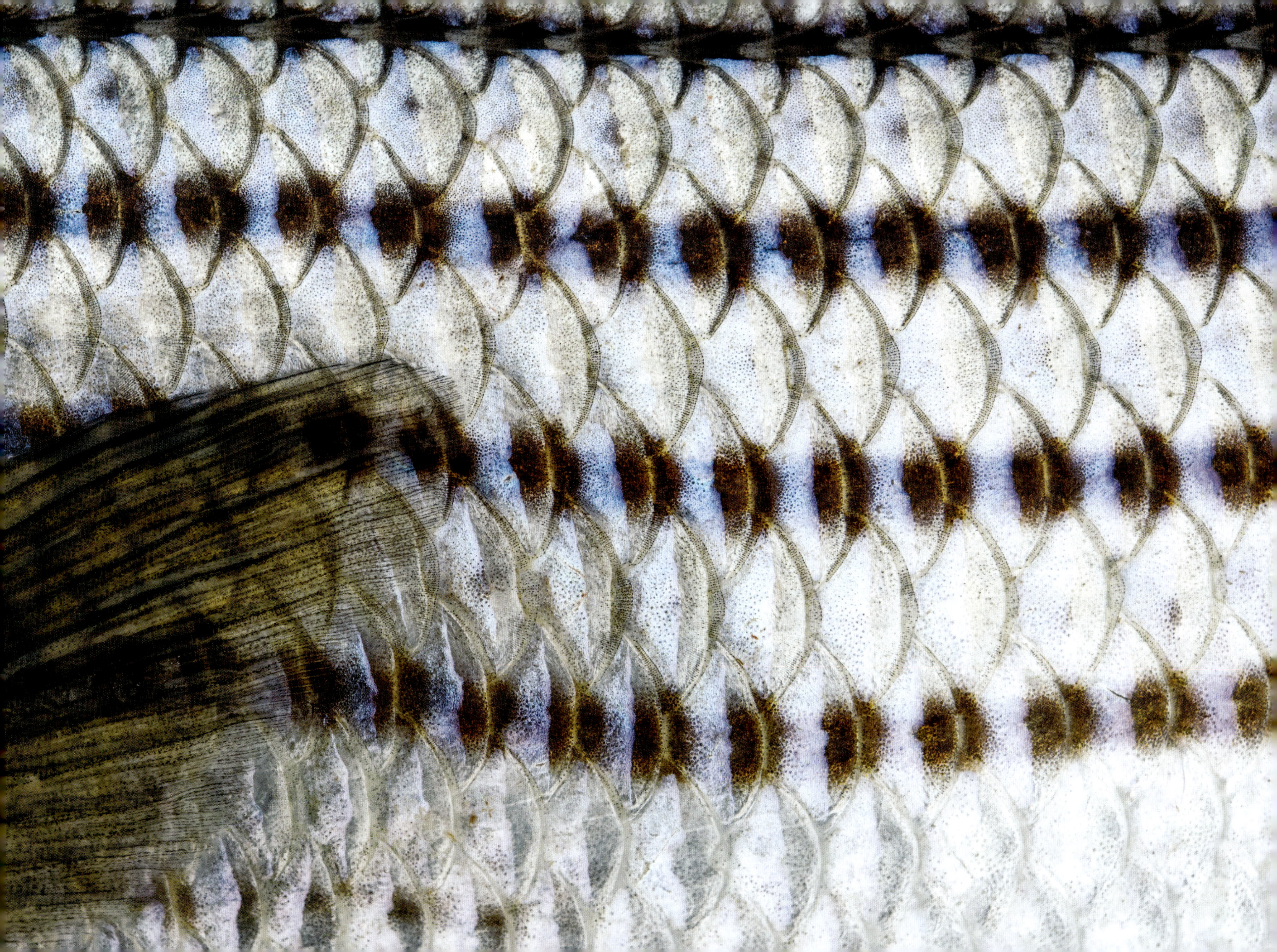

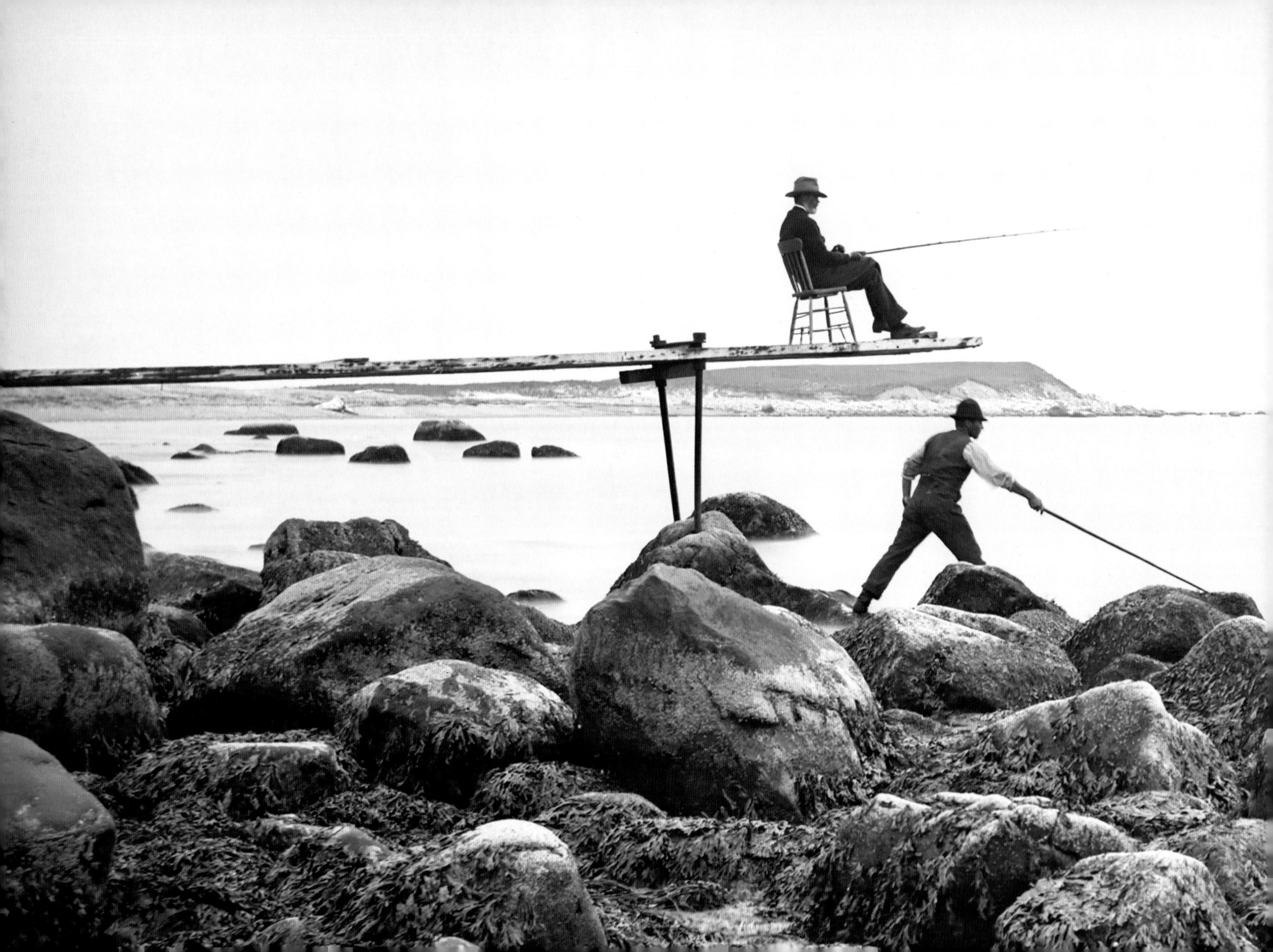

THE OLD WAYS

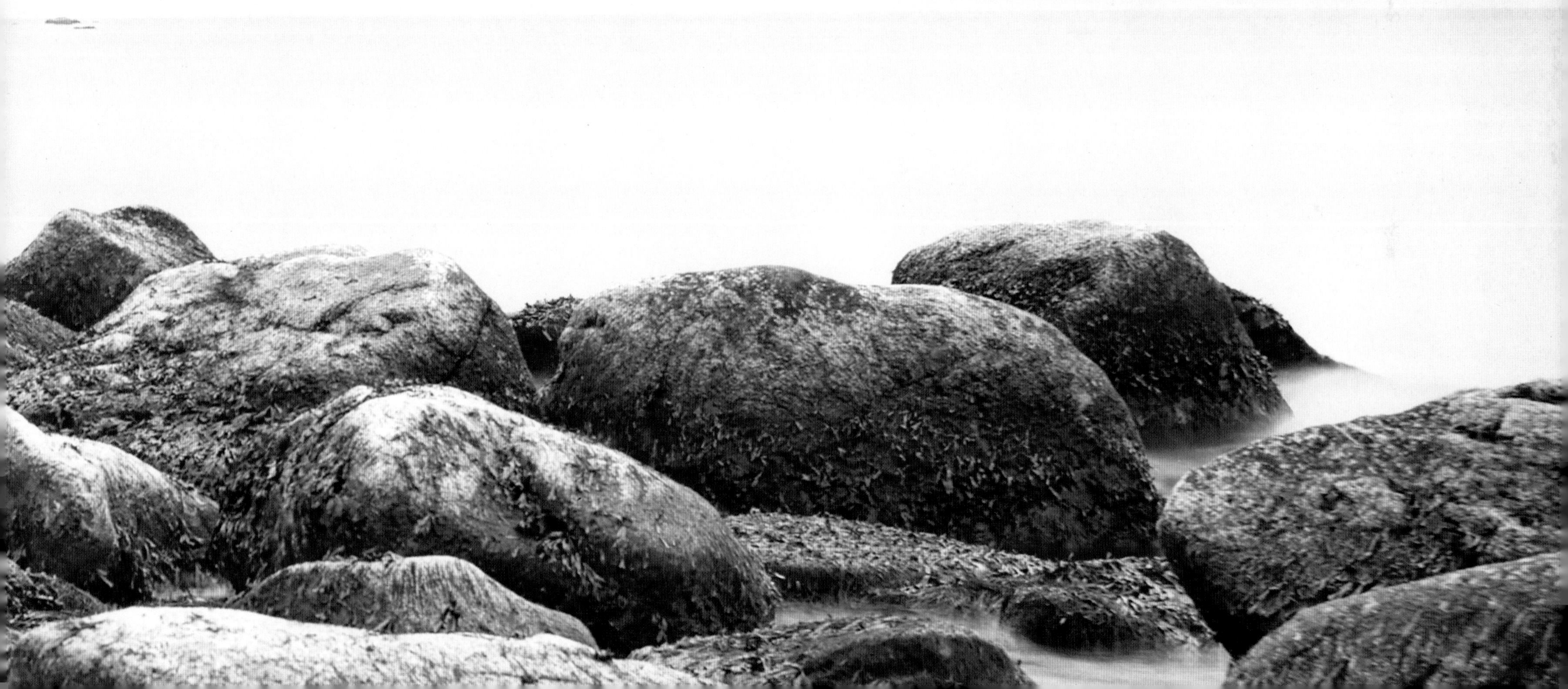

PRIVATE BASS CLUBS FOR WEALTHY ANGLERS appeared on the Massachusetts islands of Cuttyhunk, Pasque, and Martha's Vineyard in the 1860s. The clubs featured fishing stands supported by iron rods or pipes, wooden planks, and guide ropes at select spots around the rocky shores.

Locals drilled holes in the boulders using star drills where the supports would go. They also procured the lobster and menhaden used for bait, and did the chumming and gaffing for the millionaire sportsmen from New York, Philadelphia, and Washington, DC.

Rhode Island had bass clubs too: the West Island Club off Sakonnet with 12 bass stands was the best known of all of them. Graves Point and the private Gooseberry Island off Newport also had clubs. Martha's Vineyard was home to at least two fishing clubs, including one at Squibnocket.

The club on Cuttyhunk had 26 stands circling the island. In the evening, members would draw to determine their stands for the next day. Lobster-tail was the preferred bait. Chum was often ground menhaden. The chummers at the Cuttyhunk Club were paid a bonus of $1.00 per fish, more if a particularly large fish was caught.

The photo of a daily catch off the Graves Point Fishing Club (on the following spread) is a reminder of just how good the fishing could be, even with tackle considered crude by today's standards. The clubs petered out over the next 30 years as fishing dramatically declined. Some blamed it on the ups and downs of the striper's natural cycle, but the real cause was intense netting on the coast, rivers, and bays.

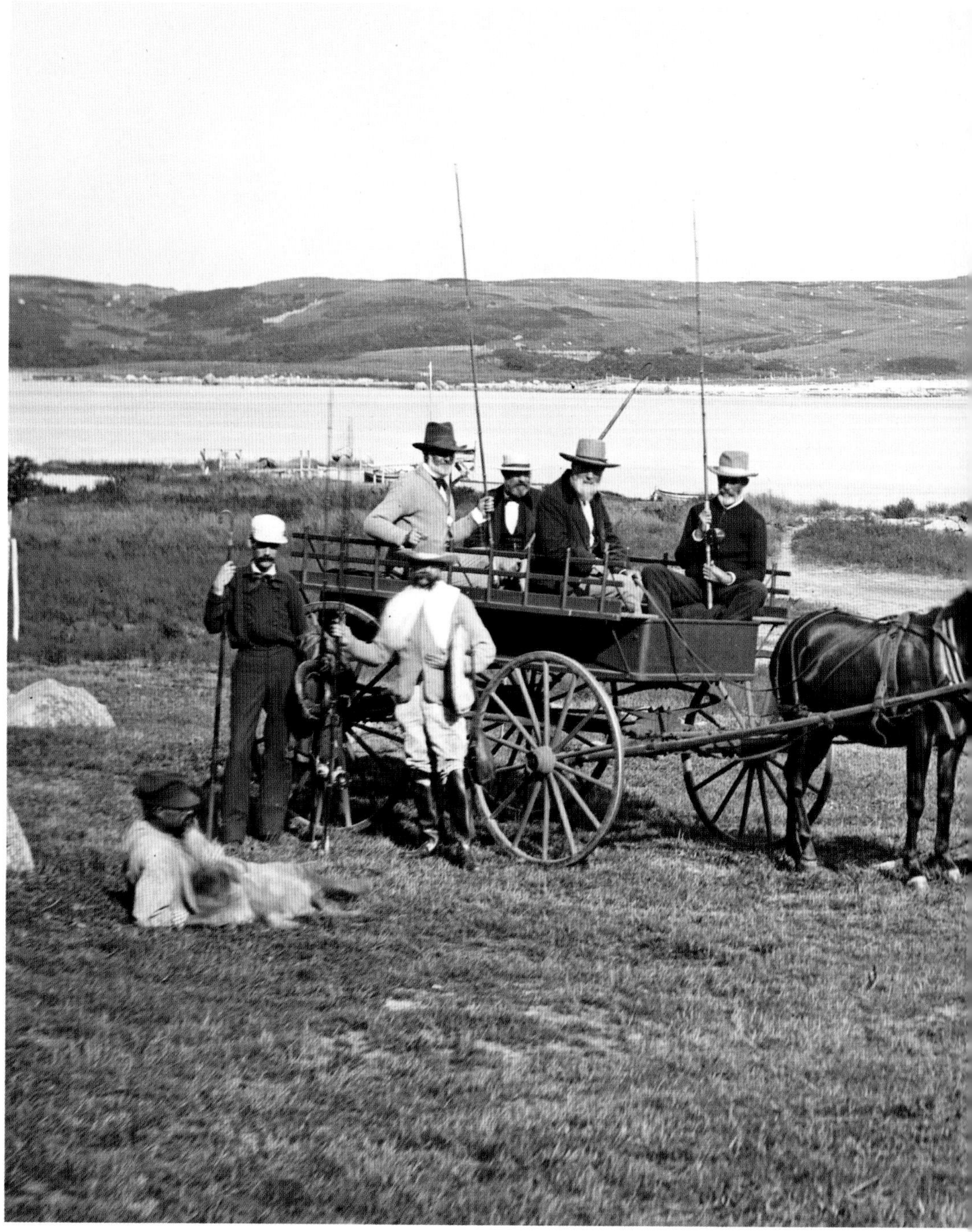

Previous spread: A bass stand on Pasque Island in the Elizabeth Islands, circa 1870. Photo courtesy of the New Bedford Whaling Museum.
Right: Pasque Island club members and locals who attended to their fishing needs near Robinson's Hole. Photo courtesy of the New Bedford Whaling Museum.

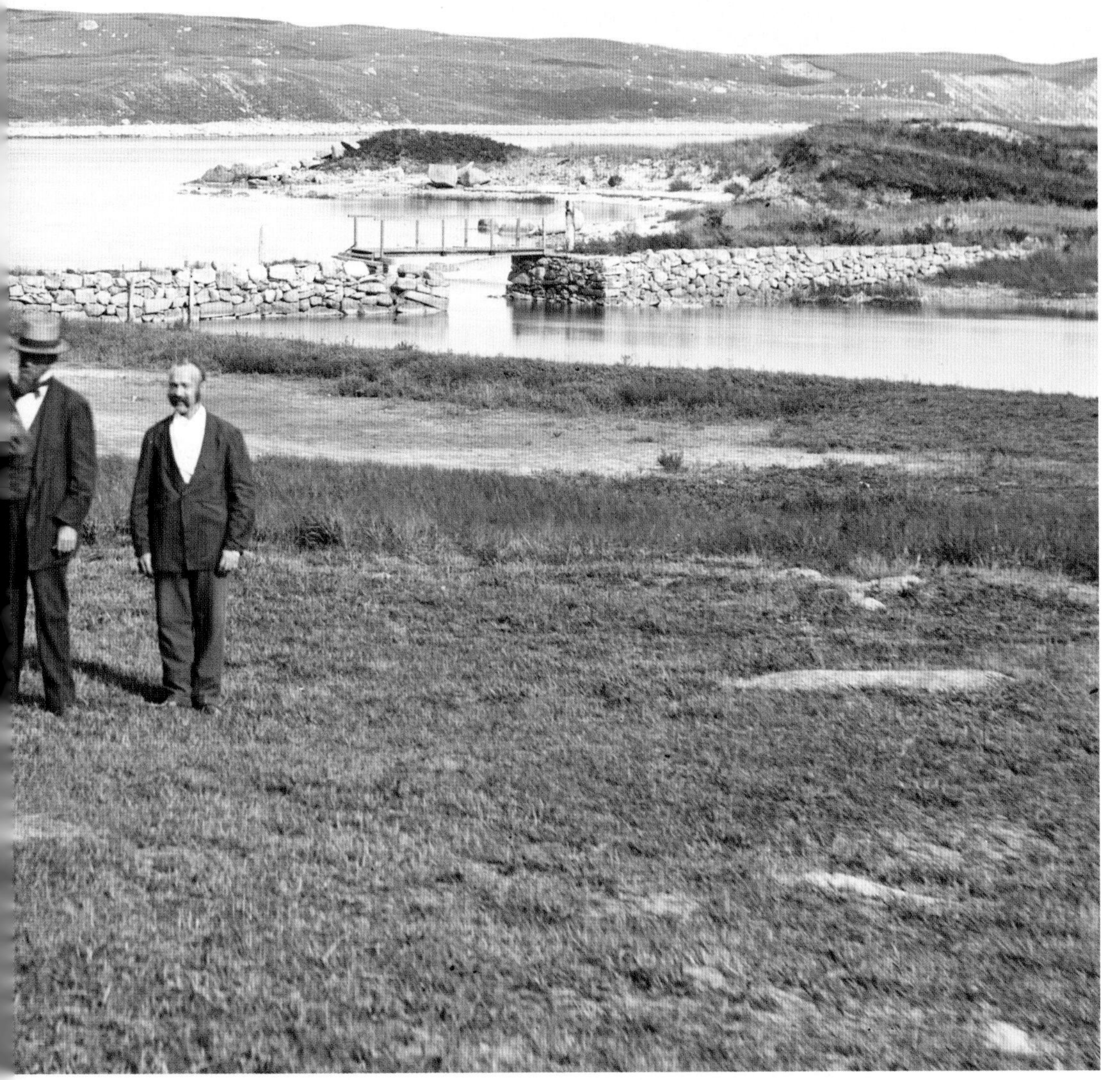

As a budding young striped bass fisherman in the 1960s, I was fortunate to inhabit a world still populated by Swamp Yankees. These longtime New Englanders made their livings as fishermen, farmers, and merchants. Swamp Yankees were a frugal, independent, hardworking lot who spoke their minds and were wary of outsiders. They could keep secrets. They were perfect role models for a young striper kid.

I am old enough to remember the Swamp Yankees of southwest Rhode Island who worked the sounds, bays, salt ponds, and tidal rivers. They netted river herring and smelt, and harvested lobsters, bay scallops, oysters, and eels. Some trapped muskrats. Others took customers out on fishing charters. At least three of my own Swamp Yankee forebears ran haul seines for striped bass along the beaches of southern Rhode Island. They had names like Peleg, Ichabod, and Ezekiel.

I grew up in this tribe and absorbed their ways without realizing it until much later. It was how they stood and moved and talked. The careful way they sized someone up. Their frugality, distance, and stubbornness. Swamp Yankees were taciturn. The ones I knew could communicate with just a look. I learned to read their eyes, their brows, the tilts of their heads. I had plenty of practice spotting the storms that sometimes clouded their expressions, the lightning that narrowed their eyes.

No population studies on Swamp Yankees exist, but their numbers have been declining for decades. Newcomers with more education and money have displaced these self-sufficient watermen, along with their rural country cousins. Old-timers were brought up eating johnny-cakes, spearing eels through the ice, and smoking buckies and bluefish. The Johnny-come-latelies wouldn't know a buckie from a bonefish.

AS A BOY IN THE EARLY '60s, my world revolved around a town dock and the seawalls of Watch Hill Harbor. There, I spent hours handlining cunners, netting blue crabs, and fishing for

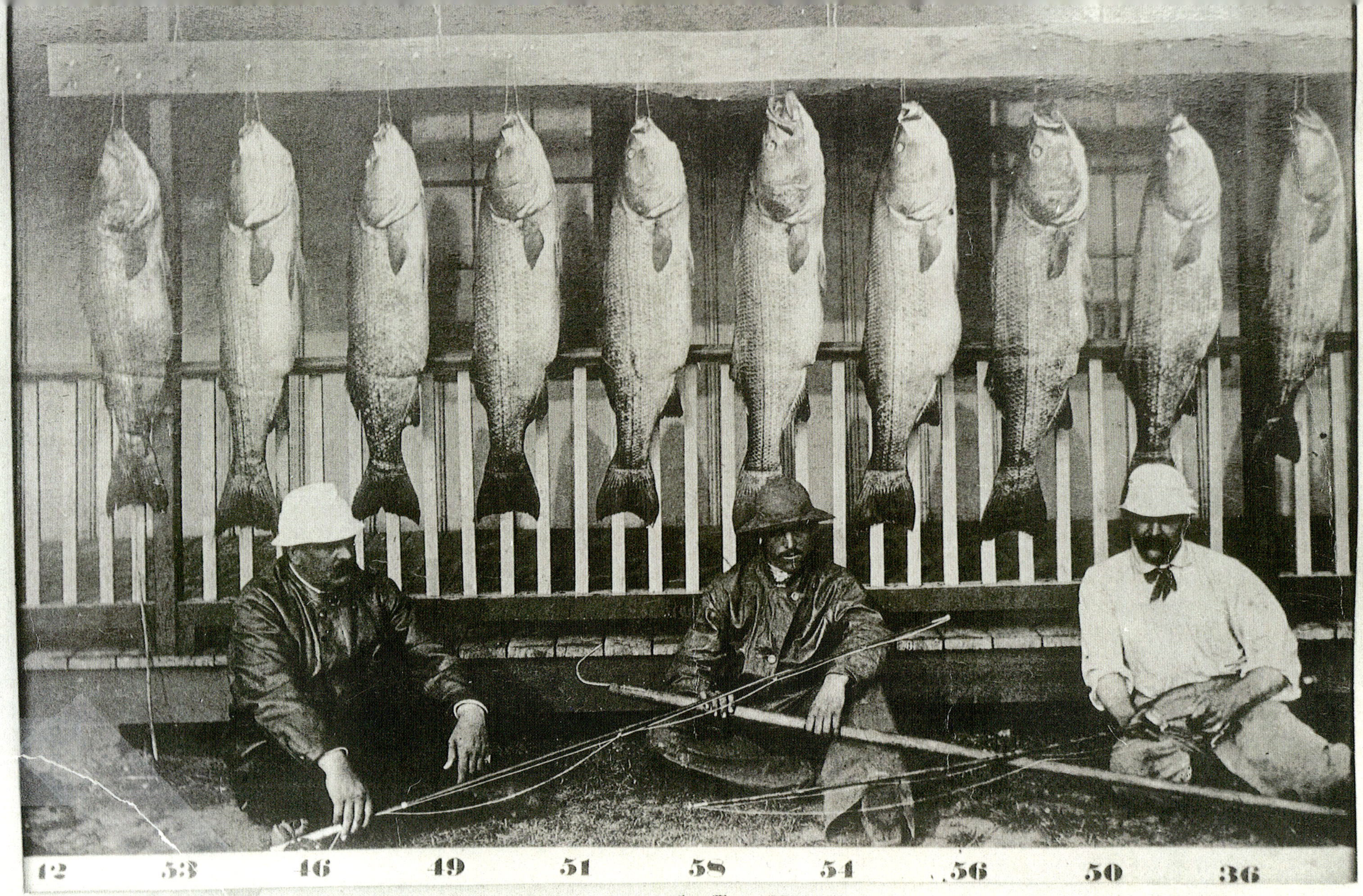

Mr. Seth Barton French | Geo. Tew (Baiter) | Mr. John Whipple

Graves Point Fishing Club — Newport R. I.

Copy of a photograph taken the day of the catch

Total weight 495 lbs.
Average 49½ lbs.

The above catch of striped bass was made on the 29th. Aug. 1881 between 6 and 11 A.M. Heavy sea on and a rising tide. This is the best day's fishing with rod and reel for striped bass of which I can find any record.

Daniel B. Fearing
Newport R. I. Oct. 1902

tinker mackerel, snapper blues, and winter flounder. The dock was also home to three charter skippers and their old wooden tubs, which to my eyes were seagoing gems. It was as colorful a collection of Swamp Yankees as you could ever find in one place. Captains Prent, Louie, and Manny were experts at making ends meet and just getting by. They cast large shadows, and I wanted to be just like them. Little did I know they were a dying breed.

The most sociable of the trio and the best fisherman was Captain Prent Lanphere, who was thin and wiry, and whose face was deeply lined and weathered. He hand-rolled his cigarettes from loose tobacco that I sold him from behind the counter in my father's general store, conveniently located across the street from the dock. When he returned with a charter, I'd be on the dock waiting to see what was swimming in his fish well, a compartment built into the bottom of the hull and flooded with seawater.

"Any stripers Captain Prent?" I'd ask. "Can I see them?"

I'd hear him sharpening his knife on a whetstone before he quickly filleted the day's catch. He was also a showman. He used to tickle a blowfish's belly, and once it expanded, he'd bounce the fish on the dock to attract tourists. Then he would try to interest them in a charter. He was known as "Old Smoothie."

I can also still picture Captain Louie Dussault stretched out on the deck of his salty little boat, his upper torso swallowed by the engine compartment, loose tools scattered around his legs. I learned not to ask the captain questions when he was thus engaged.

For years my family chartered a fishing trip with Captain Louie each summer on my oldest brother's birthday. I looked forward to the outing all year. With great anticipation, we

An exceptional one day's catch hangs at the Graves Point Fishing Club in Newport, Rhode Island. The average fish weighed 49½ pounds. Photo courtesy of the Tew family.

dropped our lines into the deep—probably all of 25 feet. That was 60 years ago, and memories of clearing the breakwater and heading west—where we bottom-fished the Middle Grounds off Stonington, Connecticut, for flounder and scup—still feel exciting.

Louie lived aboard his charter boat in the spring, summer, and fall, and retreated to an ice-locked houseboat in a cove on the Pawcatuck River during winter. As my mother and I drove through town one late fall when I was 11 or 12, I spotted the captain leaning against a light post by the road, a large bag of groceries in his arms. He wore a heavy mackinaw wool jacket with the collar turned up and a broadbrim fishing cap. It was starting to rain, so my mother pulled over. Louie climbed in the front seat. He didn't have his thumb out—my mother later told me he was too proud to ask for a ride. We dropped him off at the head of his cove, where a footpath led down to the houseboat. Unshaven, he looked tired and worn, not the rugged skipper of summer. That small encounter, when one of my heroes suddenly seemed all too human, left an enduring impression.

For many years, Captain Louie and a few other solitary men came to our house for Thanksgiving and Christmas dinners. They had nowhere else to go, and my parents had been friendly with them for years. That world is long gone. Today, a kid couldn't fish off the dock if he wanted to. A gate blocks the entrance, and a sign prohibits both fishing and any access at all unless you're a boat owner or the guest of one. And anyway, a large yacht now walls off the face dock, where old men once sat on overturned buckets and marked the passage of the seasons by the comings and goings of small fish.

THOSE STUBBORN OLD CAPTAINS wouldn't feel at home in the harbor today either. They were from the long-gone analog world, where you fished with your wits, skills, common sense, and sea smarts. A world that calls into question our notions of "progress."

I know one thing for certain: if not for those skippers and the springs and summers spent fishing off the dock and patrolling the seawall with a long-handled crab net, I would be a different person today. There, a kid could learn the basics from the bottom up through observation and trial and error. It was a laboratory for finding bait, understanding tides, tying knots, pulling apart birds' nests, mimicking baitfish with spoons, getting gouged by dorsal spikes and nipped by blue crabs, and a hundred other nuances and building blocks we fishermen take for granted. These were early fundamentals for a striped bass fanatic.

I felt utterly safe sitting between my father and my oldest brother on the old face dock, our feet hanging over the edge, each of us working a handline. We broke sea clams on the raised heads of the spikes that held the planks together and avoided the large gray splinters that penetrated hands and feet as easily as the small hooks we baited with clams.

My father was full of kinetic energy, heckling the fish like a shortstop: daring them to bite, letting them know they had met their match and were about to be caught. With each nibble, he'd snap his wrist and forearm as if making a throw to first, setting the small hook and hauling his fish onto the dock in a blur. An impatient man who played fast sports like racquetball, my father with a handline and a mess of cunners in the waters below was a catching machine. His time with us was limited; he usually had to hurry back to his store.

Once, in an antique shop, I found a tarred hemp handline wrapped on a wooden holder. Its enduring scent instantly swept me back a half century to that dock, where a boy came of age and discovered his tribe. It was just as the writer John Hersey described: "He picked up the ball of twine and put it to his nose and drew in the smell of boats, caulking smell, rope-locker smell—

A hardscrabble fishing family near Robinson's Hole.
Photo courtesy of the New Bedford Whaling Museum.

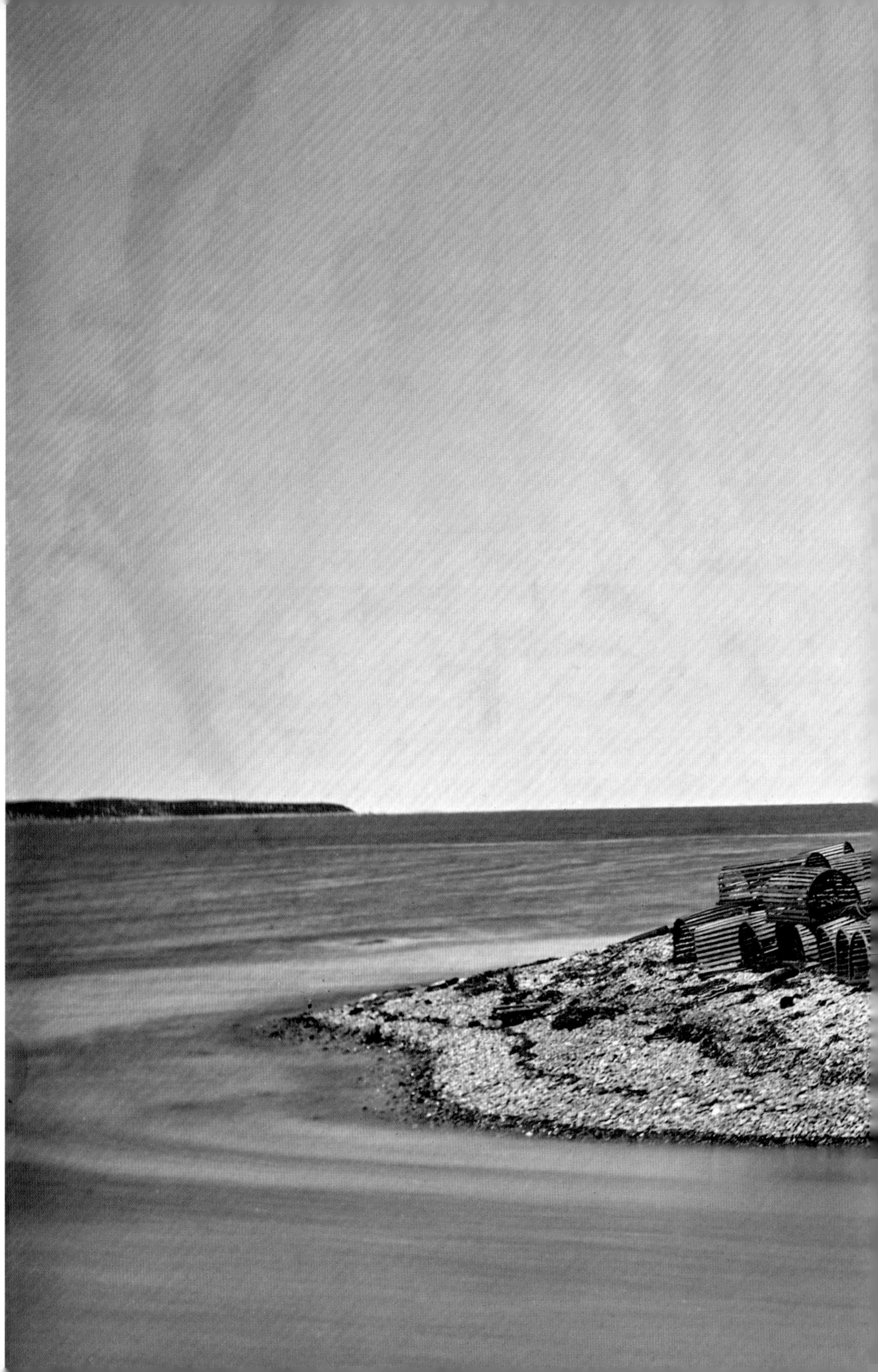

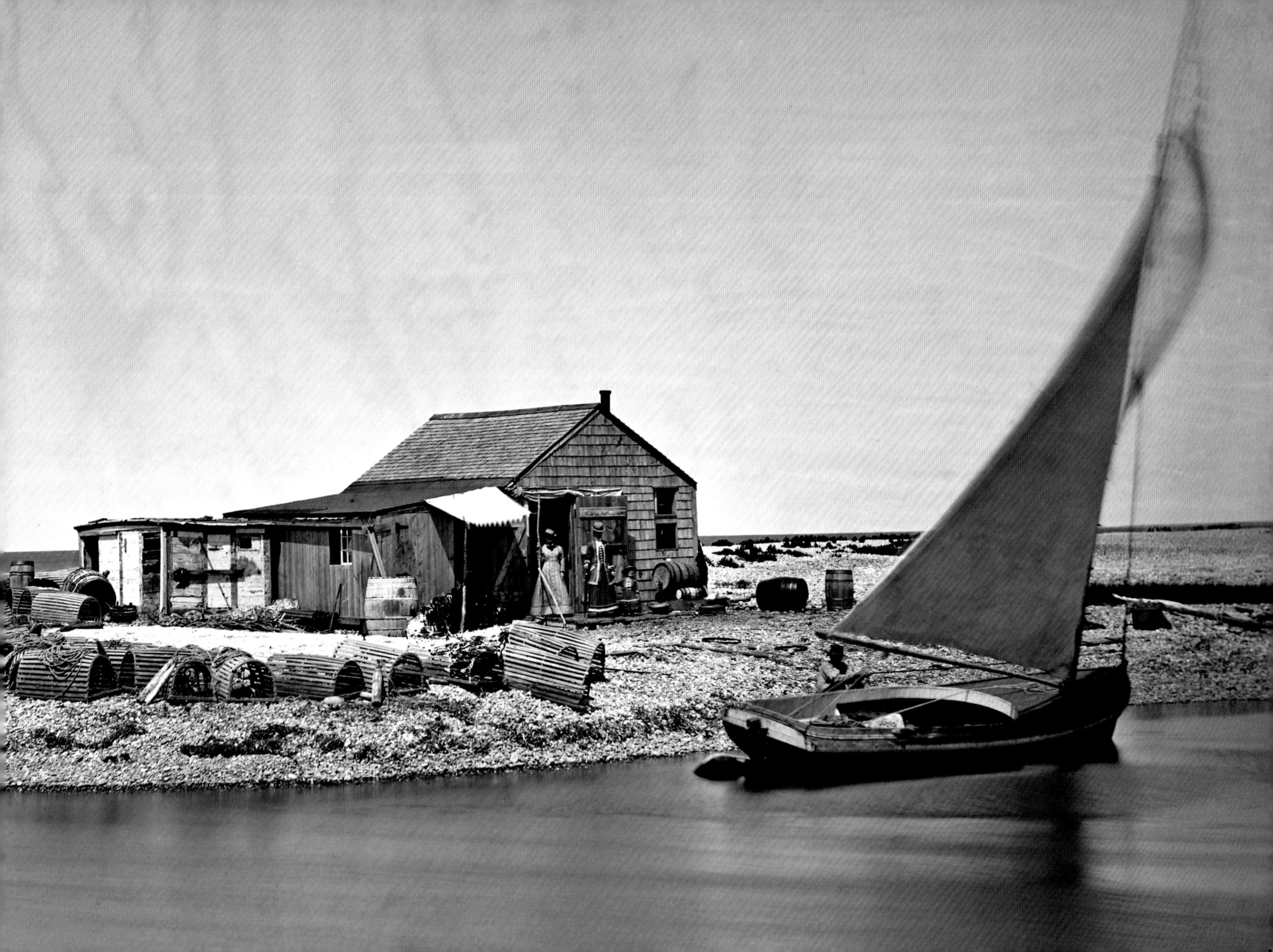

the smell which, savored in deepest gloom of wintertime, had the power of evoking faraway sunlit wavetops, a canted mast, splashing bow waves, a warm summer breeze on a helmsman's cheek."

My father descended from Quakers who fled England for Portsmouth, Rhode Island, in 1651 to escape religious persecution. He kept close to his colonial roots. He lived just 50 miles away as the crow flies, beside a tidal river in Westerly, in the southwest corner of the state. He owned and operated several businesses in nearby Watch Hill that he took over from his enterprising mother, Hattie. He was born into a family of commercial fishermen that had been shaped by loss.

MY GRANDFATHER, William Bernard Sisson, was a surfman in the U.S. Life-Saving Service (forerunner of the Coast Guard) and was stationed both in Quonochontaug and Point Judith, Rhode Island. He and his mates kept watch over the coastal waters, launching pulling boats to rescue distressed mariners. On the side, he fished commercially for striped bass and was a professional gambler.

Known as Bernie, he died suddenly in 1922, when my father was two years old—too young to form any memories of his father. The following year, my father's five-year-old brother, Billie, was struck by a truck and killed. In photos of my grandmother taken shortly after, she is dressed in black and faces the sea, my tiny father held close to her waist. Her kind swallowed their losses and moved forward. My grandmother steered my father away from the saltier relatives on his paternal side who fished for a living. Letters she wrote in the 1920s revealed her determination to ensure her surviving son and daughter would get college educations. Both did.

MY GREAT-GRANDFATHER, also named William Sisson, was himself no stranger to risk on or off the water. This eldest William Sisson was, according to his obituary, one of the youngest Union soldiers in the Civil War. Too young to enlist legally in Rhode Island when the war broke out, he instead went to New Hampshire, added a few years to his age, and joined a cavalry regiment under another name. He lost a leg on a battlefield in Virginia and returned to Rhode Island to make a living as a commercial fisherman.

A photo shows him standing on a beach, holding a cane in each hand, trouser leg pinned up, net strewn in the sand, pipe between his teeth. He levels the same hard look displayed by family members across the generations that are etched both in my memory and in photographs. My great-grandfather and his sons, commercial fishermen all, had long, sad, windburned faces. Maybe they didn't start out tough, but they were eventually tempered by their circumstances. During the Great Depression, my grandmother dropped off bags of groceries at their homes.

MY GREAT-UNCLE, Captain Ed Sisson, was another Rhode Island seine netter, known for his keen ability to smell stripers before he could see them. At 76, he died in the surf hauling in a heavy seine, literally with his boots on. Such were the times.

Captain Prent once told a writer for the now-defunct magazine *Tidings* about a day when he was helping this great-uncle haul his seine off East Beach in Watch Hill. That day, he said matter-of-factly, they netted a striped bass weighing 105 pounds. That he said it so casually makes me believe it was true. All along the striper coast are stories of linesiders of yore weighing 100-plus pounds, nearly all taken by commercial men.

The thumbprints of these Swamp Yankees still mark their descendants, revealed in their stoicism, independence, and hard bark. They bear no buttery sentimentality. We are all our father's children. My father was frugal his entire 91 years, long after there was any reason to go without. In his later years, he lamented the father and brother he never knew. I had him read the 80-year-old obituaries

A Cuttyhunk Bass Club stand, circa 1870. Photo courtesy of the New Bedford Whaling Museum.

"Casting menhaden bait for striped bass from the rocky shores of the bays, estuaries, and islands along the Atlantic coast constitutes the highest branch of American angling. It is indeed questionable—when considering all the elements which contribute to the sum total of sport in angling—whether this method of striped bass fishing is not superior to fly-fishing for salmon, and if so, it outranks any angling in the world. The method is eminently American, and characteristic of the modern angler by its energy of style, and the exercise and activity necessary to success."

—Genio C. Scott,

Fishing in American Waters, *1869*

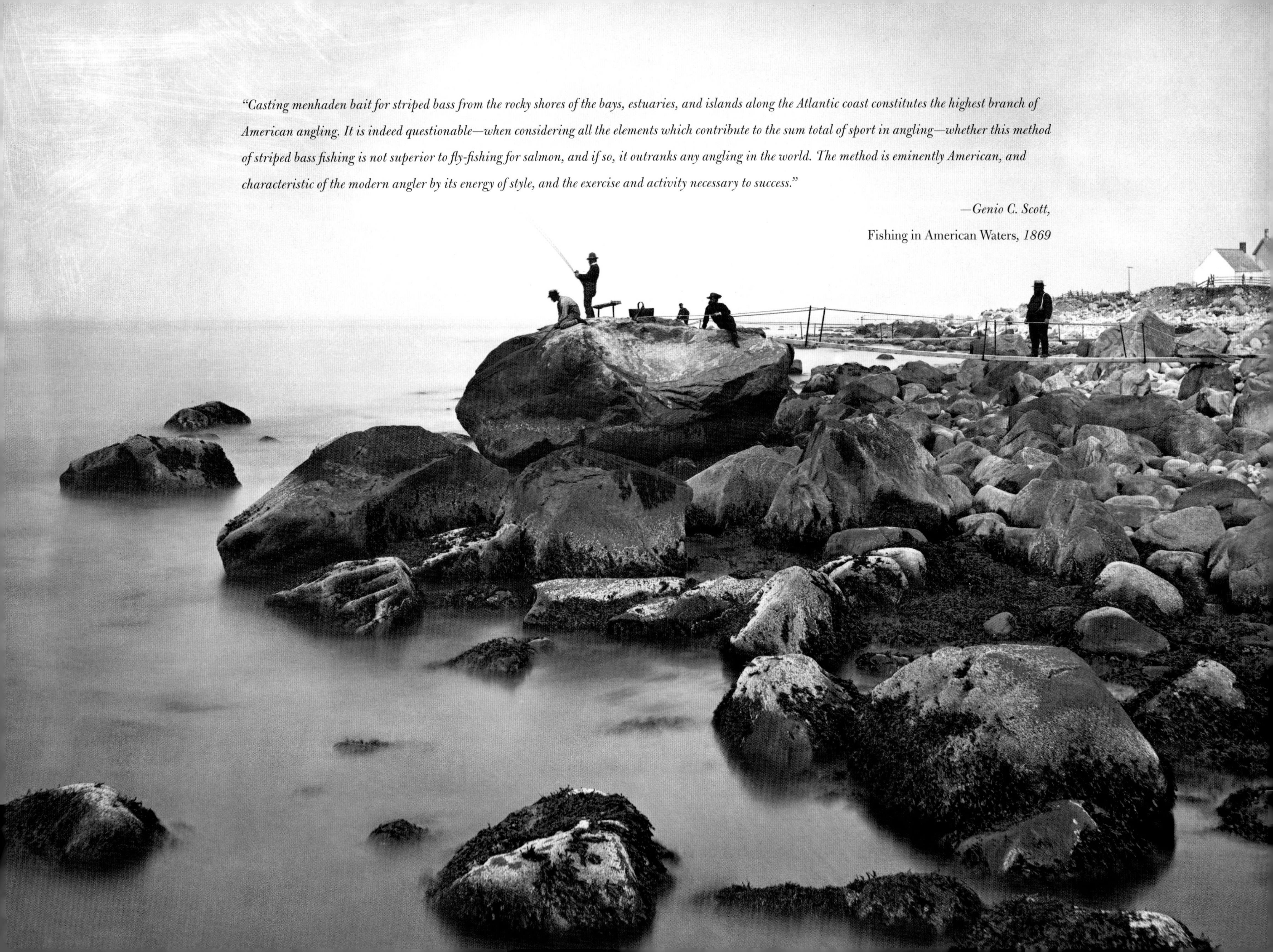

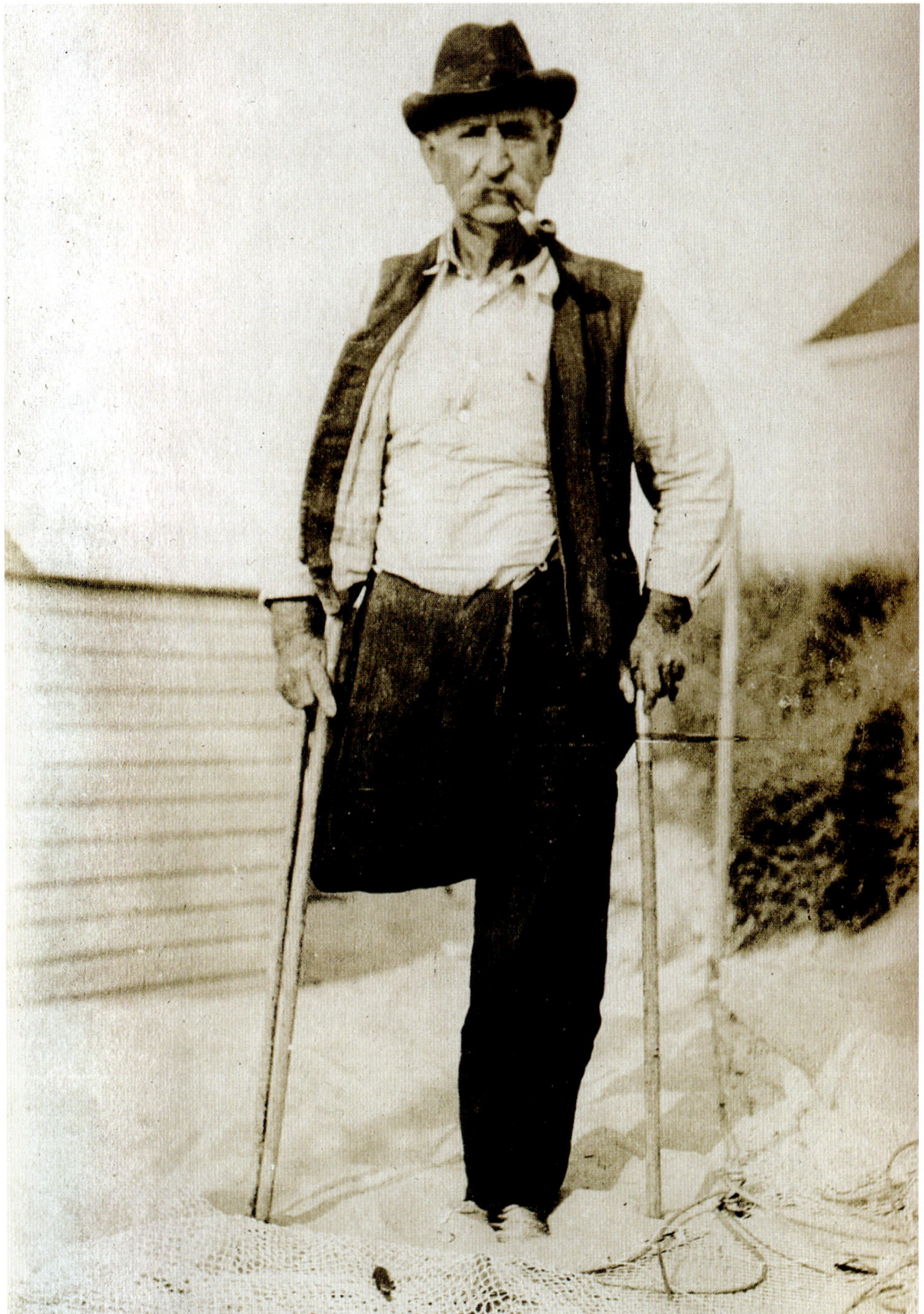

I had found in my research. He sighed and shook his head. "I never knew my brother," my father said. "I never knew my father either. Imagine that. Never knew either of them. What a shame."

IT IS FALL, AND I'M IMAGINING William B. Sisson riding beside me in my Down East skiff as the wind strengthens and the seas build with the flood. My family has worked these waters for generations. I skirt the empty rip and study the seas in the fading light. It's bigger and steeper than I'd hoped. No other boats are working the reef this evening. I'm fishing alone, except for the old-timer in my head. To keep the bow from getting knocked sideways, I drift it under power, with one hand working both the throttle and wheel, the other one holding the rod. I've fished this way before.

You can make it through there, son, he whispers. *You're not going to get any fish unless you get back in there anyway. You know that. The fish are in the second or third wave.*

My grandfather is right. A surfman and a gambler, he knows about playing the odds and taking chances. There's little to be gained by nibbling around the edges. I know exactly where the fish are lying. Either I go in after them or pack up and go home. I've got the gold pocket watch with his initials engraved on the back. I have his name. And, like it or not, I've inherited that little bit of wiring that connects us to our past.

Like my dad missing his dead father, I, too, have spent my life looking over my shoulder for the ghost of this waterman, chasing him until we meet here on a windy night with a foaming rip spread in front of us. It looks and feels fishy. The calendar and tide suggest the same. And here he is, the Swamp Yankee, standing beside me, talking in my ear.

Go ahead, boy, he says. *Get back in there. There's fish to be caught. You can make it. Move!*

Left: The author's great-grandfather lost a leg in the Civil War and fished commercially thereafter. Photo courtesy of the Sisson family.
Right: A gathering of Yankees pose for a photo. Photo courtesy of the New Bedford Whaling Museum.

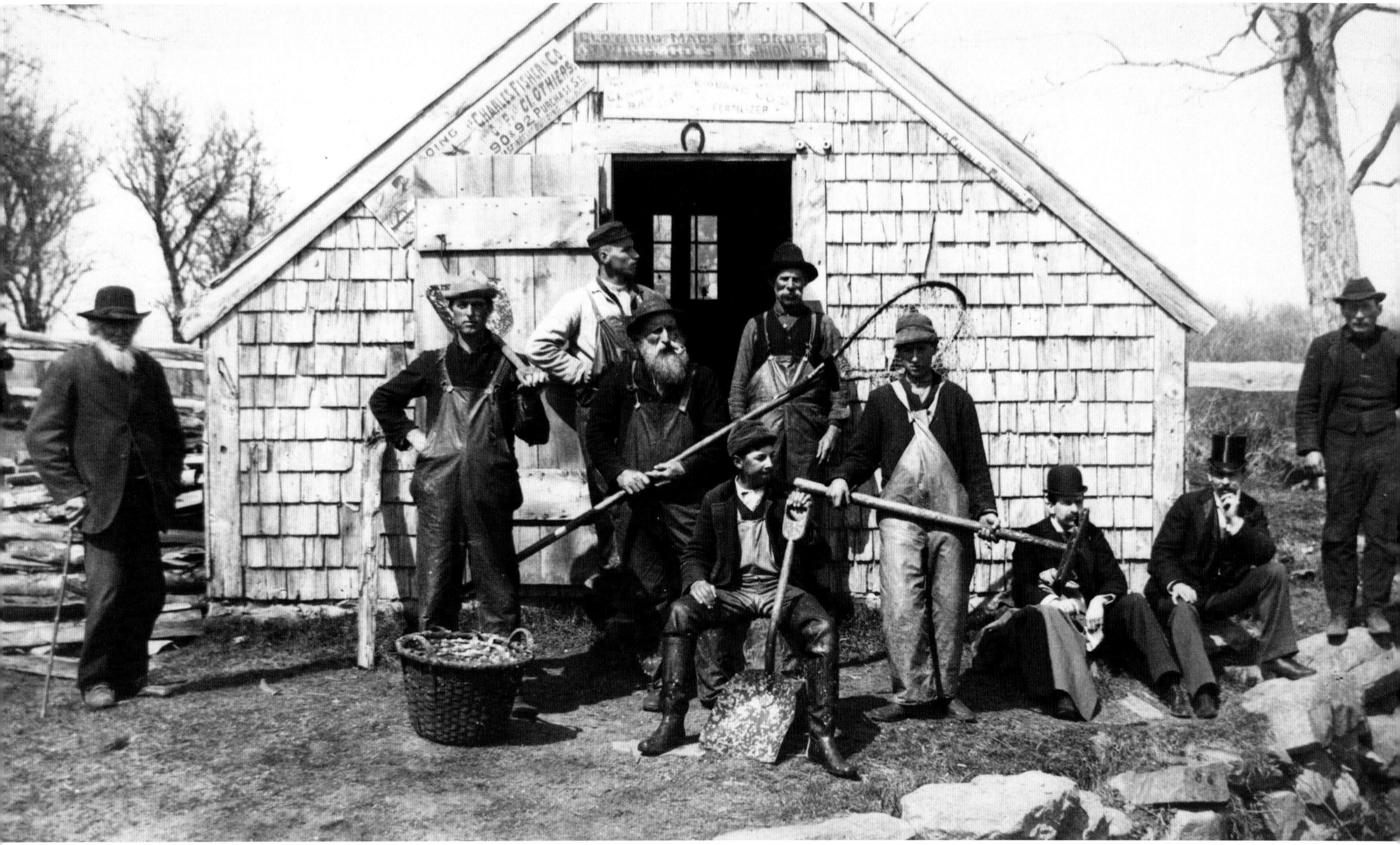
CHARLES FISHER & CO.
CLOTHIERS
90 & 92 PURCHASE ST.
FERTILIZER

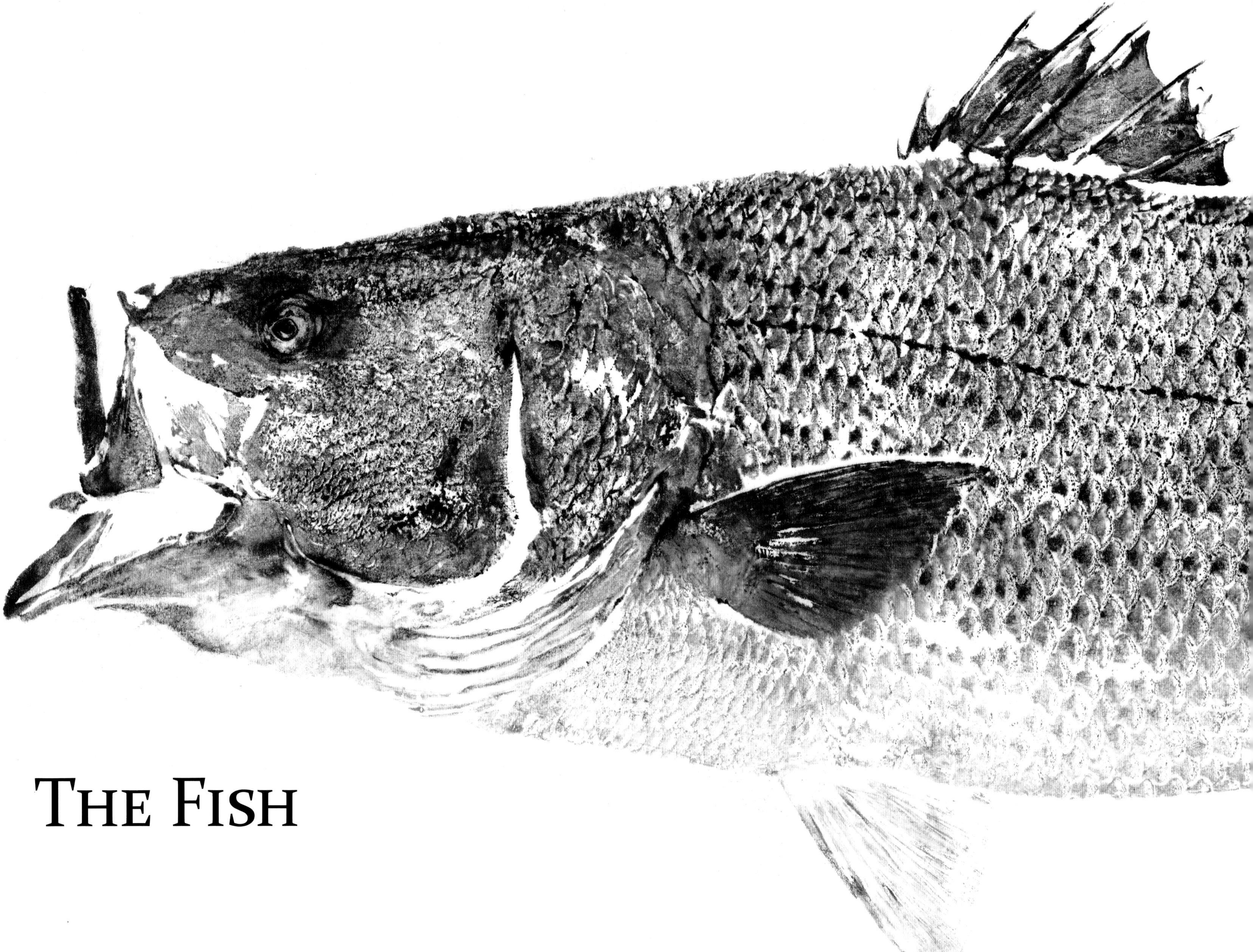

The Fish

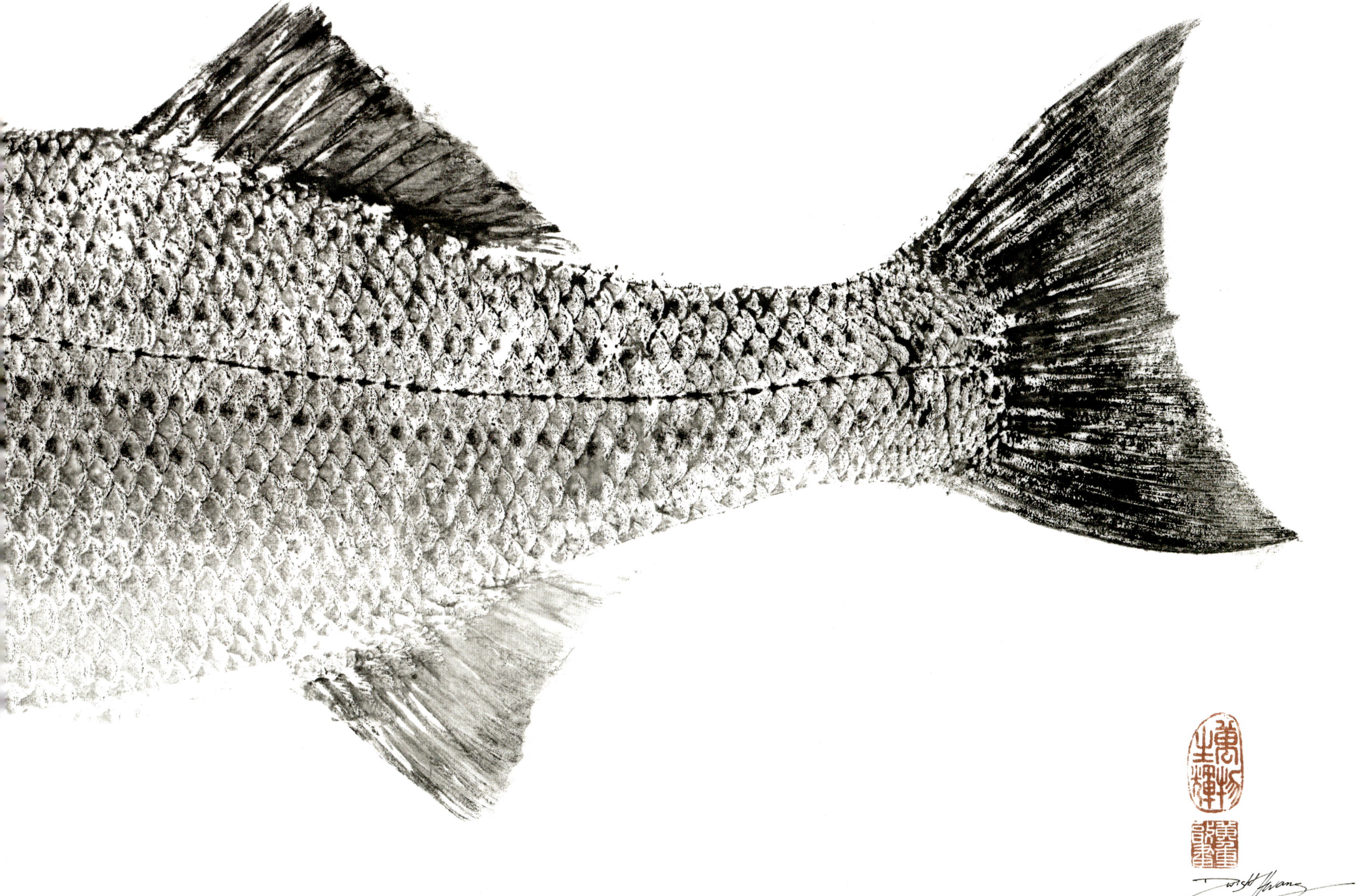

A striper is what it does. It's how the fish goes about its daily business of feeding in so many habitats and under such varied conditions that makes them so magical. I have followed stripers for a lifetime, and they surprise me every season.

What's not to like about striped bass? New York fly guide Captain Brendan McCarthy said he wishes the fish would tail more on the flats, like bonefish. A nitpick, but fair enough. Someone else told me that if striped bass jumped, he would have quit his job and left his happy home to follow the fish to his ruin.

Stripers do make an honest jump on rare occasions, but more often they pull off what one might generously call a clumsy leap—more like a barrel roll—where they partially emerge from the water and curl back over with a splash. But a true jump, like a rainbow or billfish? It's just not part of the package.

WHAT A STRIPED BASS CAN DO more than makes up for its lack of both aerial explosives and showy tail flashes. "Stripers are so well-endowed in terms of where they live and how they make a living," said John Waldman, an aquatic conservation biologist and professor at Queens College. "There is almost no habitat along the coast where they are not found."

According to Waldman, who is a longtime striper angler and also edited the book *Stripers: An Angler's Anthology*, the striped bass is the ultimate generalist. "Some species have very particular requirements, like grayling or brook trout," he said. "These damn things exist and flourish in an amazing range of geography and environments—it's just really impressive."

Previous spread: Gyotaku fish print by Dwight Hwang.
Right: Stripers in a Montauk wave. Photo by Tom Lynch.

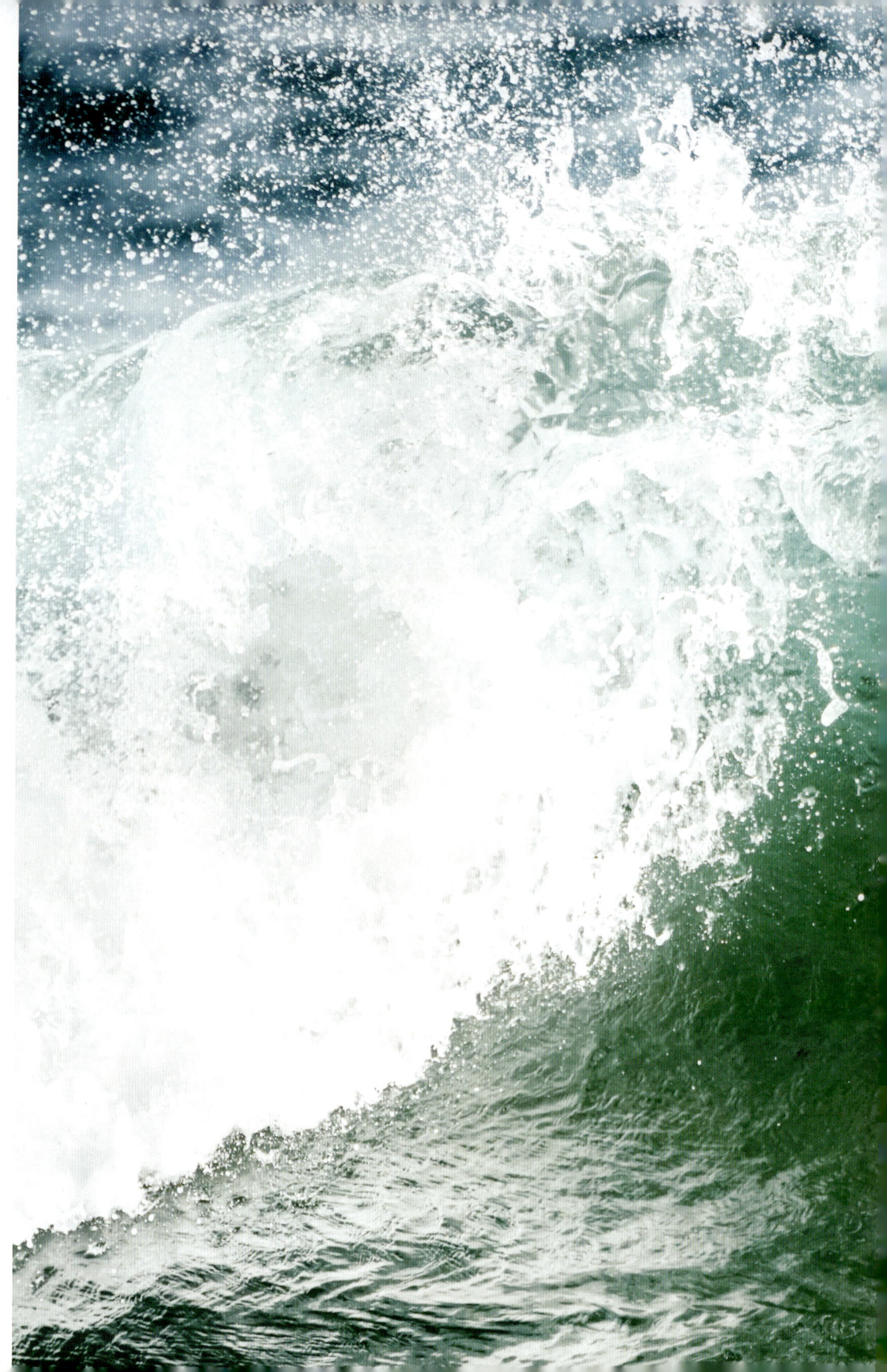

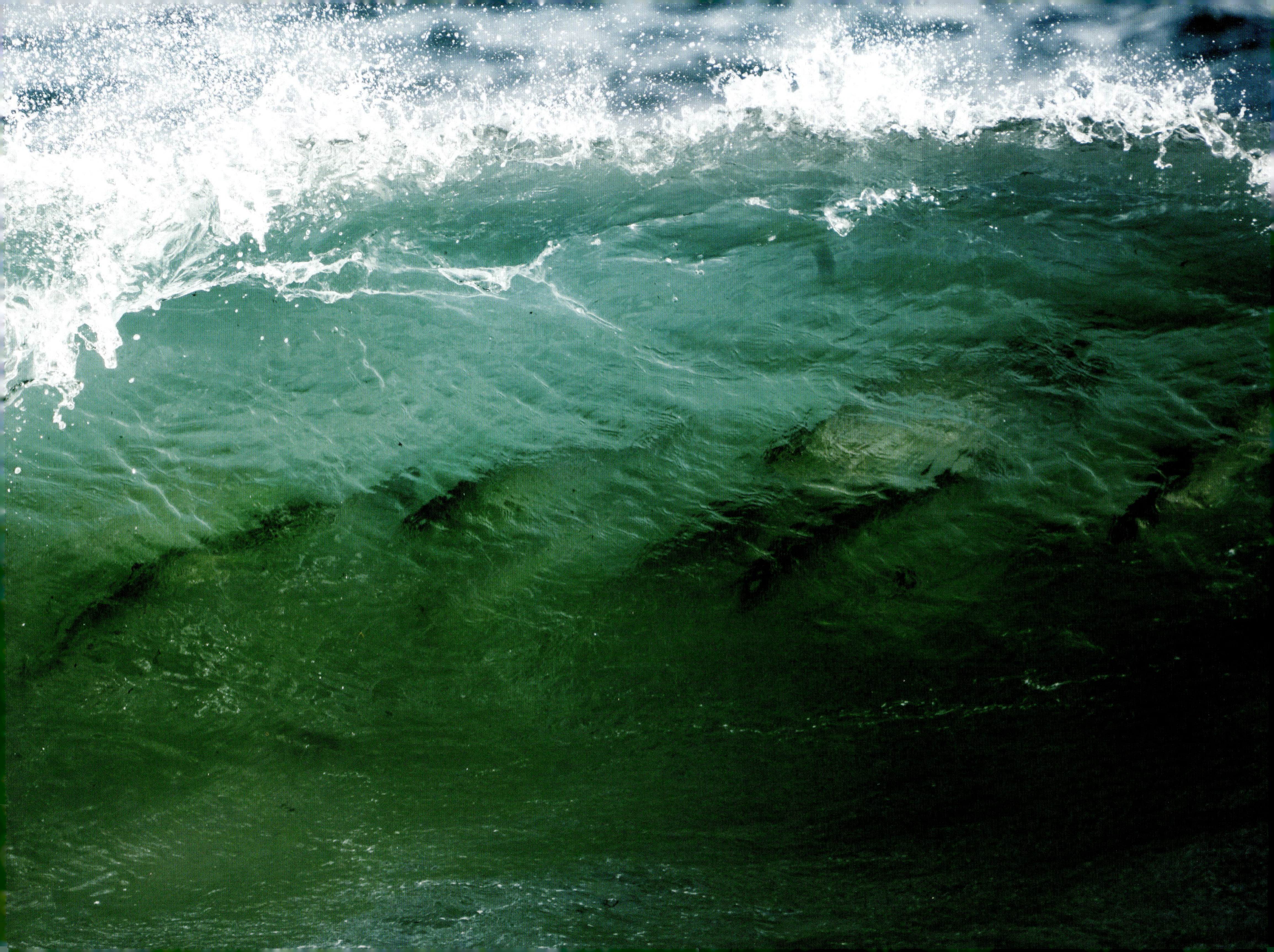

Striped bass are perfectly formed to thrive in a world of tides and currents, moving water, and breaking waves from North Carolina to Quebec, Canada. Most of us have watched them feed as if it's their last day on Earth amid nor'easters and the remnants of hurricanes, gales, horizontal rain and sleet, and gnarly storm waves. For stripers, the worst weather you can conjure is just another day at the office.

Striped bass have incredible tolerances, said Waldman, rattling off the various places the fish are found: freshwater reservoirs and lakes; rivers that drain into the Gulf of Mexico; on the West Coast; in estuaries, rocky coasts, the open Atlantic, and hundreds of miles up the Hudson and Delaware Rivers. Stripers are also regularly caught in a host of urban areas, including Boston and New York Harbors. Photographer Tom Lynch, who took many of the photos in this book, sometimes chases the fish in heavily industrialized backwater areas of New Jersey, including a former Superfund site.

"It's been called a sewer trout, sardonically, because it tolerates an amazing range of environmental conditions," said Waldman, who has studied striped bass for decades and written more than 100 scientific articles and several popular books, including *Running Silver: Restoring Atlantic Rivers and Their Great Fish Migrations*. "That's not to say it's invincible, but it's a helluva hardy fish."

I WAS BARELY OUT OF BOYHOOD the first time I saw a striper race up the back of a big green breaker, chasing bait a moment before the wave toppled in a roar of foam and spray. A year or two later, my adrenaline surged again when a bass shot diagonally across the face of a reared-up storm wave and snared my Hopkins jig as improbably as a wide receiver makes a fingertip catch. I was in my early teens, and I stood transfixed. Is there anything this fish can't do?

Stripers have evolved to take full advantage of what old-timers used to call "boisterous" weather. Long ago, dressed in waders and rain gear, I fished the rocks at a lighthouse during a booming nor'easter as waves surged up the riprap and forced everyone casting there to back against the seawall surrounding the light. I imagined we were crew on a clipper ship clawing its way around Cape Horn with the decks swept by breaking waves and green water eager to grab a careless sailor and carry him to his demise.

As water drained between the rocks, we returned to our spots and fired off casts, each keeping an eye trained for the next boarding wave. The stripers, meanwhile, frolicked through the heart of the storm, feeding on bait that was helplessly disoriented by the surf, current, and froth. How could you fail to love a fish so suited for even those bad-ass days that keep the largest sportfishing boats in their slips?

For all their ability to feed in foaming rips and pounding shore break, striped bass are equally adept at finding food in tidal rivers, bays, salt ponds, and flats. You gain a sense of their capabilities by watching them sip cinder worms in salt ponds and feed on crabs and sand eels on the flats. I once heard a story about stripers that regularly trailed a lobsterman, devouring the shorts he culled and threw over the side.

THE ABILITY OF A STRIPER TO FIND A MULLET, menhaden, or your bucktail in billows of white water, day or night, is a function of its prominent lateral line. This organ is embedded in scales, senses vibrations in the water, and allows the fish to zero in on prey that is floundering. In stripers, this line extends one-third of the way onto the caudal or tail fin, with additional short sequences of lateral line scales above and below the main one on the tail, adding sensitivity to the rear of the fish. "If you're in the middle of a blitz, it's great to know that there is something behind

A good dousing. Photo by Tom Lynch.

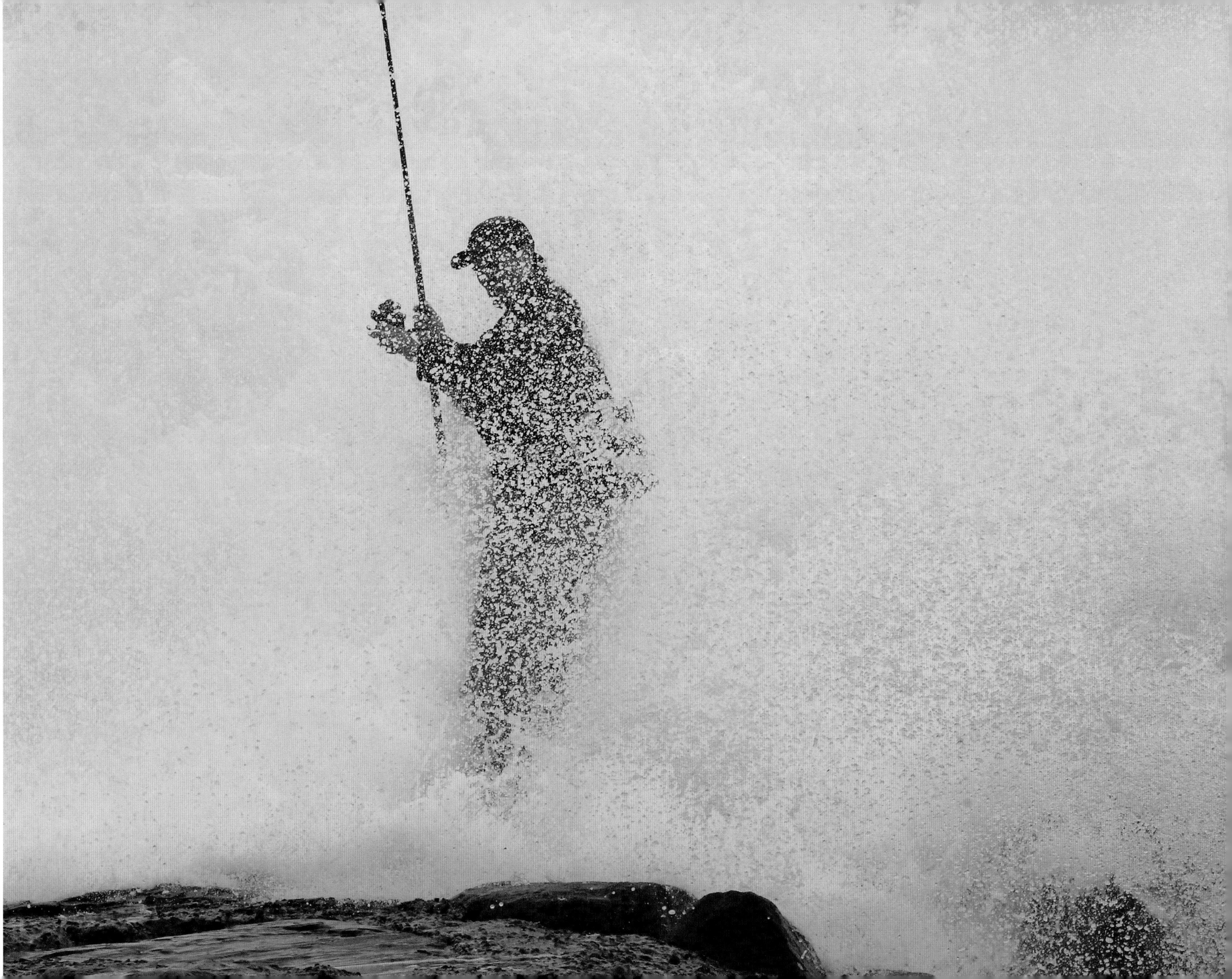

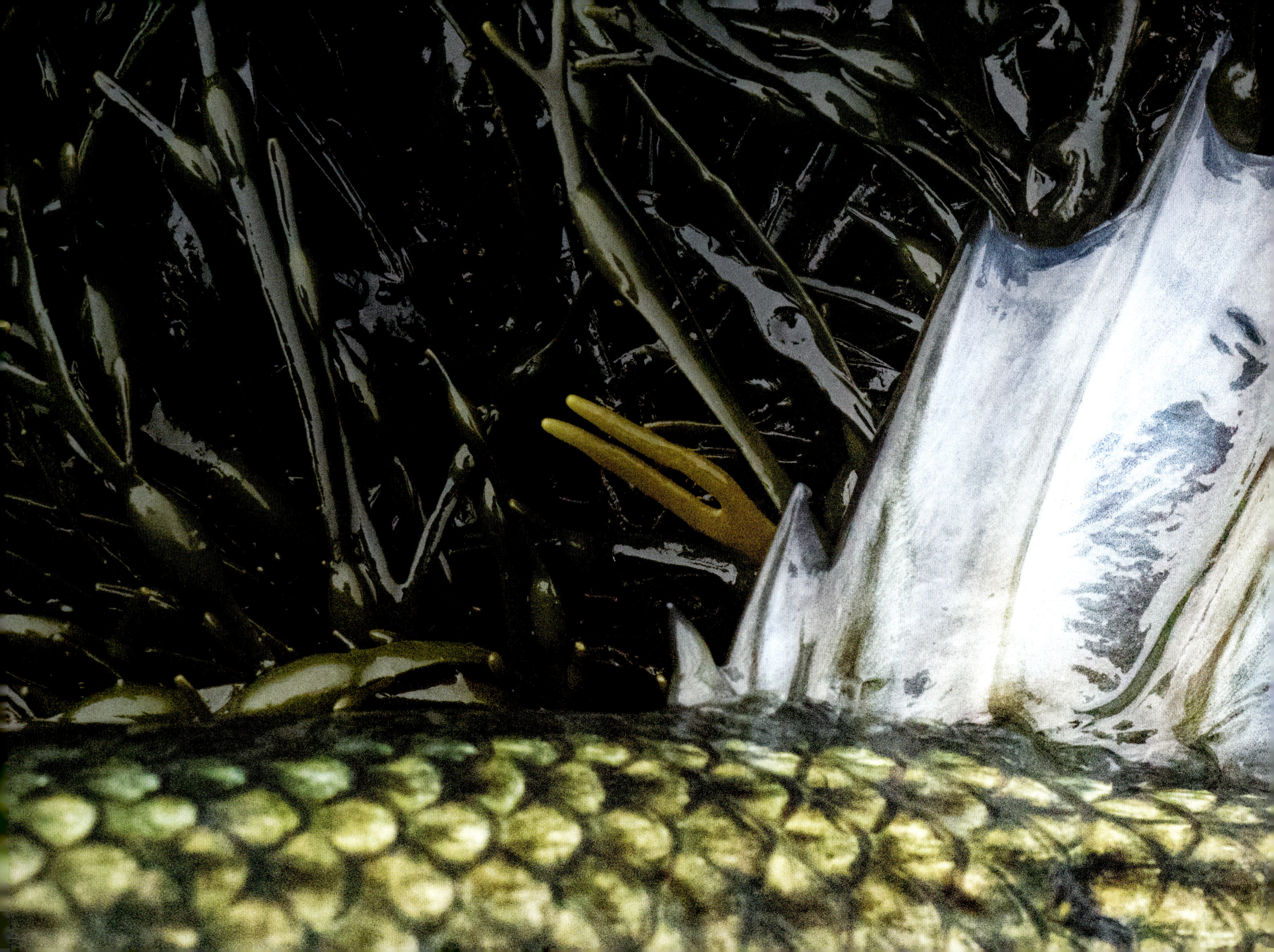

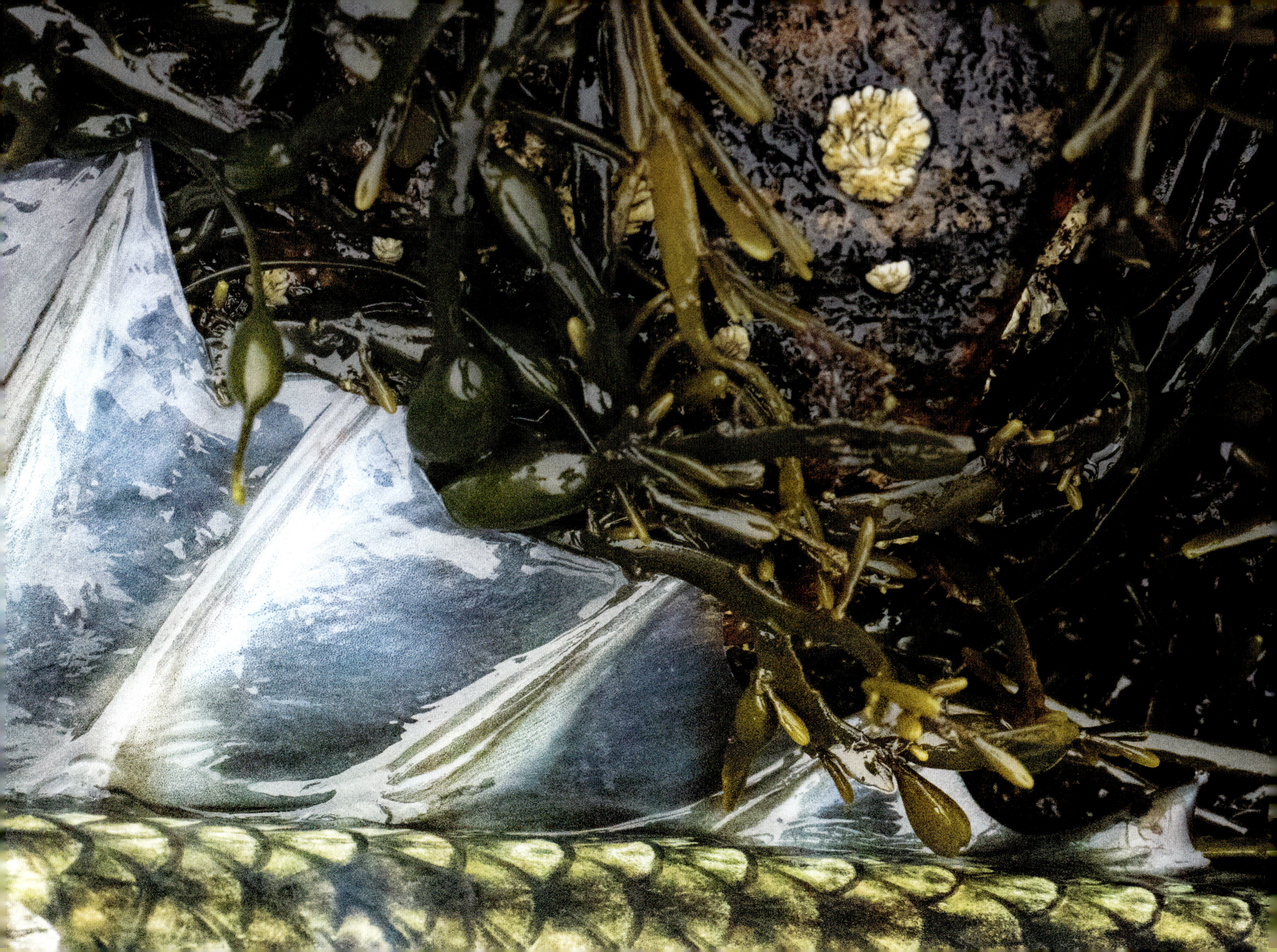

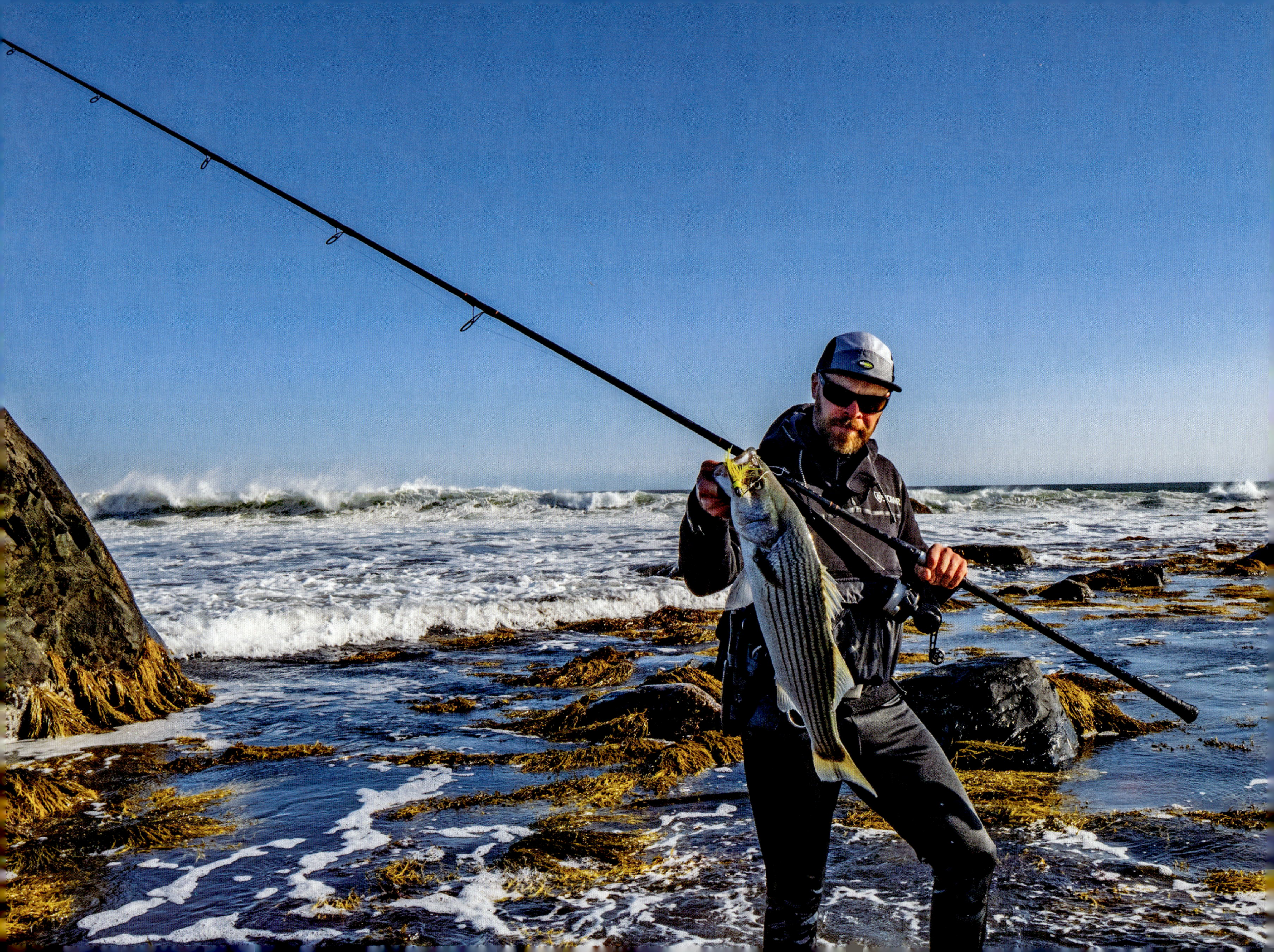

you. You can just whirl around and grab it," Waldman said. "That's a very helpful adaptation for the fish." During a day bite in white water, the fish relies on eyesight in addition to its lateral line.

I asked Waldman if he could compare a striper's lateral line to any human sense. "I don't think we have anything we can directly compare to the lateral line," he said. What might come closest, he added, is "wind on our naked body, on our arms and legs."

SOME OF MY MOST MEMORABLE FISHING has occurred when schools of discombobulated bait become trapped in broad swaths of white water between breaking waves—the stripers moving in and going ballistic, cutting through bait and foam with abandon. You time your casts so that your lure is in the air as the last wave in the set crumbles. You crank the reel handle a few times and are tight to a good fish. Those moments have the visual and auditory elements that make striped bass fishing as spectacular as any experience in the angling kingdom. Breaking waves, busting fish, wind-blown spray, panicked bait, berserk gulls, and bent rods. Those outings may be impossible to top.

"They love to feed in white water," said artist Nick Mayer. "And their big, broom-like tail is pretty remarkable. It's made for navigating in that churn. It has a lot of torque. . . . They're like apparitions that appear out of the white water."

WHEN A STRIPER GRABS A MULLET, BUNKER, or even an American eel, it usually holds tight, thanks to an effective arrangement of teeth. The fish have regular teeth along the upper and lower jaws, which feel like sandpaper. They're the ones that give us "striper thumb." The fish also have additional teeth for grasping food right on their tongue—near the tip in the soft tissue, and a pair of tooth patches on the tongue bone section.

Previous spread: Dorsal fin, rockweed, and barnacles. Photo by Tom Lynch.
Left: Island schoolie caught in the white water. Photo by Jerry Audet.

"The fact that they and the five other members of family *Moronidae* have these lingual teeth [*lingual* means tongue] makes them pretty unusual in the fish world," Waldman said. "There's almost nothing else that has teeth on the tongue. They also have teeth farther back in their gullet that can help crush a small blue crab or a fish. So they are pretty well dentally endowed."

STRIPERS DON'T PULL LIKE A TUNA, they don't jump like a tarpon, and they don't have the top speed of a bonefish, permit, or sailfish. But they bring their own brand of powerful magic as they move along the coast. This truth remains across generations: a big striper in heavy cover is a handful.

If you're going to make hay with stripers, it helps to get comfortable fishing nights both from a boat and from shore. You can certainly catch them during daylight, especially in deep water and at opportune times of the year. But the striped bass is principally a fish of night tides and moving water. It is a fish that rewards hard work, persistence, and knowledge of the tides, as well as an understanding of seasonal rhythms and patterns. Their challenges are compelling. Just when you think you can predict their comings and goings, they leave you flummoxed.

The surprises are part of their appeal. Mayer, an avid angler, remembers a blitz on the west side of Charlestown Breachway in Rhode Island, when schoolies actually beached themselves in their amped-up pursuit of peanut bunker. "They were launching themselves on the sand and flipping around until they got back into the water," he recalled.

Fish long enough and you see your share of oddities. My partner Bruce was playing a schoolie on a summer evening and his eel slipped up the leader to the swivel, where it dangled and twisted above the water. A second striper lunged a foot or more out of the water for the squirming bait, successfully snatching or knocking it free on its second attempt. That was a first.

THE STRIPER IS ONE OF THE HANDSOMEST fish in fresh or salt water. It looks like a proper fish—stout, distinctive, without a hint of the outlandish or eccentric. Ichthyologists refer to its shape as a "classic fish body." From its wide tail to its large head, the fish is, indeed, classically proportioned. A 25- to 30-pounder exemplifies the beauty, balance, and strength of the species, with its broad shoulders, striped flanks, and spiny dorsal. The skin mount of a 26-pounder that hung in my friend's beach cottage in Rhode Island was a perfect embodiment of balance, beauty, and form following function.

"If there was a Fibonacci number for fish, I think the striped bass would be the base mark," said Mayer, referring to the idea that beauty in a host of fields is related to this mathematical relationship of dimensions. "The proportions are pleasant to the eye."

"They are absolutely striking," said Bob Popovics, an innovative fly developer and striper fan from New Jersey. "There is a balance to it. It looks like a fish is supposed to look."

A Long Island charter skipper once told me that if you gave a kid in the Northeast a crayon and asked him to draw a fish, it would come out looking like a striped bass. I was one of those kids. Each fall in school, I doodled dozens of striped bass on the covers of my notebooks and in the margins of my papers as I daydreamed of racing to the lighthouse as soon as school let out.

"The fish has an indescribable look," said Lynch, the photographer and avid surf fisherman. "I'd say the shoulders and the dorsal are the two most definitive parts for me. And the big broom tail too."

The broad palette of hues and the many shades, tones, and tints with which the fish is endowed—combined with its seven or eight dark, longitudinal stripes—make it one of the world's most striking fish. "There are so many colors," Lynch said. "It's a great mix of greens, magentas

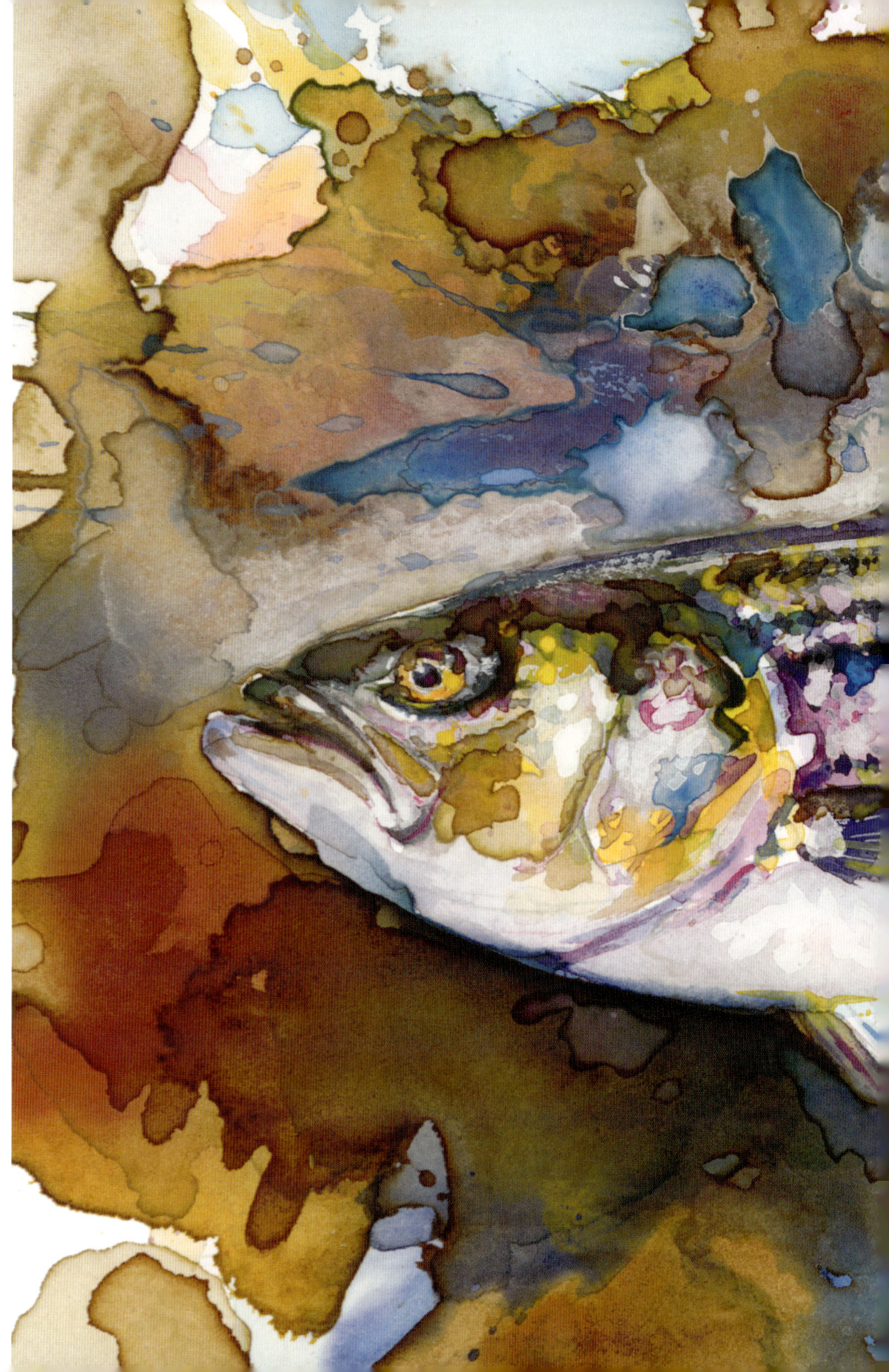

Stripers are strikingly colored. Painting by Shane Reiswig.

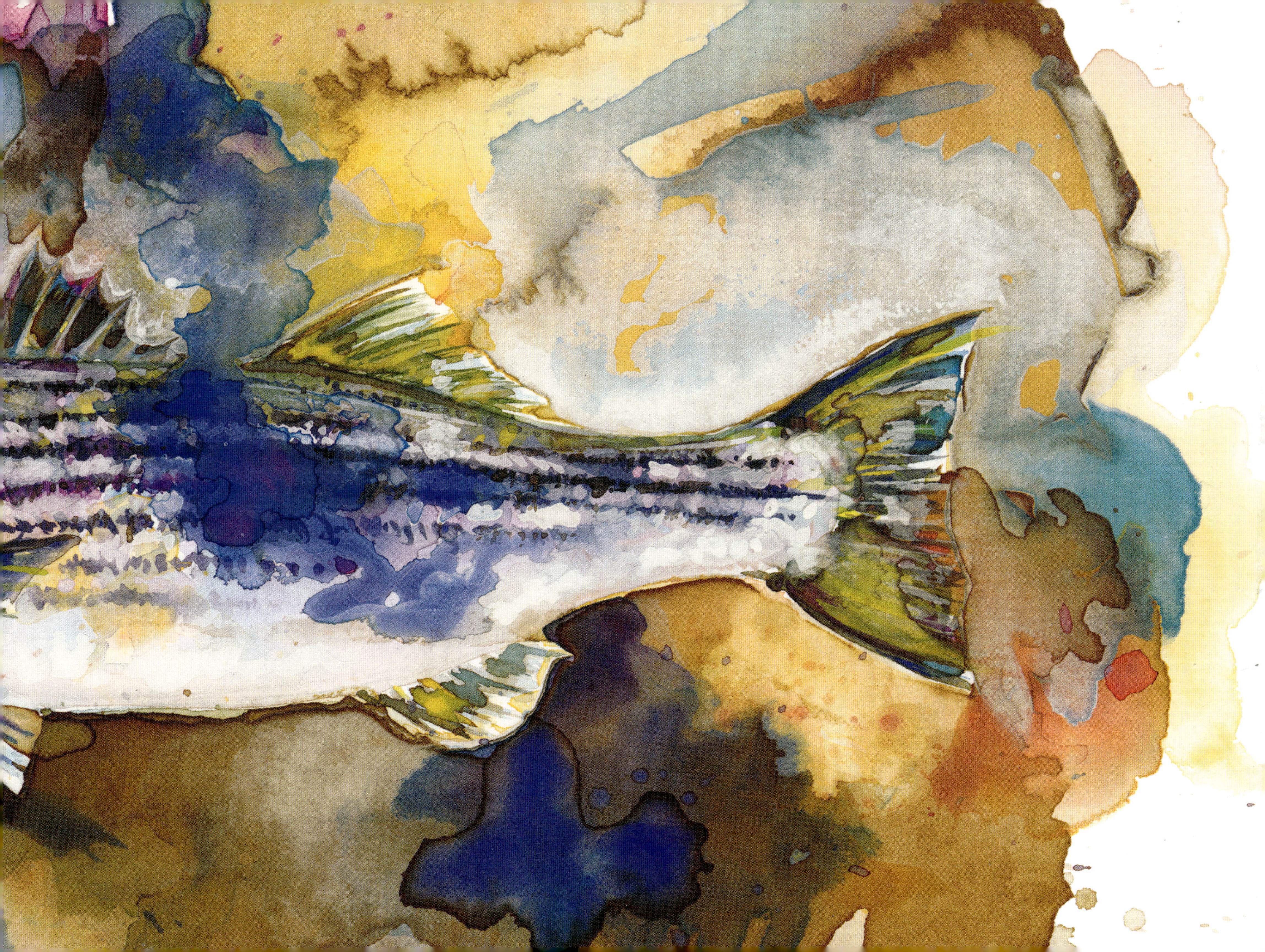

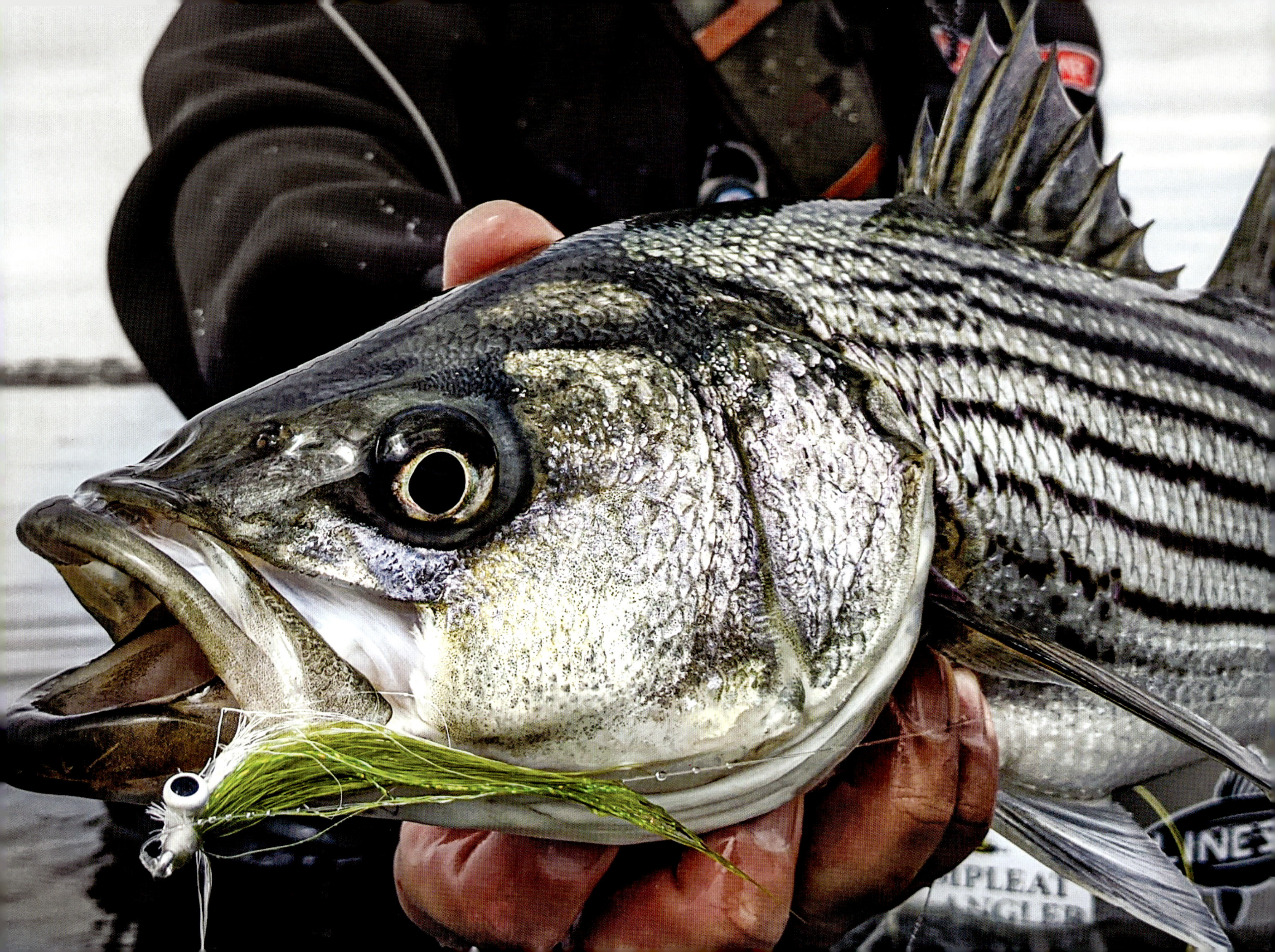

and browns, silvers, gold, and purple. There is a little section behind the eye, up high, where there are just some crazy colors."

The shades change depending on where the fish have been feeding. Darker tones point to deeper waters and rocky bottoms covered with kelp, rockweed, Irish moss, and other seaweeds. Those dark fish are strikingly beautiful in their rich robes of purple, green, and browns. On the flats, the fish are lightly colored to match the sandy bottoms and appear more mirrorlike. "You don't notice all their beauty until you hold the fish in your hand," said striper fanatic John Jinishian, pointing to the turquoise, blues, and purples around the fish's eyes and gill plates. "It's not just a zebra fish."

STRIPED BASS ARE SOMETHING OF a Goldilocks fish, neither too simple to catch nor too difficult. "It's at the elite edge of the everyman fish," Waldman said, "and that's a good place to be. They are not an easy fish. You have to pay your dues."

"They just bring it all," said Captain McCarthy, who guides out of Montauk in the fall. "They are the most everyman fish on the planet. . . . I think of them as the hungry man's can of stew."

On certain days, you can catch stripers cast after cast; on others, they are fickle, remaining closemouthed as frustrated anglers change colors, retrieves, and lure sizes, all the while speculating about hundreds of possible factors that might be at play. "They definitely can be a puzzle," said Rex Messing, 30, a striper fan and fly fisherman. "If they weren't, you wouldn't chase them."

Casual anglers as well as fanatics from a broad range of backgrounds pursue stripers: millionaires and warehouse workers, truck drivers and financial analysts, the rough-spoken and the literati, high school dropouts and Ivy Leaguers, preachers, reporters, pipefitters, scoundrels, grandmothers, and everyone in between. People catch them from beaches, rock piles, rips, jetties, piers, marshes, rowboats, beneath highway bridges, and along urban waterfronts, as well as in pristine coastal areas far from crowds.

A chunk of menhaden stuck on a single hook and flung from a $50 rod-and-reel combo bought at a discount store can yield a 30-pound striper. I've seen it happen. So can intricately tied flies or $40 hand-turned plugs cast with $2,000 fly or spinning outfits. The fish doesn't give a hoot if your guides are attached with electrical tape or if your popper is an old red-and-yellow Atom refitted with new hooks like the one I tossed last fall. You can drop a million dollars on a new triple-engine center console, or you can catch your fish from a kayak, tin boat, or single-engine skiff. The fish doesn't care.

"The striped bass is America's fish," said Jim Hutchinson Jr., managing editor of *The Fisherman* magazine, citing the striper's history in this country, including helping to fund the first public school in the Plymouth Colony through a tax on the sale of the fish.

THOSE WHO CATCH STRIPED BASS consistently have put in their time; studied the fish; paid attention to maintaining sharp hooks, good knots, fresh line, and smooth drags; and have accrued plenty of knowledge of tides, current, weather, location, and a dozen other factors that make a difference. And then there are those who are just flat-out "fishy."

"If you're fishy, you're fishy," said author and Rocky Mountain fly guide Callan Wink, speaking of the intangible qualities that set some anglers and guides apart. "This is something that goes beyond the realm of experience or even luck. This is the stuff of mysticism, and I think these people are closer to artists than the rest of us."

As to diet, stripers are not picky eaters. "They'll eat anything they can get their jaws around," the late Mario Comoli, a Rhode Island boat fisherman, once told me. I've heard Comoli's sentiment expressed dozens of times. The better question might be: "What *won't* they eat?" A four-year Massachusetts survey found 48 different prey items in the stomachs of 3,000 stripers taken from June through September in estuaries, off beaches and rocky shores, and in offshore waters.

"Crazy colors." Photo by James Manning.

WHEN THE FALL RUN IS IN HIGH GEAR, and I am surrounded by a thousand screaming gulls and acres of breaking bass, I sense the bounty that was commonplace along these shores 400 years ago. "Watching, you get some dim idea of how it all used to be, some small glimpse from the edge of winter at a world before the fall," wrote Ted Leeson in *The Habit of Rivers*, a popular book about rivers, trout, and fly fishing.

The life span of a striper can exceed 30 years. Historical accounts tell of seine and pound nets capturing bass weighing upward of 125 pounds. With stripers having few natural predators, save for sharks and seals, and little fishing pressure at the time, those reports seem credible. The current world-record striper weighed 81.88 pounds and was caught in 2011 by Greg Myerson off Westbrook, Connecticut, on a live eel drifted over a reef on a three-way rig.

Today? Biologists like Waldman and others doubt a striper can survive the gauntlet of ever-more-sophisticated gear and techniques long enough to reach those historic sizes, not to mention the environmental factors at play these days. "The environment is conspiring against that," Waldman said. "The fish would have to have spectacular growth in every phase of their life. The estuaries where they're born are not as healthy as they used to be. Length limits have forced us to catch more of the faster-growing fish than the slower-growing fish—that is, size-selective fishing pressure. Plus, our waters are getting warmer, and it takes more energy to extract oxygen from warm water than cooler water. . . . No, I think it's unlikely we'll ever see a 100-pounder again."

He's probably right, but part of me wants to imagine there are still some 100-pound fish out there—transiting the coast in small pods with the seasons but spending most of their time in deeper waters, outside the usual migration routes and beyond the many snares set to capture them. It's a boyhood fantasy that won't die.

A big Chesapeake fish. Photo by Jay Fleming.

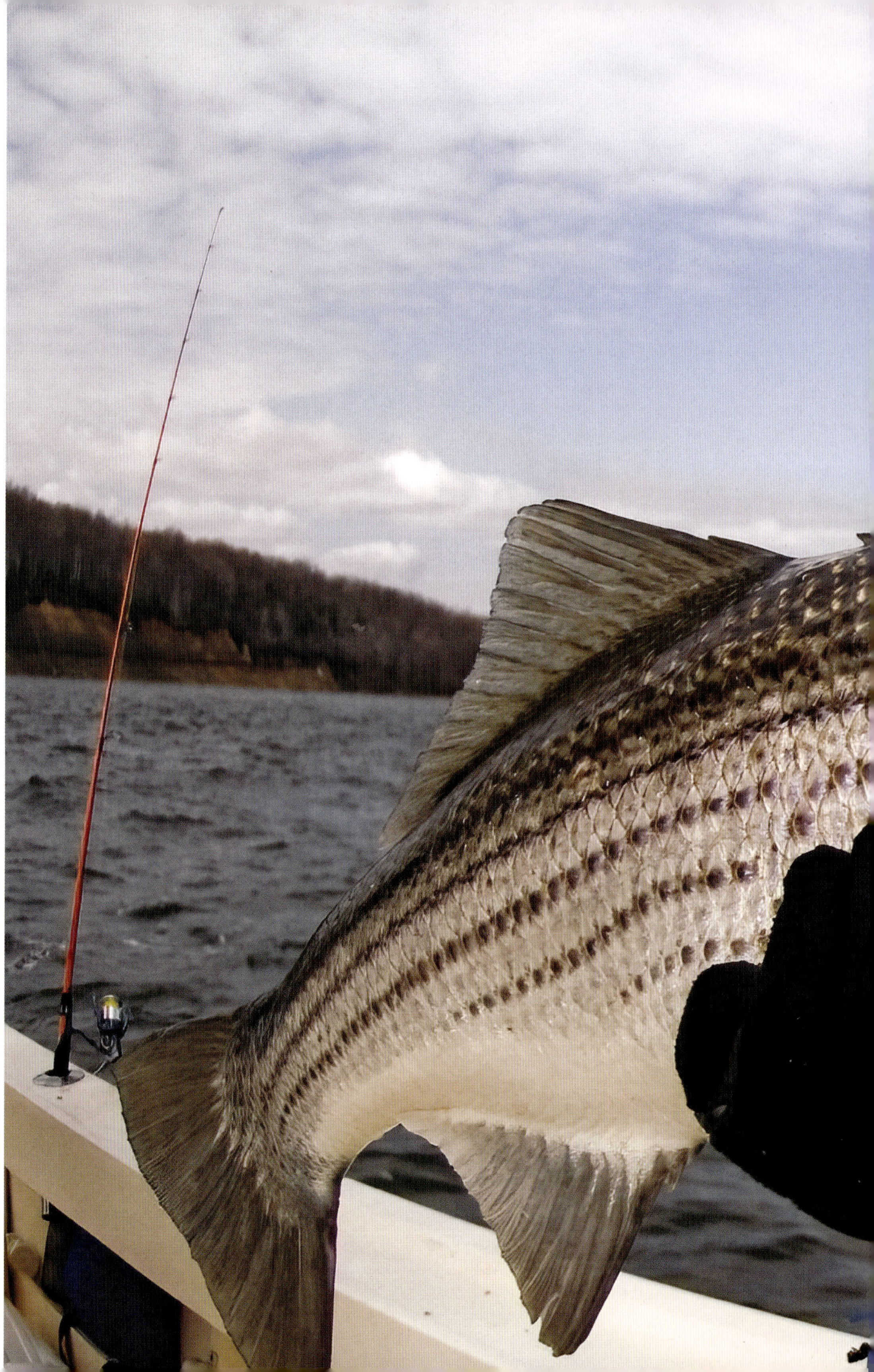

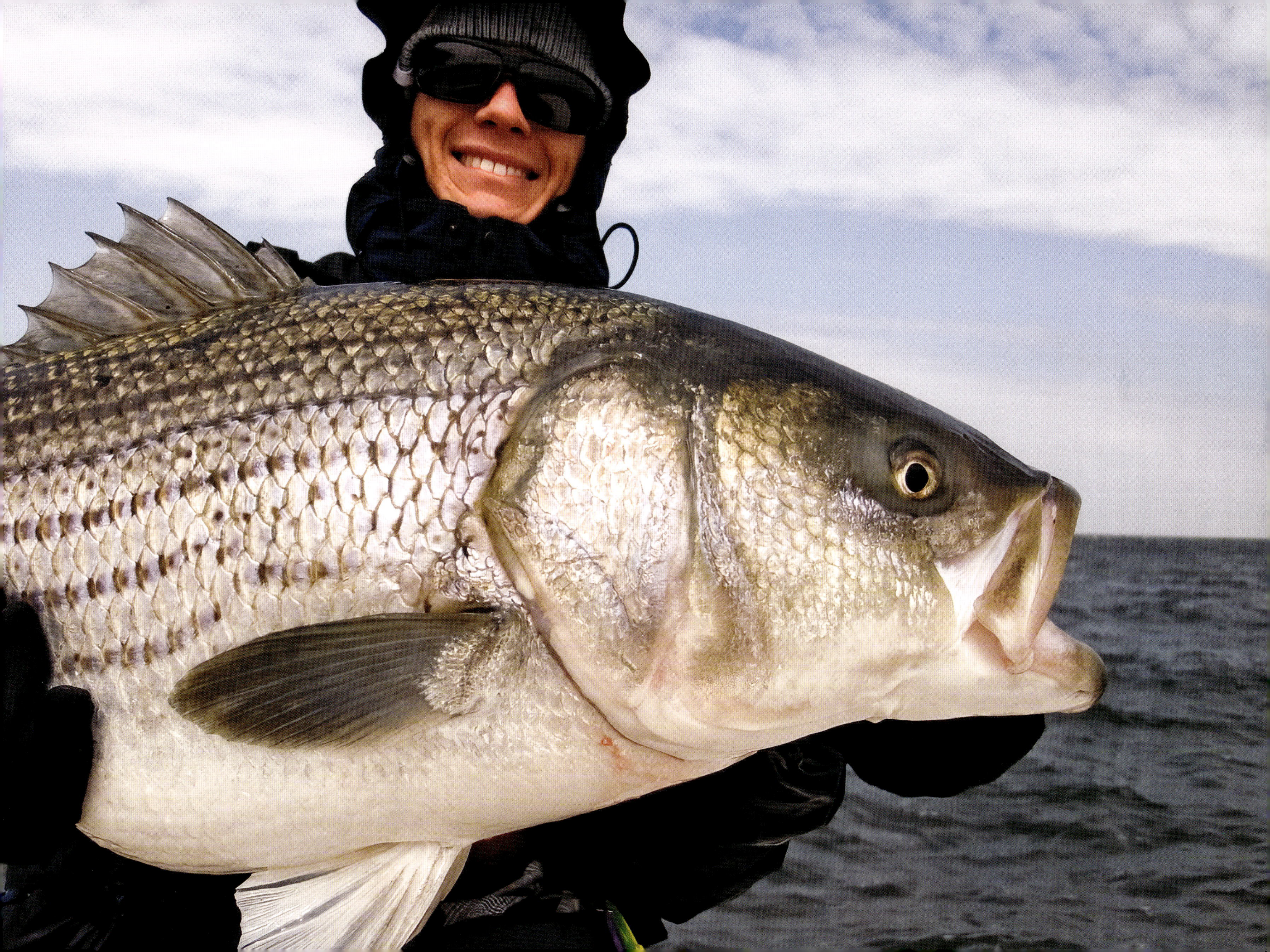

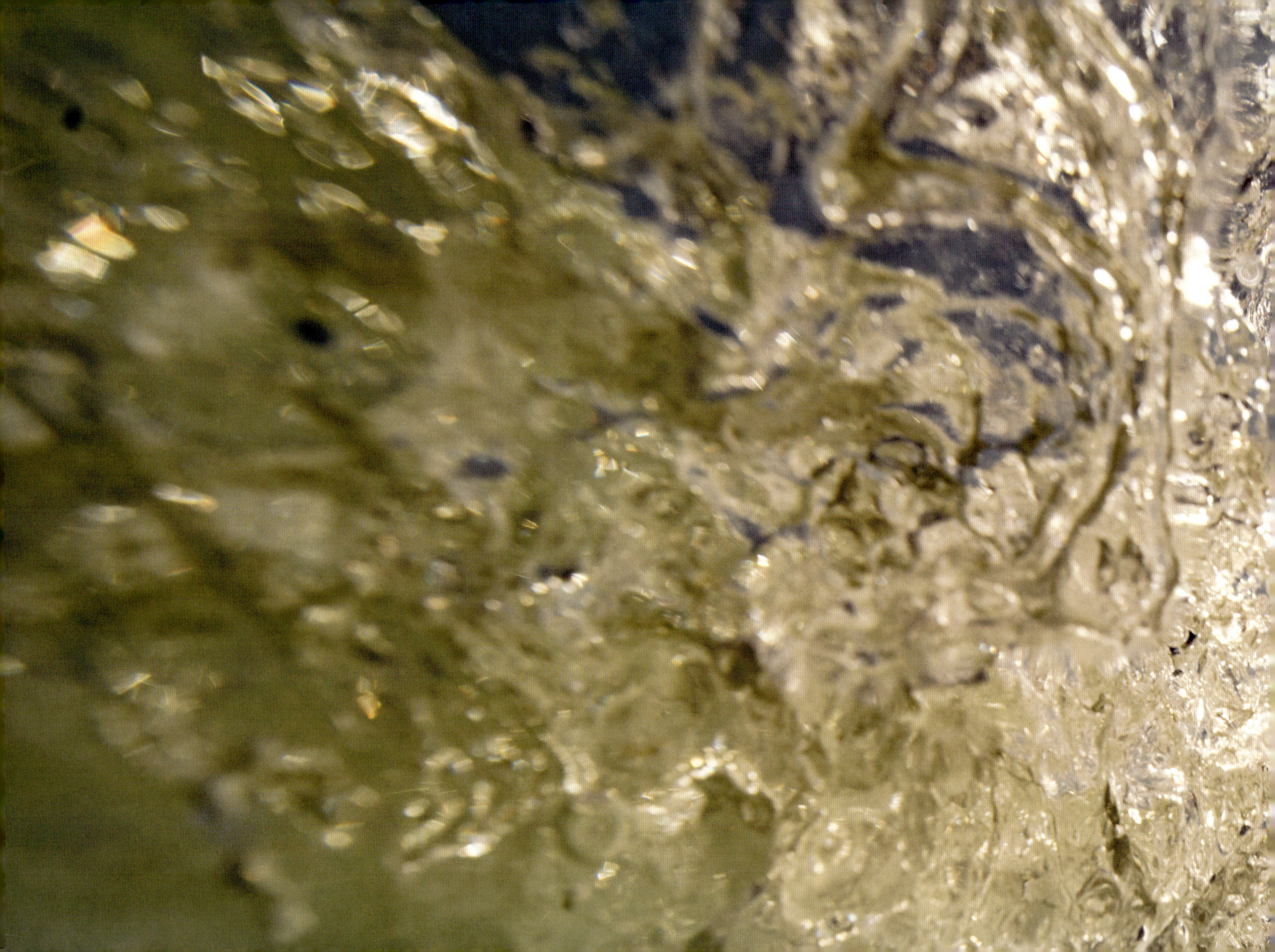

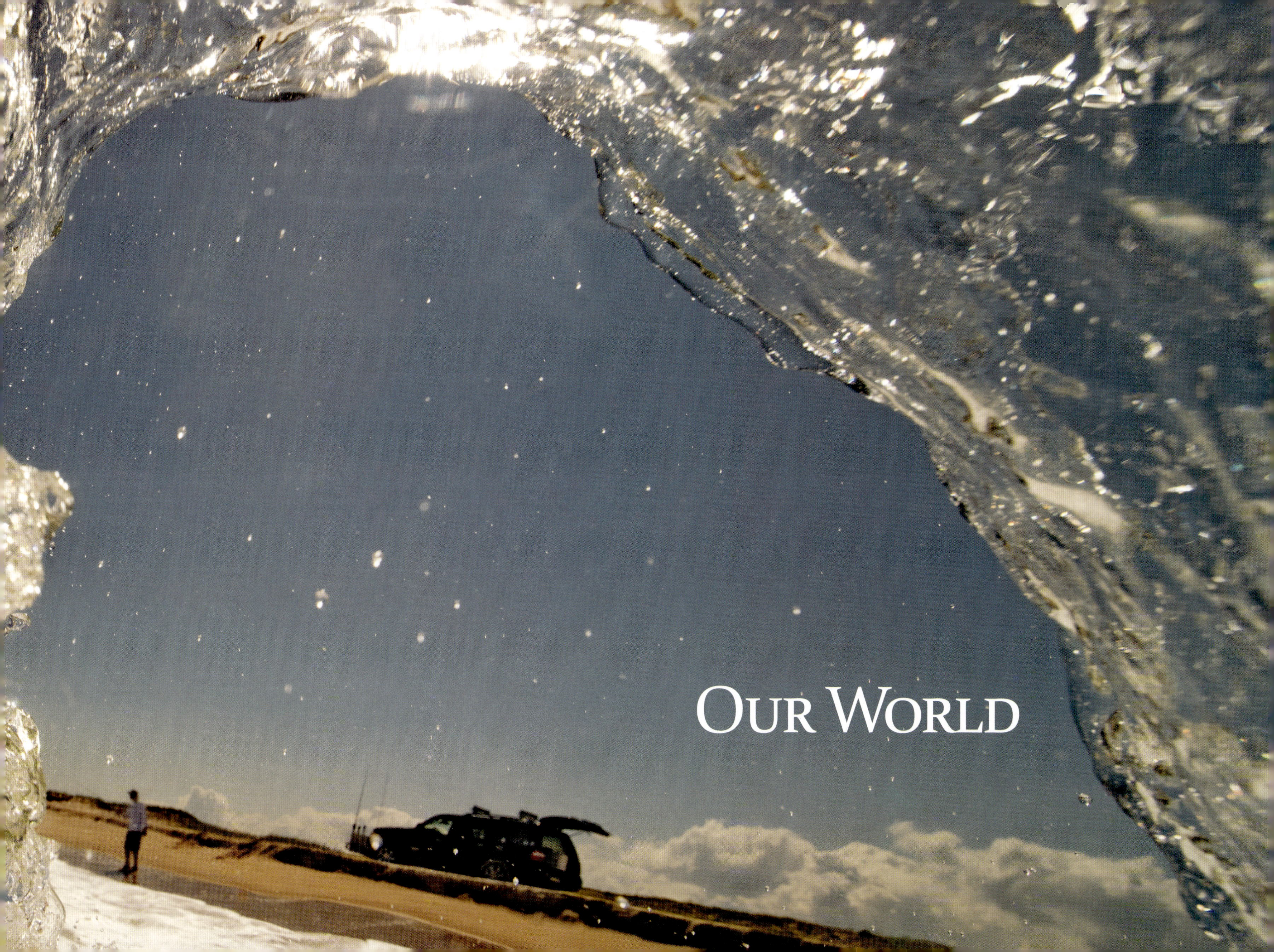

Our World

I fish in a world of secrets, subterfuge, and eavesdropping. Part detective, part spy, part mole, I constantly troll for information on striped bass. I pick up intel in a breakfast diner, standing in line at the grocery store, and sitting in the chair with my dentist and ophthalmologist, both bass guys.

Clues can come from anyone. The landscaper, chimney sweep, travel lift operator, financial adviser, shop teacher, retired cop, friend of a friend, or random person conversing in a bait shop, who sets you to feigning interest in a pricey doodad. The guile means good-natured feints and parries—and straight-out lying, where brothers deceive brothers. "If you don't know somebody, you keep your mouth closed," my old fishing friend Cuttyhunk Pete used to say. "Or you tell them something that's 10 days old. That's the way it's always been."

This world has its own language, clues, and signs. Lies and boasts, vulgarity and poetry, balderdash and bilgewater. A tip, a look, a whisper, a nod, a brush-off, two men speaking code about a night's catch, and the search, always the search, for truth. "You guys are like masons," said a boatyard friend who overheard my partner and me conversing. "You've got all the secret signs and handshakes." You give some intel, you get some back, but you respect the rules of the game: "If someone is dumb enough to ask directly," a tackle shop owner once said to me, "they deserve to be lied to." Social media is undeniably changing the rules of the game.

We search for an escape hatch from a world that places consumerism above all else. We hunt for someplace purer and wilder, for wind and starlight, weather, tides, and migrations. For a world in sync with the seabirds and the seasons, one that reminds you that you are alive. What counts in this world is a wave breaking on a ledge in the middle of the night, the slap of a

Previous spread: In the action. Photo by Tom Lynch.
Right: The striper's dorsal "flag" is a defining characteristic. Photo by Tom Lynch.

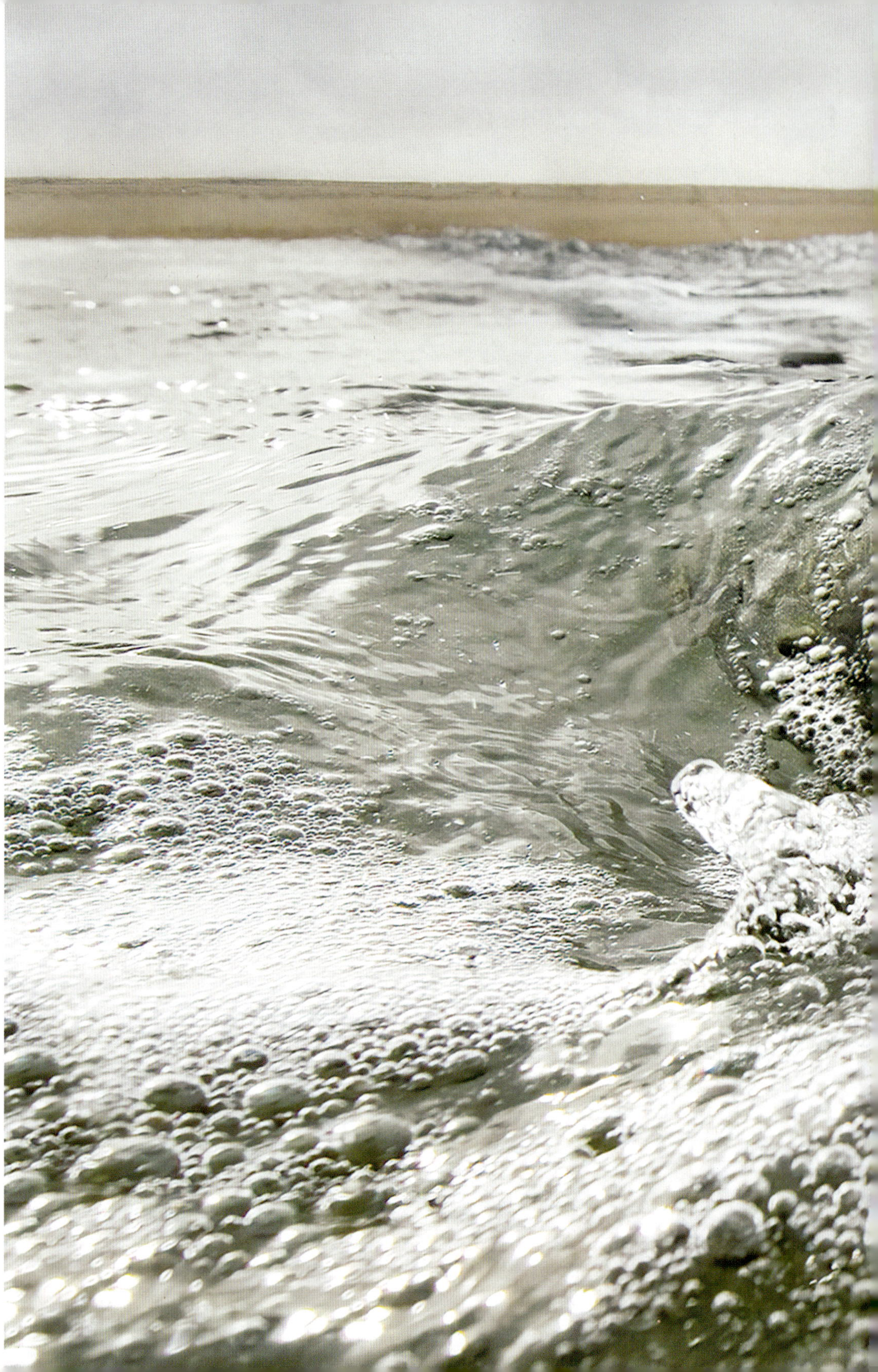

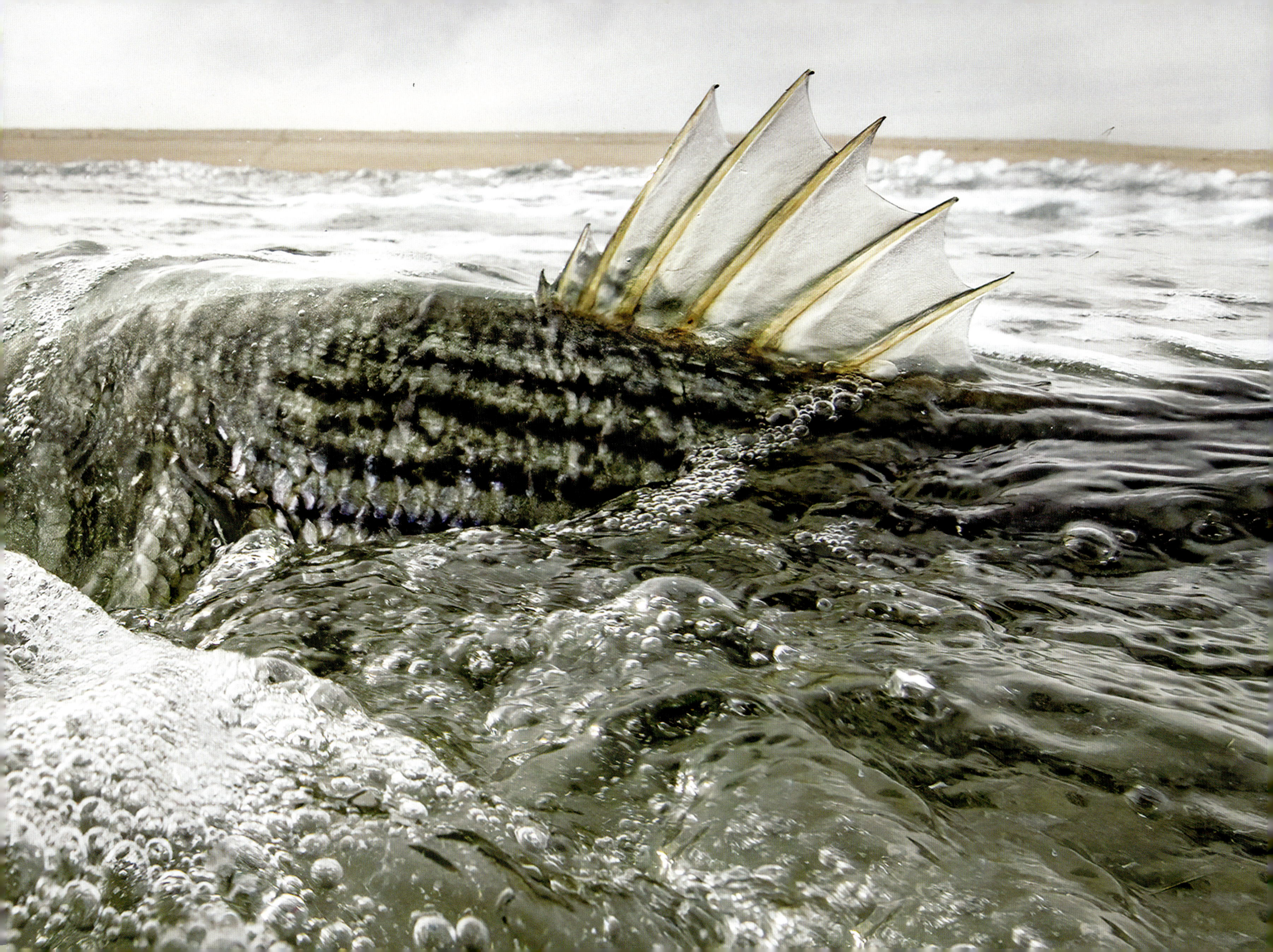

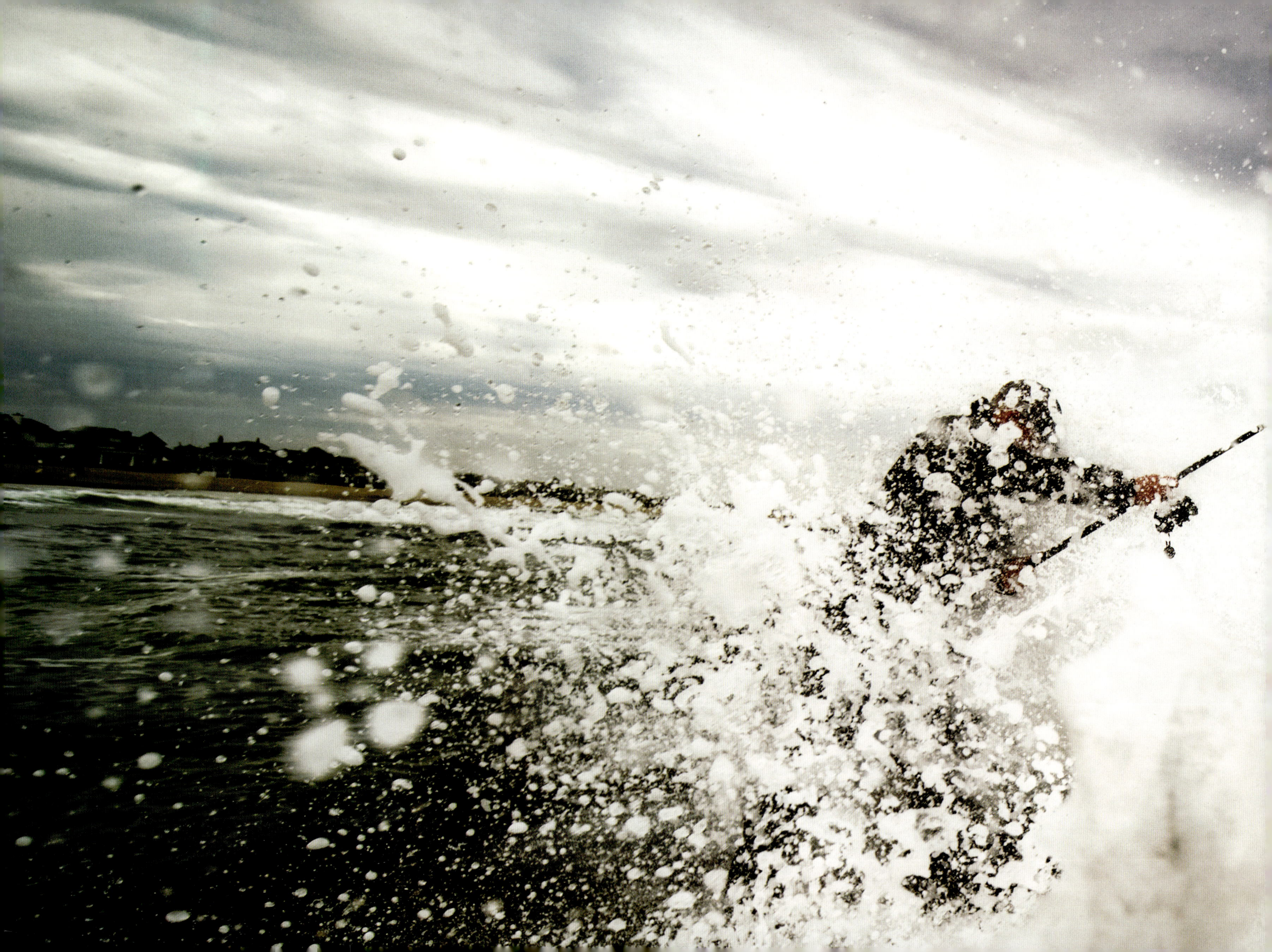

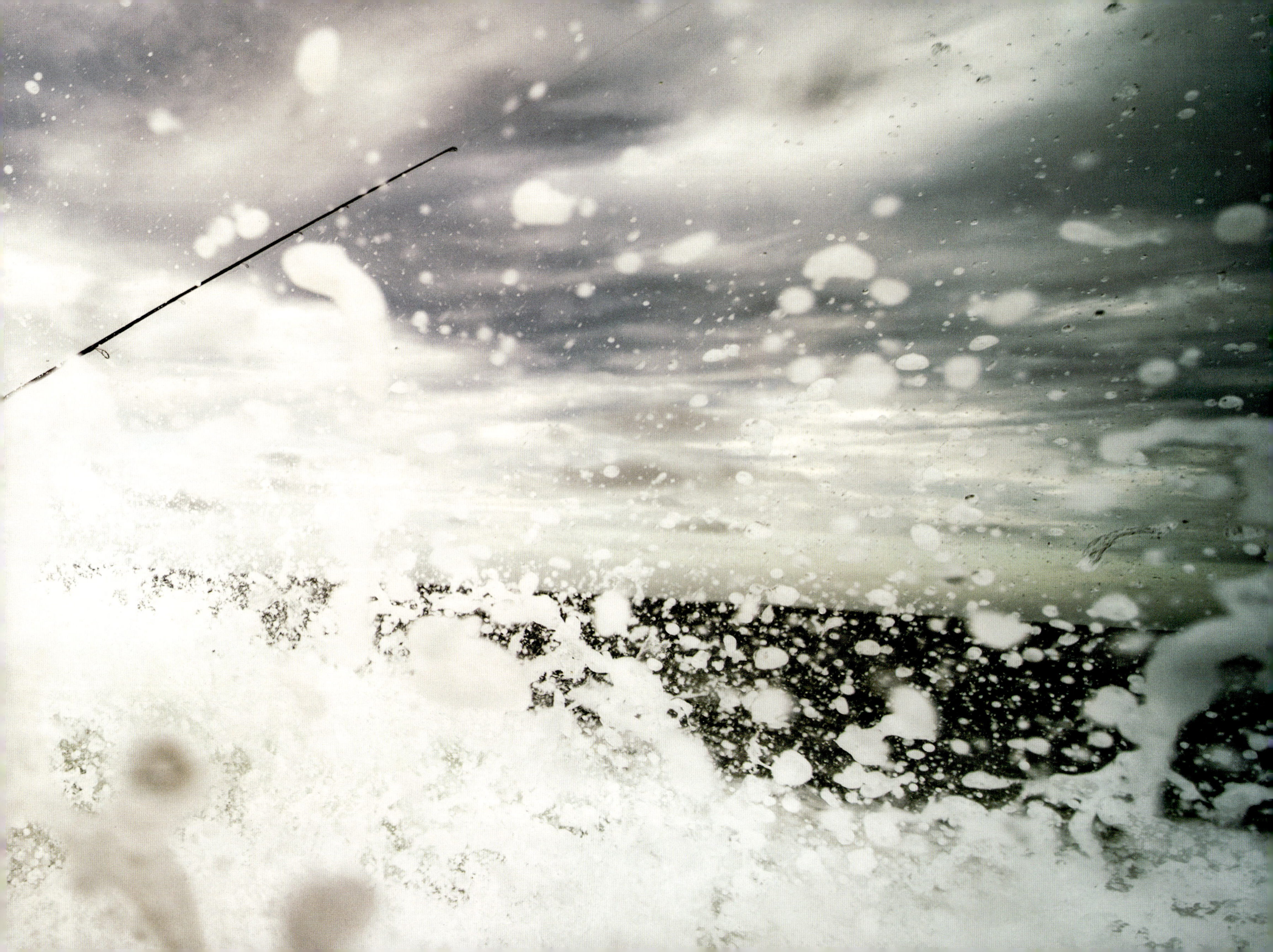

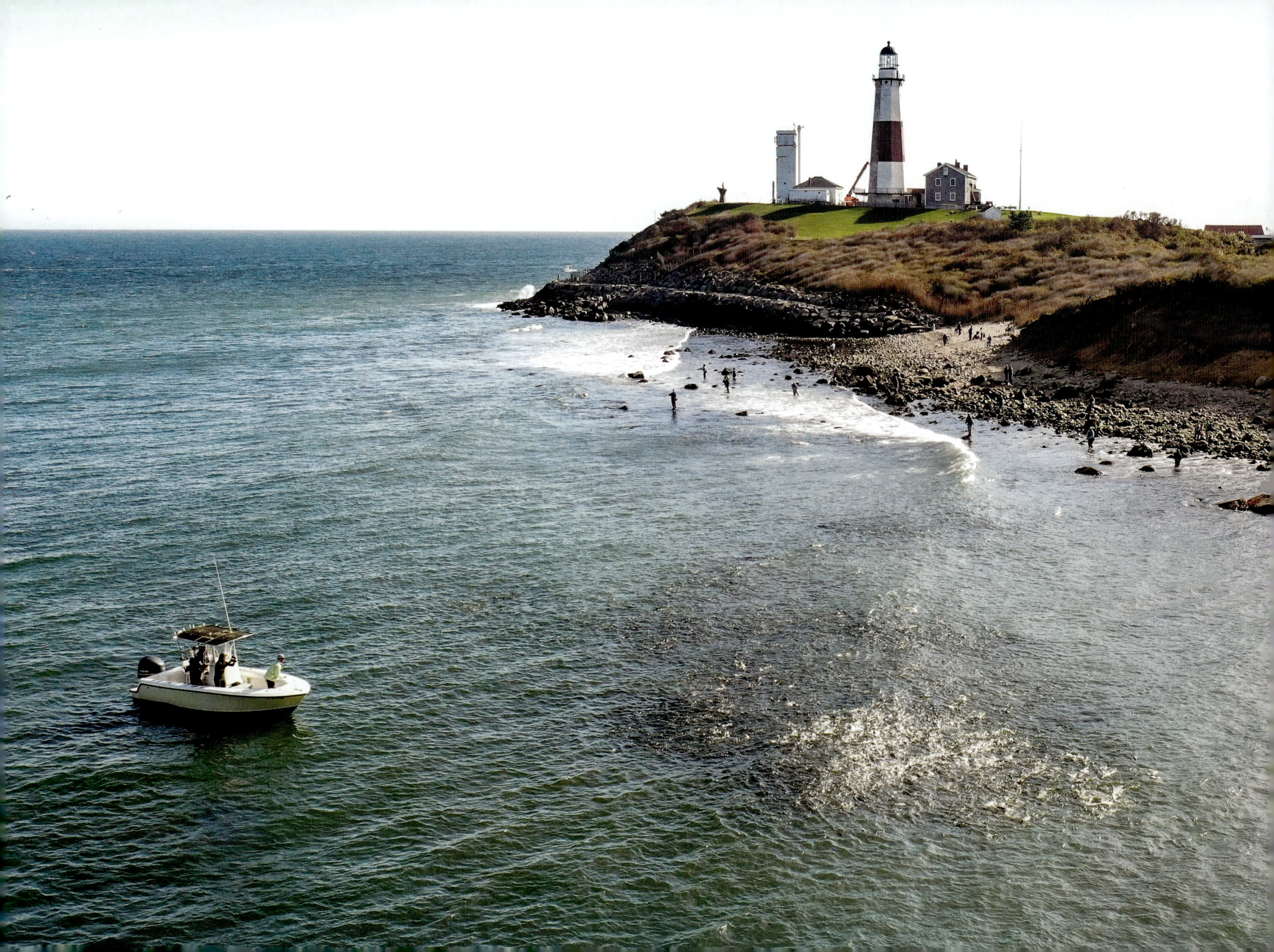

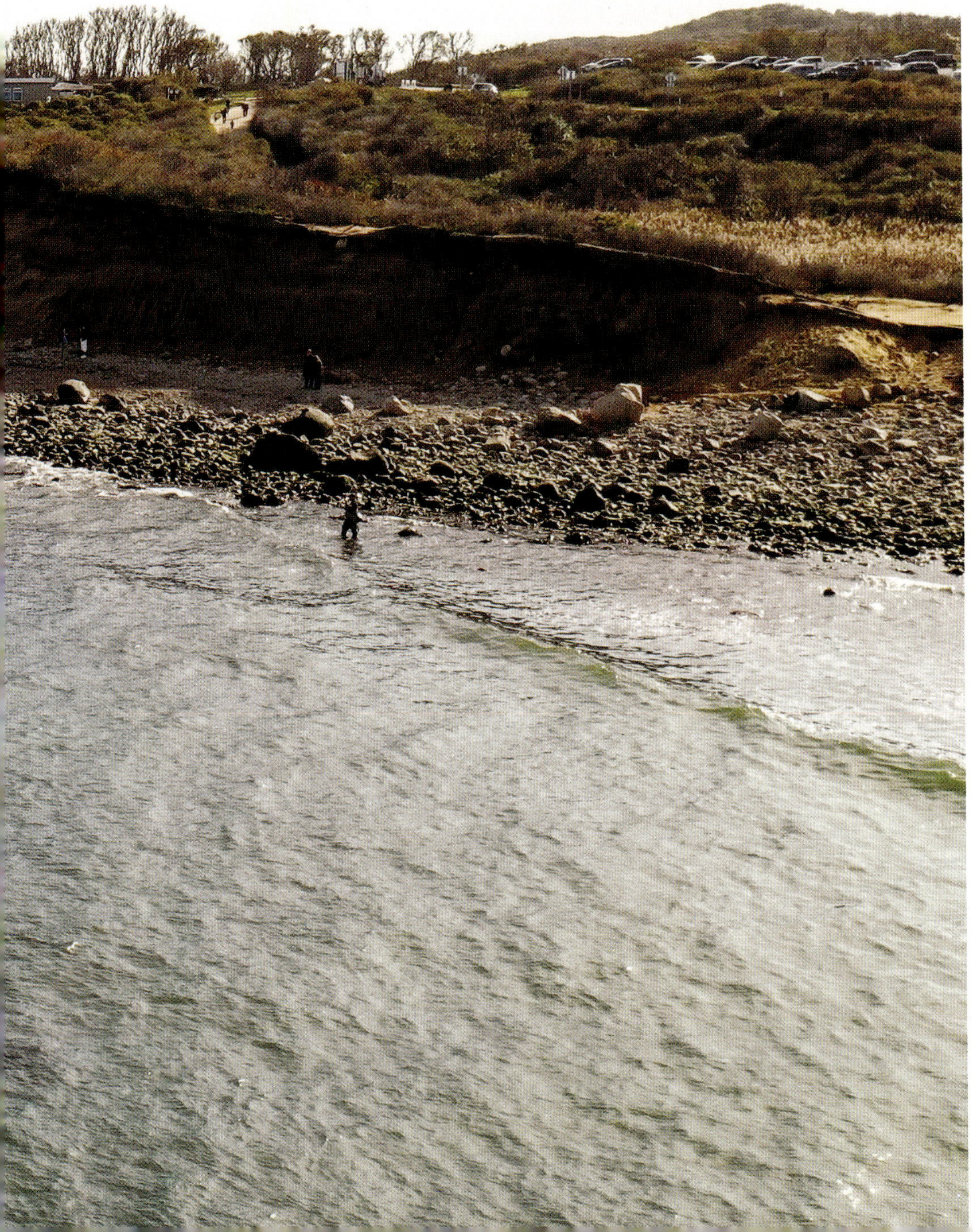

tail, the swell that knocks you to your knees, the wave that sweeps you off a rock. A train whistle from childhood that still echoes across the bay from a place whose name few can pronounce—Wequetequock. The quick prayer that follows.

I FISH IN A WORLD THAT MOVES WITH RHYTHMS as old as the tides, one based on moon cycles, water temperature, winds, and signals from plants, trees, birds, and bait. I defer to W. E. Whalley, a commercial fisherman from Narragansett, Rhode Island, whose voice from 1871 still resonates. He said he timed the setting of his scup trap nets to when dandelion buds "swelled full." And when they go to seed, he continued, the scup are gone.

"When high blackberries are in bloom, we catch striped bass that weigh from twelve to twenty pounds; when the blue violets are in blossom—they come early—you can catch the small scoot-bass," Whalley wrote. "That has always been my rule, that has been handed down by my forefathers."

A fresh breeze carries back the words of a wise old painter I once knew about the movement of stripers. "You have a calendar and a clock and a tide table in your head," said Stanley Meltzoff, a lifelong striper fanatic, diver, and one of the finest artists ever to have painted fish. "You go by time and tide, darkness, weather, and water temperature." Meltzoff taught me the fine points of "seeing" bass underwater, explaining how the brain stitches together glimpses of the fish—a few partial stripes, a dorsal, a sliver of tail—to form the entire creature.

I LIVE IN THIS WORLD OF MOVING WATER, line squalls, secret spots, and gruff charter skippers who aren't afraid to holler and curse, even at paying customers. It's a world of southwest winds, new moons, shoestring eels, silver eels, porgies, and live menhaden. This realm is dotted with

Previous spread: Paying your dues. Photo by Tom Lynch.
Left: Breaking bass off Montauk. Photo by Rex Messing.

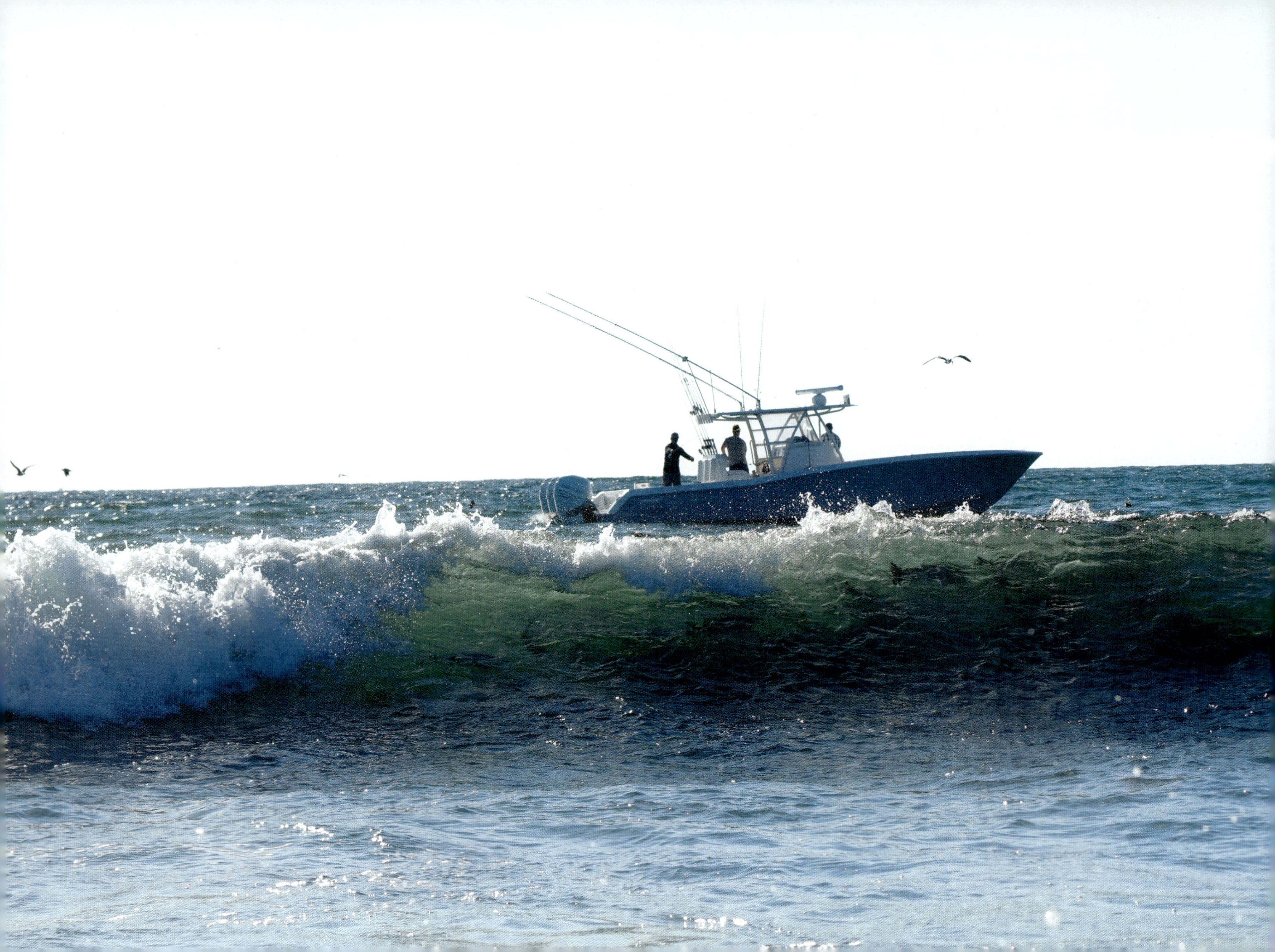

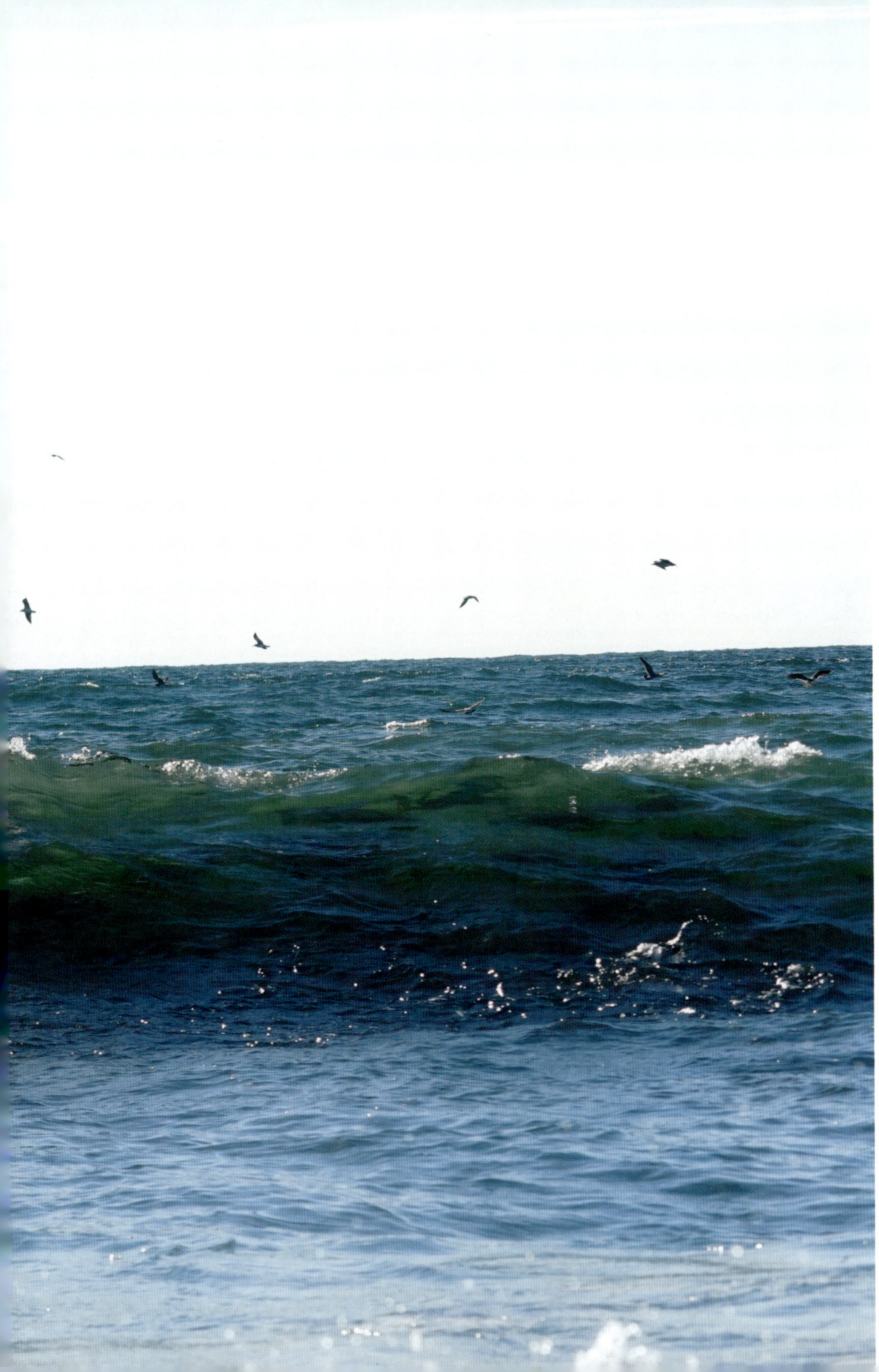

lighthouses and foghorns, double-humps and tide rips, sandbars, mussel bars, mud flats, deep ruts, and bright, windy flats where light-colored fish grub and gorge on sand eels, silversides, and crabs.

It's here where old ghosts ricochet inside my head, like crotchety Cape Codder Charles "Tiggie" Peluso remembering when 40-pound bass rushed from eelgrass meadows near Chatham, Massachusetts, to smack live pogies or menhaden in early September.

"Bam! Bam! Bam!" said Peluso, a commercial fisherman, fly fisherman, and rod-and-reel angler who was skilled in both salt and fresh water. "Like a trout taking a dry fly. Goddamn it! It would take your breath away." A few moments later: "OK, I've got to go. My cereal is getting cold."

I asked if we could talk more later. "Come see me," he said, giving me his address. "It's a dirt road, and I don't pay for no broken axles."

I miss Tiggie.

FISH FOR STRIPERS LONG ENOUGH, and eventually you get into something that makes you swallow hard and catch your breath. Where your pulse races and your mouth goes dry. *Can I swim to that rock after dark? If I drift the rip, will I fill the boat with water? Will those crazy thunderstorms and winds find me?* That's the feeling of living close to the edge, close to your bones.

The same old stories repeat again and again. Too much wind, not enough boat; too many tides, not enough sleep; too many blabbermouths, not enough reticence; too little time, money, breathing room. We fish a blue wind, a gray wind, a black wind, a darkening wind, a new wind, an ancient wind, and a sad wind. All in the ceaseless hunt for big fish.

A stormy day and the boats are stuck in the harbor. Mario Comoli is at the lighthouse surveying the wind and swell, wondering when he'll next be able to go out. He takes out his pocketknife and scrapes a shine onto an old block-tin jig, flakes of metal flying as he preaches the value of changing

Waves of fish. Photo by Tom Lynch.

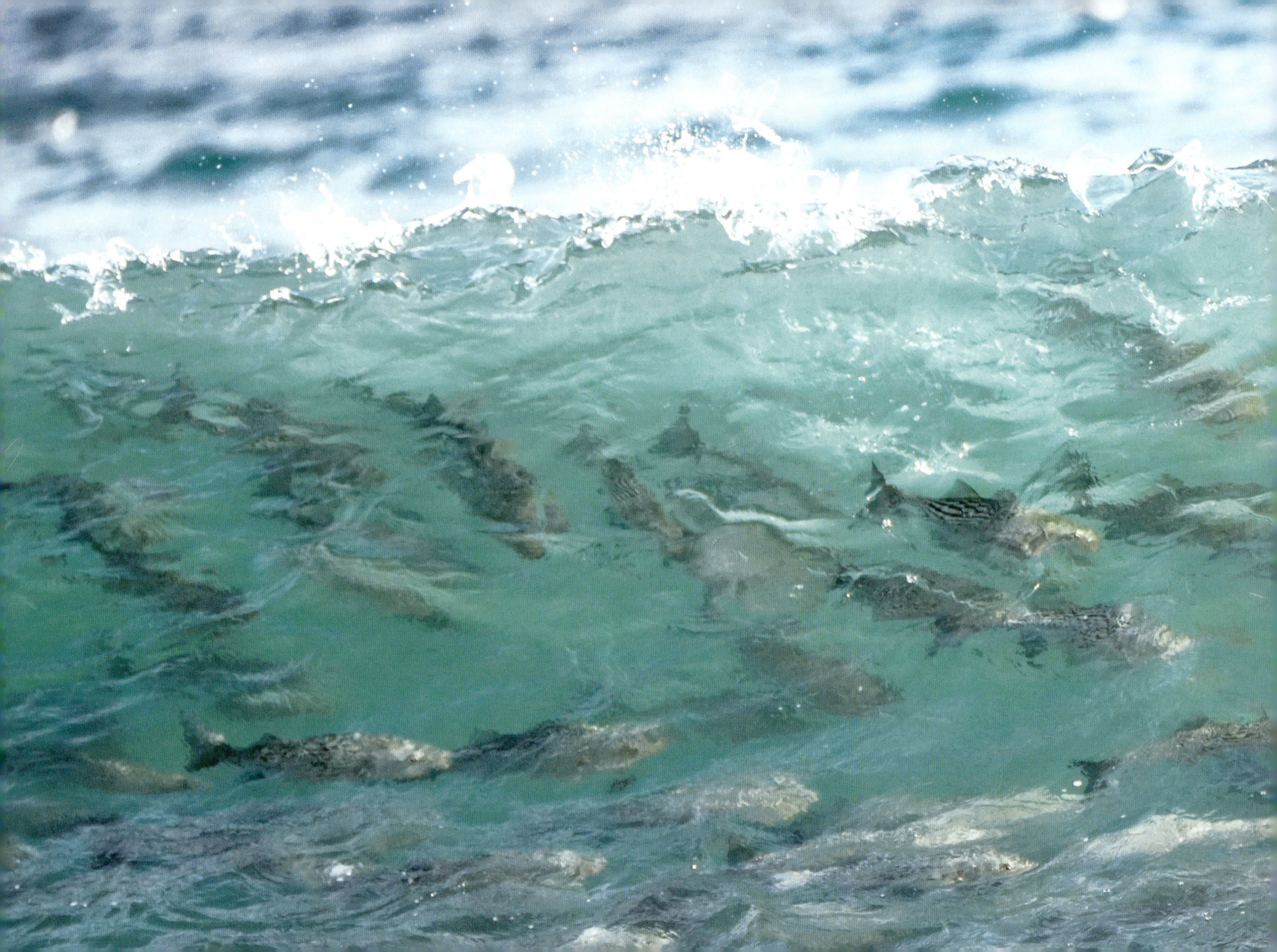

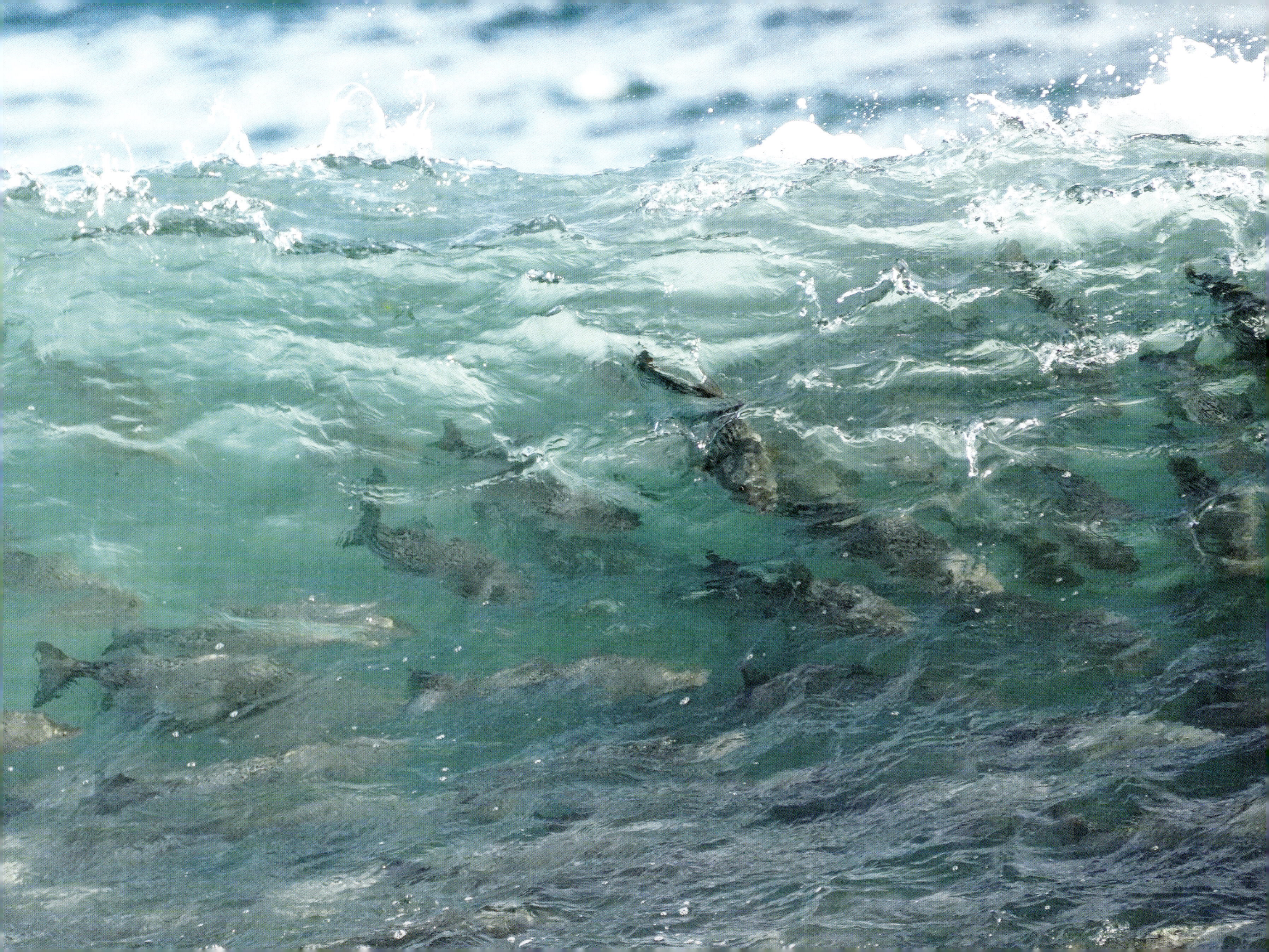

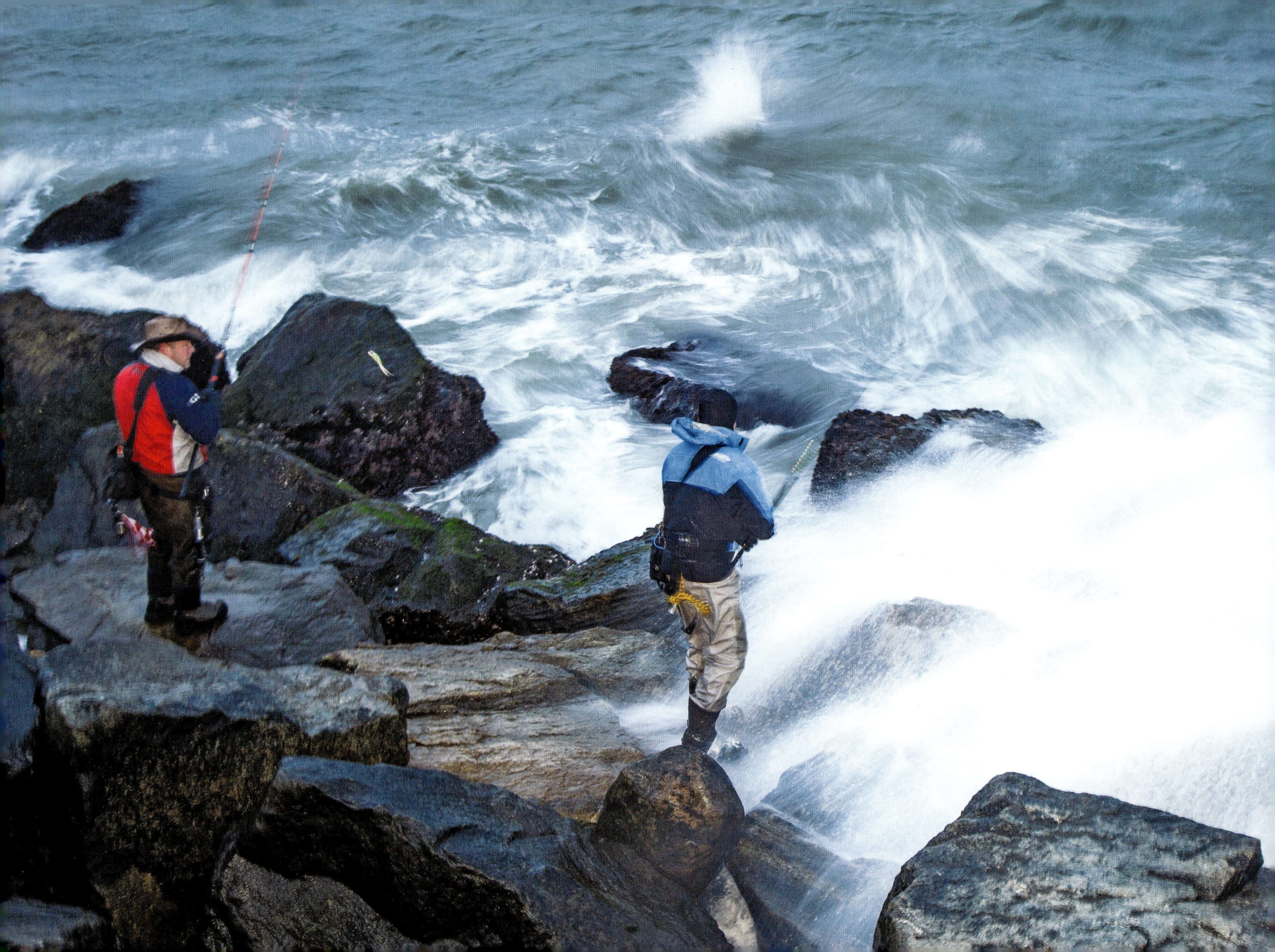

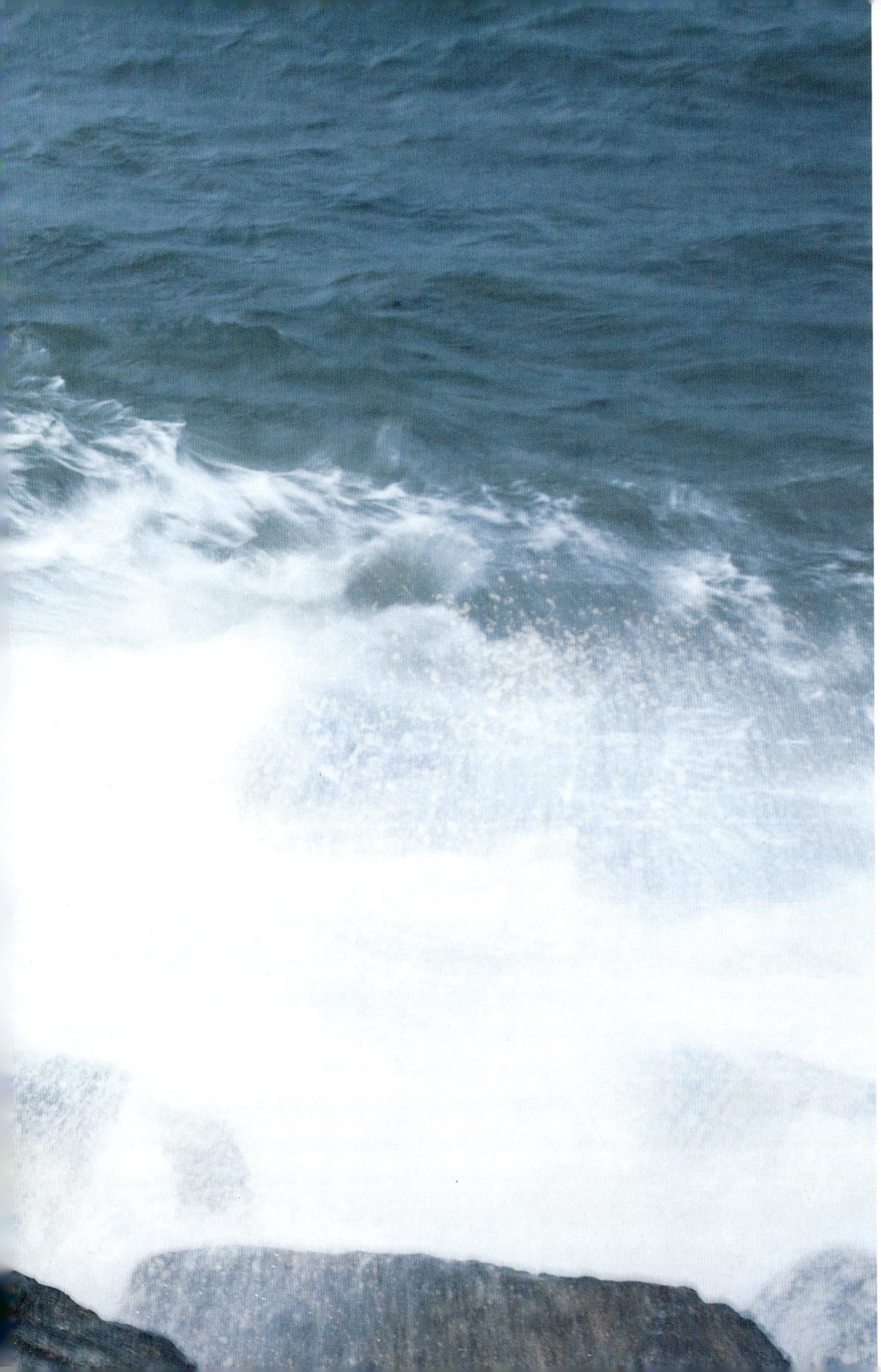

lures from time to time. "Fish are like women with a hat," said the lifelong bachelor, not known for his prowess with the *jeune femme* but hell on fish. "Sometimes they just want something new."

I DRIVE THE SANDY BACK ROADS SEEKING BAIT, bass, migrating hawks, monarch butterflies, wind and surf, a sunny corner in a lee, a friendly bait shop, and open space. I look for the green-glass waves and for narrow schools of bait flowing through the rut like adrenaline through capillaries. I come for the light, the wind, a hunch, the sun-filled front seat of the old station wagon overlooking a beach. I meet my brother, a surfer and boat captain, along one of the back roads. We pull over the way workers do in the off-season when everything slows and the roads return to the locals—tradesmen, carpenters, landscapers, fishermen, and surfers. I search for higher meaning as we talk about fish, surf, boats, wind, tides, coming weather, and friends.

Those of my ilk fish on intuition and experience, choosing spots by the way an evening smells, by shifts in the wind, by three terns hovering over sand flats in June, by following patterns that have worked for decades. Walking off a night beach in late fall, you think of an old friend you haven't seen since before the pandemic. You pass someone carrying a rod whose gait and lanky profile are familiar. "Joe, is that you?" Two friends catch up and swap intel but mostly just revel in seeing each other alive and well.

THE NAMES OF THE PLACES we fish effuse heft, meaning, and history when we roll them in our mouths and say them out loud: Wicopesset, Squibnocket, Quonochontaug, the Gut, the Swamp, the Constellation, the Guzzle, Sow and Pigs, the Aviary, the Horseshoe, Old Silas Rock,

Previous spread: A sight we live for. Photo by Tom Lynch.
Left: Late-season Montauk. Photo by Grant Monahan.

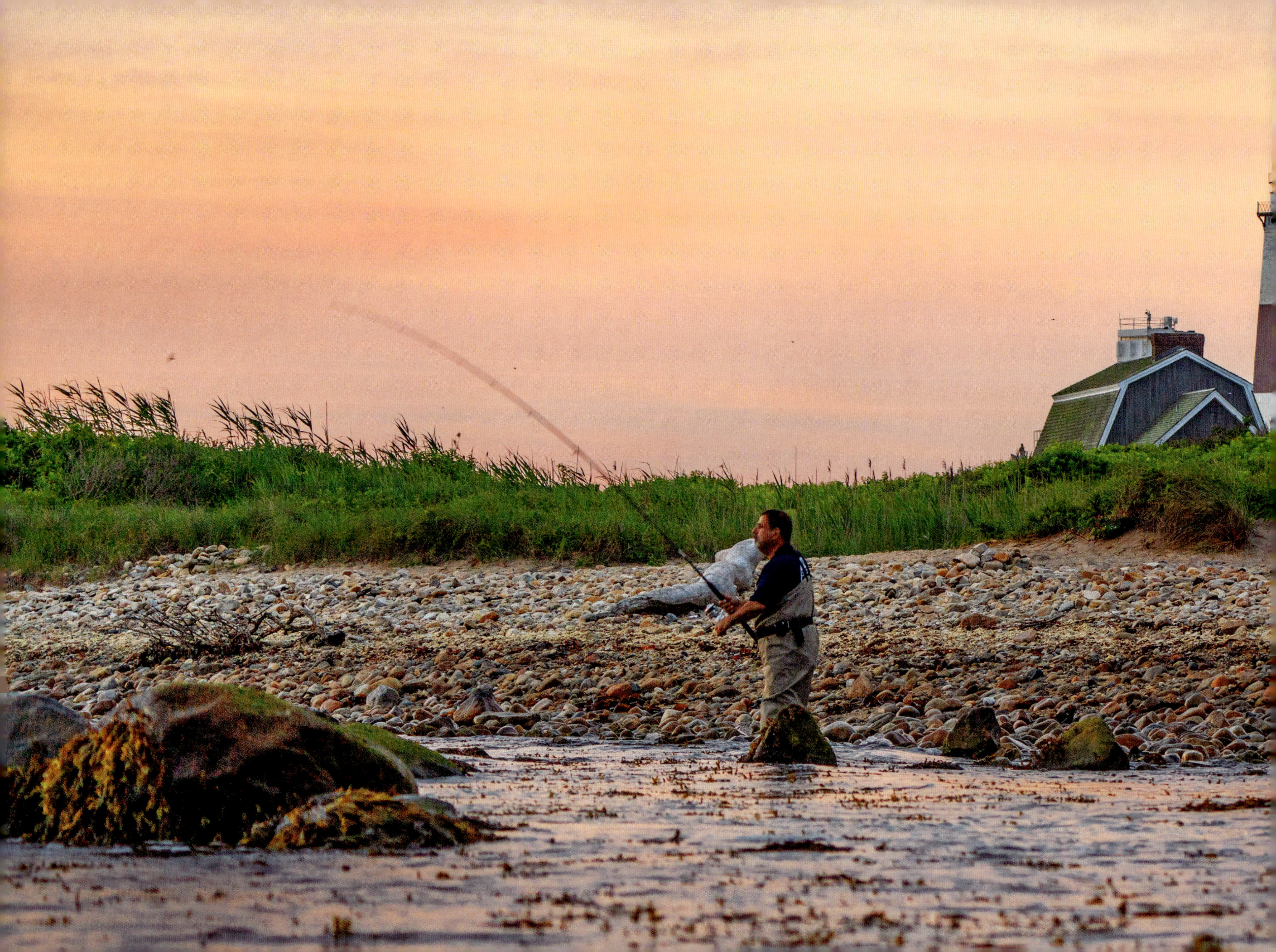

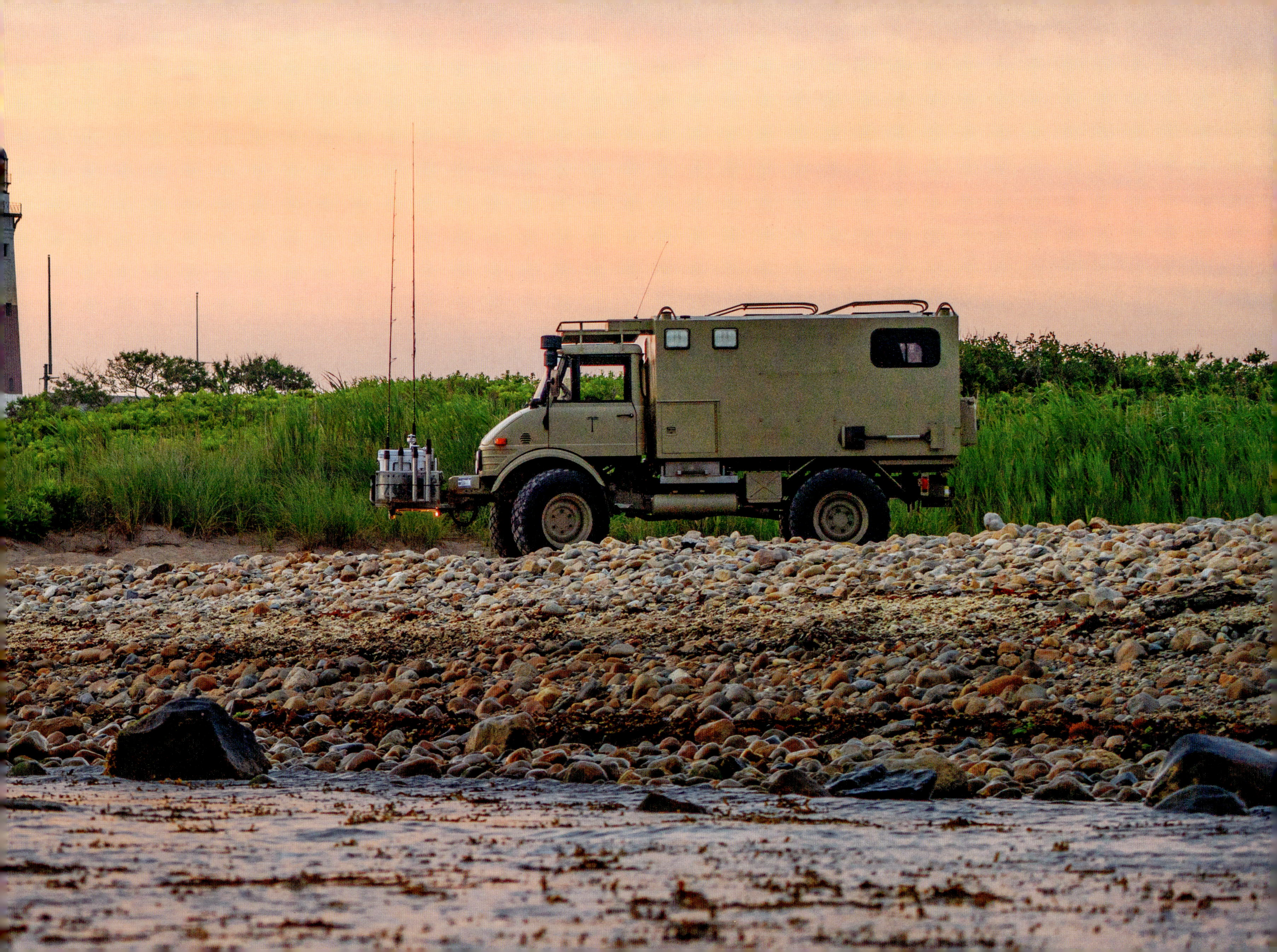

Rock on Rock, Wreck Island. A thousand other spots exist along the striper shore, some with apt names you can figure out easily, others whose origins are lost to time.

In this world, you are the first of the season to launch your boat and the last of the season to pull it, usually when ice skims the ramp and the batteries are flat. You are the last to rake your leaves, carve a pumpkin, decorate for Halloween or Christmas. By season's end, you are late in executing every household and yard chore known to domesticated mankind.

It is 1:30 a.m., and my fishing partner and I are casting from a nub of an island that is breasting a torrent of current when we flip a coin to see who gets the last eel, a runty shoestring. Two casts later, standing on a rock at the edge of the world, I'm working onto the gravel beach a fish that weighs nearly 40 pounds, one I will never forget.

In this world, a southeast gale drives fish in tight. If you know the right beaches, some nights you get lucky twice. The first when, despite a big bow in the line, you land a 36-pounder in the warm October gale. The second when you survive the late-night drive home down I-95. Window open, coffee gone, music blaring, you slap yourself in the face and still manage to nod off. At the last moment, the chatter strip near Exit 74 rips you back into the wide-awake present, adrenaline flowing out of your scuppers for the rest of the ride.

THIS WORLD WILL SURPRISE YOU WITH HOW QUICKLY things happen. Casting eels one night on a new moon with the drag cranked down tight, a big fish yanks me to the edge of the boat, where my knees dig into the gunwale, preventing me from tumbling into the drink. The fish rips off line that I have trouble hand-pulling from the reel and after a few moments is gone. I recall that fish from time to time, not so much as the one that got away, but rather for its strength and speed, and for the lovely dark night and big tide on which I encountered it.

You follow the fish down the rocky spines of terminal and recessional moraines, where the waters are full of both glacial debris and current, and where, after dark, there is still little company. The fish are big and willing. You win some, and you lose others. You go confidently with your bravado intact, and the rocks, swift waters, and heavy fish remind you that you are just an interloper.

This world can find you guessing wrong on the wind because you are certain big fish are on the little island in early October. And before you have the opportunity to find out, you nearly send the boat to the bottom of the sound in the building sea. With darkness rising, you spin the boat around just in time to retreat and pound your way home into two miles of sawtooth waves and windblown spray. You reach the dock with your tail between your legs, hubris rinsed from your socks. "The wind's not that bad," you had said dockside a few hours earlier, thinking you were sheltered from its full brunt but deep down knowing better.

DENIZENS OF THIS WORLD GET TO witness spring worm hatches in the salt ponds, wet-wade under meteor showers in summer, drift the passage reef on harvest moons, and wear wool socks and watch caps in the rips of late November when all the fish are bright, voracious travelers racing the season and the stars on their way south to who knows where.

On soupy mornings, with moisture beading on the brims of our caps, we drink breakfast beers, and I smoke a cigar while we slow-troll on the inside grounds. My friend sets up on another fish. "It's a good one, Will."

I remember still nights on back bays where mosquitoes and no-see-ums eat us alive, right through our damp, DEET-be-damned shirts, as the fish powder a green-and-white streamer to tatters. We hear the chaotic choruses of gull rookeries and get to visit scrubby little islands that smell of nesting cormorants. Our companions are fireflies, heat lightning, June bugs, and a goofy Newfoundland, who carries his own sizable colony of flies, lying at my feet while I glass the offshore waters.

Previous spread: A Unimog at Montauk. Photo by Tom Lynch.
Right: Astrid deGruchy with a 51-pounder. Photo courtesy of deGruchy.

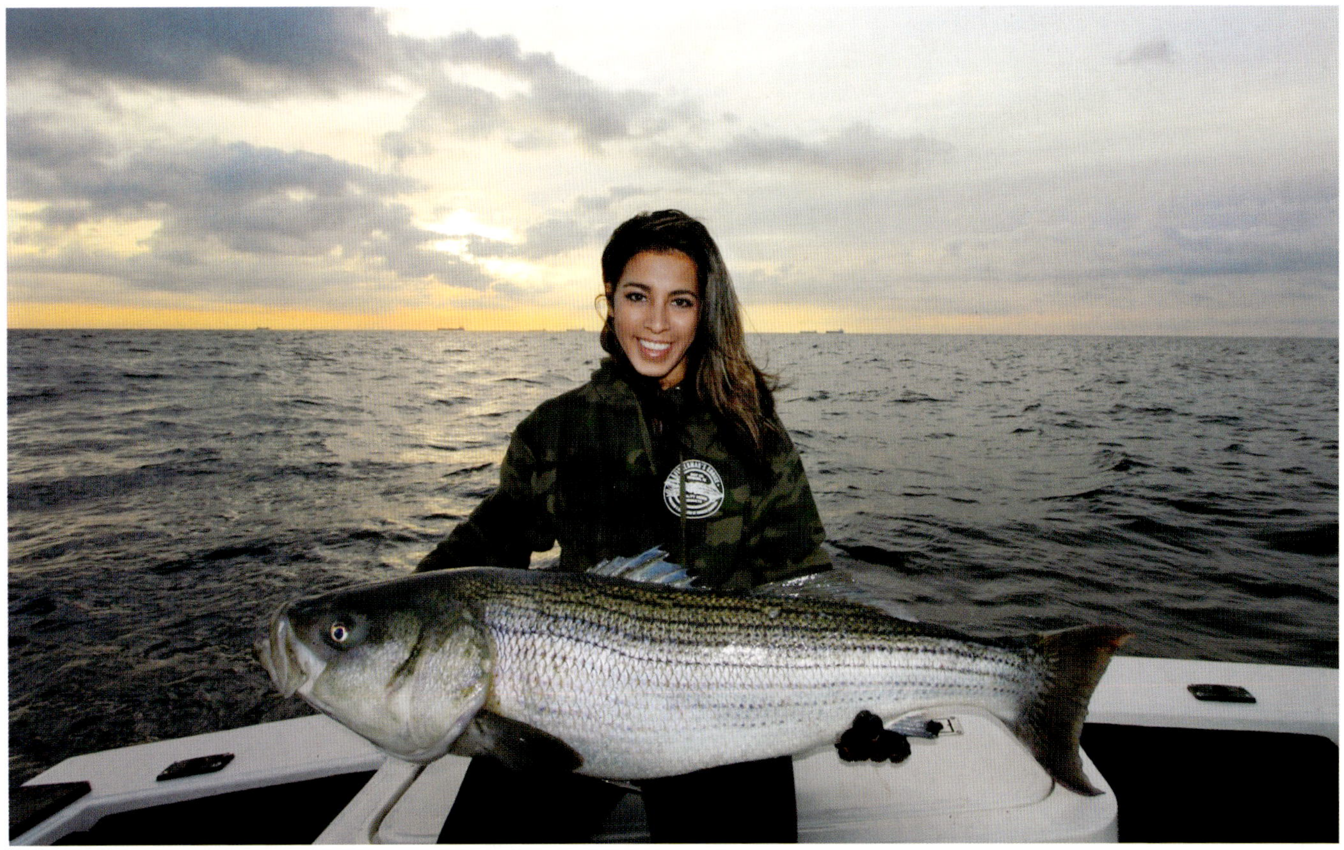

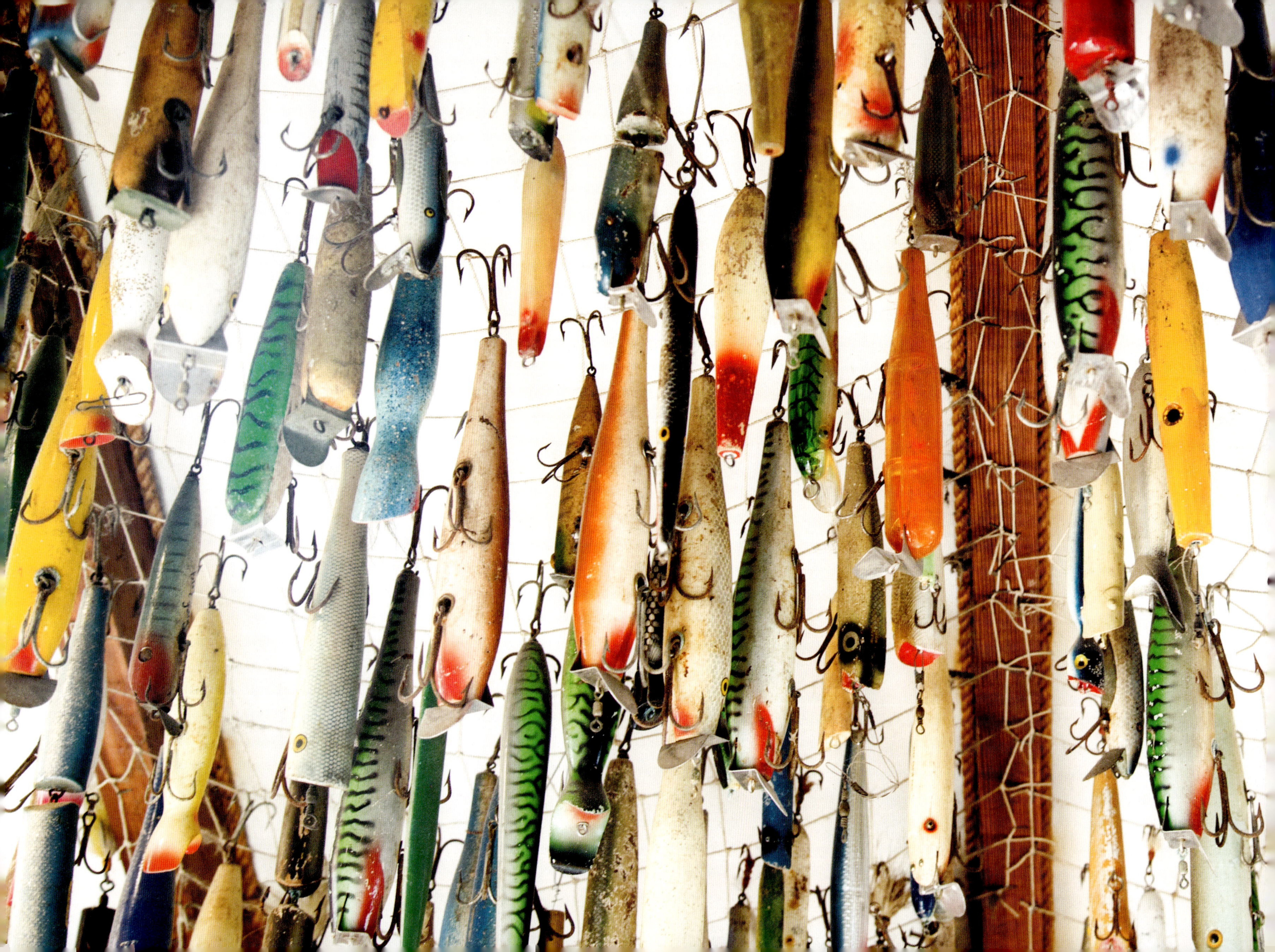

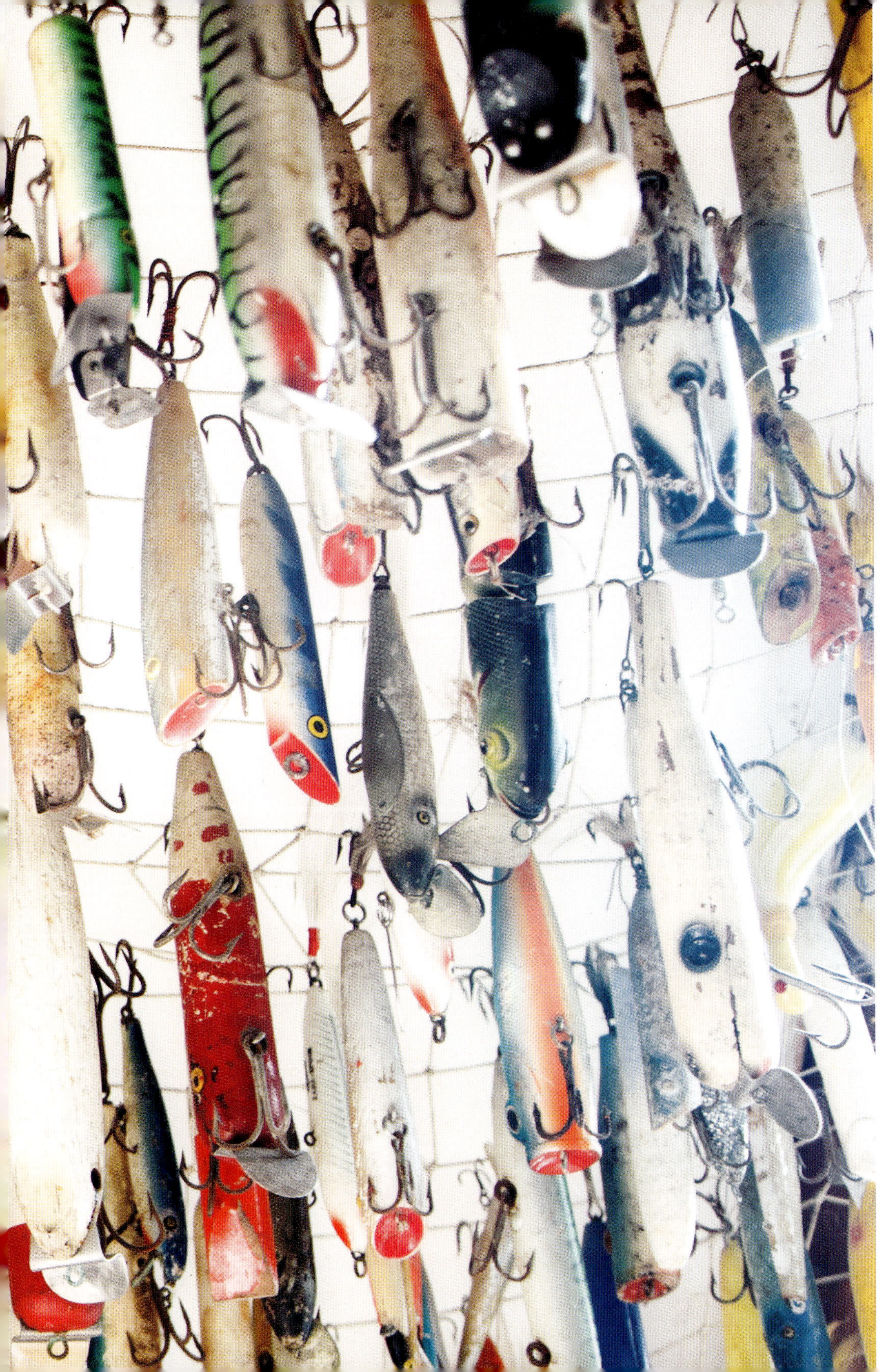

Some days it's boat talk and fish talk from sunrise to sunset. "You know how you buy a lobster boat?" a guy on the island fish docks asks me one morning. "You wait until you hear someone say, 'I think I'm just going to plant petunias in her.' That's when I buy." Been there, done that.

BLACK DECEIVERS, METAL-LIPPED SWIMMERS, needlefish, a silver popper worked on a foggy day through big swaths of white water covering a boulder field in autumn, water still in the low 60s, three or four good pops and they're on it—cast after cast.

Blue and white, through-wired with no bucktail, rough homemade poppers raise fish as lethargic as Lazarus. "Make 'em talk," my old friend Pete, well into his 70s, hollered at me from the helm. "Make 'em dance."

ONE MOMENT I AM SITTING IN 10th-grade biology class in 1969, and my tough-minded teacher is telling me to "pay more attention to the books and less to the bass." Travel forward 20 years. The sun has set, we are crabbing along the lively North Rip off Block Island, Rhode Island, and the rods are going over with newly arriving spring bass. At the helm is pioneering charter captain and my old teacher, Captain Al Anderson. We forged a friendship that started in high school and lasted more than 50 years. We fished together dozens of times on several of his charter boats in his 47 years as a working captain. All were named *Prowler*.

An inductee into the IGFA Hall of Fame, Anderson was not only a talented fisherman, but also a conservationist, writer, and fish tagger. In all, he tagged more than 60,000 fish, including more striped bass and bluefin tuna than anyone. He was smart, outspoken, and competitive—and he could yell with the best old-school captains. You either loved him or you didn't. He died in 2018, and his ashes were scattered in his beloved North Rip.

Old bass plugs hanging in Bill Beattie's attic. Photo by Michael Cevoli.

I often reflect on a simple truism he uttered one day. "I felt rejuvenated after yesterday's trip," he told me after an April outing on a tidal river where he tagged and released 52 stripers. "Like all was well with the world. It's amazing what a few floppy fish will do for your spirit." Well said, my friend.

IN THIS WORLD, WE ARE THE LOCALS who grew up trapping mummichogs and eels and netting blue crabs to sell to visiting yachtsmen. We knew where to find grass shrimp and dig soft-shell clams, quahogs, and big surf clams; as boys we caught cunners, tinker mackerel, snapper blues, and smelt. We knew which dogs to avoid when our bikes were loaded with fish and tackle, and we kept rocks in our pockets for the ones we couldn't out-pedal. Homegrown, we knew where to stick a car to avoid getting towed. And we never forgot the low spots in the stone walls, the shortcuts through the dunes, and all the other end-arounds you learn as a kid growing up in a beach town.

We knew exactly where the wind might catch you crossing the salt marsh; where the current would rock your skiff as you rounded the headland; the location of the alley behind the summer restaurant where Greek dishwashers in stained aprons smoked on their breaks. We recognized the pungent odors and loud voices coming from behind the fish market, and the old cavernous wooden garage where you could buy the coldest eight-ounce bottle of Coke on Earth after fishing an evening tide. You'd drink the first one down without stopping and savor the next while standing beside your best friend, recapping the evening and trading small-town gossip with old Charlie, the Yankee proprietor now long gone, along with his garage.

I remember these things now not sentimentally, but as pieces that fit together to make a place a home. These are the pieces that imprint an identity and craft character, that shape the world I know.

Fresh tracks. Photo by Tom Lynch.

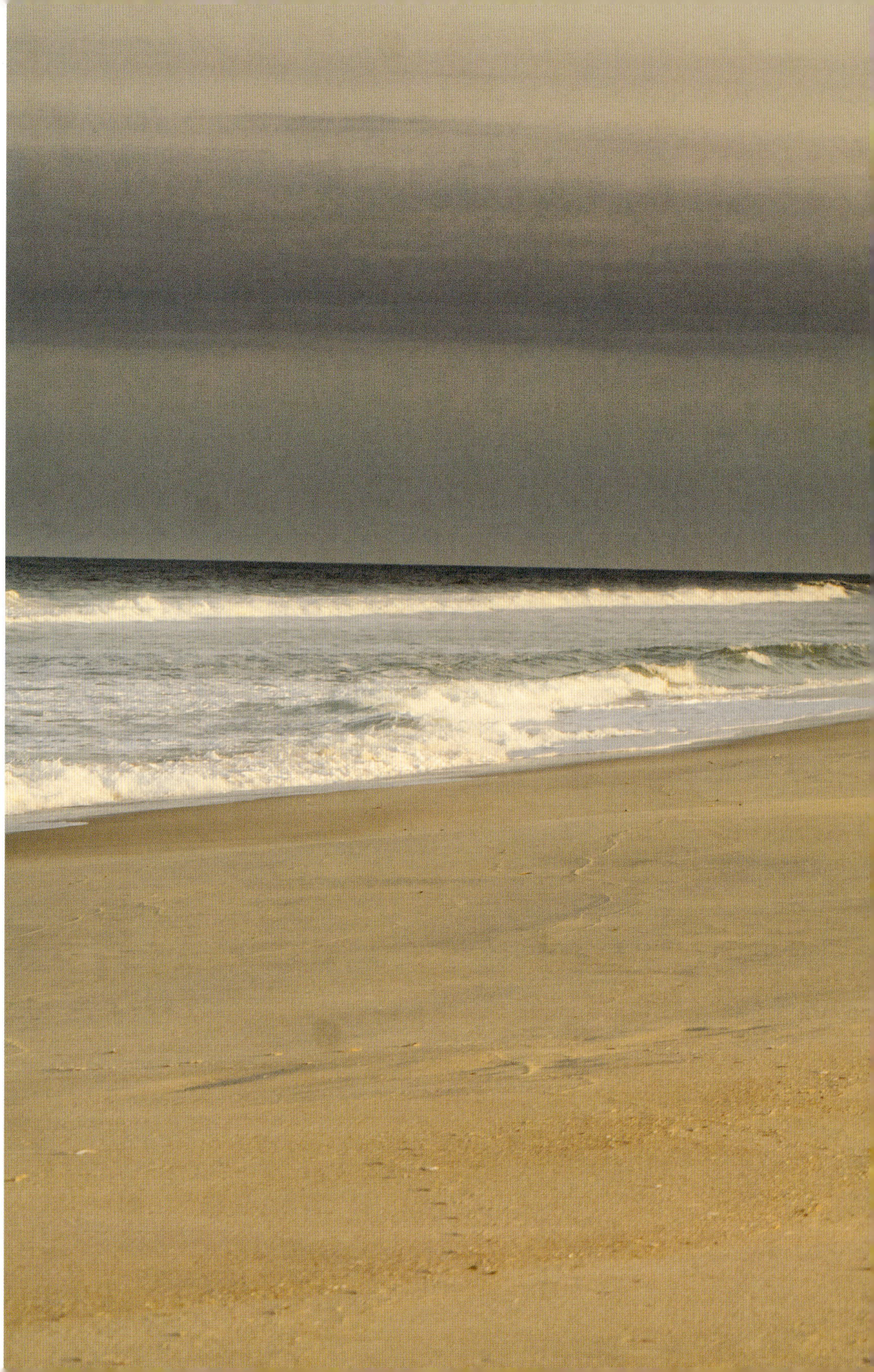

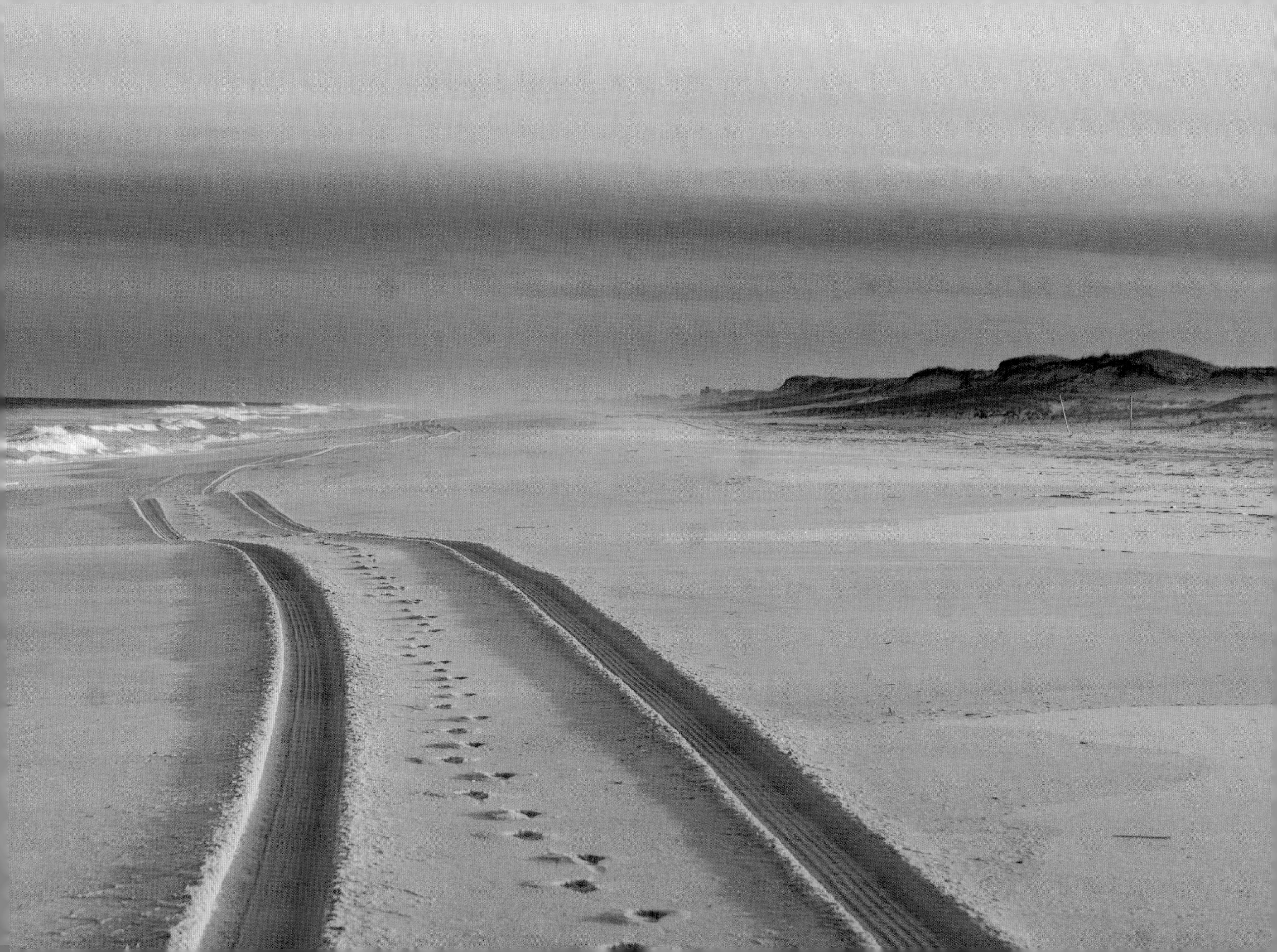

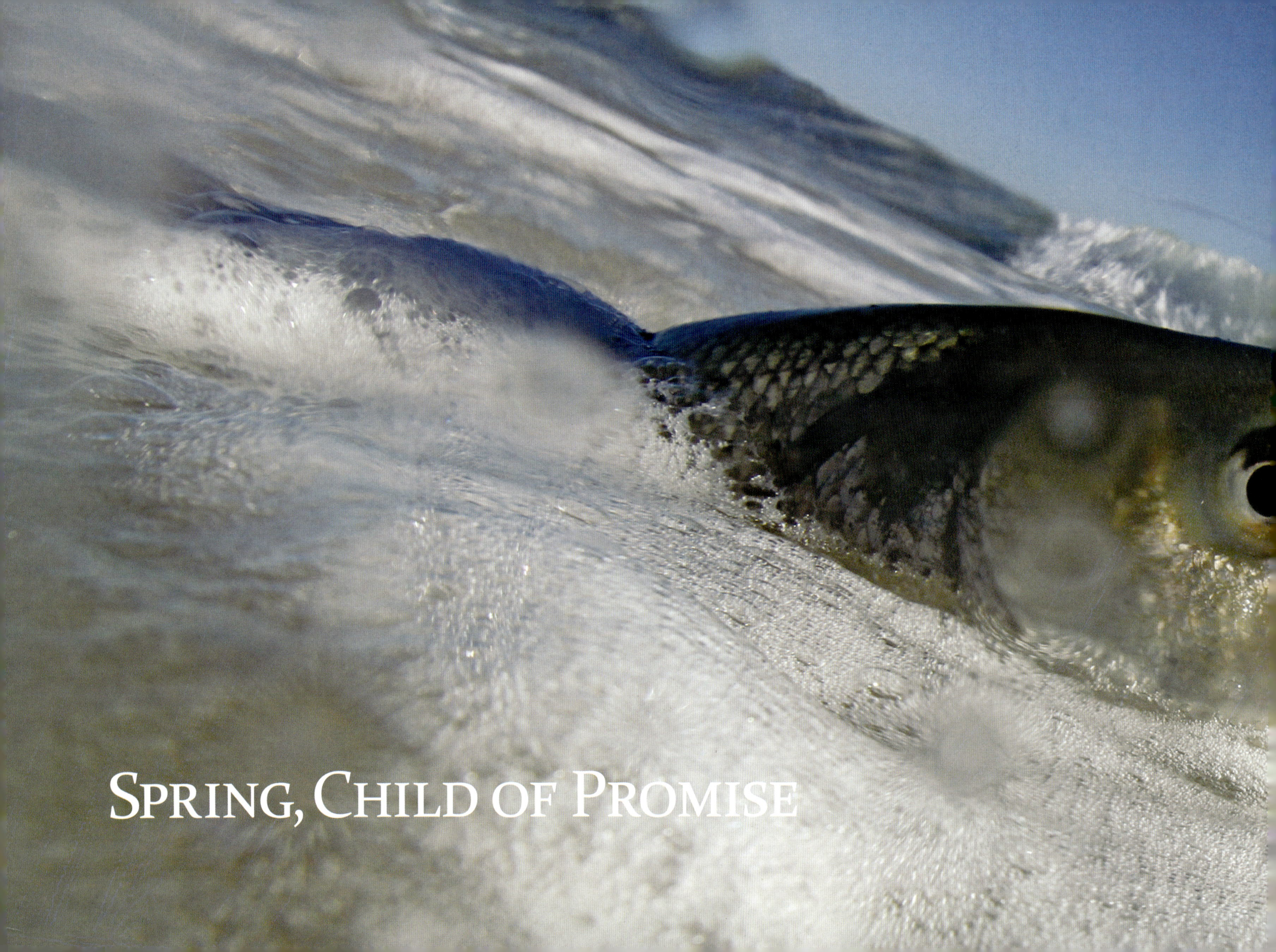

SPRING, CHILD OF PROMISE

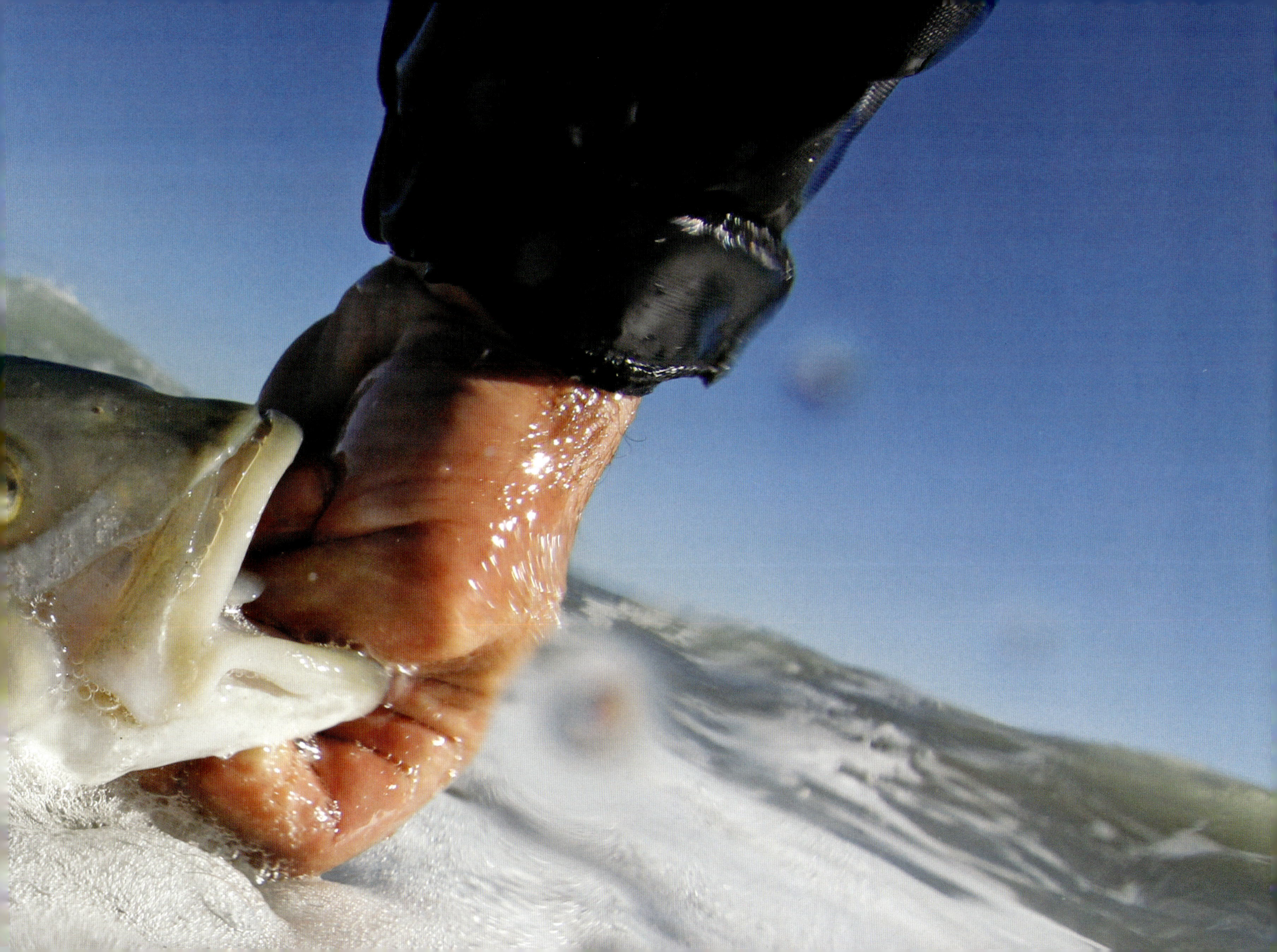

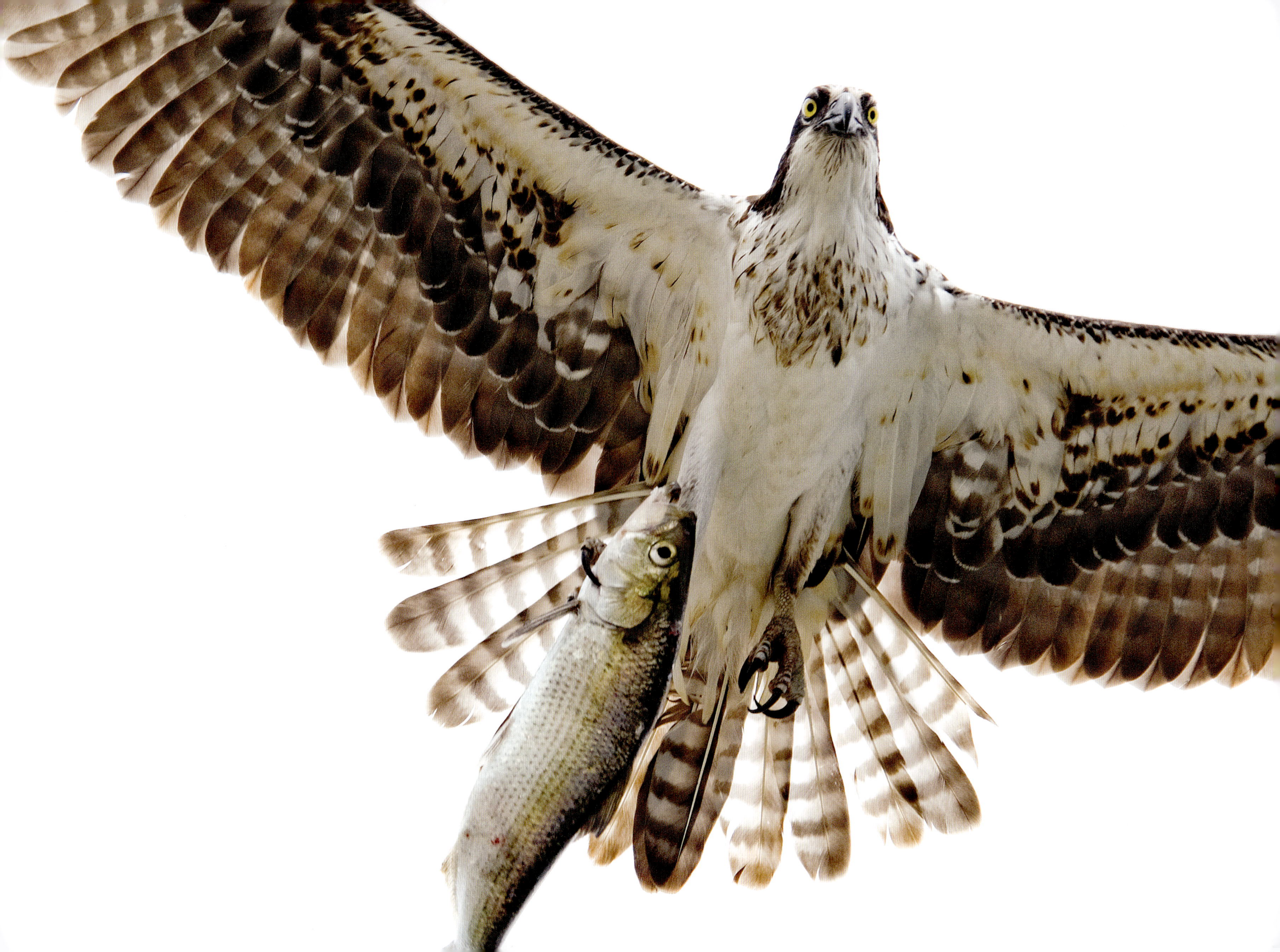

There is nothing finer than running up an empty tidal river in the May twilight after an evening spent catching schoolies. The fishing is easy and relaxed, with stripers from five to 12 pounds hitting flies, soft plastics, and bucktails in the shallows along the eastern shore of the lower Connecticut River.

Water works its way up the bow of my skiff and blows aft as a friend and I speed past the small, gray floats that mark eel traps, leaving a submerged rock pile to starboard, and then sailing past a shallow reef that has yielded many nice fish. The sun is almost down, the wind has dropped, the river is smooth, and the little skiff is running like a top. What could be better?

Spring is the child in whom you see nothing but promise and possibility. When you live in a region with clearly defined seasons, everything still lies ahead in spring, poised to unfold like the shadbush, apple blossoms, and mountain laurel that soon will color the banks of the rivers. The scent from the land and the tidal marshes is rich and fragrant. Lilac, honeysuckle, and wild rose mix with spartina and the dark river mud exposed by the falling tide. The smell is intoxicating. Make the same run in a month, and the bugs in your spotlight will be as thick as rain.

AS THE STRIPERS SPREAD NORTHEAST from their spawning grounds in Chesapeake Bay and the Roanoke, Delaware, and Hudson Rivers, they flood the sounds and coastal waters, tidal rivers, and bays from the mid-Atlantic to New England. Eventually, they move into New Brunswick and Nova Scotia. They shake off the vestiges of winter and feed with the vigor of the new season.

On the water, you lock into these fish and their migrations with land, sea, and sky blooming once more. The still-cool ocean waters smell fresh and alive. Thousands of informal networks begin blinking as scores of anglers wait for word that the fish are back. Reports trickle in of stripers caught in those predictable places where they first show up each season. The familiar refrain: "Are they back yet?"

Your truck magically knows its way to the boatyards and tackle shops, where you catch up with old friends, compare notes, and get to work. Everyone is aching to get back on the water and into fish. "March is an acquired taste, but a good day in March is about as good as anything you'll ever get," said conservationist and Chesapeake Bay angler John Page Williams.

As temperatures warm and days lengthen, the waterfront comes alive. I grew up in a small riverside village with three boatyards within a half mile of my family home. Each spring, the sounds of pile drivers and power tools serenaded us, along with a chorus of hammering, scraping, and sanding, and the smells of bottom paint, resin, varnish, creosote, and two-stroke outboard exhaust. Heavenly sensations for youngsters and old-timers.

SPRING IS FULL OF STARTS AND STOPS as the seasons grind past one another. It snows one day in April in southern New England, as temperatures dip into the 20s and ice reappears in the corners of my boat. The salt marsh is again ringed in a thin silvery-white glaze. Not a good day for striped bass larvae on the spawning grounds, but the birdsong at 7:00 a.m. is loud and mesmerizing. Daffodils and budding trees herald the inexorable arrival of a new chapter, despite the falling snow.

Eventually a few warm days string together. Then a week or two, and suddenly the fish are everywhere. Famished from a long winter of no fishing, we catch them on flies and light tackle in shallow waters or pull them out of surging 60-foot tide rips on bucktails and live bait. When tides, moon phases, and water temperatures line up, stripers feed with abandon and precision on tiny cinder worms in salt ponds, where the heavy thud of breaking surf from over the dunes echoes the undulations of the cosmos.

Previous spread: Lipped. Photo by Tom Lynch.
Left: Osprey and hickory shad. Photo by Jay Fleming.

"The bass are in—or should be—and you and the fish have a new lease on life," wrote surf-fishing pioneer Frank Woolner nearly 50 years ago in *Field & Stream.* "Baby the first one. Whether you keep him or turn him loose, the first striped bass of a fresh new season is a mightily important fish."

STRIPERS FEED IN COUNTLESS NOOKS AND CRANNIES, and through broad swaths of tidal and coastal waters—on reefs, along beaches, in rivers and sounds, in the shadow of tank farms on industrial riverfronts, along lonely barrier beaches, at the mouths of inlets and rivers, and off scrubby little islands where ebony cormorants are nesting. Where there is food, you can find striped bass.

Muscling forward in waves, they arrive in all sizes—foot-long fish hitting lures almost as long as they are, medium-sized rock-and-rollers weighing from the mid-20s into the mid-30s, and big cows that rip off line until you wonder if they'll ever stop. Laughter and camaraderie bloom, too, when you lip a big striper at the boat and a swoosh of her tail shoots river water into your partner's face.

OSPREYS FISH ALONGSIDE US ALL SPRING, tossing their distinctive cries of *cheep, cheep, cheep* into the skies. I watch a fish hawk dive with the fury of an Old Testament god on alewives spawning on a pollen-crusted mill pond. Its controlled abandon reminds me of the farm kids I watched leap from a bridge in the Willamette Valley of Oregon on a long-ago hot summer day. Wearing sneakers and cutoffs, the boys scaled the riveted structure to the top, where they laughed

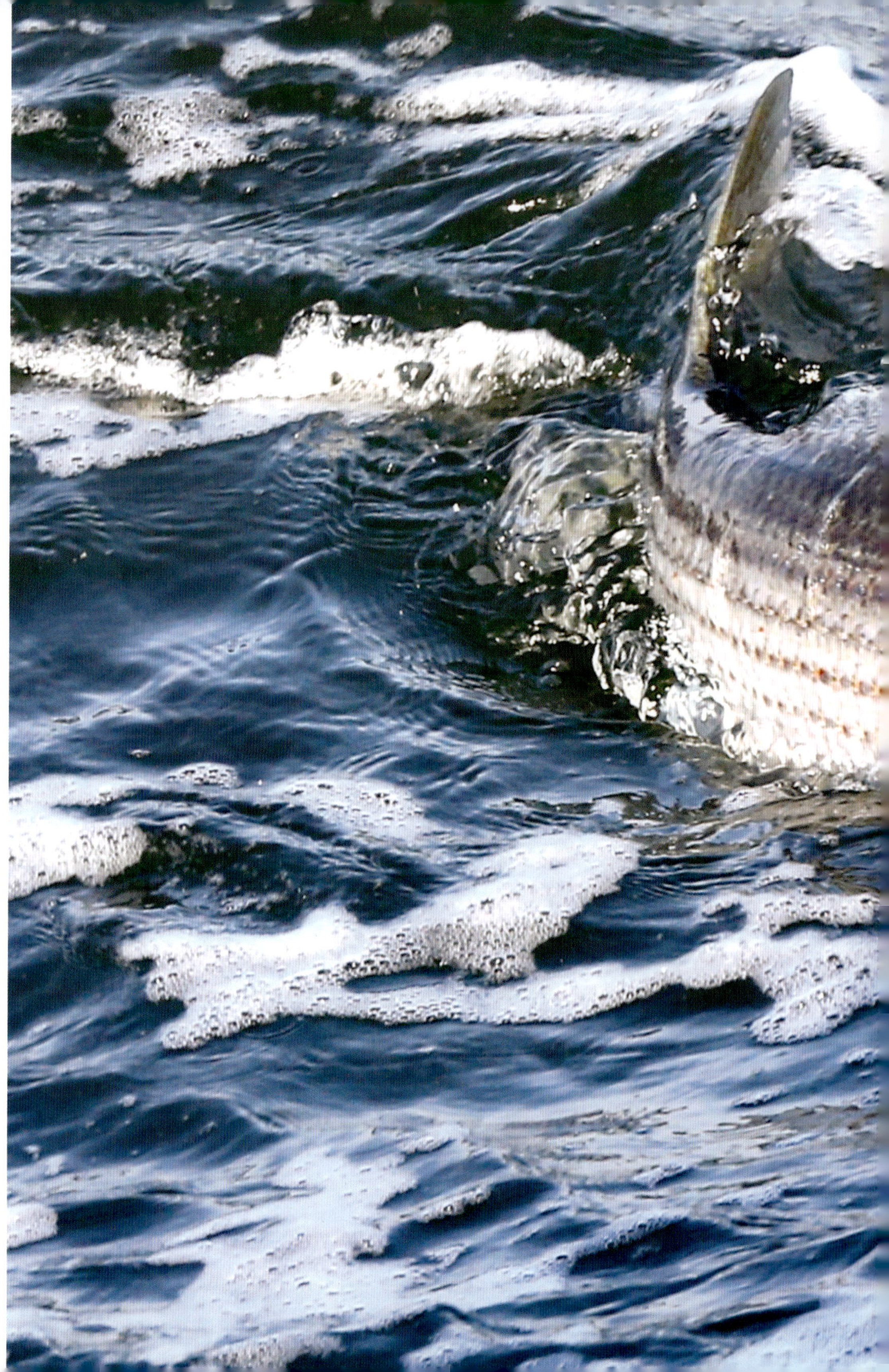

Chartreuse is the color. Photo by Tom Lynch.

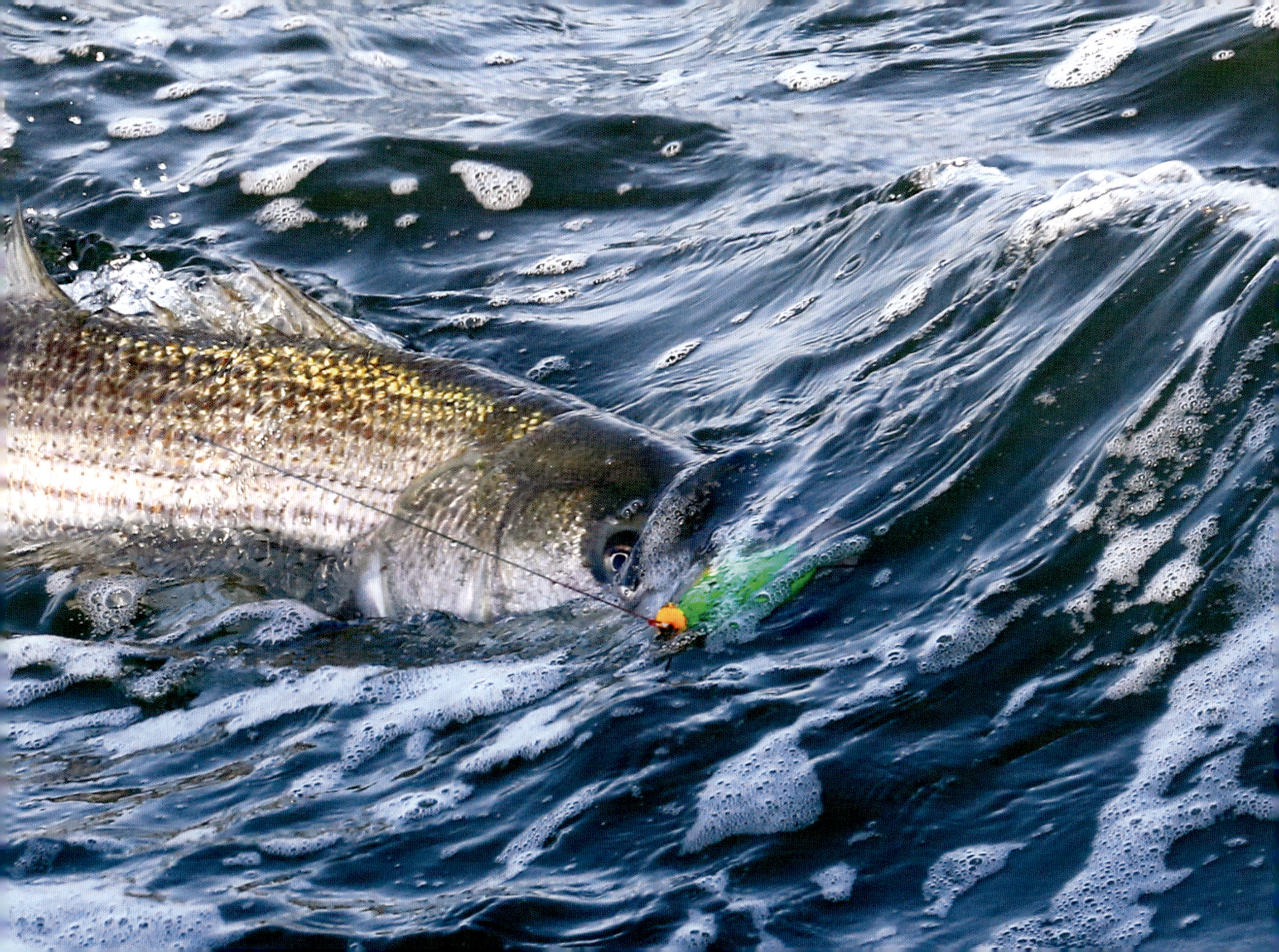

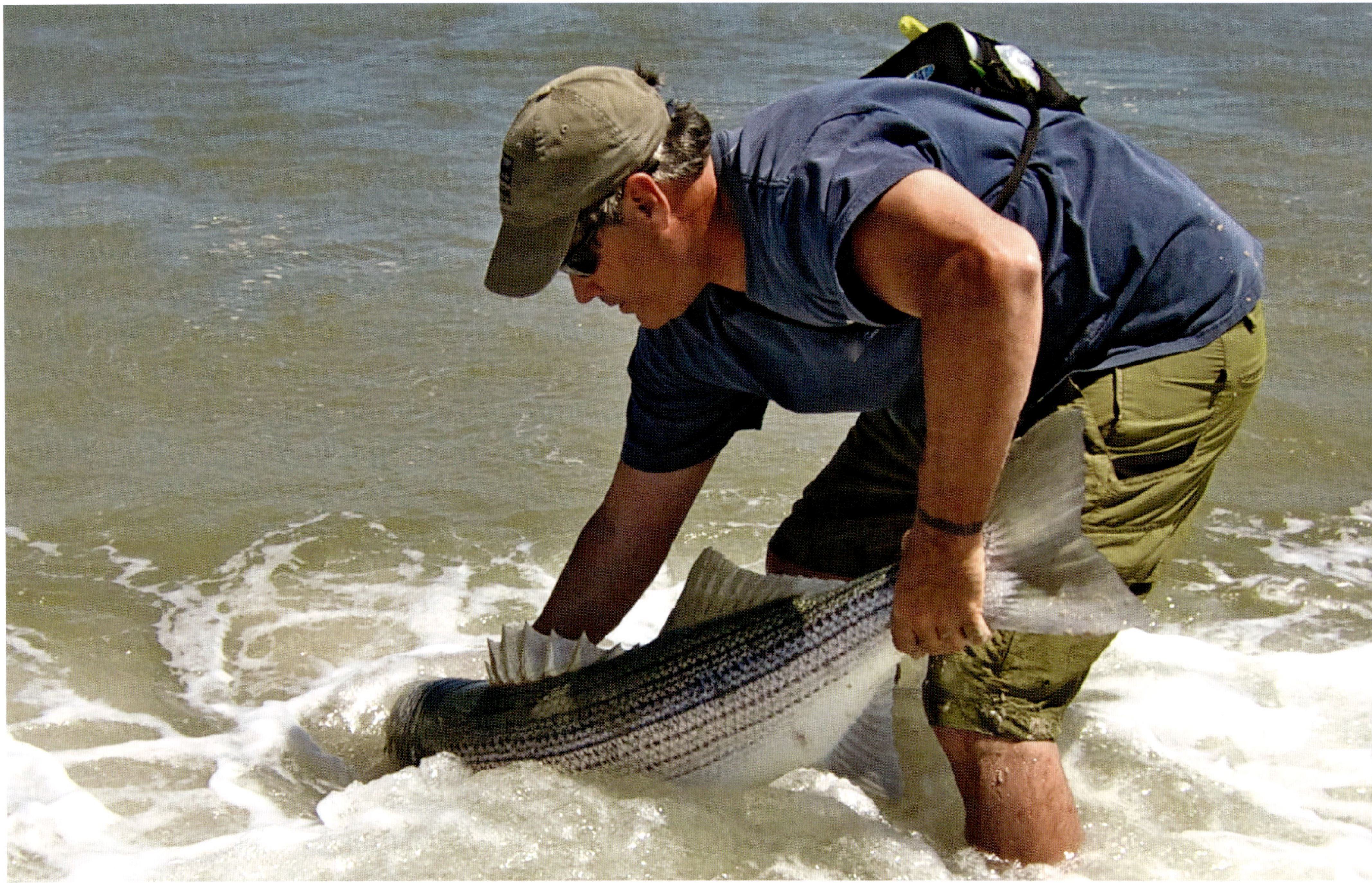

and preened as they readied themselves. These boys leapt feetfirst, and I could scarcely believe their boldness or the height. I held my breath, like when watching an osprey plummet from eight stories. Graceful, under control, arms feathering to maintain their balance, the boys fell like the birds—letting gravity carry them to the water.

STRIPERS CONNECT PEOPLE AND PLACES across generations. As a kid, I started catching small bass in late April or early May in a cove on the Pawcatuck River in Westerly, Rhode Island. According to my boyhood journal, I took my first of the year on a ⅝-ounce popping plug on May 3, 1968. I was 13 years old. I'm certain I could catch a bass today at the same spot within a day or two of the same date.

Two of the people who were fishing beside me that day were Larry Maderia and Joe Manette. More than 50 years later, the three of us once again gather by the river; I have not seen either in 20 years. Manette is now a 67-year-old fly fisherman and a former high school classmate. We fished the river in junior high school, when Manette and I were in eighth grade. "You sat right in front of me, and we talked stripers," recalled Manette. "I remember you used to bring a Penn reel catalog to school." Simple times for fish nerds. Maderia was five years older than me, had a license and a car, and mentored me in the ways of striped bass, for which I am eternally grateful.

I STILL FISH HARD IN MAY AND JUNE from a kayak on the lower section of my boyhood river, where the fish are plentiful and there is never a crowd. The first mile from the mouth is small-boat country—mostly tin boats, kayaks, or guys in little center consoles who nibble around the edges of the channel, fearful of losing a prop to the many rocks hidden beneath the tannic waters. The smart spring crowd slow-trolls tube-and-worms along the edges of the channels and through the coves, taking their share of keepers. Some cast small lures or flies.

As several terns start squabbling, three men putt-putt close past me, trolling sandworms from an aluminum skiff. One angler is in a wheelchair. The man in the stern with the outboard tiller stares at me. I stare back.

"Well?" he finally asks.

"Little slow," I answer.

"Low tide," he croaks, the Rhode Island accent coming through. "But hey, it's a beautiful day."

Their raspy laughter that drifts my way on the southwest breeze, along with their hunched, slouch-shouldered postures, reminds me of a trio of black-crowned night herons. The men are drinking beer, enjoying the sun, and looking for a little stretch of water that holds bass. These are the types of men with whom I grew up and went to school. They are the ones I understand. To me, this is home.

IT'S THE THIRD WEEK OF MAY and the second day of temperatures reaching into the 90s. My phone rings at 7:30 a.m. A friend who lives near a salt pond in Rhode Island is calling to tell me the worms are beginning to hatch.

"When can you make it?" he asks.

"How about tonight?" I answer.

As the long evening unfolds, I stand on the bow with a fly rod in hand as the stripers glide smoothly out of dark shallows to inhale worms, making for the surface and then slipping out of sight in a graceful dance. They feed with a precision that you rarely witness during their usual

Released. Photo by Ray Kerico.

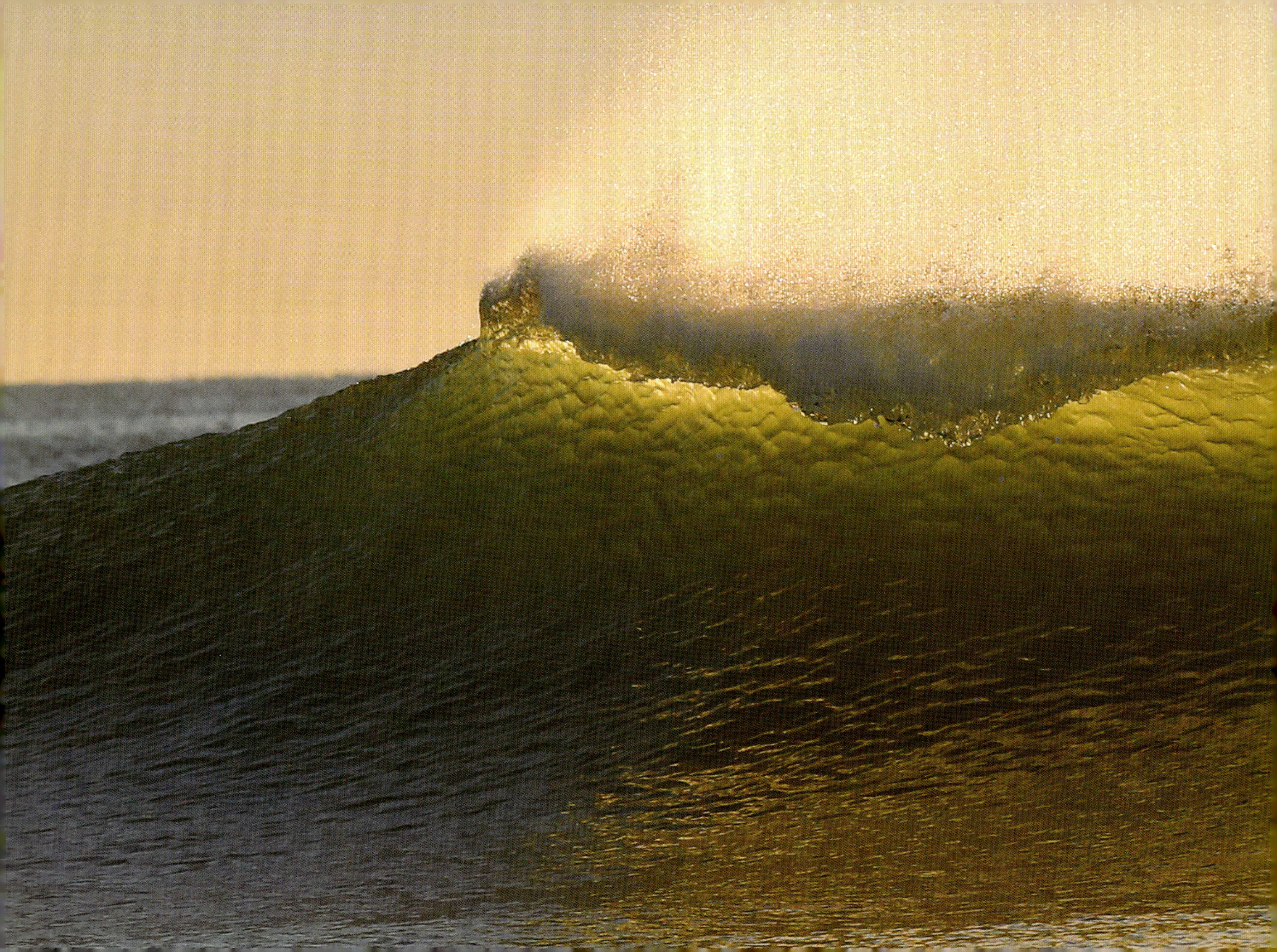

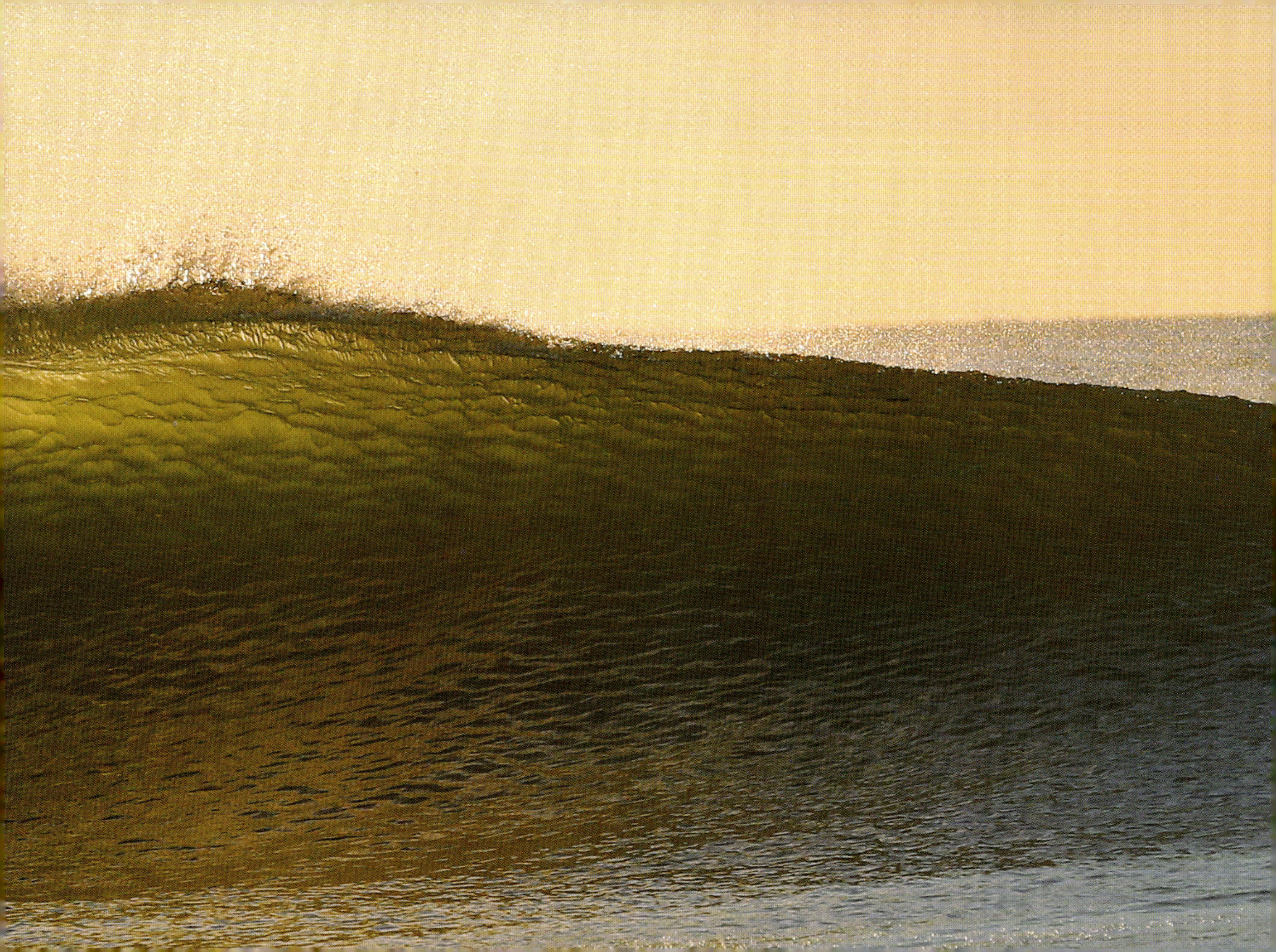

frenzies. More like trout than bass. With patience and persistence, we both take fish, but it's not the catch that I remember so vividly. It's the swift, graceful movements of predator and prey on a soft spring evening that are unforgettable.

ONE MEMORIAL DAY MORNING makes me thankful to give up sleep. Staying in bed would mean missing the half-moon, pale and fading as morning brightens; the soft dabs of high clouds; the birdsong that flutes into my consciousness before the alarm goes off at 4:45 a.m. The scratchy and melodic chorus from the thicket in my yard is in full throat by the time I roll out of the driveway for the tidal river.

Had I slept in I would have missed a tern resting on a piece of driftwood ahead of my skiff and a cormorant drying its wings on the rotting piling at the mouth of the cove. The sun is an orange smudge as it comes over the hills to the east, and I smell the banks of the river starting to bloom.

I feel the first puff of a westerly breeze as I move downriver to fish a shallow reef. The wind builds steadily so that by 10:00 a.m. it is snapping flags and pennants, and carrying the unmistakable parade sounds of fifes and drums down the tree-lined streets and across the coves of this old river town. Close your eyes, and the music carries you back to June 1776, when the young republic's colonial warship *Oliver Cromwell* was launched in Essex, Connecticut, where I am fishing on this day more than 200 years later.

I'm thankful I didn't miss running my finger down the dark-purple, iridescent scales of a 40-inch striper that snatched the live eel I drifted over the rocky bottom a couple of hours earlier. Soon, I am hurrying up the street in my fishing boots to catch my daughters marching

Previous spread: Beach-break peak. Photo by Tom Lynch.
Right: Trophy striper on an eel. Photo by Tom Lynch.

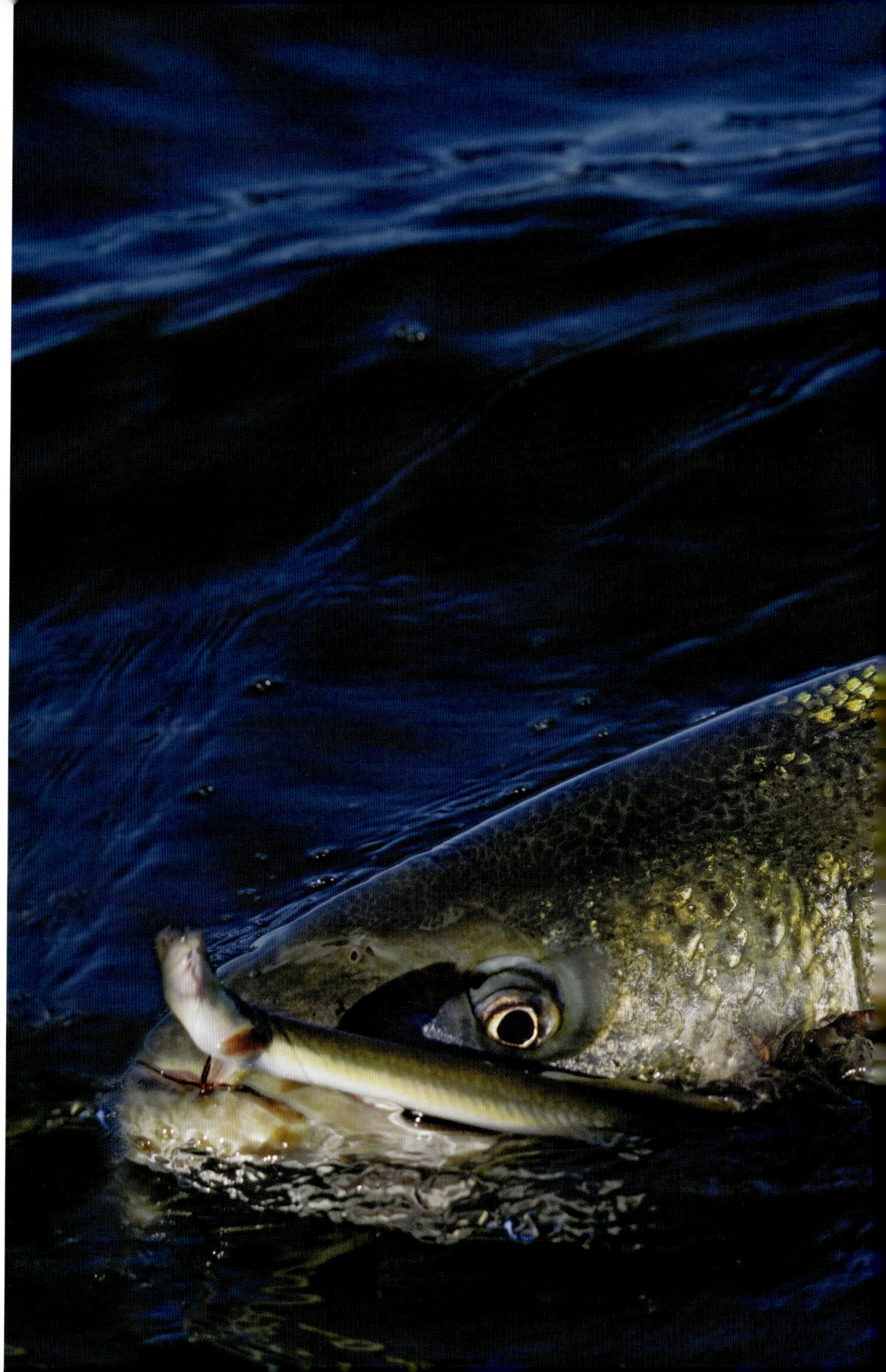

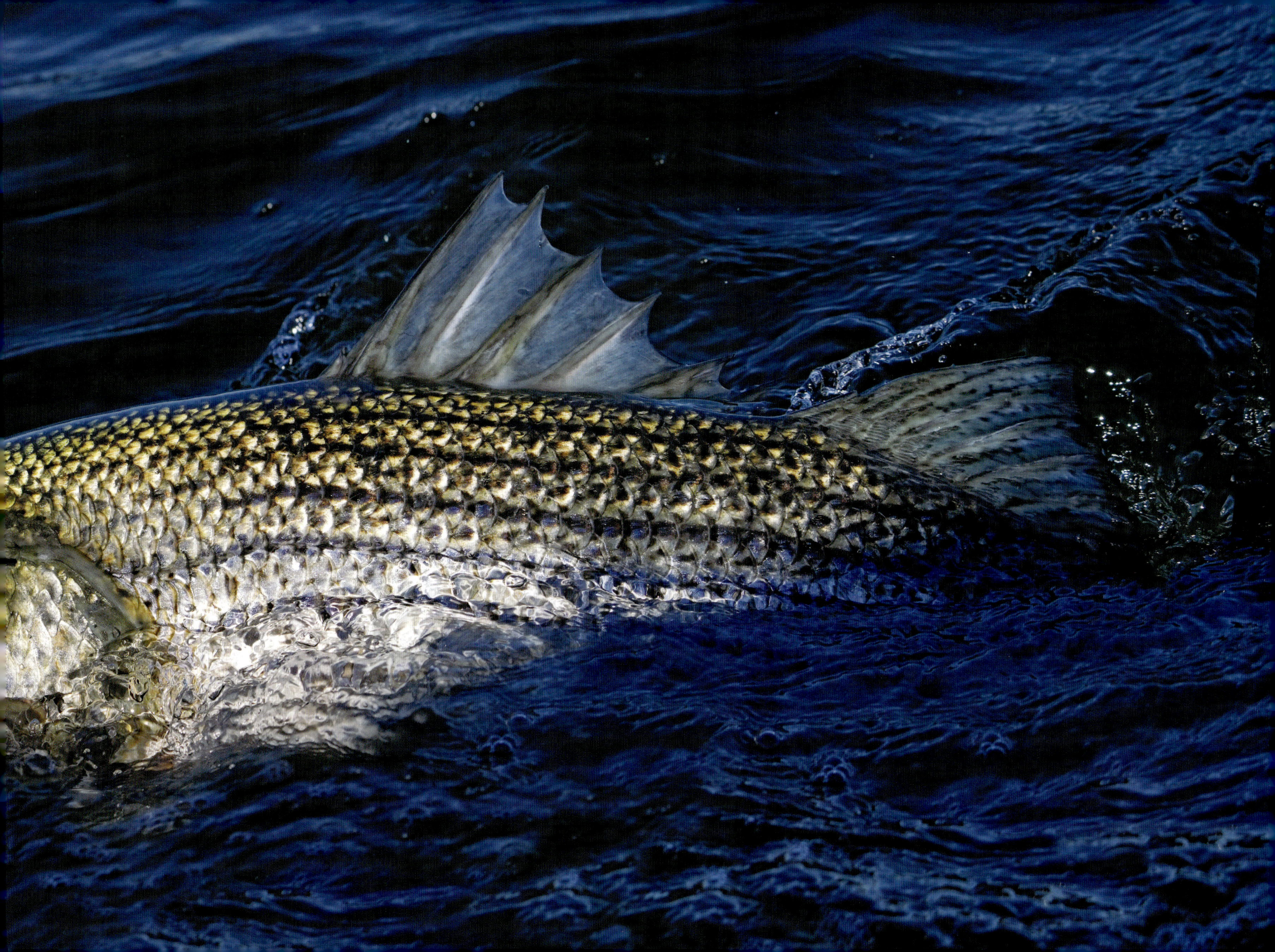

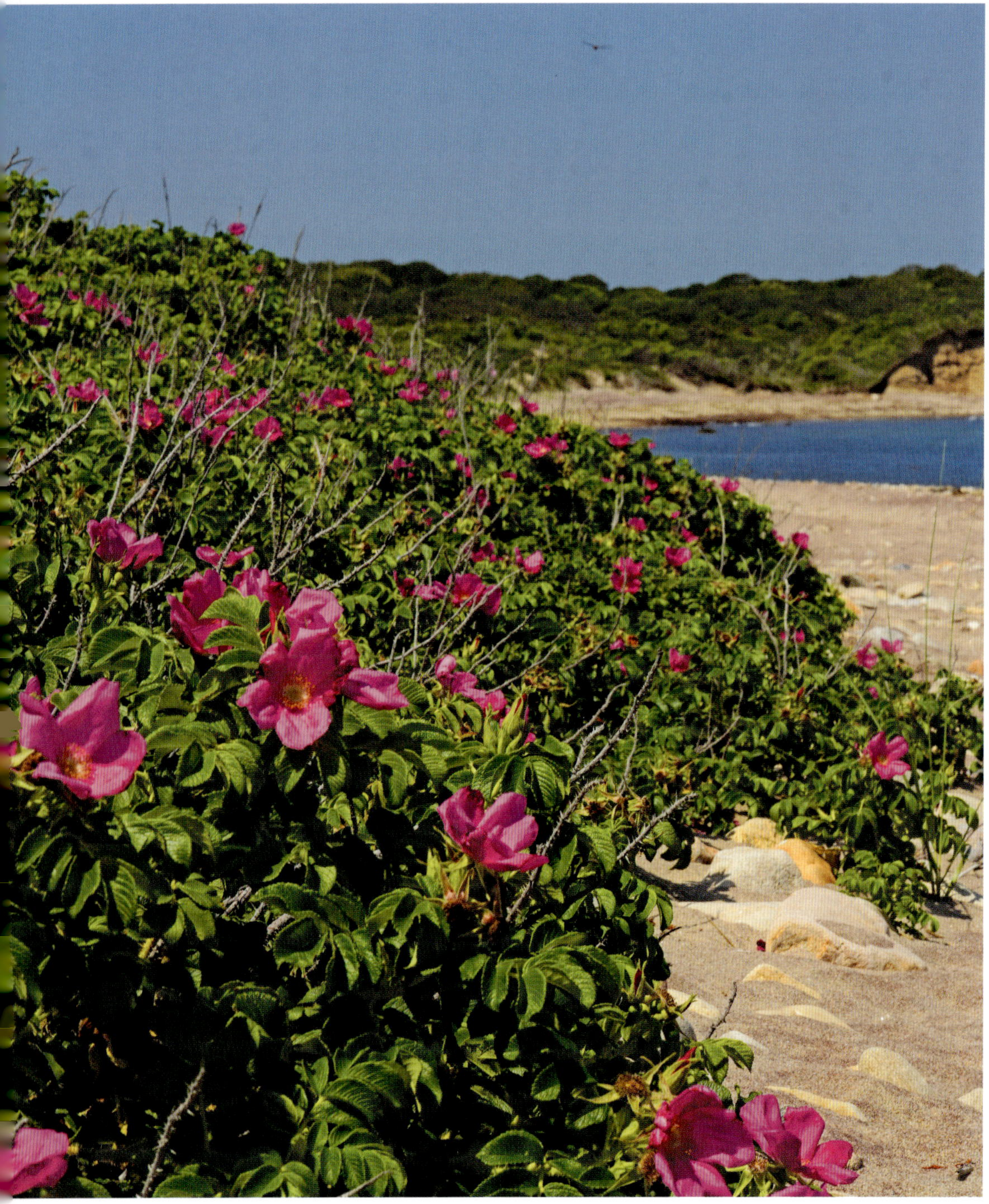

past in the parade. My oldest child mouths, *Were you fishing?* before her eyes answer her own question. She blushes and turns away. My younger daughter waves without embarrassment at her shabbily dressed father; I am wearing my favorite fishing pants, ripped wide open at one knee.

WHILE THE BOUNTY OF SPRING STRIPERS seems endless, it is but a small remnant of the wave of anadromous species—salmon, sturgeon, alewives, blueback herring, shad, striped bass, and others—that once moved upriver to spawn in fresh water. Pollution, habitat loss, overfishing, dams, and other factors have taken a toll on the runs of these important fish.

Stripers are predictable on some days, maddeningly fickle on others. Some days they hit cast after cast. Other days they are impossible to fool, prompting endless speculation about where they are or why they won't eat. The truth is no one knows, but the appealing mystery would all be lost if we could accurately predict their every move and feeding whim. Better to scratch your head and speculate with friends than to find legions of bass eager to gobble everything you throw at them on every trip.

"They have to run a gauntlet," said Todd Towle, a fly fisherman and guide from Maine. "By the time they get up here, they've seen everything thrown at them from New Jersey to Maine. They have a PhD. It's like asking a pretty girl to dance, and she says no. It's heartbreaking, but you keep coming back."

I've returned for a half century of springs, and plenty of tides still leave me perplexed.

Left: Beach roses. Photo by Tom Lynch.
Right: Fox and striper. Photo by Jay Fleming.

ONE TERN IS ALL IT TAKES to stop me on a May evening. The bird hovers like a drone, head bent, its eyes fixed on the darkening water. And then it drops, which along this barrier beach is a good sign. The light is low and fading, but I think I see a fish roil the surface.

The fog that mists my glasses is settling in, and I am freezing my backside off. I am eager to get back to my truck, an hour's walk away, to crank up the heat and thaw out. I didn't really want to stop and cast. I've been wet-wading up to my waist in a large bay behind the ocean-facing dunes for more than an hour. In my rush this afternoon, I forgot my shortie wet suit, and now I am shivering. My feet and fingers are numb.

The high tide is starting to ebb when I wade ashore and cross the dunes to check the ocean swell I've heard break all evening. I am ready for a change of scenery on the walk back. The ocean smells fresh, and the two- to three-foot waves are peeling off sharply as they break. Then the tern appears. Some signs you just can't ignore and still call yourself a striper guy. "Those little gulls are the ones who give them away," an old-timer told me a lifetime ago, referring to the terns.

My first few casts produce nothing. I throw a floating swimming minnow as more bait dimples the surface. The fish are feeding selectively on small bait, which I never identify. I switch to a half-ounce unpainted jig head onto which I thread a four-inch purple curly-tailed worm to imitate the worm hatches going off in the salt ponds and bays. I've never fished it before, but it seems like a promising combo.

I hook up on the second cast. After that things go crazy, with nothing showing on top. I seldom go more than a few casts without a fish or a hit. It's foggy, and the lights from the nearby village are weirdly distorted as twilight deepens. I repeatedly scan the mile-long beach for the lights of approaching fishermen, but none appear. The stripers are well-proportioned and weigh between 10 and 20 pounds. I release almost two dozen. With water temperatures in the mid-50s, the fish are feisty, carry sea lice, and are full of the season. They hit hard, strip line, shake their heads, and dog it to the sand.

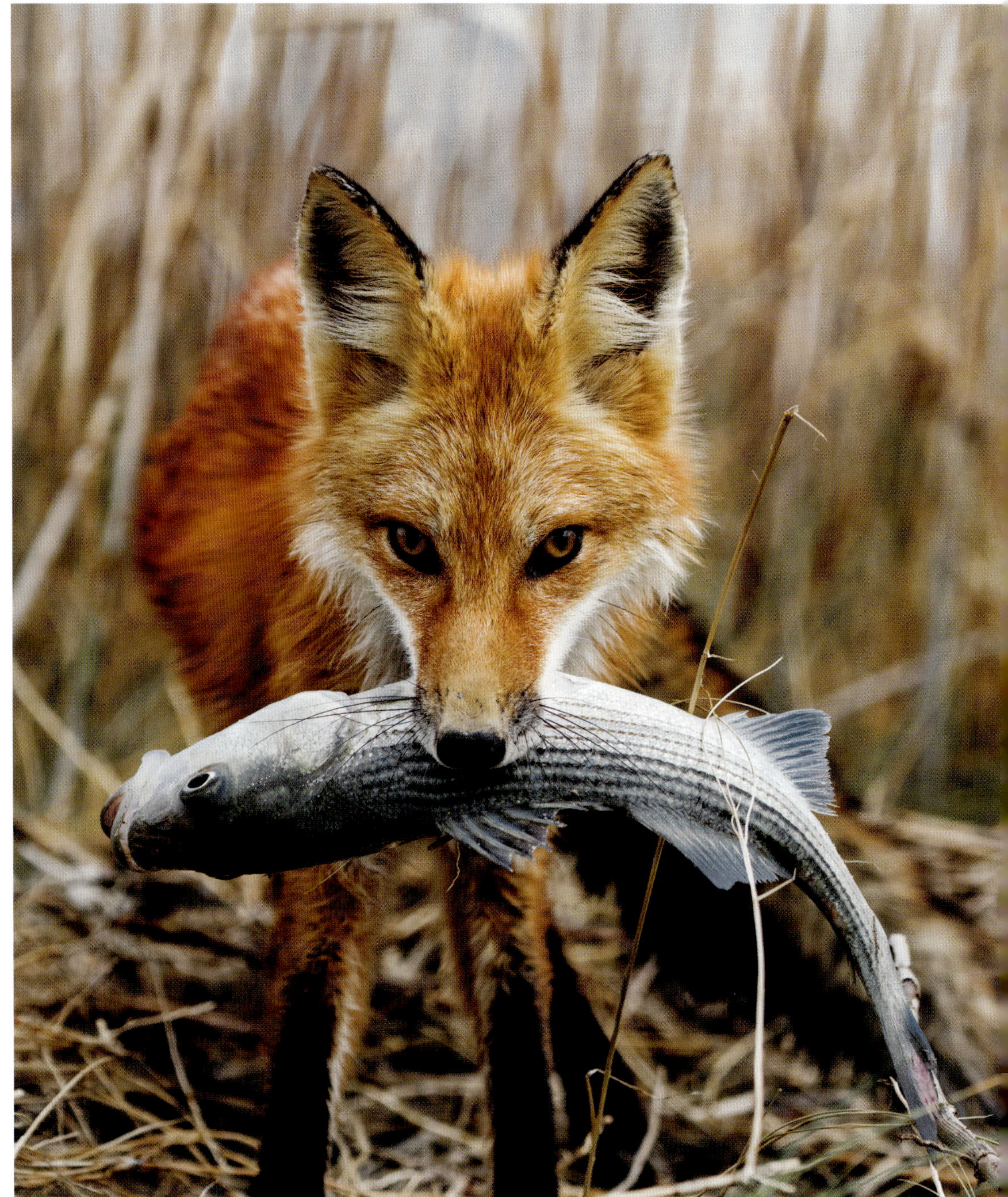

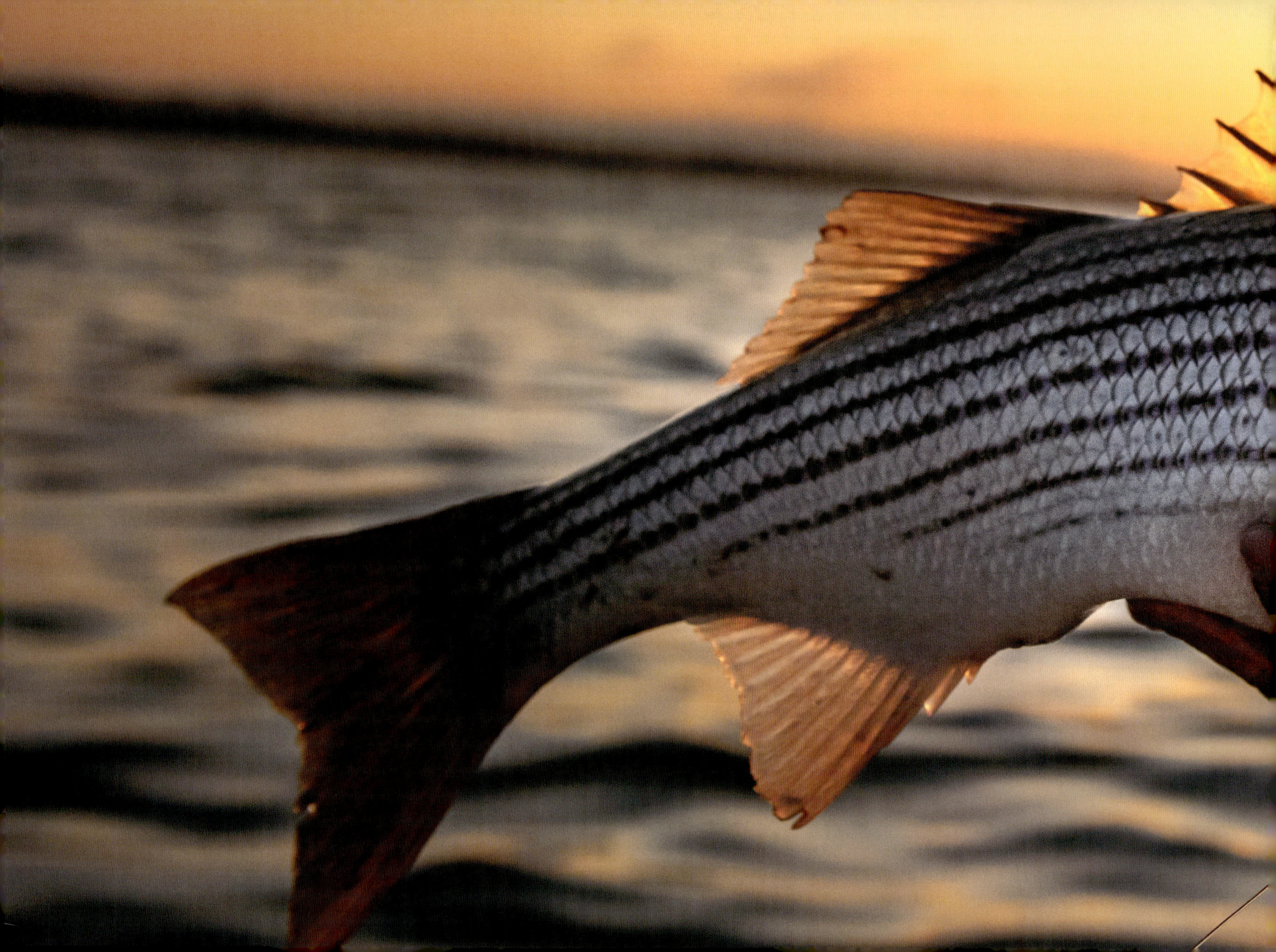

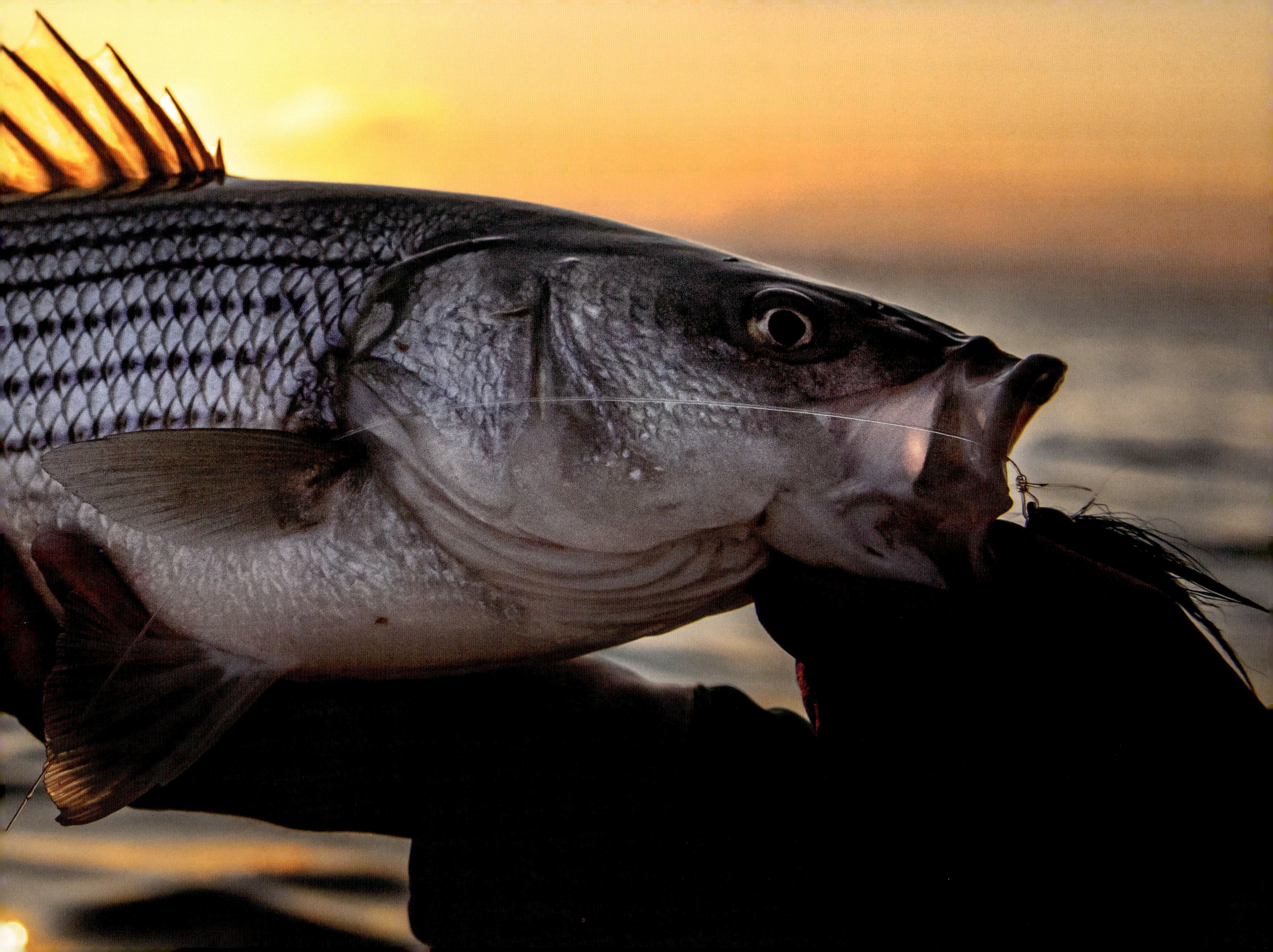

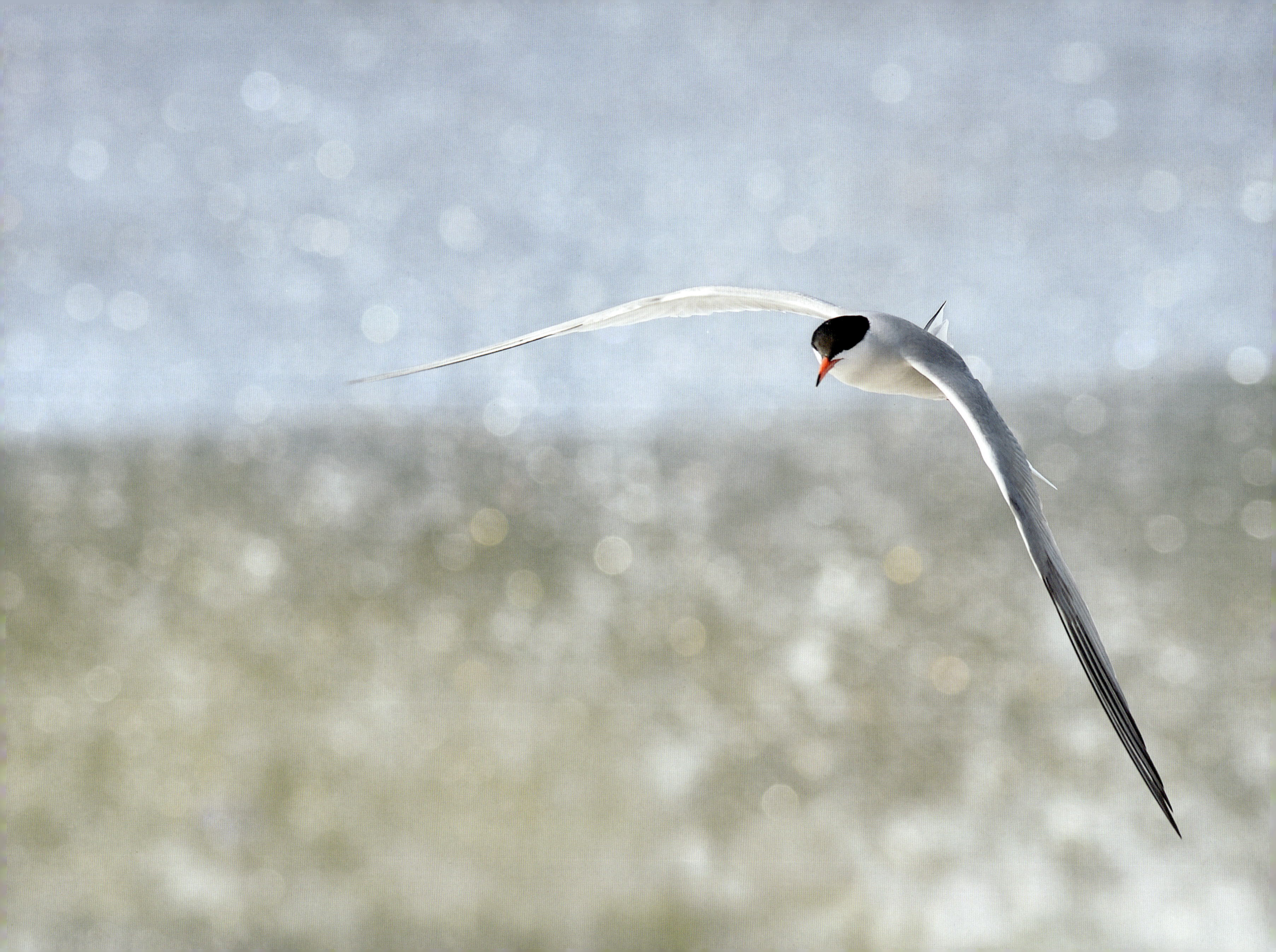

Darkness rises, and the water grows slick calm. The waves sharpen as the tide ebbs, and foam from the breakers shoots up the steep beach. The only noise is the surf, the murmurings of settling shorebirds, the sound of my drag, and the clang from the red channel marker nodding sleepily in the tide. It is one of the best spring evenings I've experienced. I've taken far bigger fish, and on occasion taken more this early in the season, but none are as bright, chunky, and full of zing. And never in a lovelier setting.

SOMETIMES A FLY ROD, a pair of waders, a few streamers, and a good little boat are all you need to tap into the magic of the striper world. One early June evening, all I want is for the damn wind to settle. I want to disappear into the night to stop the chattering inside my head. I attended a funeral mass for a friend this morning, then made tracks to this bay in southwest Rhode Island where I go whenever the continents start drifting.

It's shortly after 8:00 p.m. when I slip the dock lines and move downriver against the tide. I run down the channel for a couple of miles and then turn north toward an island, skirting the broad sand flats. I am drawn to small islands that are overlooked or difficult to reach. This little rise of sand, broken shells, and beach grass is easy to find but unreachable without a boat. And to fish it properly at night, you need to wade. The island is low and constantly changing. It has been drifting to the northeast ever since it was severed from Rhode Island by the Great New England Hurricane of 1938.

I ANCHOR OFF THE EAST SIDE. With a flooding tide, I set the Danforth well up the beach and pull the skiff close to shore. This is a raucous, noisy world. Each spring, thousands of shorebirds hitch a ride on the migrating sandbar to scratch their nests in the sand, lay their eggs, and fledge their young. Day and night, the breeze carries the cries, warnings, and trills of gulls, terns, plovers, peeps, oystercatchers, and others. I don't know what they are saying to one another, but their collective racket shouts, *We're alive*!

Horseshoe crabs crawl up the beach during moon tides. The males clasp the carapaces of the larger females to perform the mating rites, which include burying greenish eggs in the damp sand. Dating back more than 400 million years, the ritual is as timeless as anything I will witness short of birth and death. They often bump into my boots in salt ponds and bays, the males sometimes mistaking a foot for a female.

I scuttle like a crab across the flats to intercept schoolies, which I try to coerce into taking my fly. Sometimes silently. Other times out loud. "Come on. Come on. Take it. There! Ahh!" I'm all focus as the line swings in the current, waiting for a light tap—an inhalation, really. We call it a hit, even though it is nothing like what you feel on a hard lure or a bucktail.

I TAKE EIGHT BASS ON THE BIG flood before the moon clears the hills of the sleepy harbor village around 11:00 p.m. It is a lovely evening. The fish hit in waist-deep water and sprint away. Some run with the tide, and others against it, racing in the shallows behind me before falling back into deeper water. I am alone, with no worry of anyone dropping by. You don't get surprise visitors out here once the sun goes down. All of my senses are working. I use one foot to probe for the edge and keep me from stepping off the shallow flat and winding up over my head, 100 yards from dry sand with only a flock of uninterested birds to hear my expletives.

AS I MOVE AND CAST, I CONTEMPLATE: *Why do I like islands? Why do I enjoy spending so much time alone at night? Is there something wrong with me?*

Previous spread: Handsome schoolie. Photo by Rex Messing.
Left: Common tern. Photo by Don Schroder.

Damn it—I miss a fish.

My senses are sharp and alert. I am moving with purpose; I'm taking nothing for granted. I think of my friend who was buried this morning. I don't know where we go when we die, so I ponder a question I do have a chance of answering: *Should I switch to a black deceiver or stay with the green and white?* I'm not looking for the meaning of life, but rather for feeling alive, which I have found tonight on this shifting bar with the permanence of a sandcastle.

When my youngest daughter was five, she learned a new word.

"I know what infinity means," she said one day.

"That's a big word," I answered. "What does it mean?"

"It means a long time."

"Yes, my dear," I said. "It means a very, very long time."

Whatever happens when we die, it's for a long time. For keeps. Another reason not to leave this wonderful night quite yet. The water is close to topping my waders. The moon keeps chugging higher. I cast and move, sliding along the drop-off, feeling for the edge with my foot, alone and happy, waiting for the heavenly tug of a spring fish.

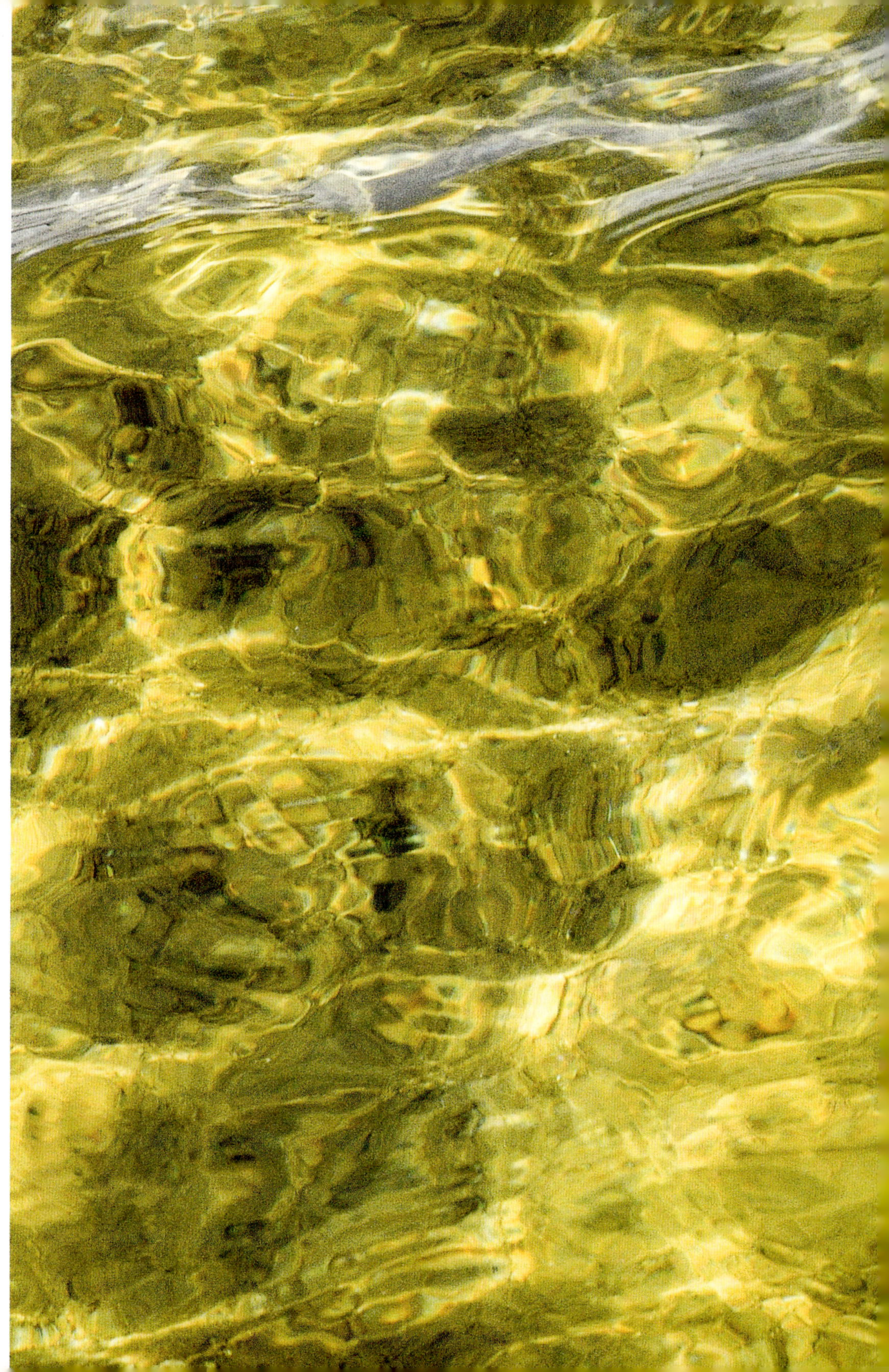

Schoolie on sunny shallows. Photo by James Manning.

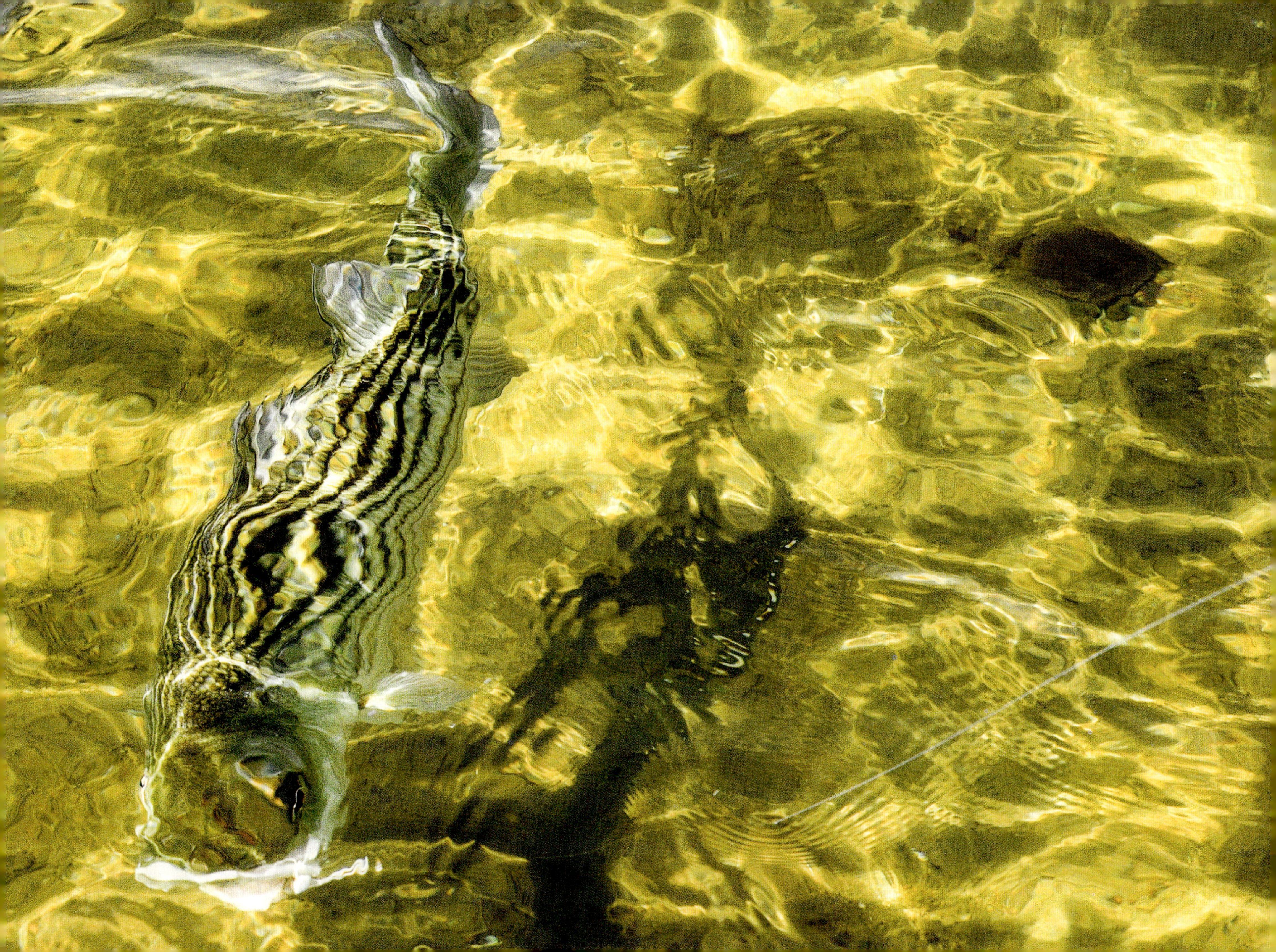

On the Fly

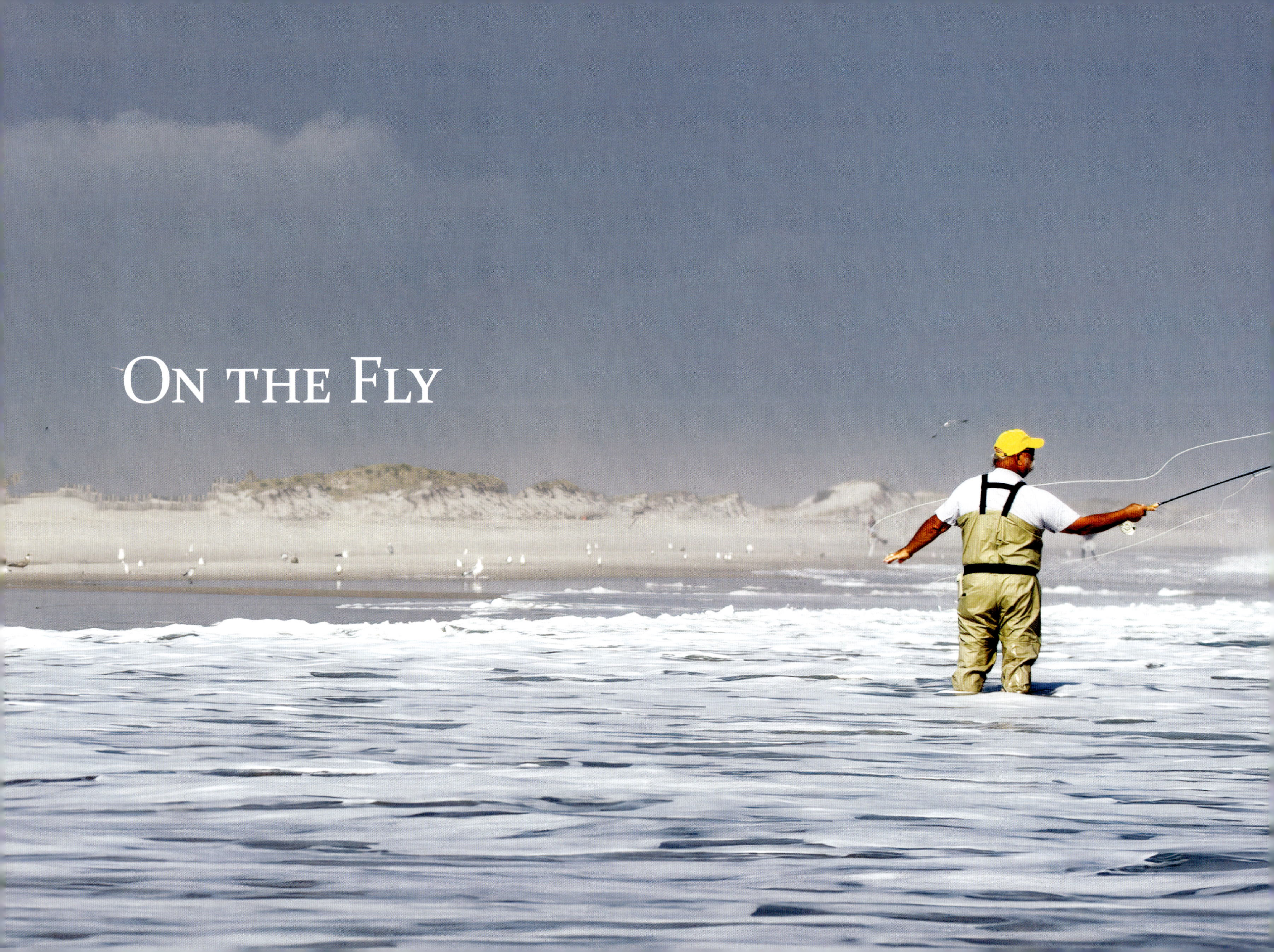

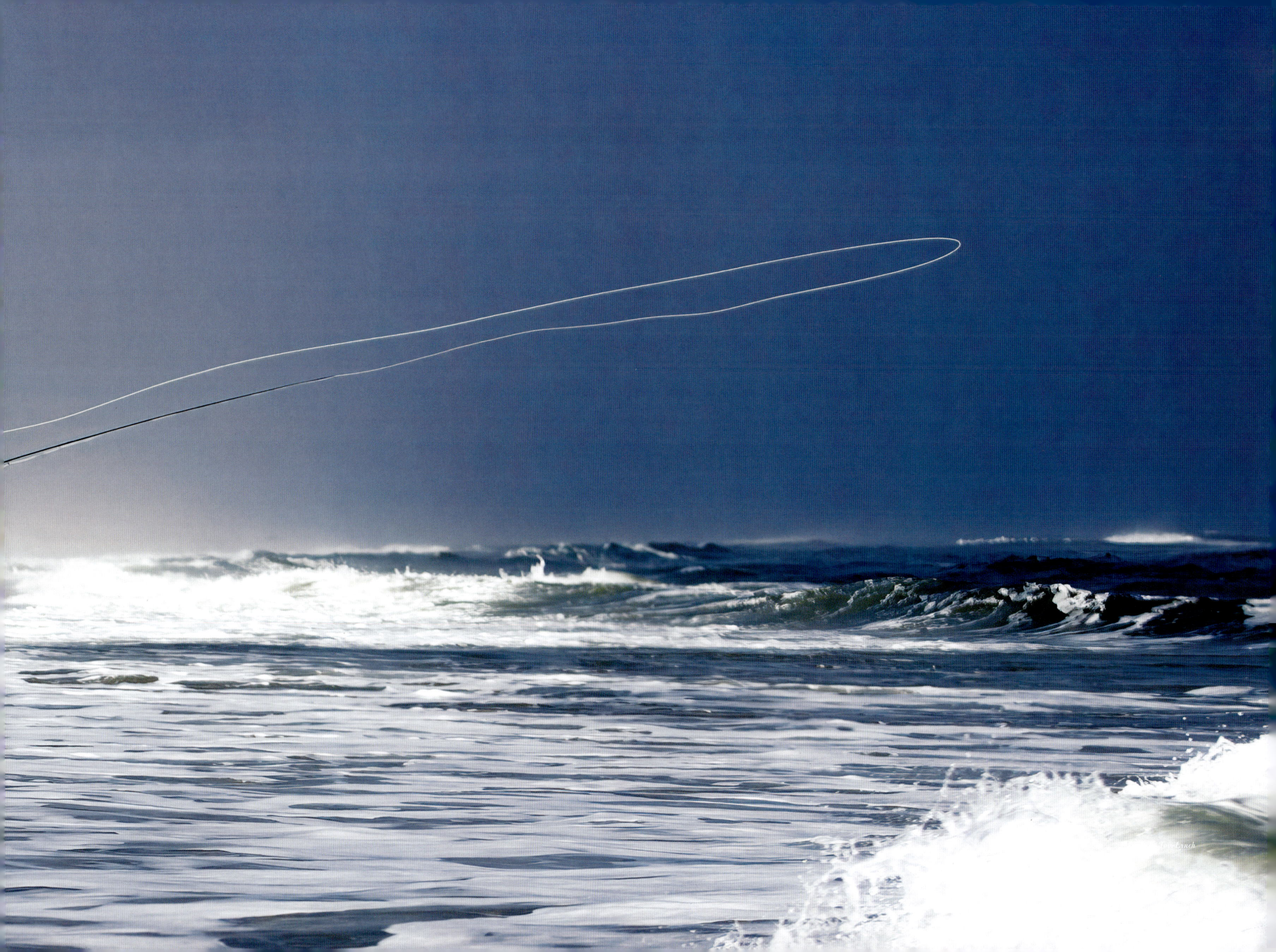
Lynch

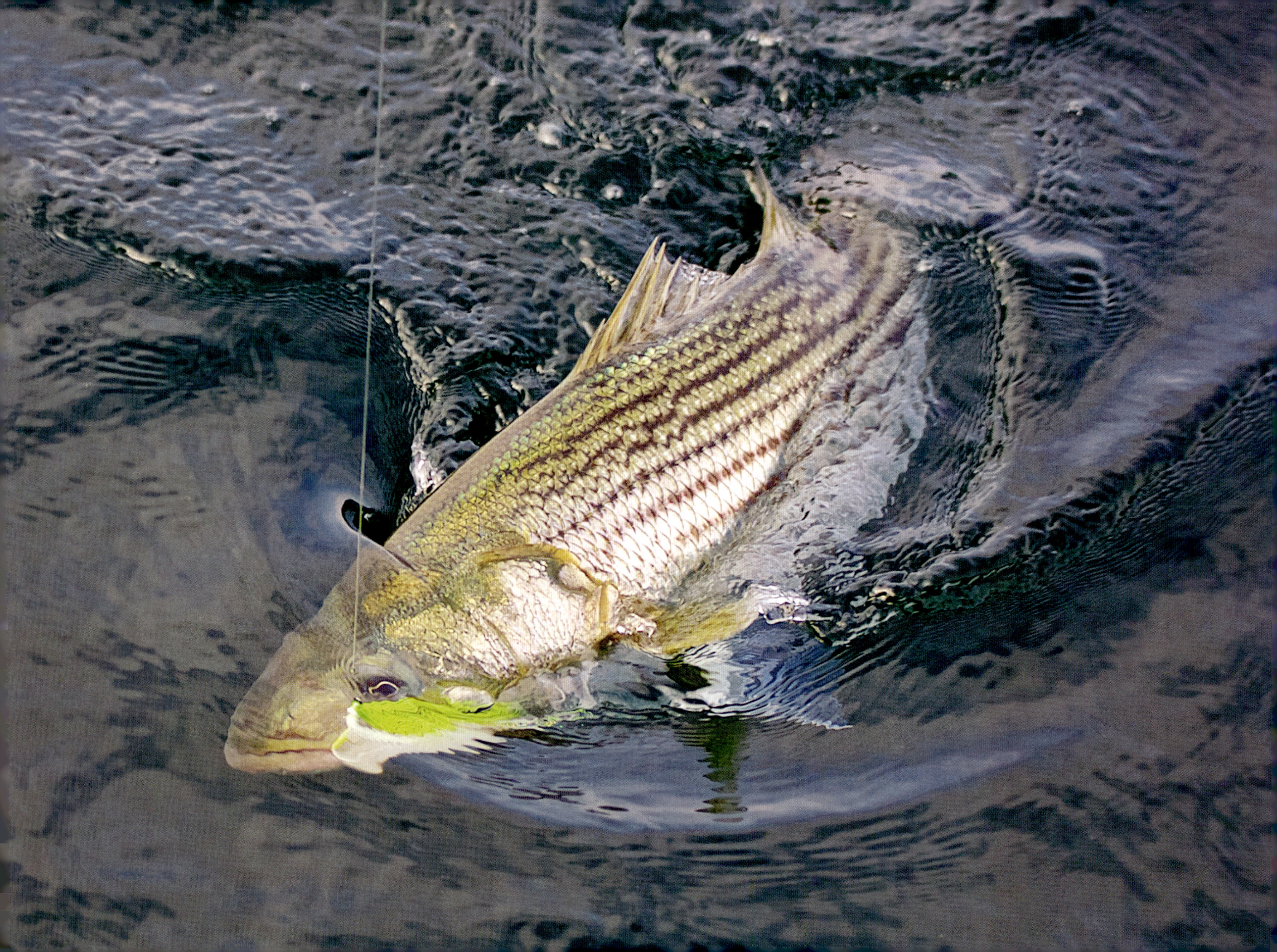

Three stripers persistently swim through the memories of a trio of anglers, regardless of the scores of bass they have taken. In two of these cases, decades have passed. The stripers ranged from 20 to 50 pounds, and all three were caught on flies.

A thread ties these stories together. The enduring memories say something about striped bass and fly fishing. As the late *New York Times* outdoor writer Nelson Bryant said of fly fishing when I interviewed him one November afternoon, at his house on Martha's Vineyard, Massachusetts, "It's a fascination with what's difficult."

My fish was one of these and, at 20 pounds, the smallest of the three. Although nothing distinguished its appearance from the many others I have caught, I can conjure memories of that fish more clearly than almost any other I've taken, including those more than twice its size, although they were not taken on a fly.

I FREEZE AND HOLD MY BREATH on that long-ago morning. A short cast away, a striper is feeding head-down on sand eels in about three feet of water. It is sunny, the water is clear, the breeze light, and a dark meadow of eelgrass lies 30 yards beyond the fish. I am wet-wading the flats on north Monomoy Island off Chatham, Massachusetts, for the first time. This striper, with its healthy girth and broad shoulders, is the first fish I stumble upon as I meander the sandy shallows.

I stare, disbelieving my early luck, as I begin pulling line off my reel. This is no schoolie. This is a good fish, and I really want this bass. I am so entranced that I eschew my usual prayers to the fish gods. All I can think is, *Don't eff this up*. The striper is perfectly content, going about its breakfast business and oblivious to my ogling. I hold a 9-weight with an epoxy sand eel tied to a long leader in my right hand. The cast has to be short, more like a flip than a cast.

The morning is still, and I don't want to spook the fish by moving or making a poor presentation. In my best stealth mode, I make three casts. The first two fall short, but delicately so, and the bass doesn't notice. What are the odds? On the third cast, the sand eel lands softly in a spot where it will drop near the striper's feeding zone. The water is so clear and calm that I follow the slender fly as it twinkles in the sun on its slow descent toward the action.

I MOVE THE FLY SLOWLY and see a bright red flash as the striper turns its head, flares its gills, and inhales the imposter. The quiet scene shatters as I come tight and the striper kicks into gear, speeding off as if I've hooked the rising sun. I worry about a buoy to my right that is attached to a line; I have no idea what it is doing here, but I don't want the fish to wrap itself around the line. Instead, the striper streaks for the eelgrass, and I follow.

I don't remember the details of what happens next. The bass is hooked well, fights with the intensity you'd expect for a fish that size, and stays out of the eelgrass. I take my time and finally get my hand in its mouth and clamp down hard. I can't believe my luck. I had made three casts to the first fish I'd seen on the flats, and now the striper is in my hands.

The memory of that encounter remains vivid. It was the largest striper I'd ever taken on a fly. I still see the bass as it appeared when I first stumbled upon it feeding. And I've never forgotten the burst of red as the striper's gill plates opened and it vacuumed in the fly. I fished the island flats for four or five more years and caught my share of fish, but none as large or as memorable as that first one.

AS THOUSANDS OF PROPONENTS will attest, striped bass and fly fishing are made for each other. And the number of skilled, young fly anglers I see casting from shore and boats

Previous spread: Expert caster Bob Popovics in the surf. Photo by Tom Lynch.
Left: At the boat. Photo by Pat Ford.

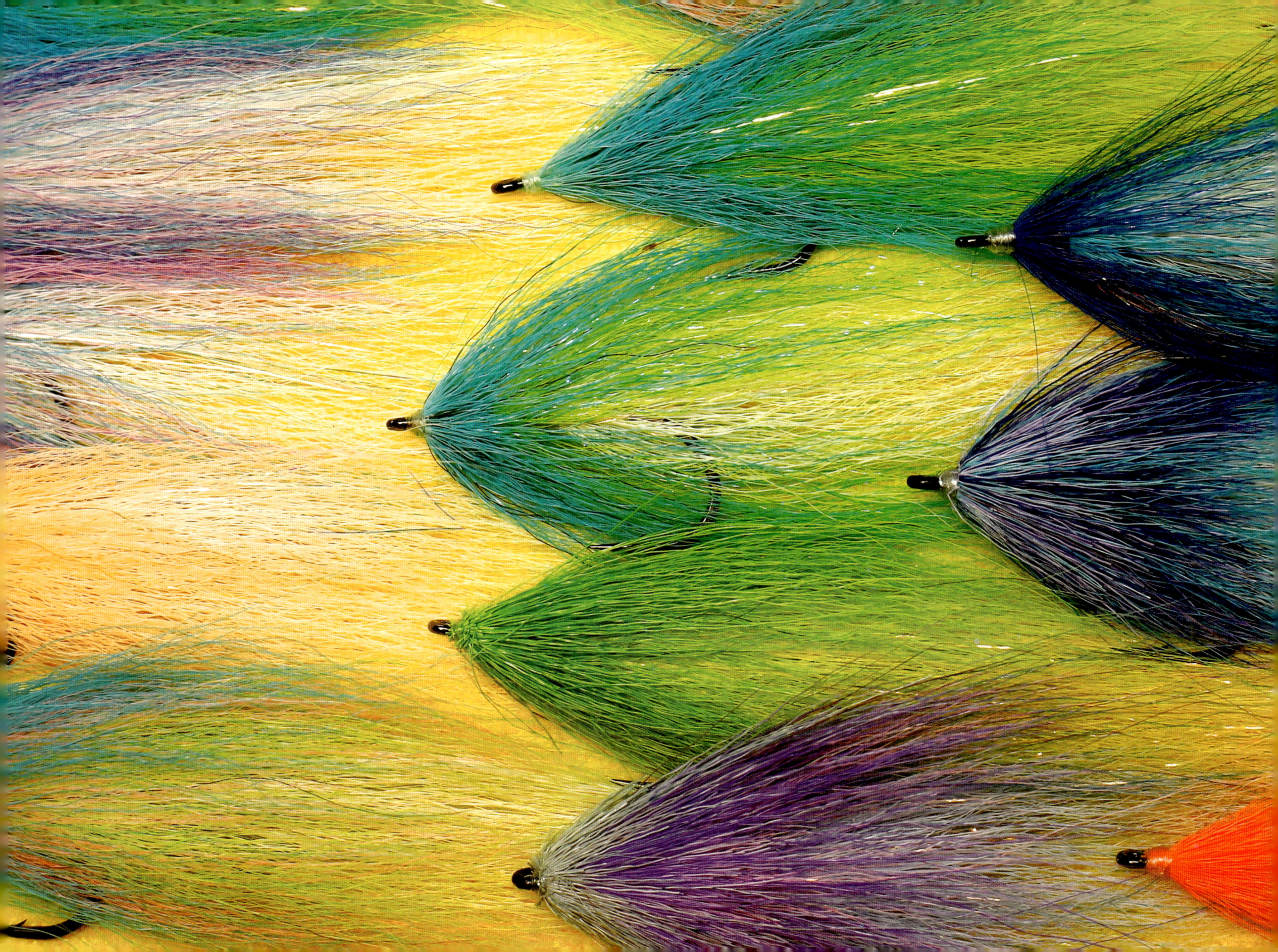

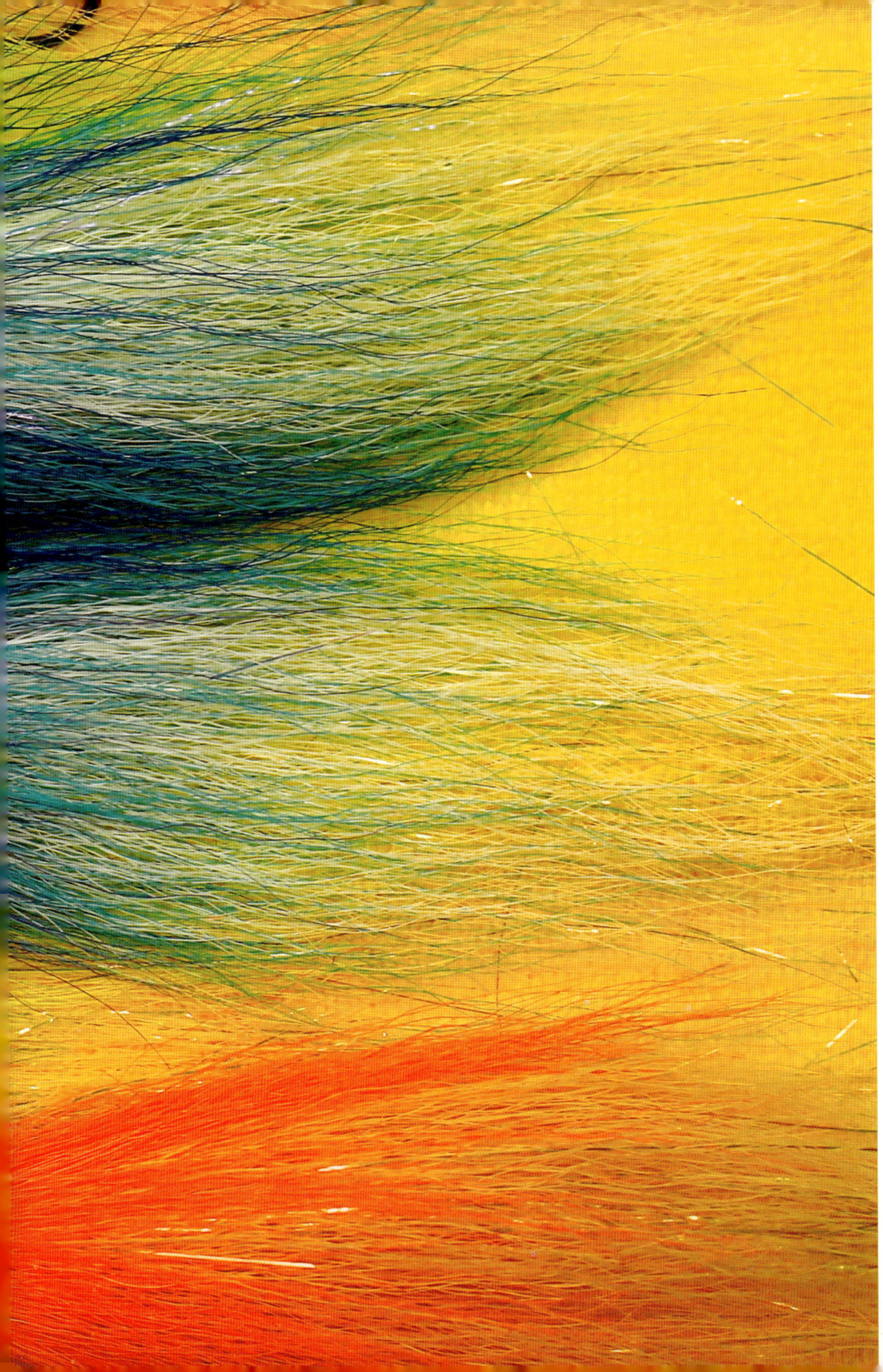

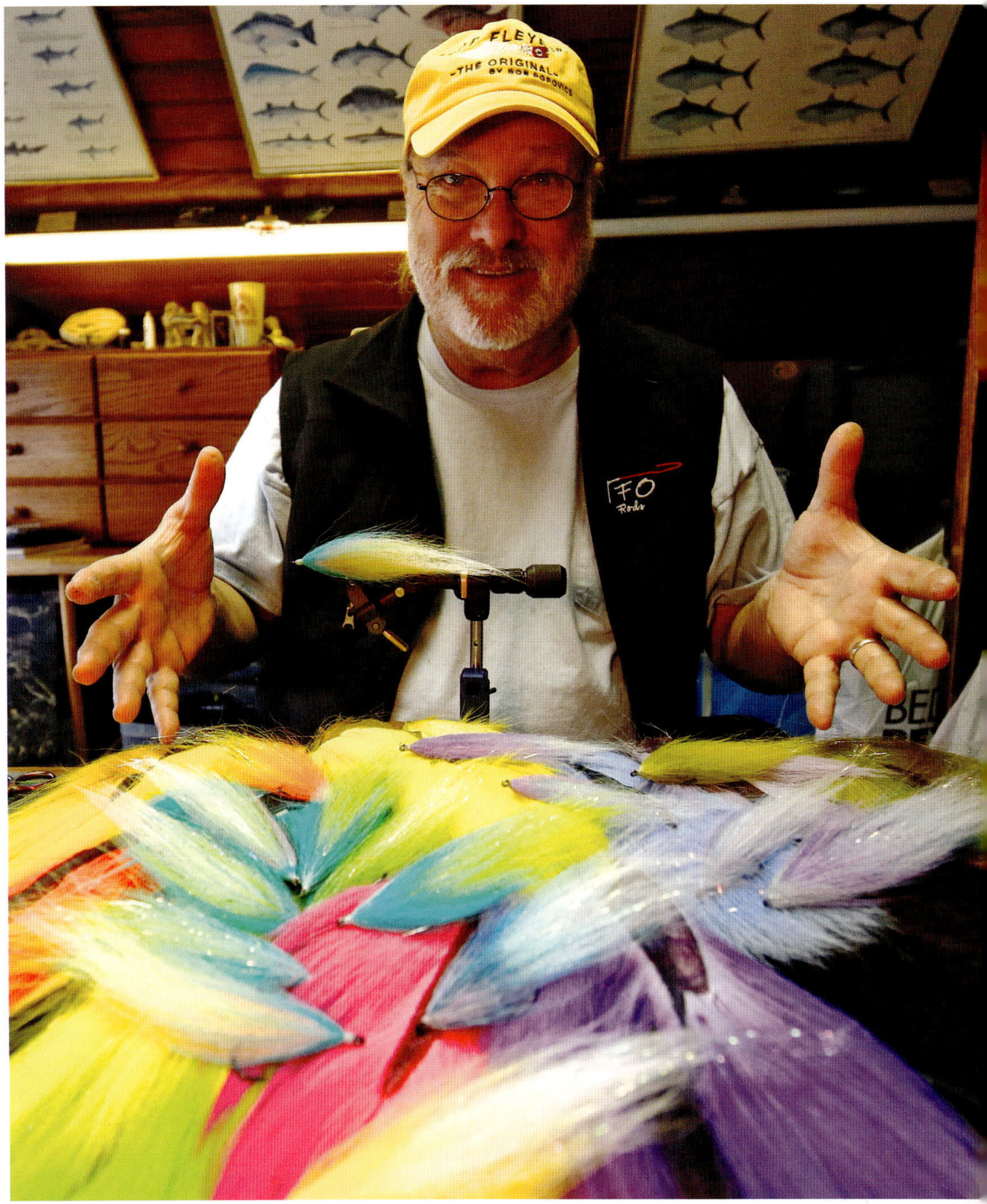
THE ORIGINAL

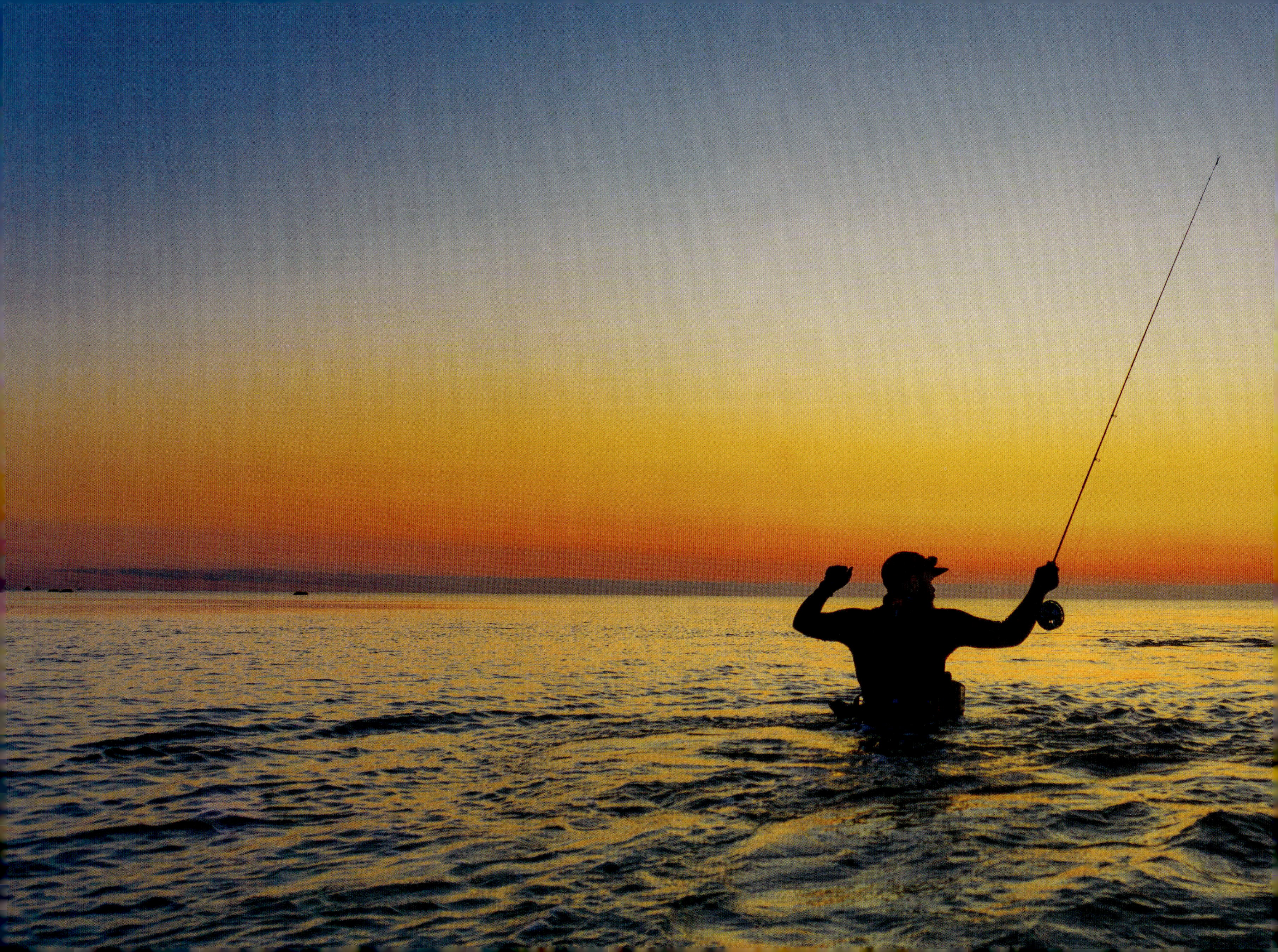

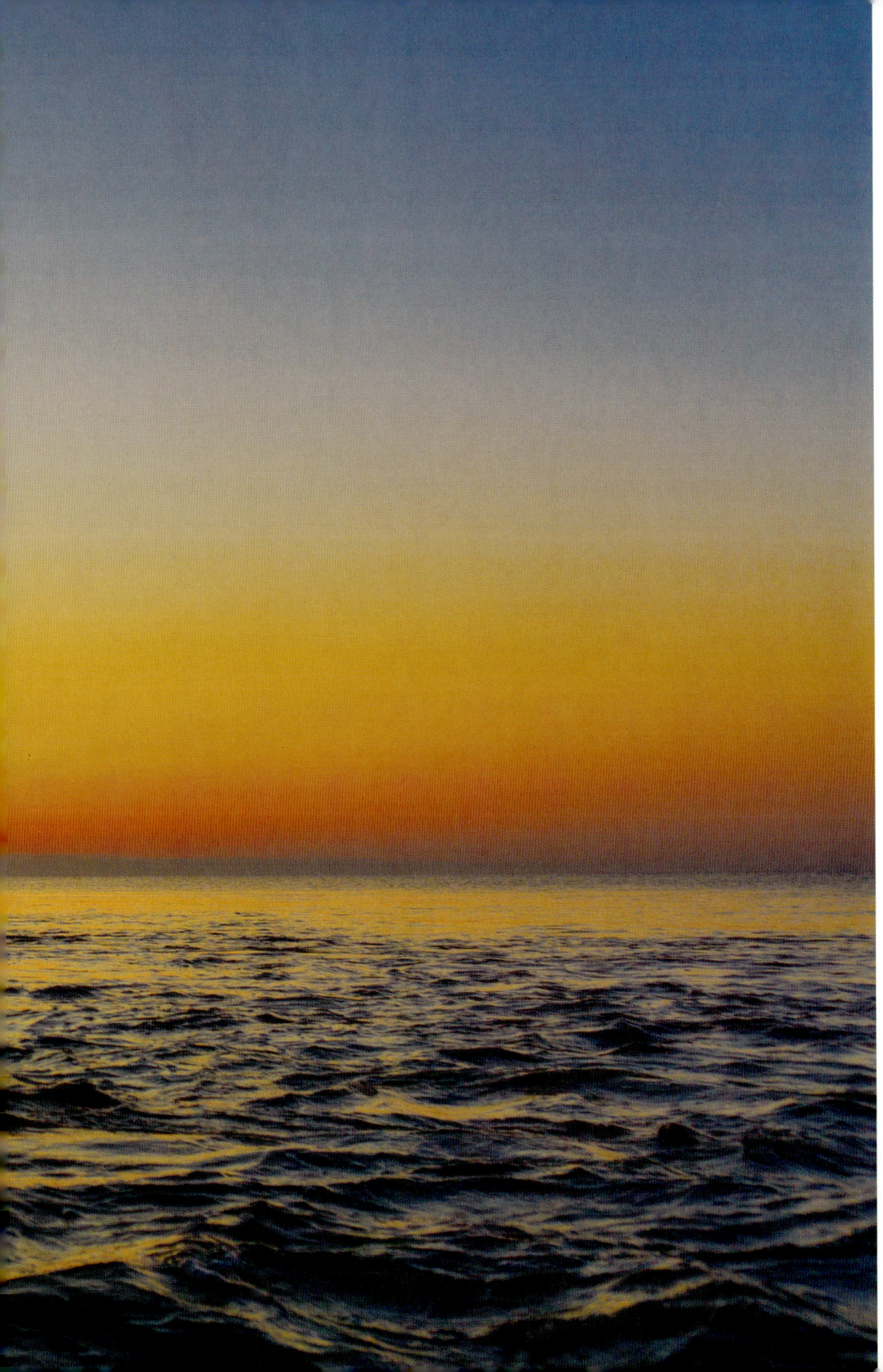

reinforces that notion. John Jinishian, who is 31, has been fly fishing for bass for half his life. An accomplished fly angler, Jinishian caught his largest striper—one that measured 45 inches—off Monomoy from a boat.

"The fly rod is the best tool for presenting small baits and suspending them in the water column and not spooking fish," said Jinishian, who grew up in Connecticut fishing Long Island Sound. "And stripers are such a good fish for the fly."

Jinishian has fished spring worm hatches for a dozen seasons, developing flies to match the cinder worms with cream-colored heads that emerge in his home waters, which are colored differently from those found elsewhere. "I've spent a lot of nights fishing worm hatches," he said. "They were my escape."

During summers, Jinishian runs float trips for salmon and trout in southwestern Alaska. "I love fly fishing because there is no sense of mastery of it," he said, echoing Bryant's thoughts. "You can always improve. But you can't be perfect at it—ever."

STRIPED BASS REMAIN A FAVORITE, even though Jinishian has caught tarpon, permit, bonefish, big rainbows, and all five species of salmon found in Alaska on a fly. "I respect this fish so much, and it's been part of my life for so long," he said. "I think of the countless days and years I've fished for them. It's a lot of time to spend with one species."

The skills that he and others have honed catching stripers have served them well as their fishing expanded into other waters and species. "Striped bass get you used to the strip set and streamer fishing," Jinishian said. "And it prepared me for reading the water, looking for structure,

Previous spread: Bob Popovics is known for his innovative fly patterns. Photo by Tom Lynch.
Left: Wet-suit fishing. Photo by Jerry Audet.

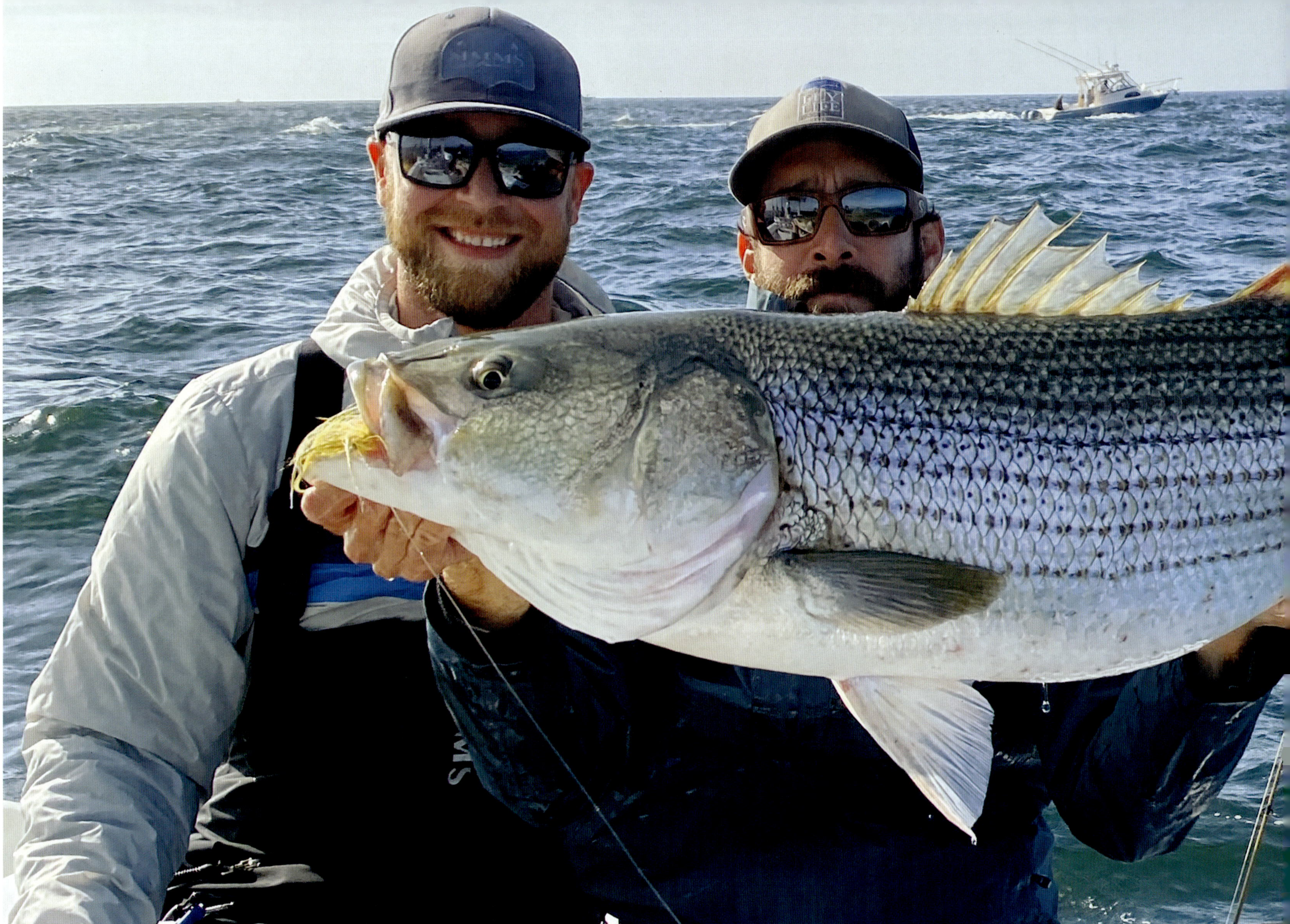

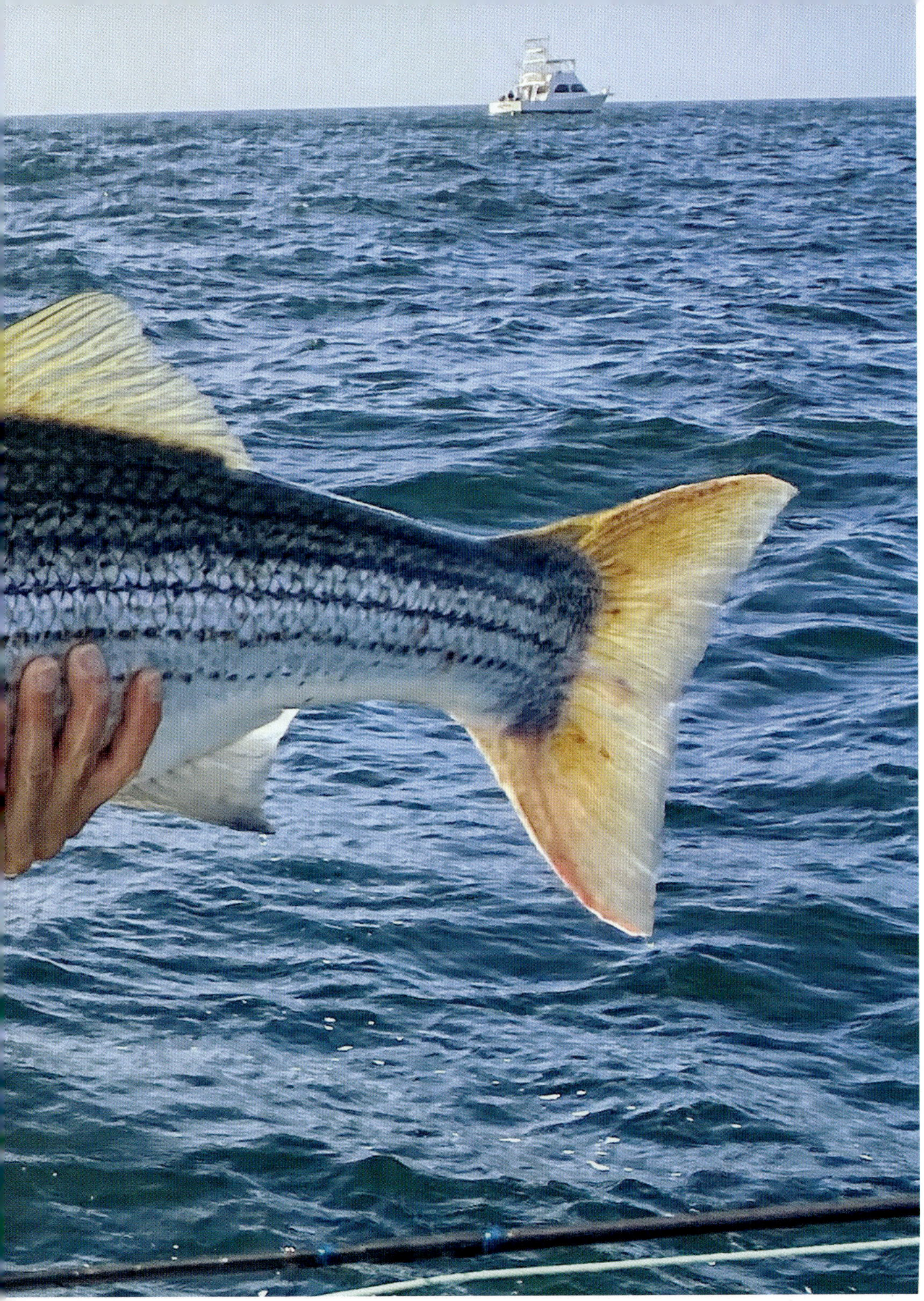

and endurance fishing." And night fishing, he noted, is one of the best ways to develop your cast. "You can't see your loops and you have to go by feel. You're doing everything by feel."

EACH SPRING AND EARLY SUMMER, I fly fish for stripers in salt ponds and bays in Rhode Island. I love the quiet tidal waters early in the year. Most of my fly fishing begins in the evening, as twilight lengthens and the fragrance of spring and wakening waters hangs in the air and lasts well into night. The chatters and cries of terns, oystercatchers, and ospreys provide a background serenade that is accompanied by the deep thumping of ocean surf wafting over the dunes.

After 30 years, chasing early stripers on the fly has become a tradition. Spring doesn't feel complete without my bending to inhale the sweet scent of *rosa rugosa* and then wading into the shallows, bumping into spawning horseshoe crabs and scaring up a bunch of scrappy schoolies. Those evenings immerse me in perfect little worlds, with a mix of bass, bait, birdsong, cool moving waters, and seemingly all the time in the world.

No matter the season, there is nothing like a solid strip set on a good bass, feeling the line race through your fingers as the rod bends, the drag comes to life, and the fish streaks into the darkness. It's hard to ask for more.

BOB POPOVICS RECALLS THE DETAILS of his own unforgettable striper, caught more than 20 years ago while fishing a New Jersey beach on a hot Fourth of July weekend.

For several days, Popovics, an innovative fly-tying legend, had been catching stripers in the 14- to 16-pound range that were feeding on calico crabs in the wash along Island Beach State Park. He was fishing an 8-weight with a T-200 line and a 12-foot, 12-pound fluorocarbon leader,

Rex Messing, left, caught this large striper on a Beast Fleye off Montauk while fishing with Captain Vinny Catalano, right. Photo by Jeff Amorello.

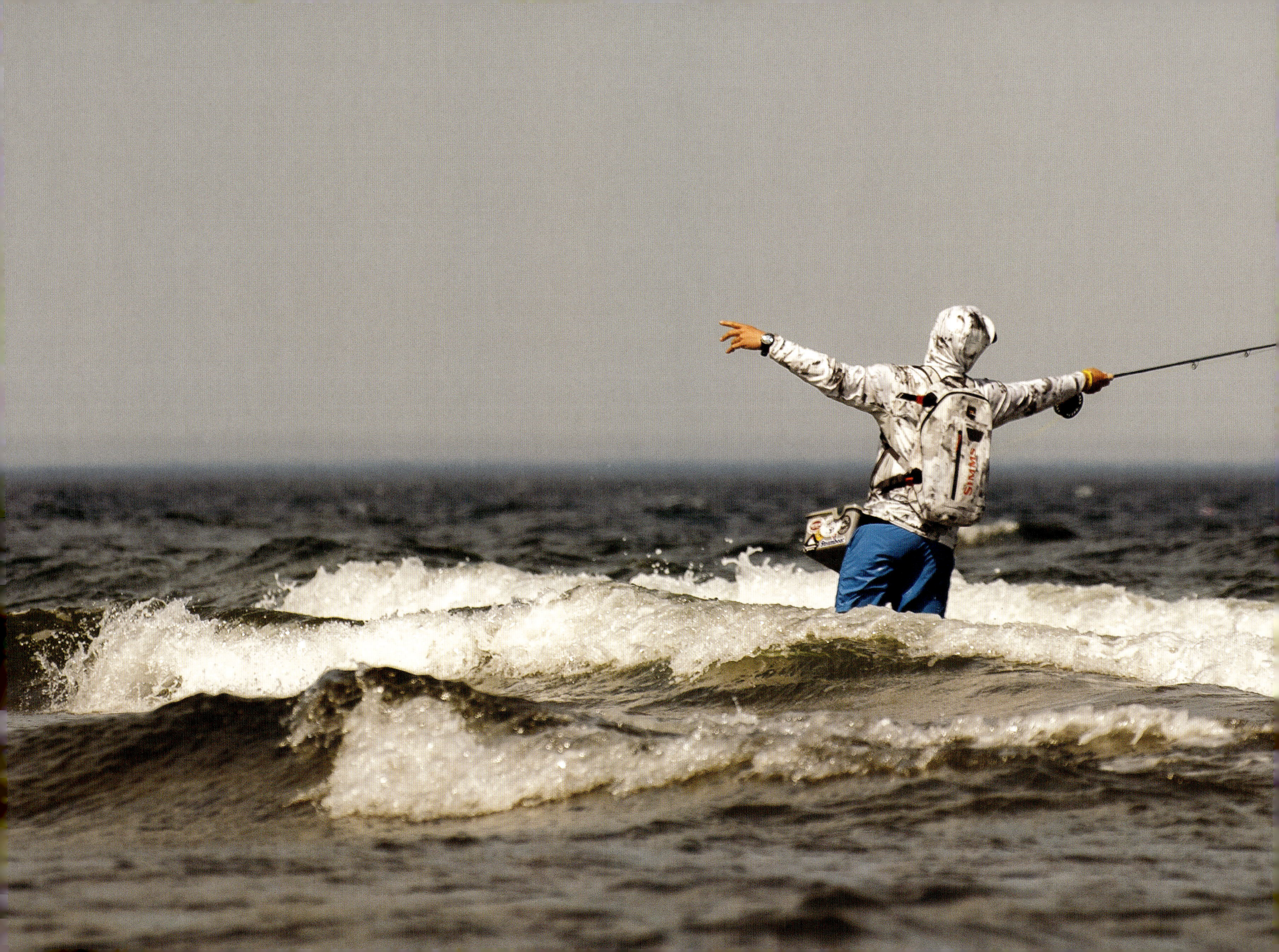
SIMMS

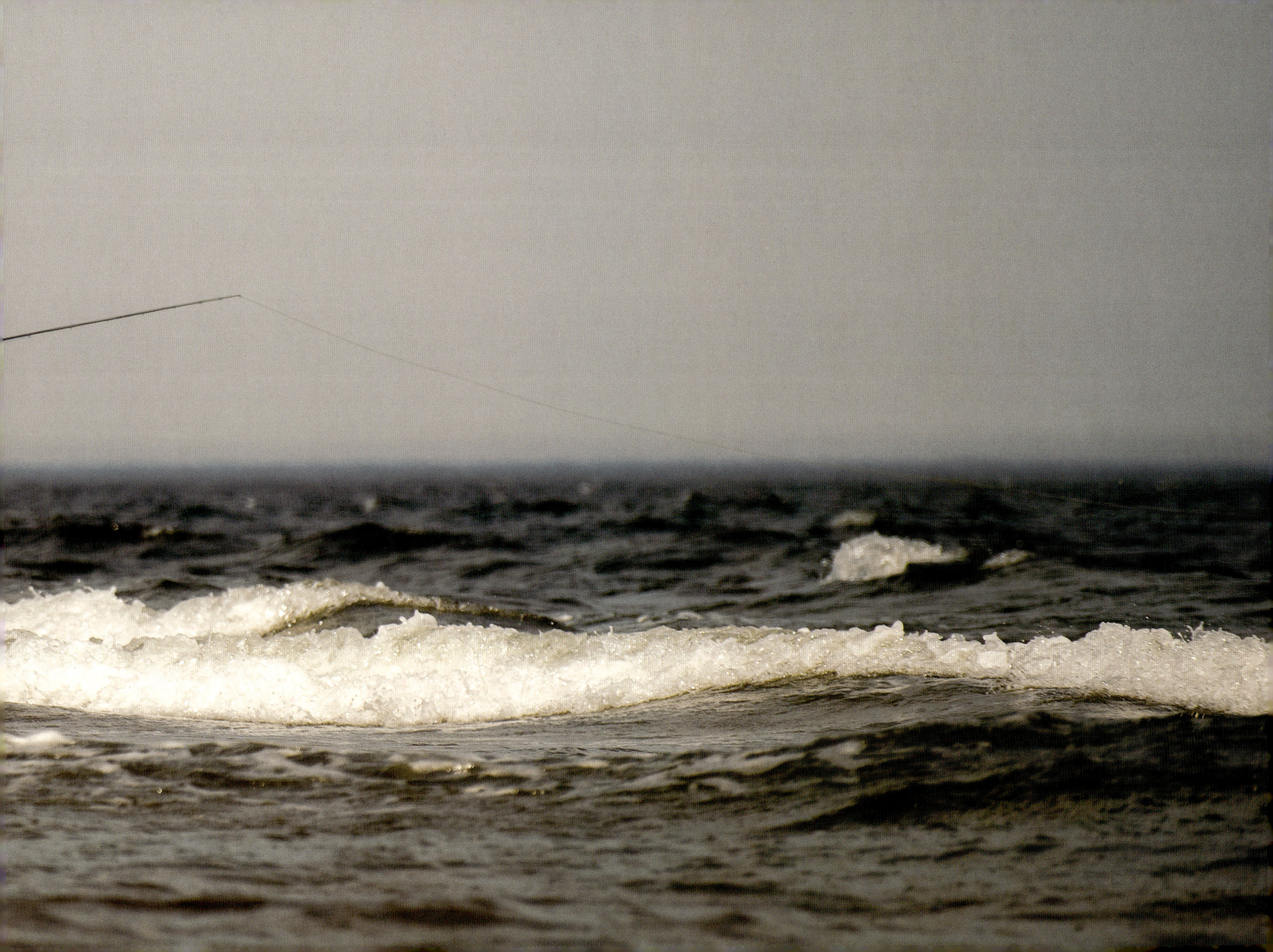

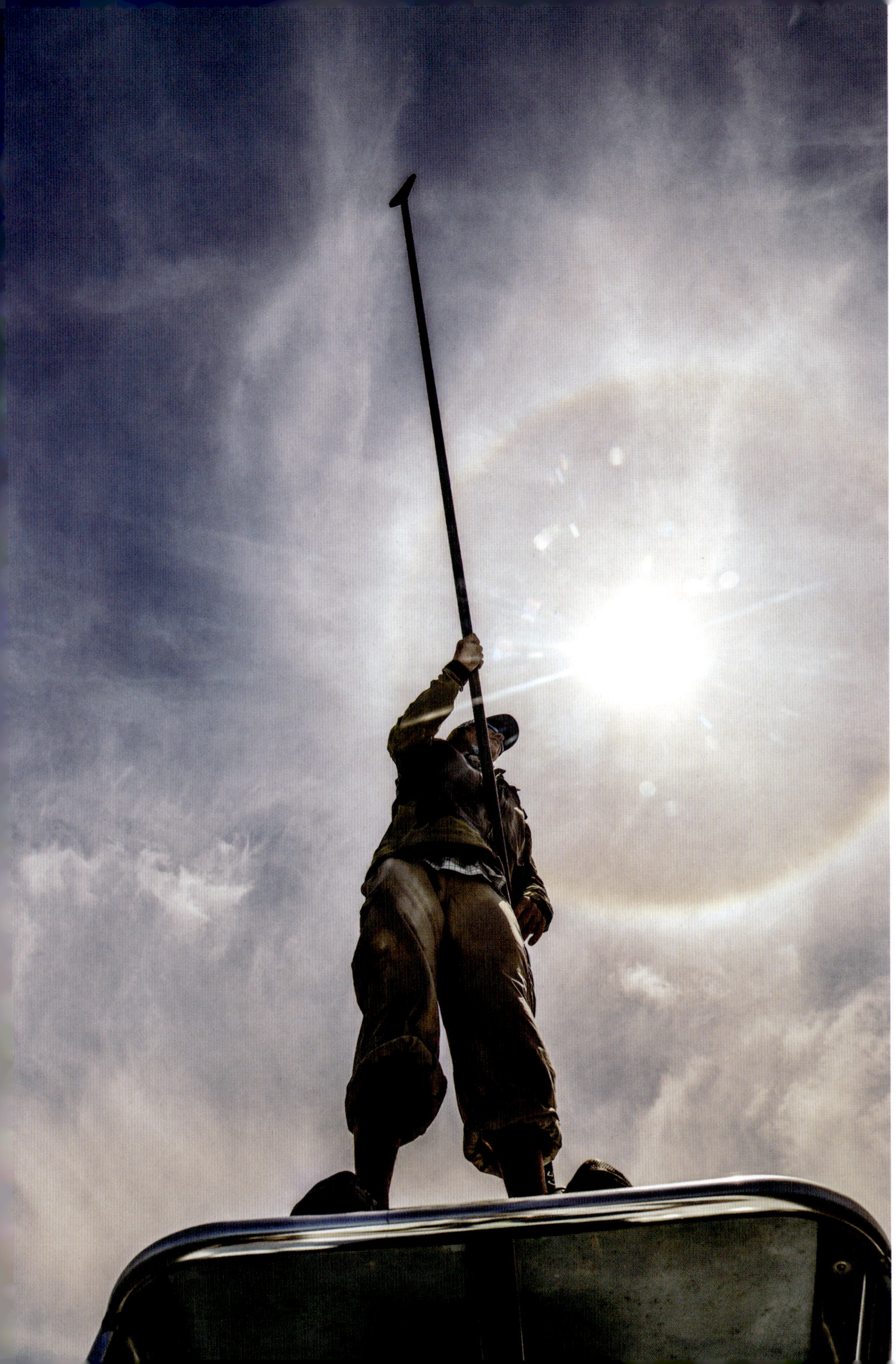

throwing one of his signature Crab Fleye patterns. On this morning, Popovics, an excellent caster, was standing on an elevated section of dry sand along the high-tide line when he spotted three stripers on a bar about 80 yards away. They were coming his way.

"The water was rarely this clear," recalled Popovics, who is 74 and lives in Seaside Park, New Jersey. "I mean, it was clearer than clear. I saw these three fish and said, *Oh shit, they look big*."

He kept watching as the trio approached. He held his fly in one hand, and the line hung free. As the fish came closer, they moved off the bar toward the wash. Knowing they were about to feed, he cast. "And I saw one of the three peel off and come to my fly," Popovics said. He gave the fly "a long, slow draw, like the crab was walking away." The striper charged and ate it. "It tore off like crazy. It was just wonderful. I can still go through the whole catch and see it all over again."

The fish weighed 24 pounds, and although Popovics has taken larger fish—he once caught a 35-pounder from the beach with a wind knot in his leader—none has been as memorable. "It's the most favorite fish I've ever caught," he said.

WHETHER YOU ARE FISHING THE SURF, flats, or from a boat, your ability to cast, read the water, and think like a fish will determine your success. "If you want to be a better fly fisherman, you have to be better at using your tool," said Popovics, who is generous in sharing his knowledge. "And be a better observer. Keep your eyes open. Look at everything. Pay attention to everything. It's usually not obvious. The fish gives you a signal, no matter how subtle it may be."

For years, he netted mullet, silversides, sand eels, bay anchovies, crabs, shrimp, and other baits, studying how they swam and interacted with the surf. He also filmed striper blitzes and

Previous spread: Working the Massachusetts surf. Photo by Rex Messing.
Left: Paul Dixon. Photo by James Manning.
Right: A good strip set. Photo by Rex Messing.

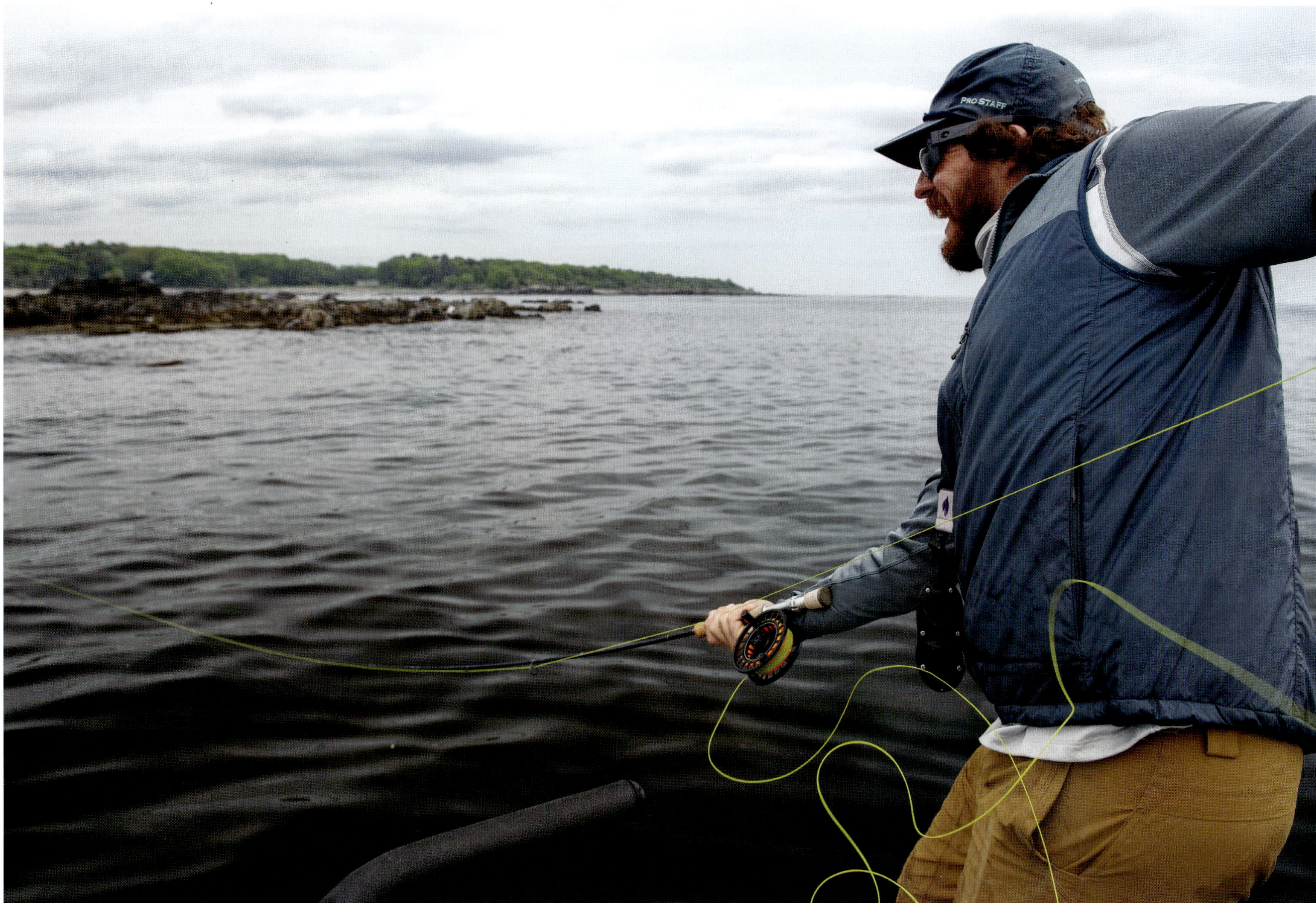
PRO STAFF

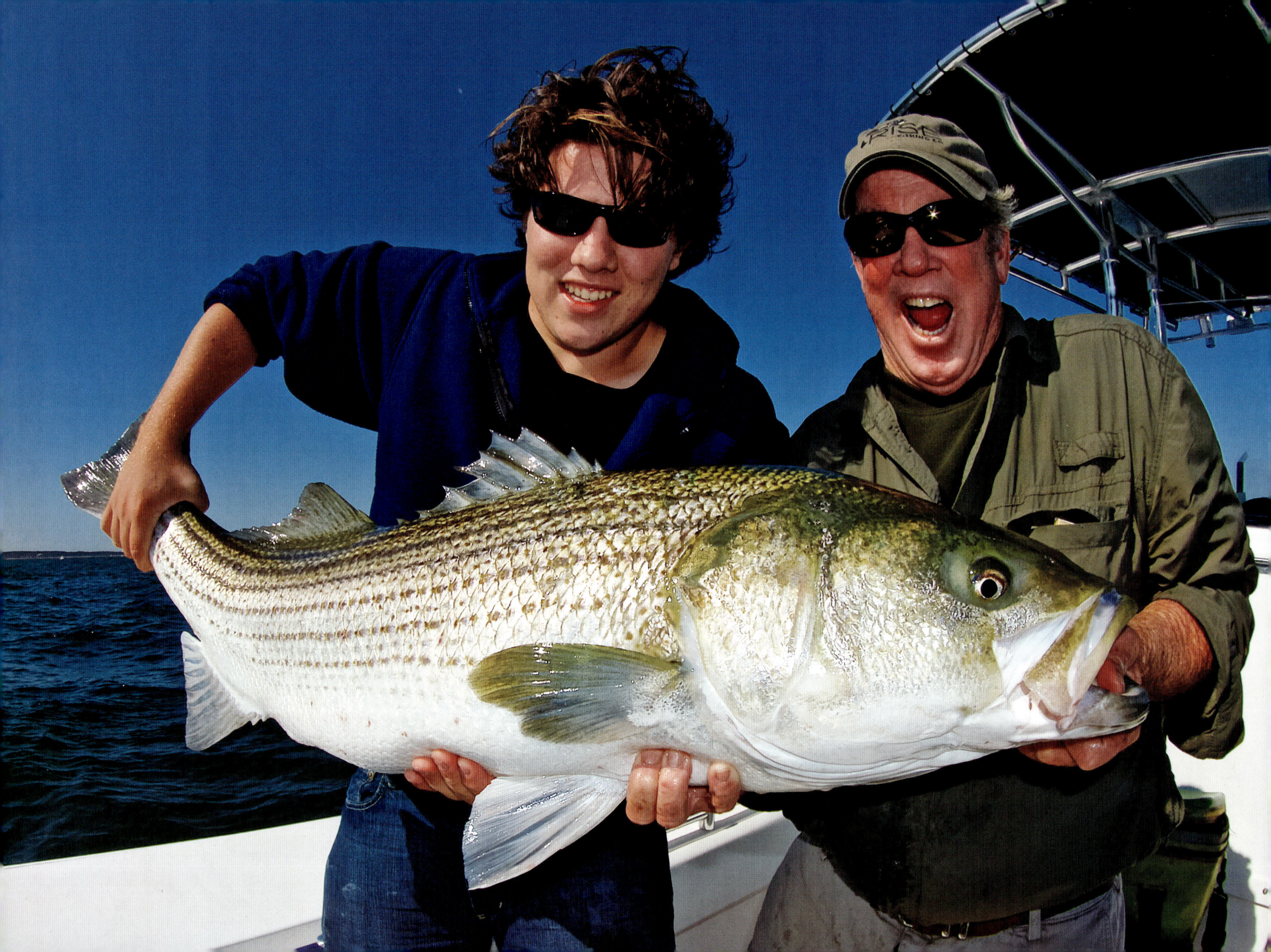

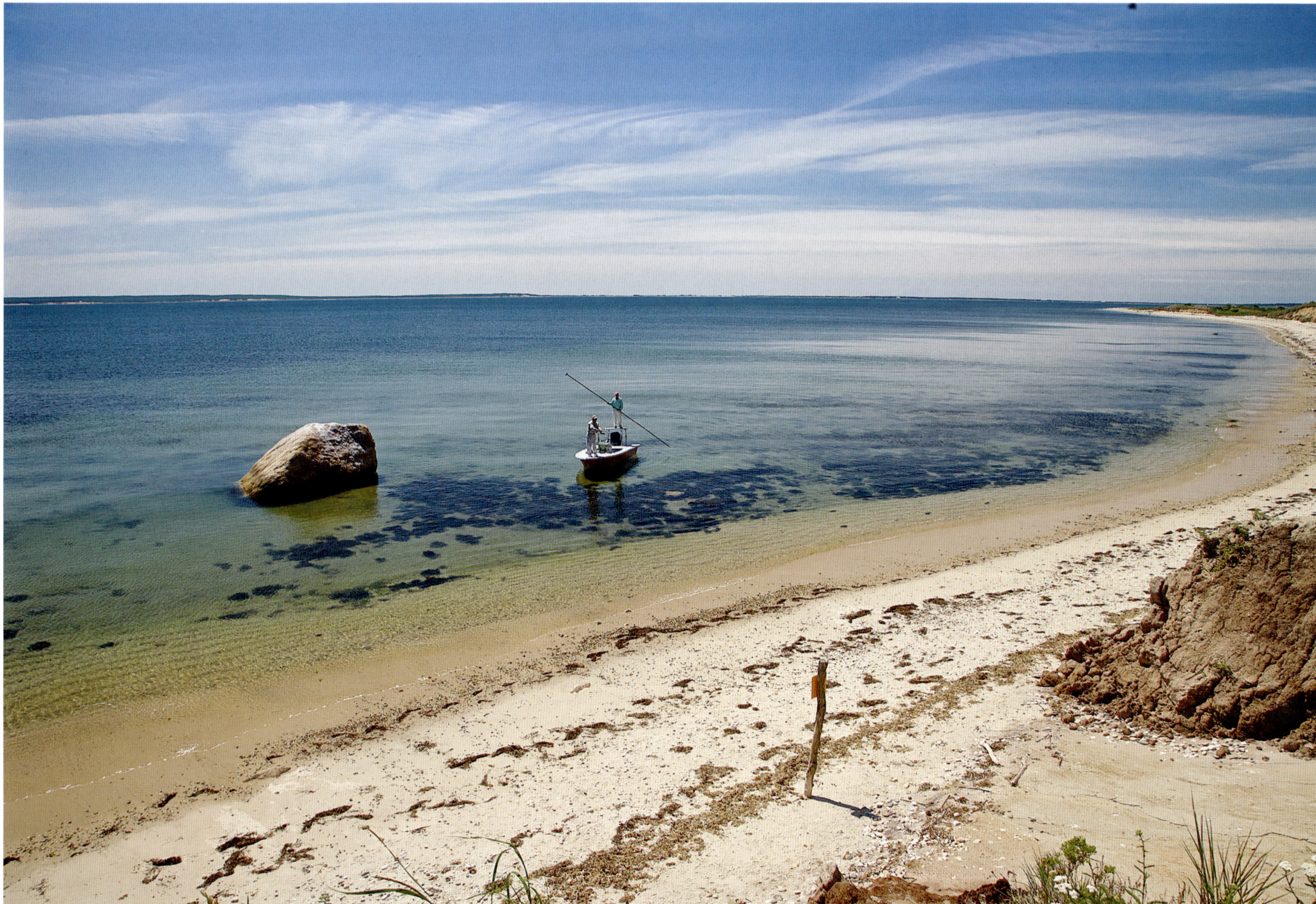

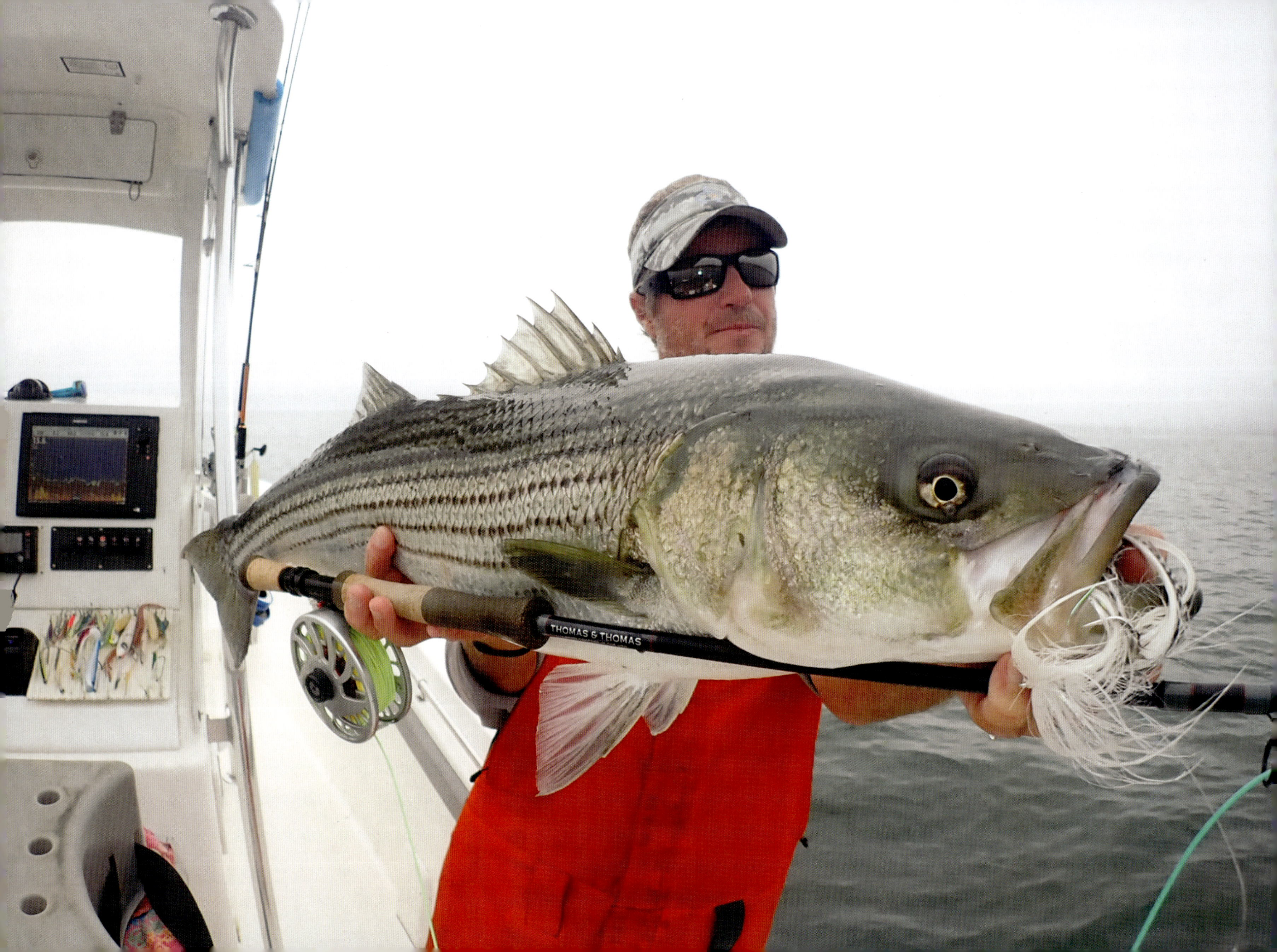
THOMAS & THOMAS

how his flies and bait moved through the water. "Presentation is number one," Popovics said. "All these flies will work. You just have to work on your presentation." That includes finding the proper depth and retrieve and positioning yourself to put the line where it needs to go.

REX MESSING AND A FRIEND were fishing with guide Vinny Catalano on a magic day off Montauk in late September 2020. Messing, who is 30 and works as a content production specialist for Simms, had booked the date six months earlier. His timing couldn't have been better.

Catalano gave them two choices that morning. They could chase albies, as planned, or they could run farther out and look for large stripers, which had shown up the previous day. They made the right choice, racing several miles off the point at first light to a rip where the tide was making up. Fish were just starting to show, and the anglers worked a switcheroo with a large surface plug, hooking a few fish between 15 and 25 pounds. The bass were feeding on adult bunker, and the action continued to heat up.

"Over the course of two hours, the whole damn ocean came to the surface, and it was all bass," Messing said. "There seemed to be more bass than bunker." The fish got larger too. The two friends released bass in the 30- to 40-pound range. "It's funny, they just seemed to get bigger and bigger," he recalled. "There were huge fish everywhere."

Messing was fishing a seven-inch yellow-and-white Beast Fleye on a 10-weight with a 40-pound tippet. He remembers standing near the transom and watching a pod of about 15 stripers push bunker to the surface. He cast into the center of the action, and the largest fish in the group came for the fly.

"I SAW IT EAT AS CLEAR AS DAY," Messing said, still excited by the memory. "It was gigantic. Absolutely enormous. Vinny called to me, 'Holy shit, that's a monster. Biggest fish in the group.' It ate 30 or 40 feet off the back of the boat. I was probably three strips in. She went straight to backing."

They were drifting in 60 feet of water, and the big fish ran off 50 yards of backing, then bulldogged for the rest of the fight. "We put the bones to it quickly," Messing recalled. He had the large fish beside the boat in about 10 minutes. They estimated the weight to be 50 pounds.

The memory of what may be a once-in-a-lifetime striper is likely to stick. "That fish is ingrained in my mind," Messing said. "I can see the fish eat it, and I can see it alongside the boat with Vinny reaching over to lip it."

It's often the case that the fish we best remember are the ones that manage to get away. As sportscaster Vin Scully once said, "Losing feels worse than winning feels good."

Not always. Sometimes the fish we manage to bring to hand last a lifetime. As the poet W. S. Merwin wrote, "What you remember saves you."

Previous spread, left: Noted guide Paul Dixon and his son Andrew with a nice fly-caught bass. Photo by Pat Ford.
Previous spread, right: Tight to Gardiners Island, New York. Photo by Pat Ford.
Left: Martha's Vineyard guide Jaime Boyle with a trophy. Photo by Justin Pribanic.

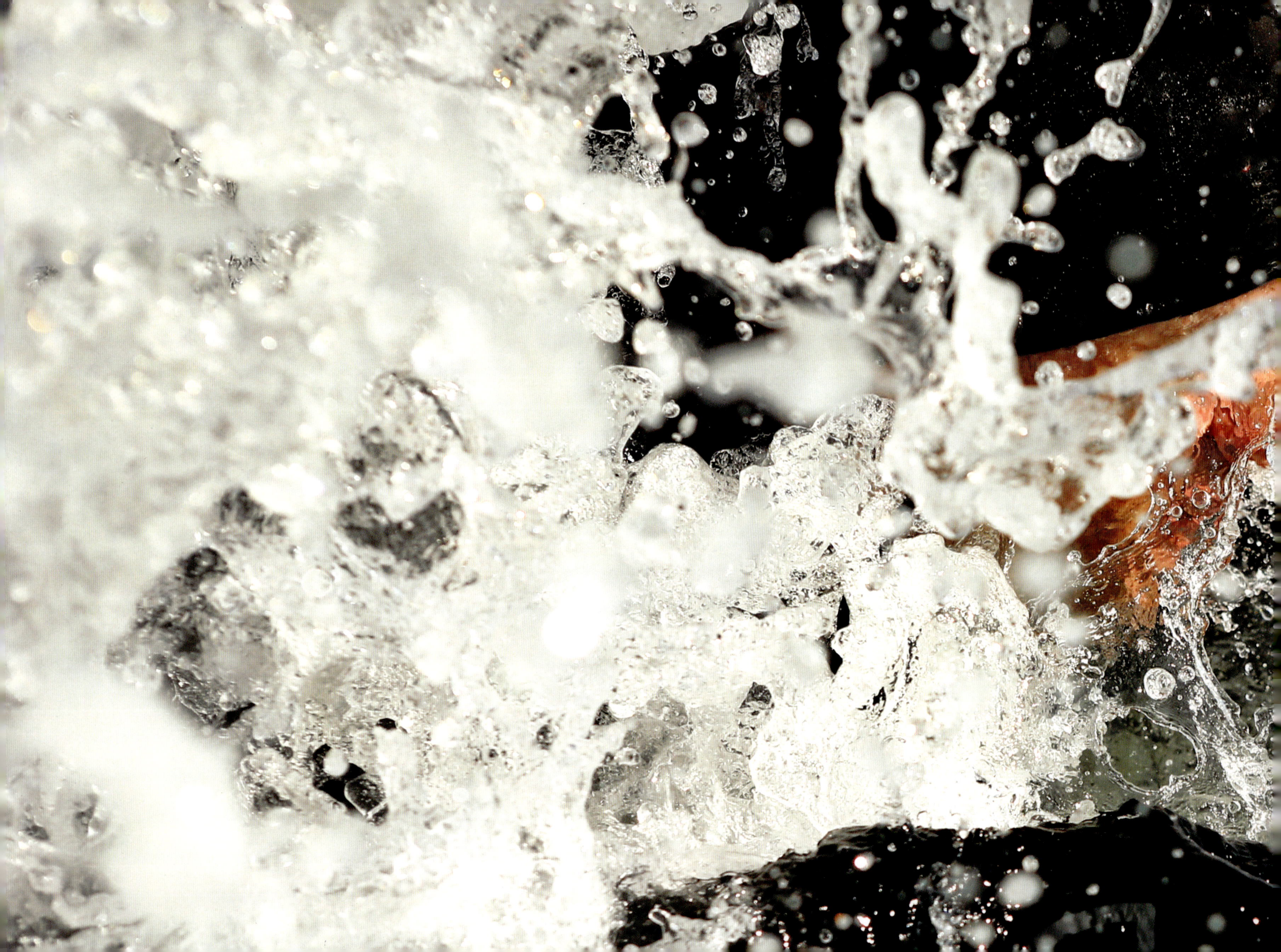

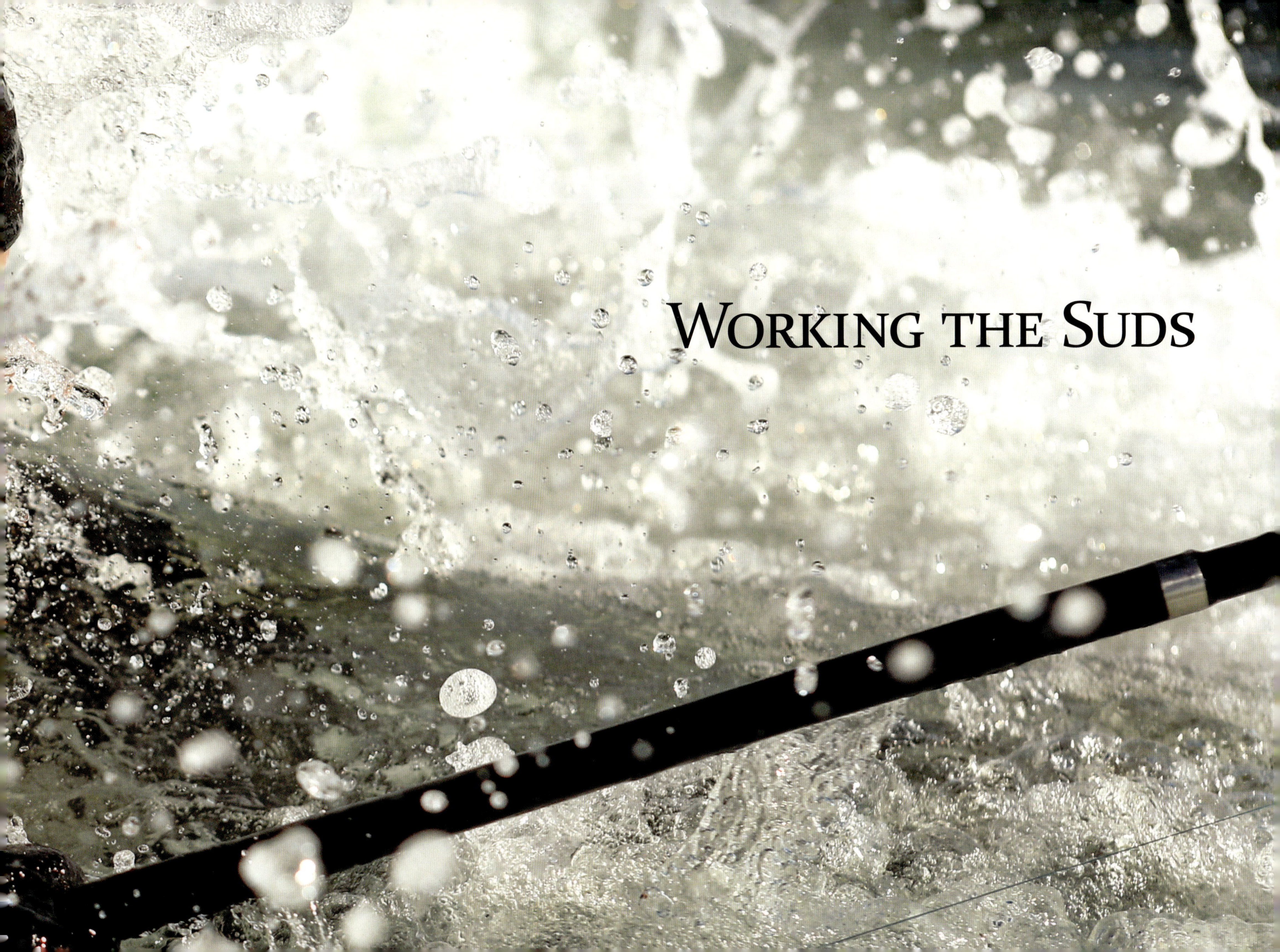

Working the Suds

The remnants of a tropical storm roll ashore in mid-September in the form of waist-to-shoulder-high waves that clean up nicely once the tide and wind drop. Then the glassy waves fill with bait and break with heavy wallops. The stripers go bonkers.

The stretch of beach I call the "mussel bar" is on fire this afternoon—bright sun, bass pounding the bejesus out of baby bunker, and I'm the only one here to partake of the wonderful chaos. Sometimes you just get lucky with the timing; the lack of other anglers owes more to the mile-long walk in the sand than anything else. I've fished this stretch of sand and rocks for more than 50 years, long enough to both recognize the patterns and to have gained enough wisdom to avoid becoming overconfident.

I recently fished a couple of nights here in late October with nary a bump. It's an old story: you need to put in your time in order to catch.

IT IS A BLESSING TO RETURN TO A PLACE season after season. To a fishing spot that has felt like home from adolescence through my hard-charging early, middle, and late-adult years. Once as sure-footed as the best of the surf crowd on the slick rocks we routinely traverse, I now catch a glimpse of my unavoidable future as I stumble like a newbie over the obstacle course.

The mussel bar remains one of my go-to surf spots, even though its name barely applies any longer to its rocky bottom, home to far fewer mussels than in times past. It is but one piece of a broader topography—a large, current-swept, surf-smashed mess of sand and glacial rubble that makes for good but tough fishing when everything is firing.

I've traveled the world since I first cast a popper into the wedge-shaped waves that define the mussel bar, but I still relish fishing hard in this familiar spot from September through

Previous spread: Fall surf means wet suits and dry suits for some anglers. Photo by Tom Lynch.
Right: Insulated for the late season. Photo by Tom Lynch.

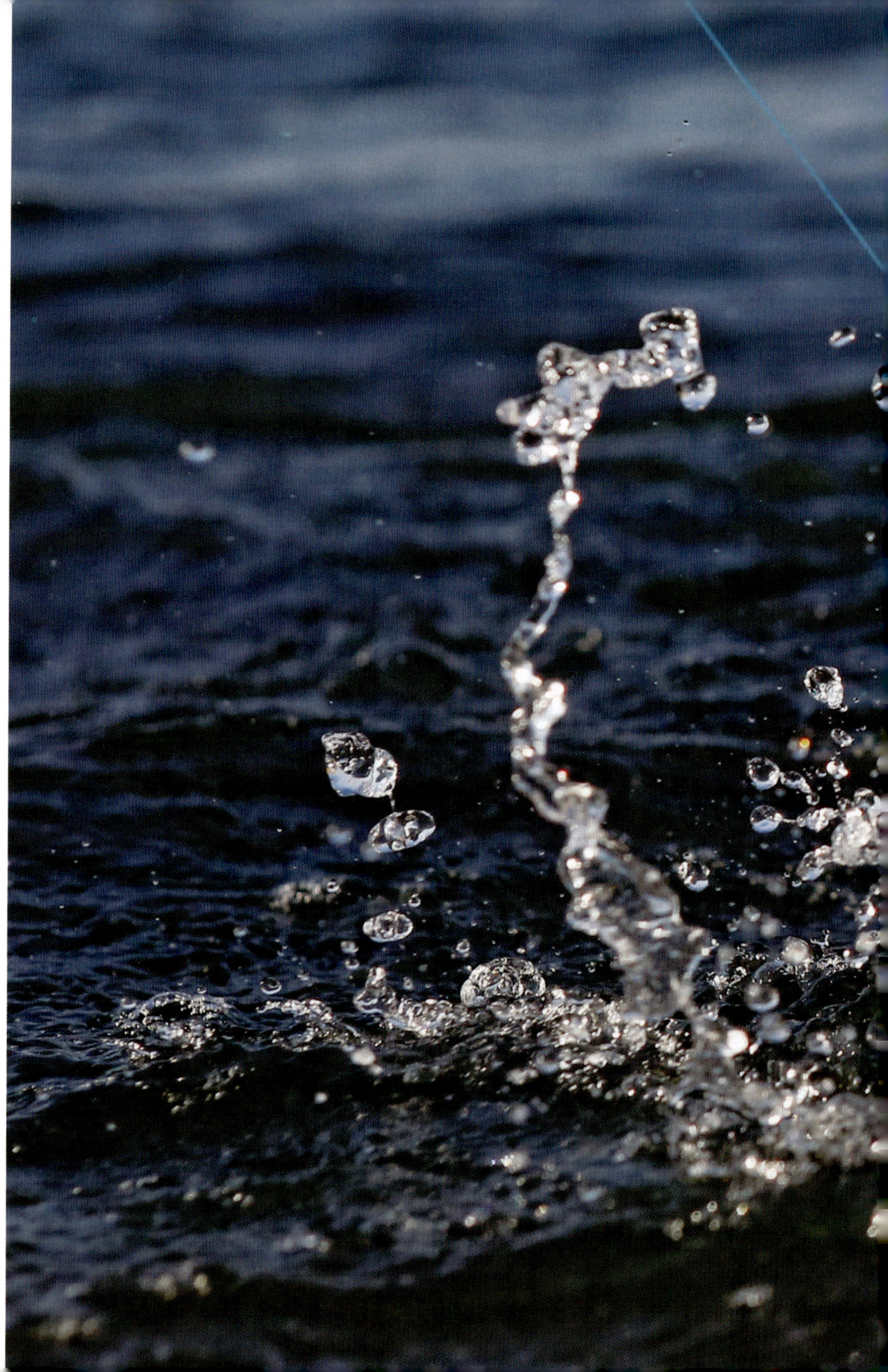

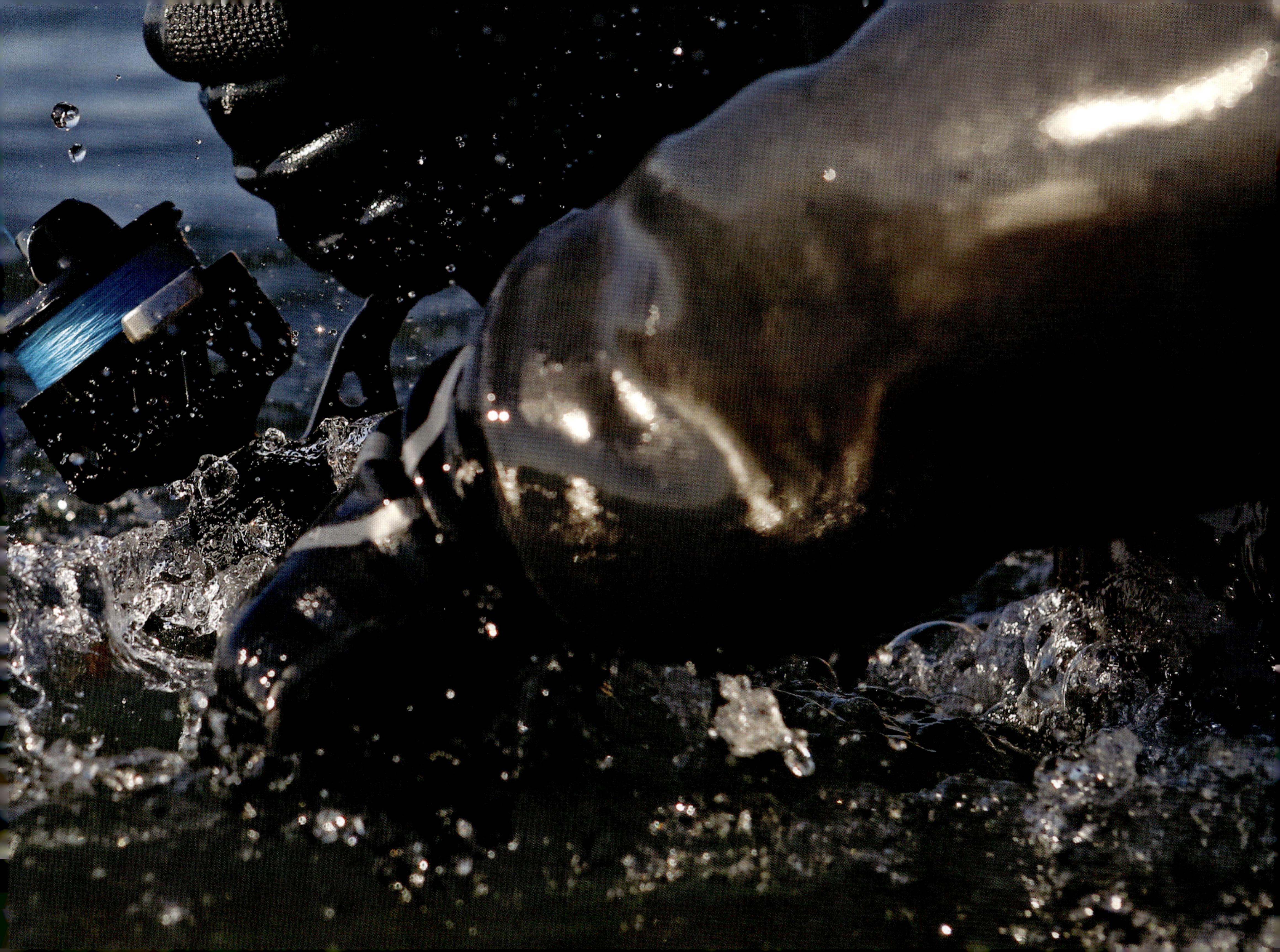

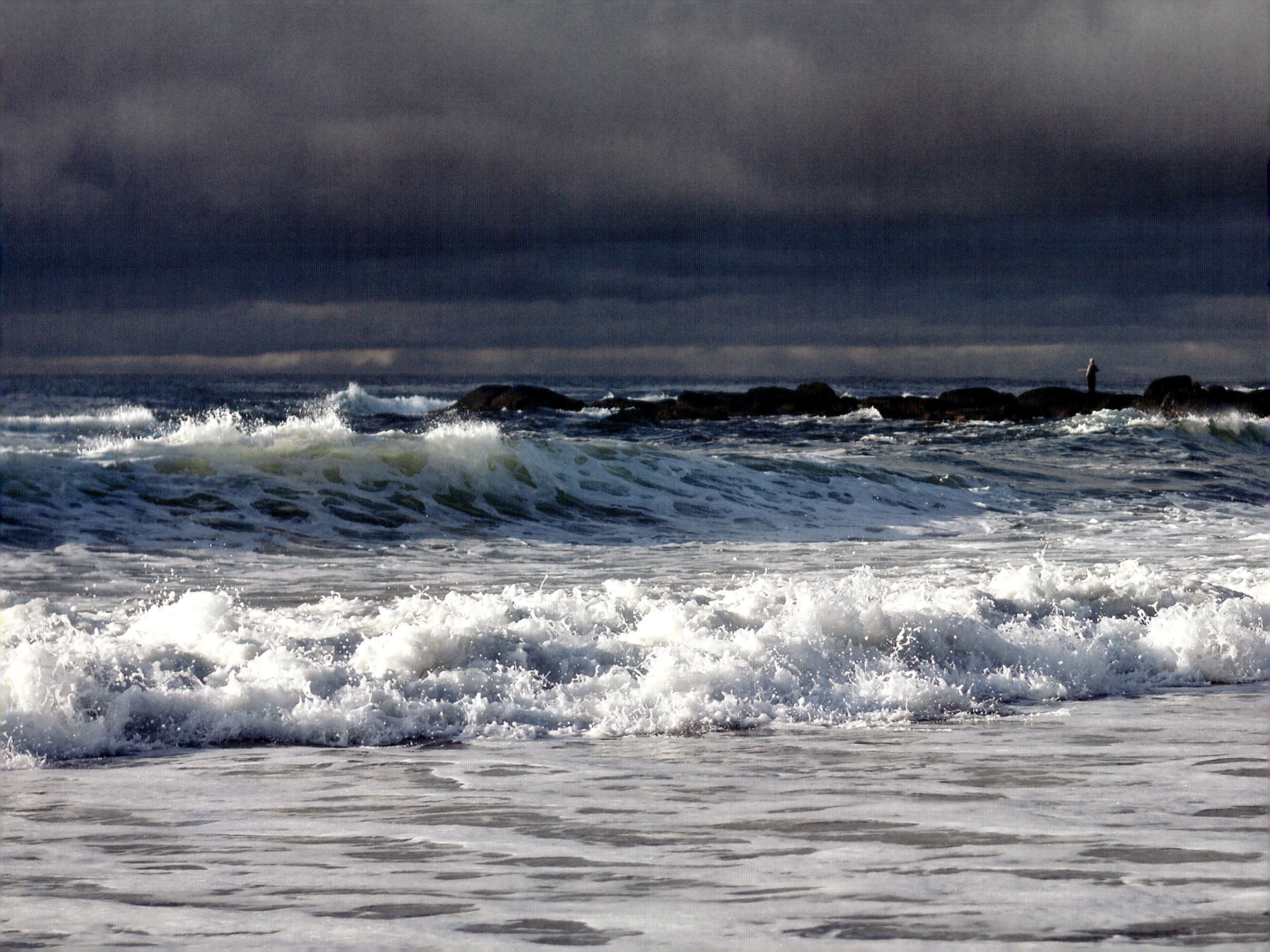

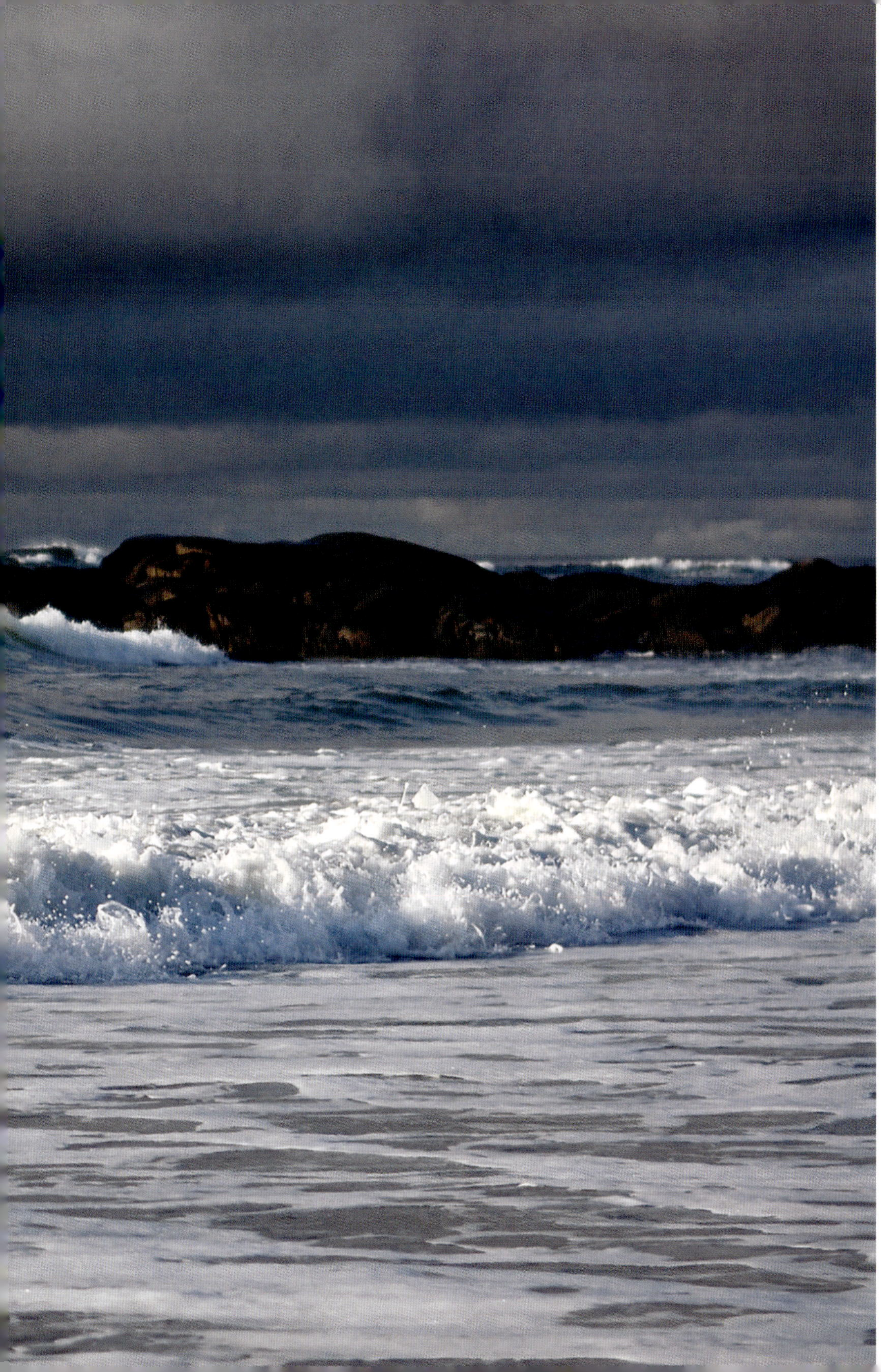

November. For as much as things here have changed in my lifetime—and change is a defining characteristic of barrier beaches—the bones of the place have remained anchored in place by a glacial headland. The whole shebang may one day find itself submerged by rising sea level, but these boulders aren't going anywhere. And if the future continues to fill these waters with striped bass, those fish will glide among the rocks, kelp, currents, and shifting bars that define this rugged seascape.

I STARTED MY STRIPER FISHING in the surf, and days like this one are why I will fish the suds until I drop. On this mid-September day, the temperature is in the 70s. I fish in a bathing suit until late afternoon, when I lean my rod against a beach log and bodysurf until almost dark. The see-through breakers radiate the pale green of early fall, when everything the light falls upon springs to life. Monarch butterflies and dragonflies wobble and weave on the northeast breeze toward distant wintering grounds. Between fish, I take a moment to scan the deep-blue fall sky for migrating hawks riding thermals.

The surf pounds; the gulls shriek, hover, and wheel; my drag chimes in with its tiny mechanical voice; a half-dozen cormorants dodge my casts; and small menhaden skitter across a broad carpet of white water. I toss a weighted soft-plastic swim bait that is a dead ringer for juvenile bunker on a lightweight 12-foot rod matched to a spinning reel with 30-pound braid. It's the ticket for large surf and school fish. A big set sweeps over the sandbars, rolling and tumbling the mass of small pogies, and the bass go nuts once more. I try to time my casts to land just after the last wave in the set breaks. Twice, stripers ascend the backs of waves to snatch my lure just before the comber pitches forward and collapses. I grin and holler into the wind.

Maine surf. Photo by Todd Towle.

The revelry moves back and forth along a quarter mile of beach. The bass sometimes drift beyond casting range, then rush back to thrash the skittish bait stretched along the impact zone. I fish for three hours, stopping only to cut back chafed leaders and retie lures, or to change out a mangled swim bait. Others join me, but the beach remains uncrowded.

The fish are revved up school bass between about five and 12 pounds. Not large, but handsome, healthy, with plenty of kick. They rip off line in short bursts before fighting stubbornly to the sand. I release more than 20 bass, give away some soft baits to help a pilgrim hook up, and help a disabled teen unhook his first bass. The kid and I are pumped. We'll both remember the fish and the afternoon.

YEARS AGO, AFTER I LANDED my first striped bass from a boat, I apologized for the way I'd taken the fish. "It didn't really count because I caught it from a boat," I said to my elders. I remember the eye rolls from patient adults as I blathered on, explaining the distinction between boat- and shore-caught striped bass.

Before I'd even caught my first striper, a cadre of surf fishermen at the Watch Hill Lighthouse in southwest Rhode Island had indoctrinated me into their gospel. It stipulated that one surf-caught striped bass equaled six or a dozen bass taken from a boat. The insinuation was clear: catching bass from a boat was so easy it was almost *cheating*. That was the actual word one of them used. Worse still, I had hooked mine trolling, which in their eyes was the lowest form of boat fishing.

This first striper struck a sandworm threaded on a Niantic Bay spinner that was weighted with a pound of bank sinkers. We were trolling around the Watch Hill reefs on a family friend's boat when the rod bent over. At first I thought we'd hooked bottom again. But the heavy rod was

A wave full of bunker. Photo by Tom Lynch.

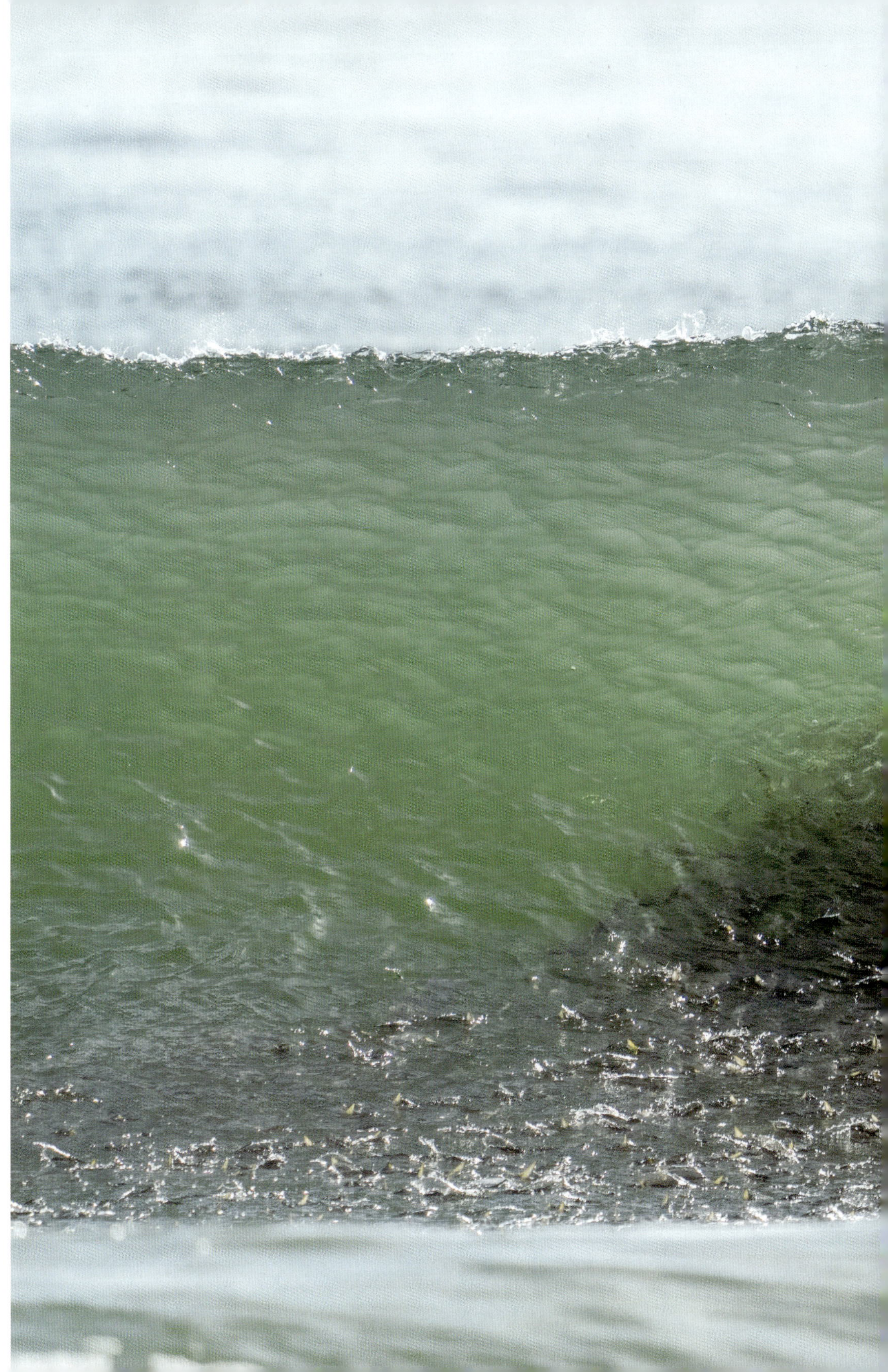

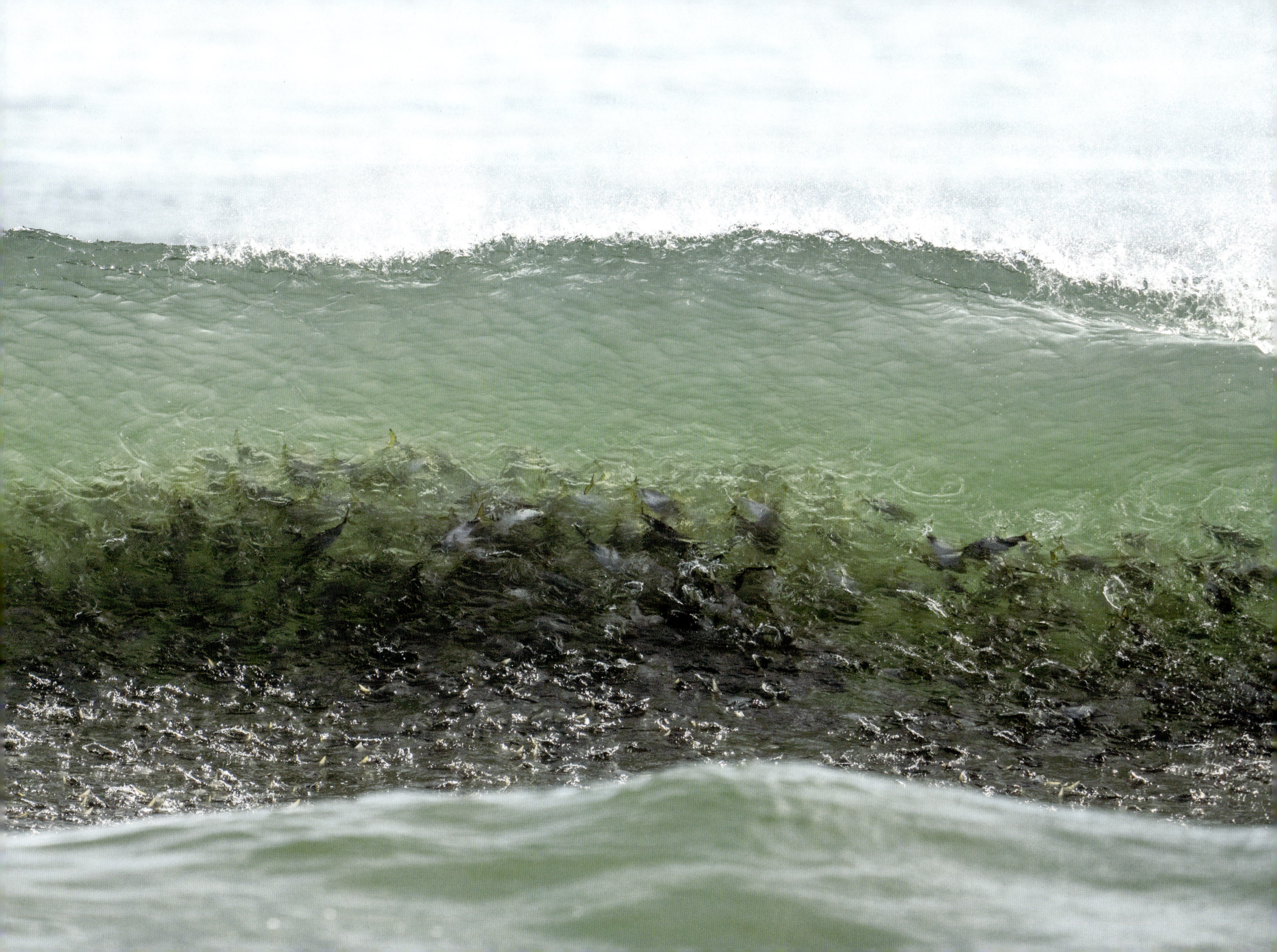

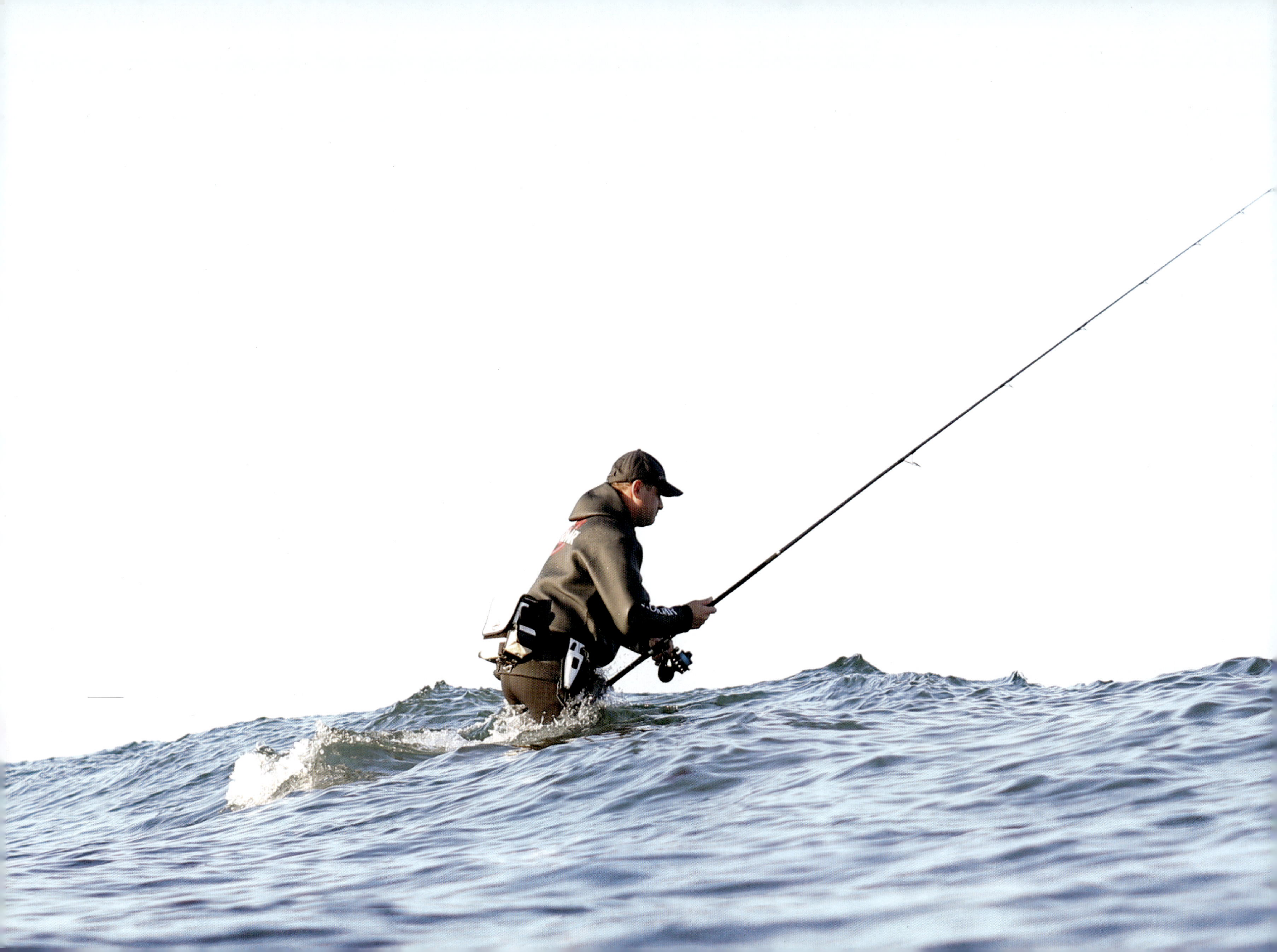

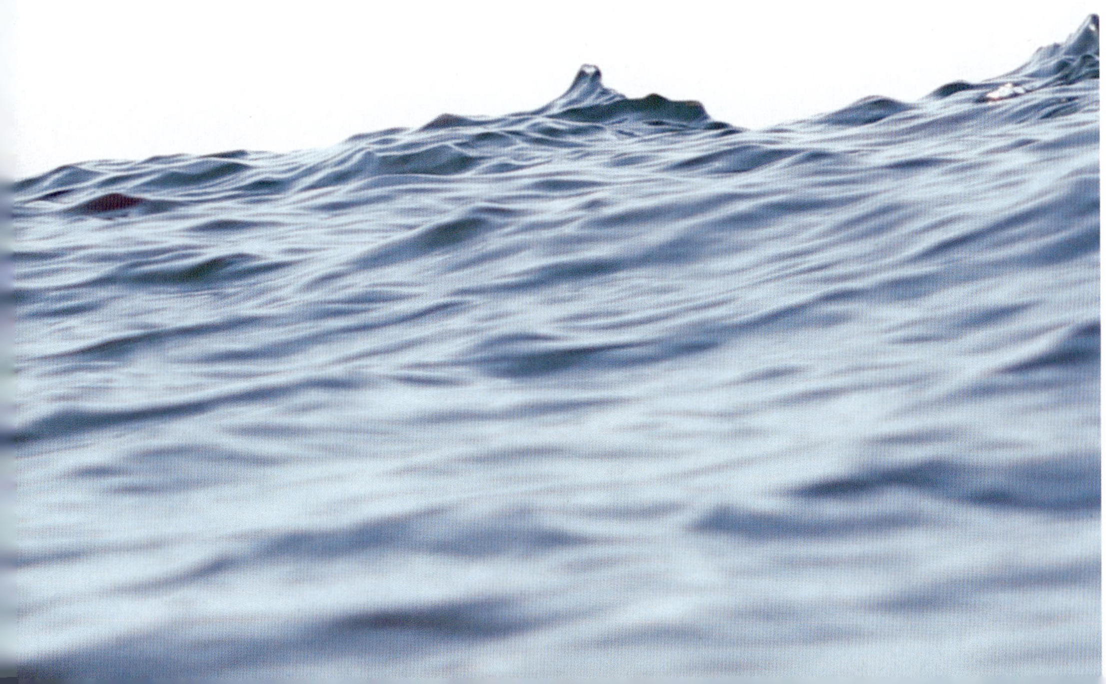

alive and throbbing, and the skipper was suddenly shouting orders. My fish weighed 15 pounds and fought like hell, partly because the skipper never let up on the throttle. I dragged it around for half a day showing it off to neighbors and friends. I still have a black-and-white snapshot of that fish.

What's funny is I knew the truth even then: the boat caught the fish, not me. I just happened to be holding the rod and cranked it in. Two months later, I caught my first striper from the surf, and all my apologizing for a boat-caught fish vanished.

Having owned fish boats for 40 years, my views on boats versus surf are more realistic today. Beach or boat, you still have to find the fish and get them to hit. And I've been skunked as many times with sand on my boots as I have with water draining out of the scuppers.

AS A KID, I LEARNED TO SURF FISH from men whose main idiom was vulgarity. This was at the Watch Hill Lighthouse, and these were largely blue-collar stalwarts—mill rats, carpenters, plumbers, landscapers, masons, and carpet layers, along with a contingent who built submarines in Groton, Connecticut. They were hardworking, lunch-pail men who were no strangers to a shot and a beer. My mother called them *salt of the earth*. Some fished well. Others did more talking than casting.

At their elbow, I learned to swear like a stevedore while they introduced me to their arcane ways: How to work a swimmer, popper, and metal lure. How to adjust the lip or eye on a plug. The proper way to use a gaff. What were the best colors, knots, and retrieves, along with a hundred other things, which later proved equally as spot-on as dead wrong.

Back then, you earned your place in the tight picket line that formed on the lighthouse rocks when the fish were blitzing by having paid your dues: learning to cast straight, respecting the elders, and acting neither as a smart-ass nor a pushover. When it was your time, you grabbed

Beyond the swells. Photo by Tom Lynch.

a spot, held your ground, swung your nine-foot rod like a grown-up, and took the fish you'd earned. Those formative years provided fuel to keep me fishing the surf hard each fall.

From a distant past, I pull a memory of a nice fish lying on the seawall surrounding the lighthouse, its big white belly facing the surf. In my mind, I see the awkward kid who took it on a tin squid during what Old Norse sailors called "witch-wrought weather," when snow fell in big, wet flakes and the wind shook the boy from his hood to his boots. He tried to blink the water from his eyes while the foghorn bellowed and icy snow stung his face. It was late in the season, and there wasn't a boat in the rips or another soul on the point, just the kid and his fish.

He continued casting, but kept looking back at the snow-coated striper, which weighed a hefty 18 pounds. He caught a few flakes on his tongue. He also kept glancing over his shoulder to see if anyone was coming around the corner of the seawall. Part of him hoped another fisherman would turn up to admire his catch; another part wanted the place all to himself. Finally, he used the length of clothesline he kept in his bag to drag the fish up the hill at dusk. He remembers the shingles lifting on the corners of the white house at the top of the road and the stop sign that shivered in the gusts.

The imprint of that snow-squall striper still pulls me into the gloaming as another season hurries to a close, even though the odds favor only a small fish or two. Stubbornness defines the diehards who are the last to give up on the season and leave the beach.

HUNDREDS OF LOCATIONS ALONG the coast bear the generic name "mussel bar," but I have a long, varied history with this particular stretch of hard bottom. I fished it as a youngster,

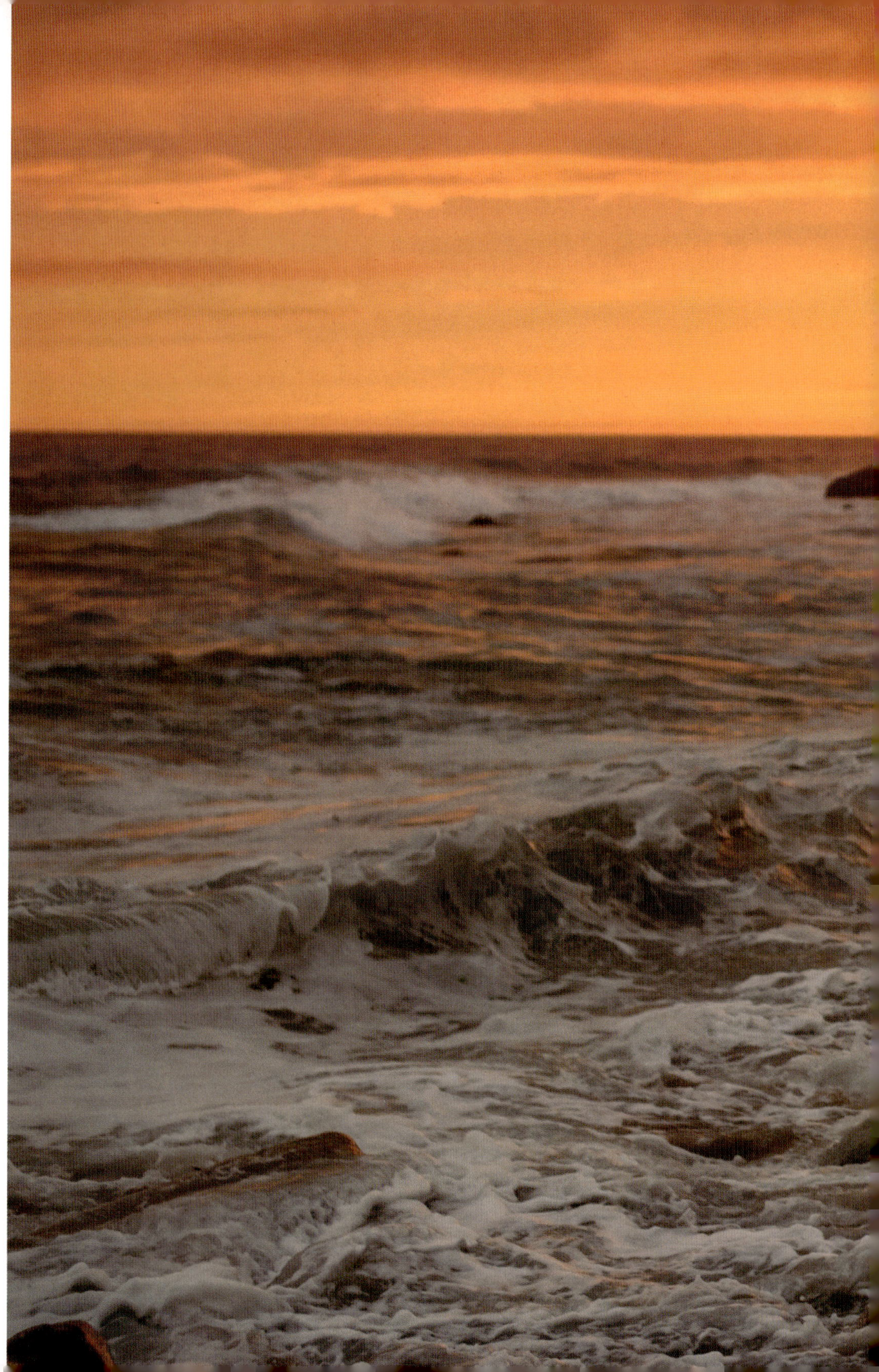

Block Island surf. Photo by Jim Leedom.

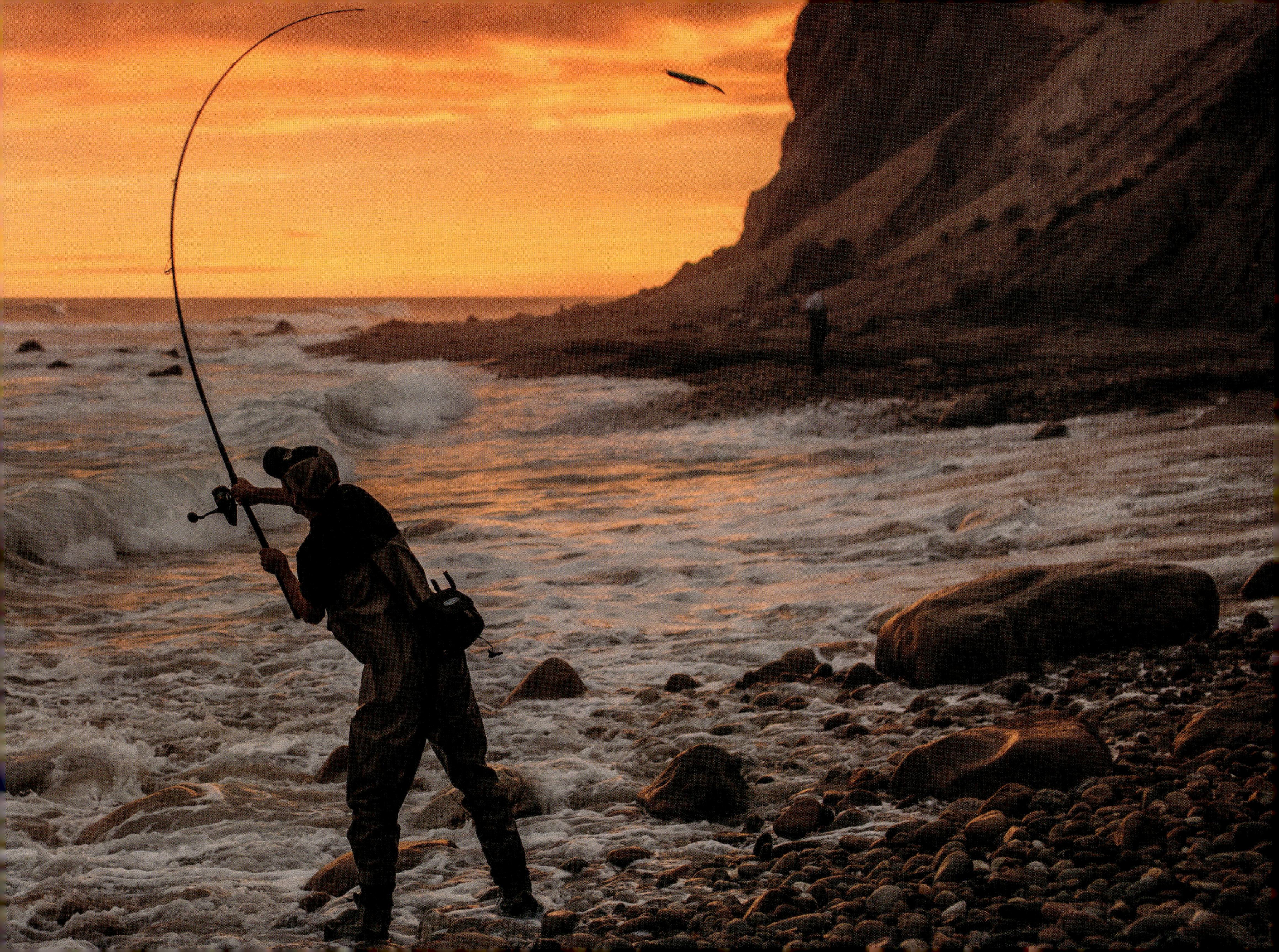

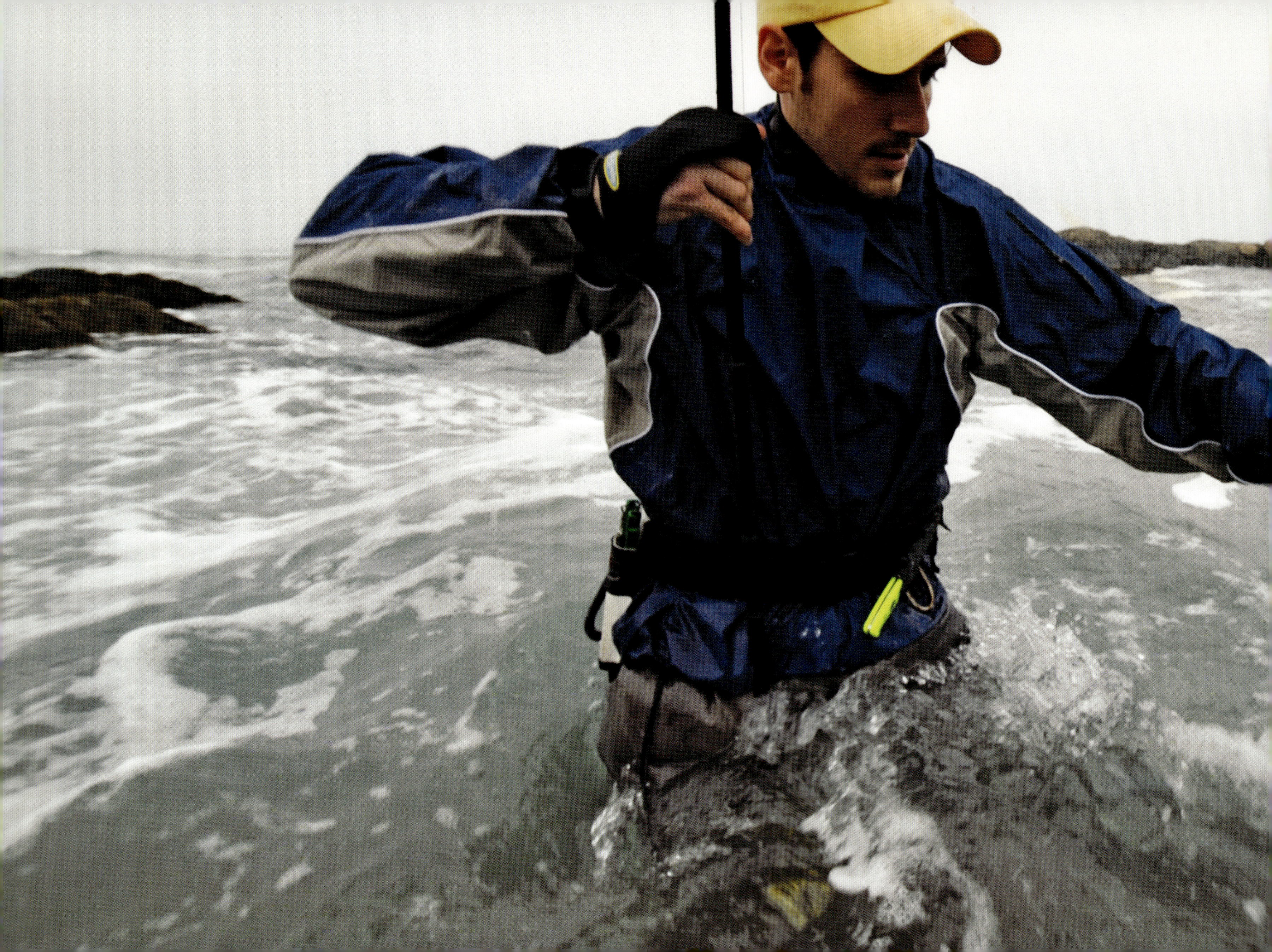

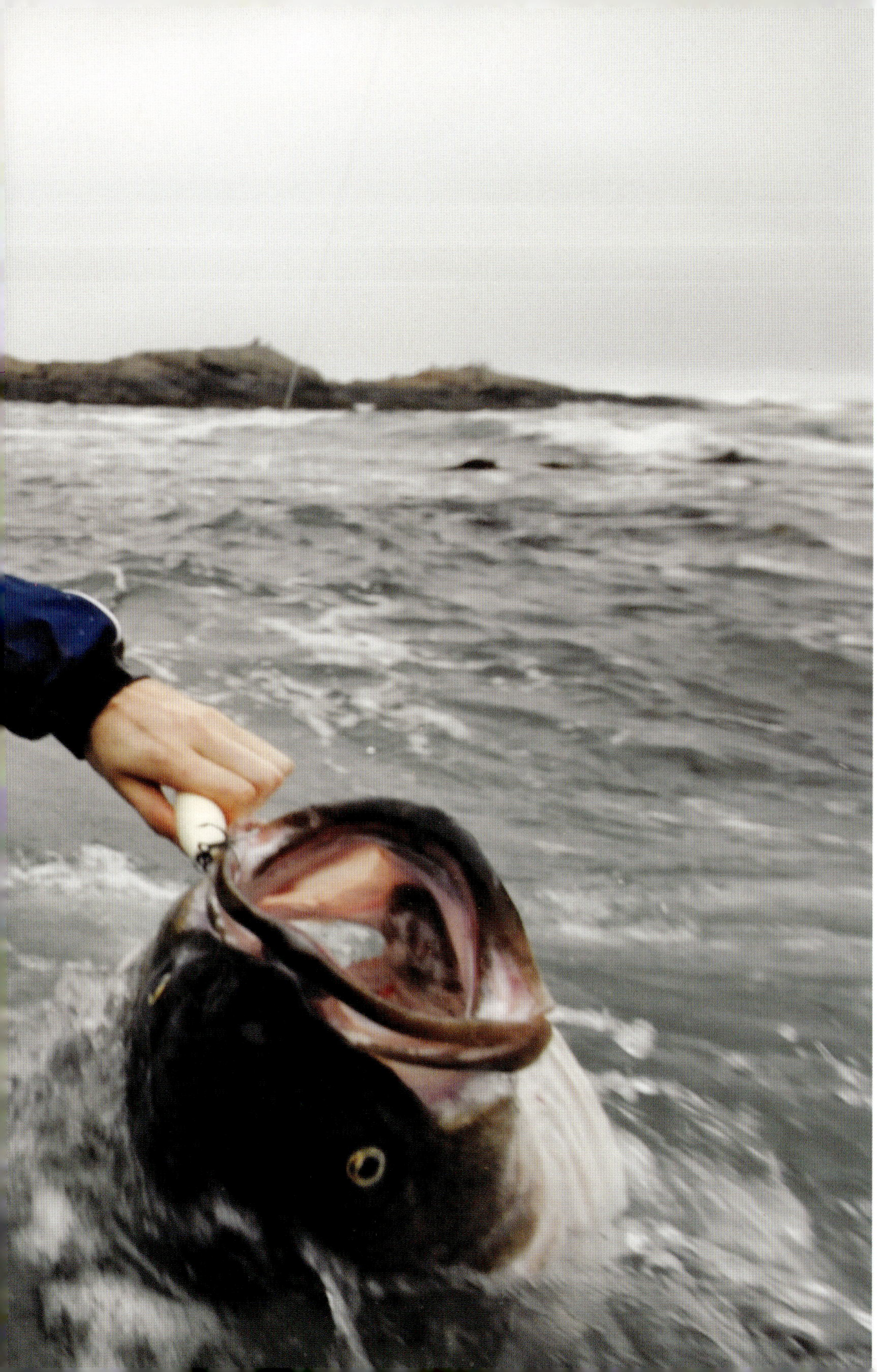

surfed it as a teen, and got to know the bottom gliding over it, donning mask and snorkel, while hunting fish with a speargun. This stretch of sand, rocks, and waves has been in my life for half a century. Before that, my great-uncle Ed Sisson was a beach seiner who kept a fish shack on the back side of the dunes around the turn of the last century. It was swept away in a storm, never to be rebuilt.

My brother and I started surfing the spot in the late 1960s. When a big swell rolled in, we'd jog out in the morning before the wind came up, carrying our boards alternately under our arms or over our heads. The waves were short, steep, and wedge-shaped. Some days they were big enough to scare us, but the break was always rideable if you had the stones.

My oldest fishing buddy took the biggest striped bass he'd caught up to that time in the rocks out there and buried it in the sand to avoid revealing anything about the night's fishing. He dragged the 30-pounder back to the parking lot past midnight, then drove to my house, where he proceeded to lay on the horn and flash his headlights outside my bedroom window.

Later in my life, nearly 20 years ago, I walk out one afternoon with my 14-month-old daughter riding in a backpack. My wife, who is pregnant, walks beside me. We pass someone walking back from the point who delivers a breathless report: *Fish are breaking everywhere*!

When I reach the bar, birds are diving and bass are busting. I walk right into the surf with the baby on my back and quickly hook a striper. I back up and carefully bend at my knees to release it, then head back out and hook a second fish. That's when a breaking wave knocks me sideways and causes me to stumble. I figure it is a sign that my daughter should join her mother on the sand.

A 42-pound bass taken from the rocks off Newport, Rhode Island. Photo by Earl Evans.

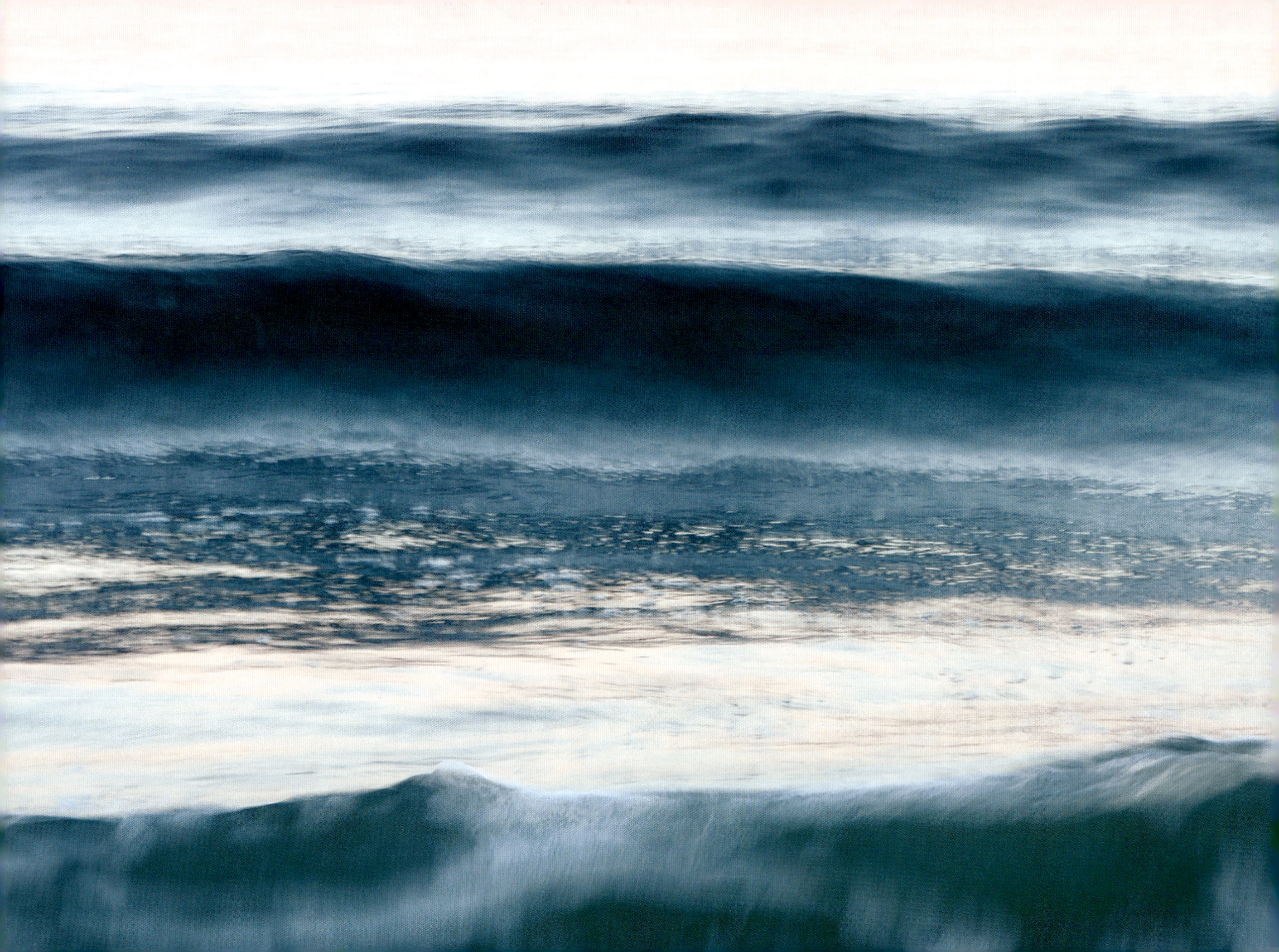

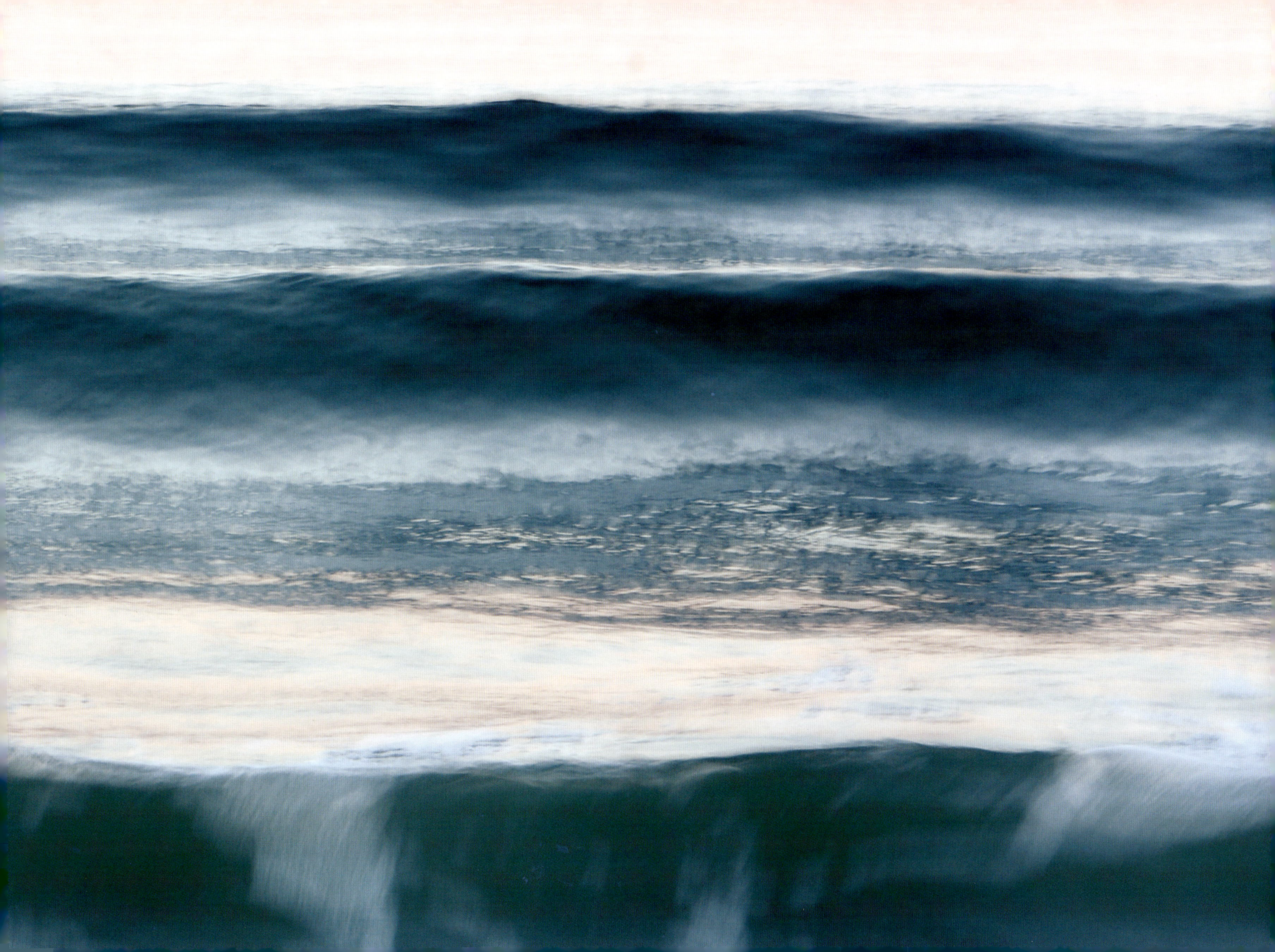

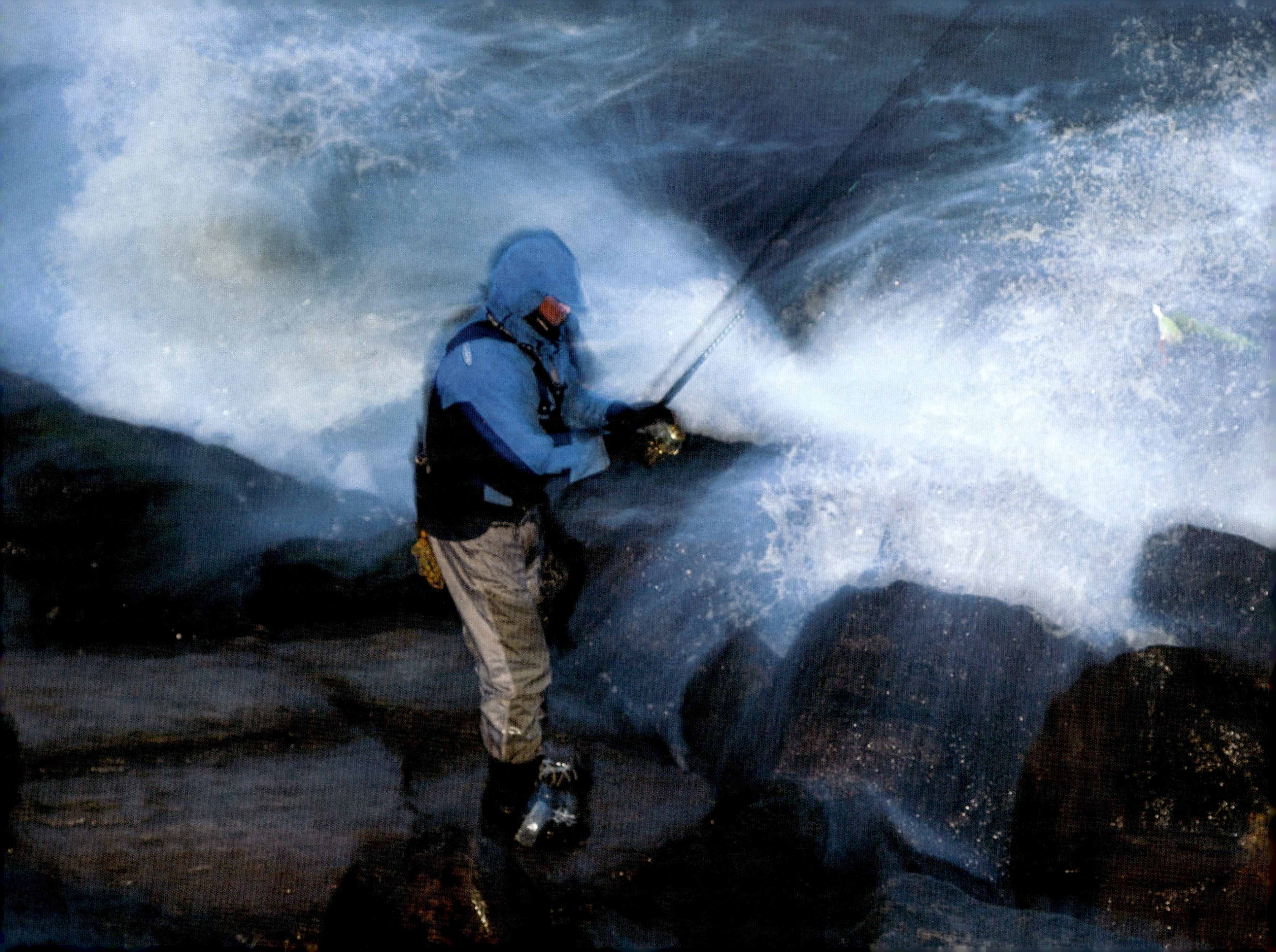

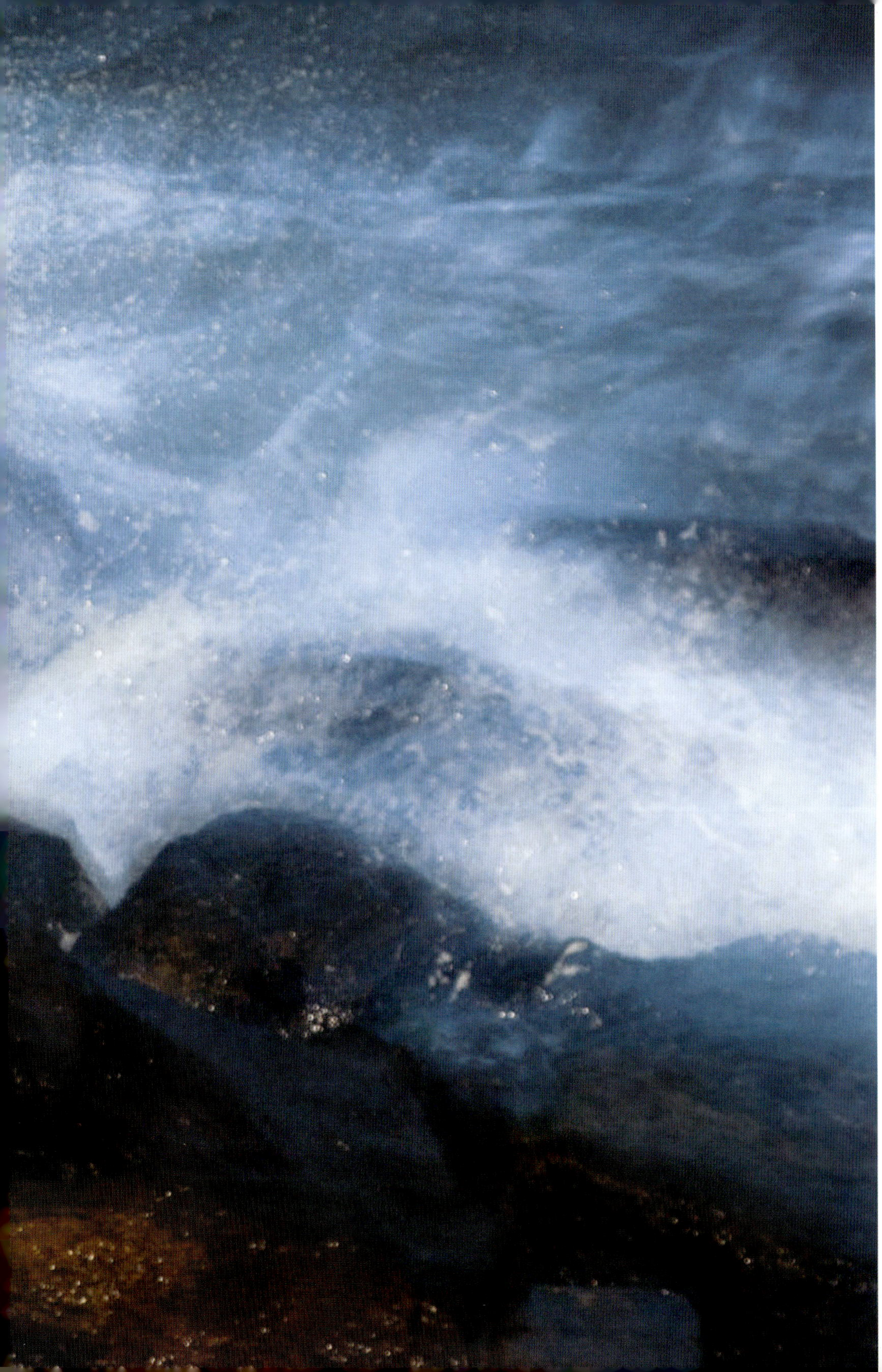

WITH THE BULK OF STRIPED BASS GONE by early November and more leaving daily, you never know what you're going to find from one night to the next. The burnt orange on the western horizon deepens, and it's not like earlier in the season, when you're working on resident fish and you're dialed in to a place and a pattern.

Once the sun is gone, you move into another realm, one that exists just to the side of the everyday world that you and everyone else normally inhabits. To enter, you have only to cross the dunes and follow the sound of breaking waves and the footprints of shorebirds.

The surf is up tonight, and spent waves drain through the pea-size beach gravel. "The beach hisses like fat," wrote Elizabeth Bishop in her poem "Sandpiper." The stripers I chase in the final days of this season range from Nova Scotia to North Carolina, as at home feeding in pounding surf as they are pushing up coastal rivers and bays. What will it be tonight? A 20-inch fish? A 40-pounder? Nada? I pull a knot tight, trim it in the light of a headlamp, and resume casting.

I fish three spots tonight without so much as a tap as I make my way toward a rocky point, where I cast six feet from a large rock in the shape of a mountain saddle. The end nearest me is angled so that every 10th wave or so that breaks on it showers me with spray. It has been doing that for 40 years. I've come to regard the surf-smoothed erratic as an old friend, annoying when the surf is up but part of the family. I put up with its wet insults because this is the best ambush spot along the east side of the point. Tonight, the dousing is for naught; the fish are absent.

I return to the sand and tie on a black plug. I intend to revisit the three spots along the beach now that darkness has settled in. The surf has been large and sloppy, but once the tide trips

Previous spread: Swell symmetry in Maine. Photo by Todd Towle.
Left: Late-season morning at Montauk. Photo by Grant Monahan.

and the wind shifts to the north, the swells clean up and snap to attention. Emboldened with the energy of the flood, the sets roll into the shallows with renewed vigor, the largest waves climbing head-high and packing into their steep faces the energy of yesterday's 50-knot gusts. They break with a crack, peel off left and right for a few seconds, and finish their lives with a resounding wallop. Tonight's music.

This is the time of year for some moxie in your makeup to offset any illusions of balance, grace, or summer warmth. You put your head down like a plow horse, place one foot in front of the other, and trudge into the wind. So what if the odds are against you finding a fish tonight? This is exactly where you need to be, fish or no fish.

Tonight, I am chasing the end of the season and looking for the boy who now feels the aches of an older man. I'm also hunting the one-legged ghost of my great-grandfather, a Civil War battlefield amputee and seine hauler whose imprint I still see coursing through our family members five generations later. There is an unyielding quality in all of us. A child of the Great Depression, my father was driven by hunger his entire life. And he could never wrap his head around catch-and-release fishing.

A typical conversation would go like this:

"How many did you get?" he'd ask.

"Five," I'd answer.

"What'd you do with them?"

"I let them go."

He'd shake his head and snort, "Stupid."

I'd laugh, shake mine, and try to explain to him that times had changed.

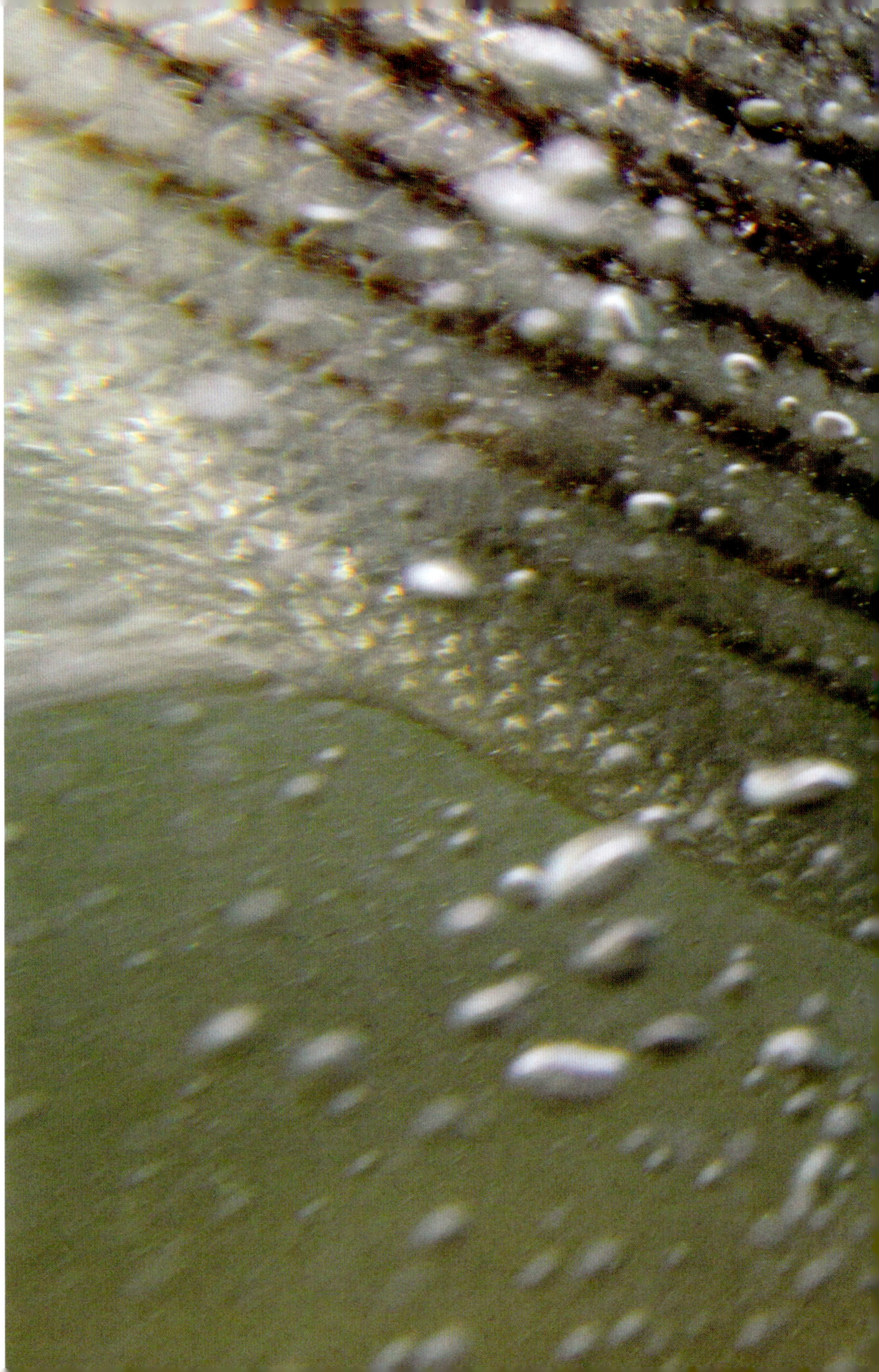

Headed for the bottom. Photo by Tom Lynch.

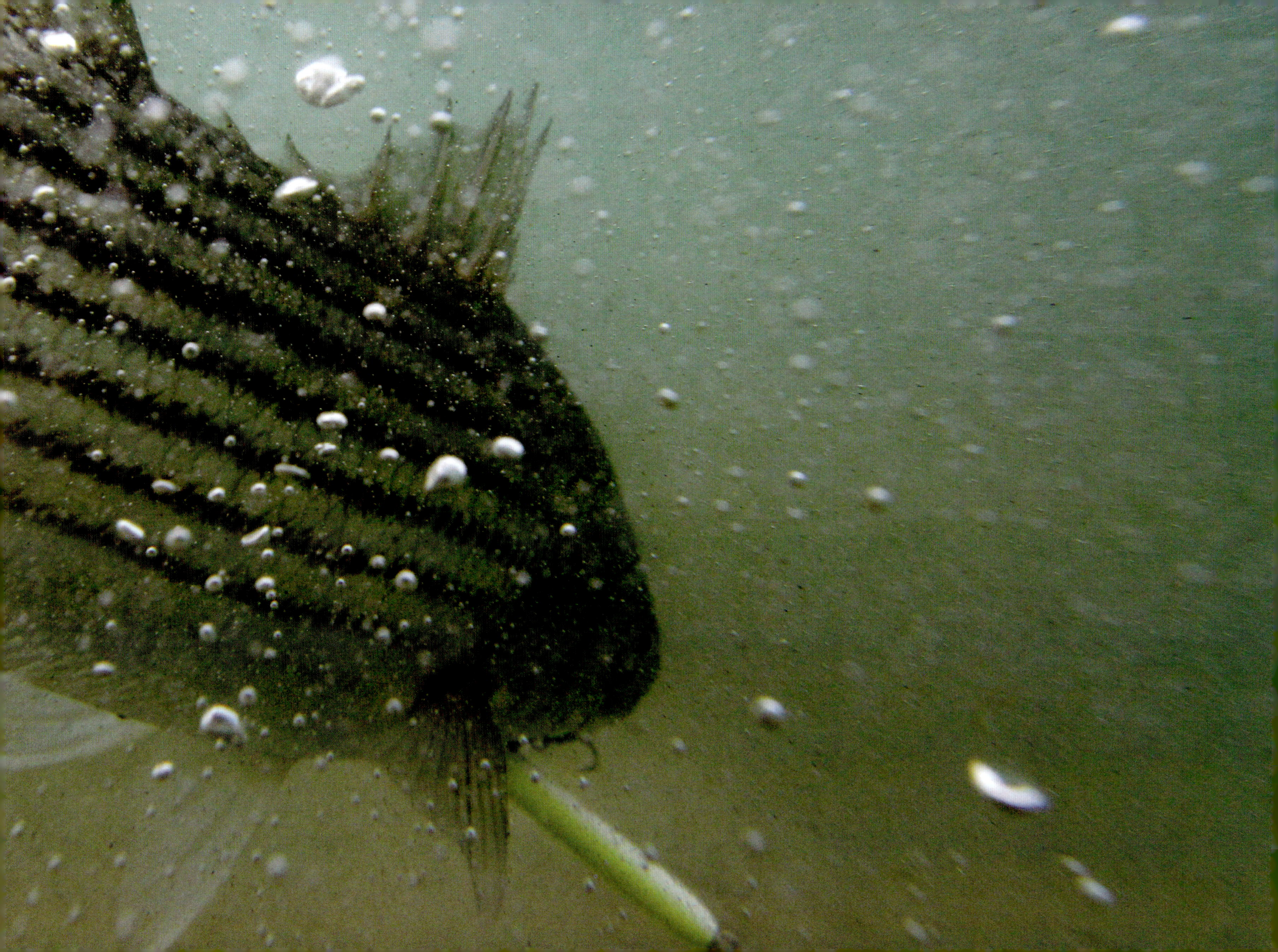

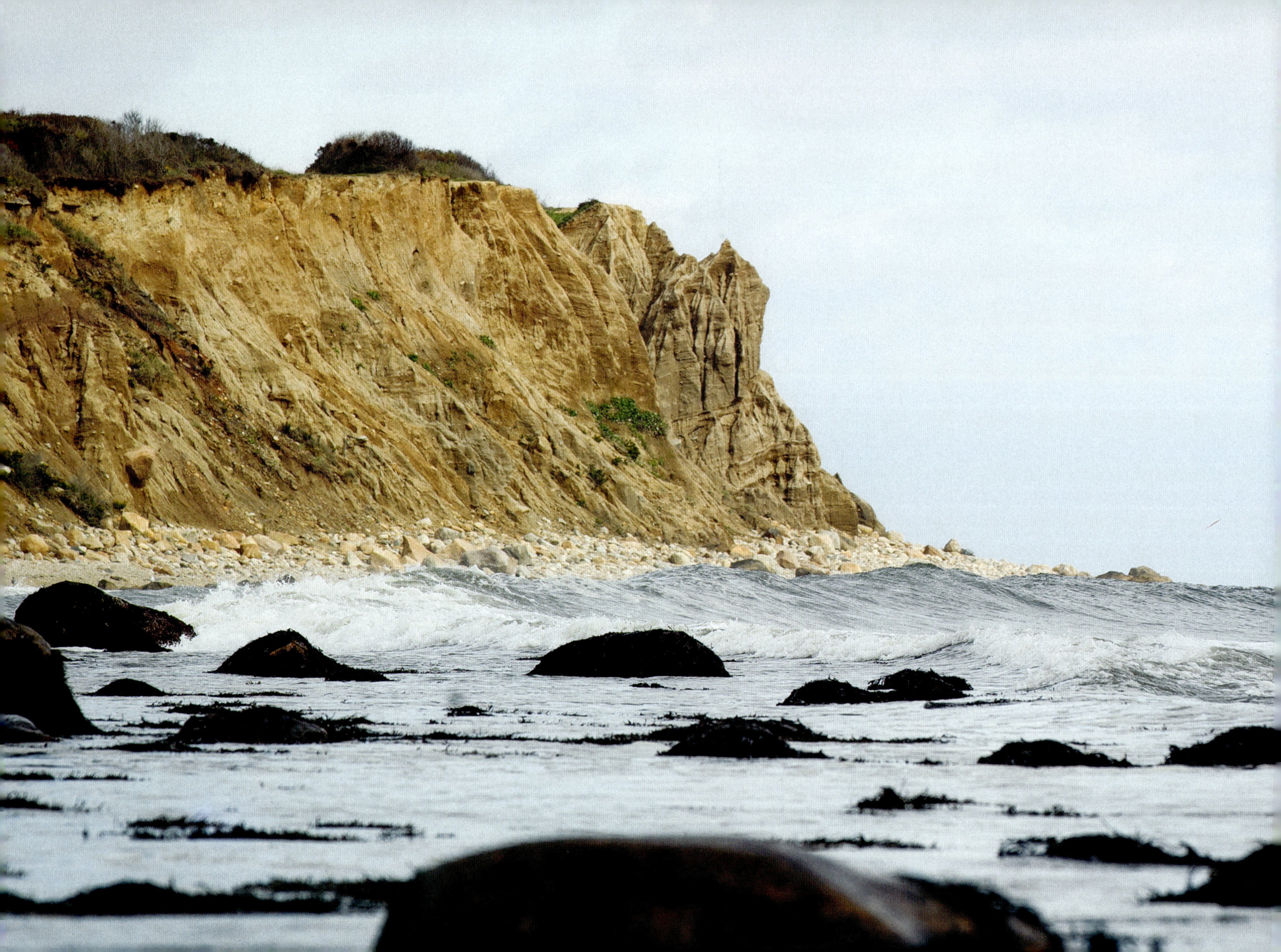

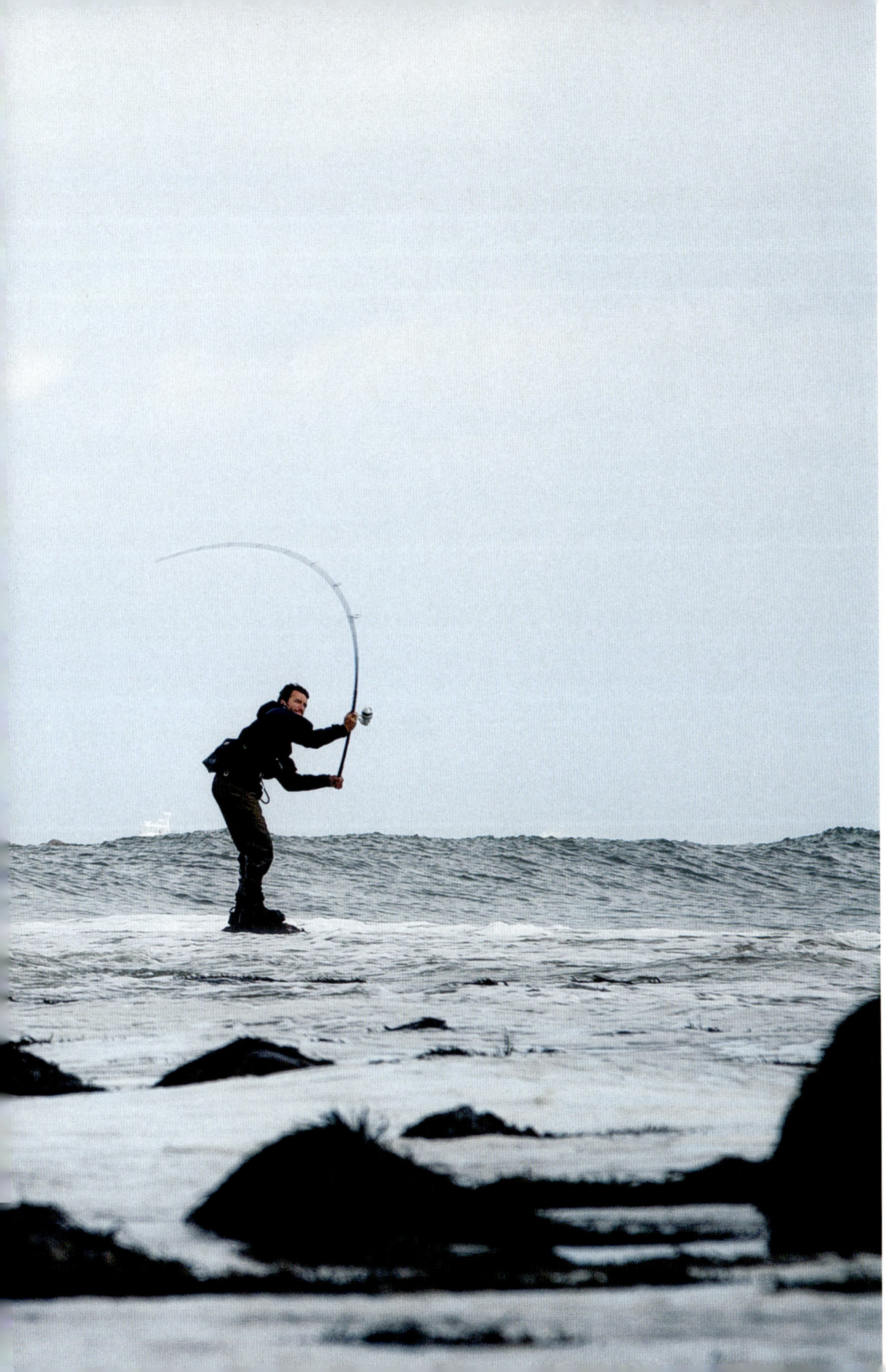

THE SHADOWS MERGE and grow longer each day. The beach is cold, windy, and empty, but beautiful just the same. The last spot I fish holds the forgotten remains of a gun battery built 120 years ago as part of a Spanish-American War fort. Time, hurricanes, winter storms, and waves have reduced this gun emplacement to chunks of rubble, visible only on the lowest of tides and decipherable only to a handful of graybeards who grew up listening to the stories told by long-dead old-timers. Each season, less of it remains.

Snorkeling over the flooded battery 15 years ago, I found a four-foot iron rod with a large nut fused to the threaded end, one of several supports that we theorized helped hold in place the five-inch pedestal-mounted guns that could send 59-pound shells seven miles seaward. The iron rod is now part of a sculpture in my brother's backyard.

Tonight, the spot is pounded by waves, and small stripers are crisscrossing it like a game trail. They smack my black needlefish, and I take six hard-won fish before the action slows. Owing to the topography, the waves that roll into this spot are unlike those along the rest of the mile-long beach. They build into short, pyramid-shaped waves and sometimes double up. In daylight, this surf is easy to read—you retreat a few steps or slide to the left or right as a wave set approaches from a funny angle. On a dark night, you can't see diddly. You think you have it figured out, and then you see the lip of a foaming breaker. You turn your face and hunch over while the wave hammers you to your knees.

You stumble to your feet—happy to find your eyeglasses still attached to a cord around your neck—retreat, regroup, and pull yourself together. Some nights you surrender and slosh off the beach. Other times, you go back for another dozen casts, more if the fish show interest. Such is the life the surf caster embraces each fall on an empty, windy beach.

Balanced below the bluffs at Montauk. Photo by Grant Monahan.

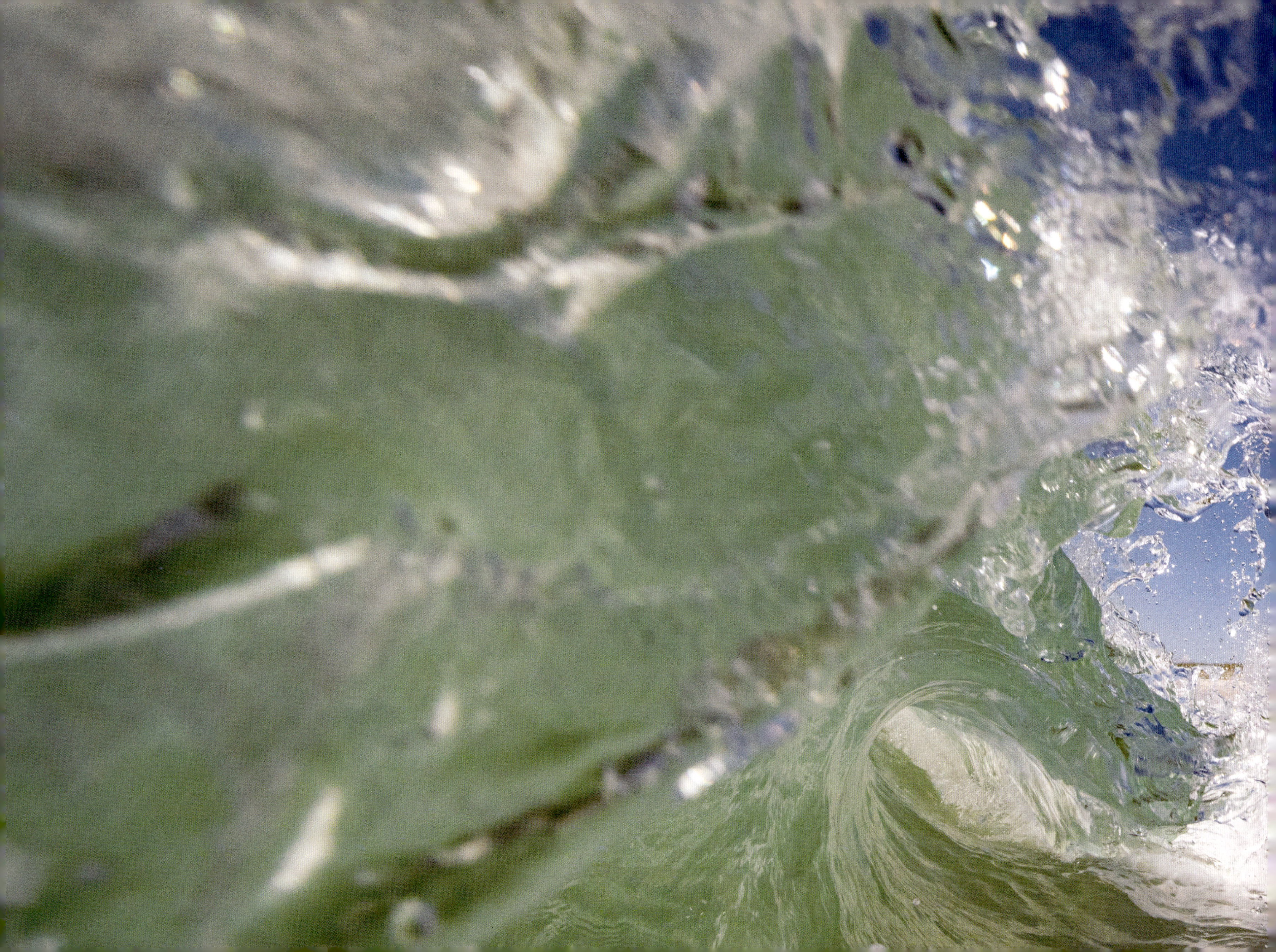

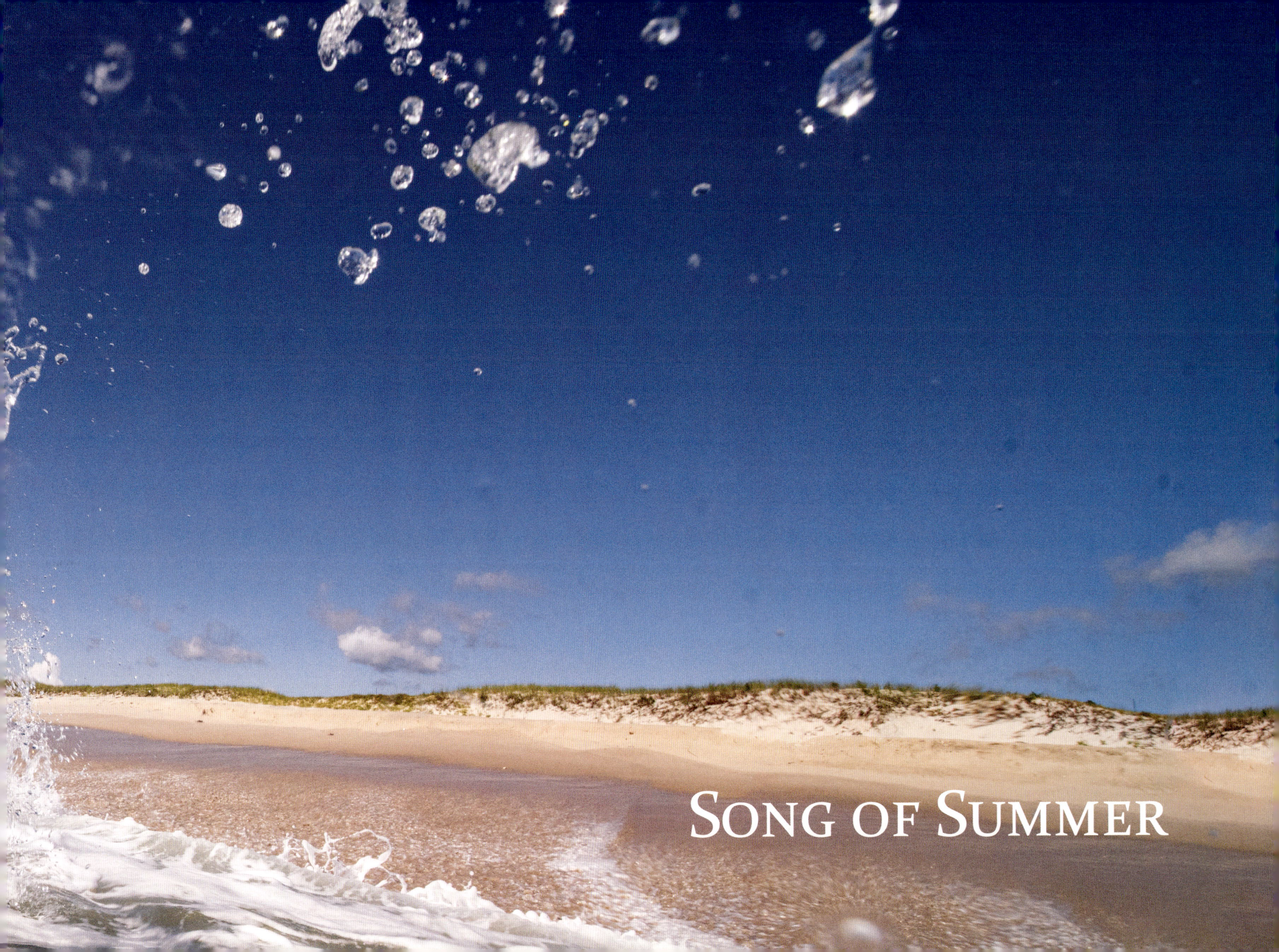

Song of Summer

I walk down a dusty island road to the water, geared up for a night's fishing, feeling in my bones as if I have "an appointment at the end of the earth," to quote Isak Dinesen. Inside my head, a dozen ghosts chatter away. They are part of a motley crew of striper fanatics: friends, forebears, and a host of old-timers who pop up regularly in stories told by other old hands. Gone. All of them gone now.

We are so busy talking to ourselves that we often forget to notice the world moving around us. Forty yards offshore, a white splash catches my eye—fish? There it is again. Yes, they're fish. My ghosts disappear, and I am back in the present and on the hunt.

Someone has drawn the shape of a striped bass in the moist clay of a drying mud puddle. Perfect folk art—here today, gone tomorrow, much like the fish. I'm not surprised to find it on Cuttyhunk Island, which once embodied this fish of dreams as much as any place along the coast.

I have a good idea where I'll cast tonight. My favorite boulder in the striper universe is on this easternmost island in the Elizabeth Island chain located off Massachusetts between Buzzards Bay and Vineyard Sound. The rock is about the size of a compact car and just big enough for two people. I first climbed aboard the glacial erratic many years ago, when I was learning the island. I fished it hard at night with live eels. During the day, I'd cast plugs, plastics, and eels, and swim to promising rocks to gauge whether I could fish them safely after dark.

This spot has been good to me. I've hooked more large stripers weighing between 30 and nearly 50 pounds off this rock than any other I've fished from. I weighed some of the big fish on a Boga, then carefully resuscitated and released each one.

Sometimes I'd dance a little jig on the boulder after midnight when the fishing was good. Although it's submerged on big tides and swept by white water on a good swell, the rock is never precariously slick. Its lower flanks are armed with barnacles. I view it as my lucky rock at the edge of the earth.

I'VE FISHED CUTTYHUNK FOR 18 YEARS, but it took only one trip to discover that it's not an easy place to work from shore. And it doesn't matter whether you're in waders, a wet suit, or a bathing suit. You'll do a lot of walking, sweating, slipping, and scrambling, but the results for persistent surf anglers can be exceptional, especially for fish 25 pounds and larger.

Cuttyhunk also taught me to change my tackle if I wanted to have a chance at landing the larger fish. On my early trips, I fished a light Lamiglas rod and 20-pound mono, and had my ass handed to me by every good fish I hooked. I eventually switched to a stiff 10½-foot Loomis rod with a Penn 706Z and 68-pound braid, 60-pound leaders, and circle hooks, which the fish couldn't get much leverage on. The heavier tackle better matched the size of the fish and the rocky, weed-strewn bottoms the larger fish dove into, chafing and rubbing their way to escape. After thrashing the surface and making a good first run, the fight often became a slow grind as the fish dug in and I worked to dig them out. It sometimes felt like winching cars out of a quarry. If only I could have hooked one of those big fish on sand.

I also fished lighter eight-foot rods with 30-pound braid for schoolies, occasionally brandishing them at night until I fully learned my lesson about being undergunned.

I feel at home on this island in the darkness, climbing over the wrack-covered rocks, buffeted by a big southwest wind and rolling swells, gazing at fireflies searching for mates along the bluffs.

Time slows on Cuttyhunk. Maybe it's the long days and the equally long nights. You eventually move to the rhythm of the island and the patterns of the tides, winds, and fish.

Wind and waves shape, smooth, and sculpt everything they touch on this island. Boulders and cobbles, old timbers, rusty bulkheads, a smashed aluminum skiff at the foot of

Previous spread: Beach break. Photo by Tom Lynch.
Right: Cuttyhunk bluffs and rocky shore looking east toward Nashawena Island. Photo by Jerry Audet.

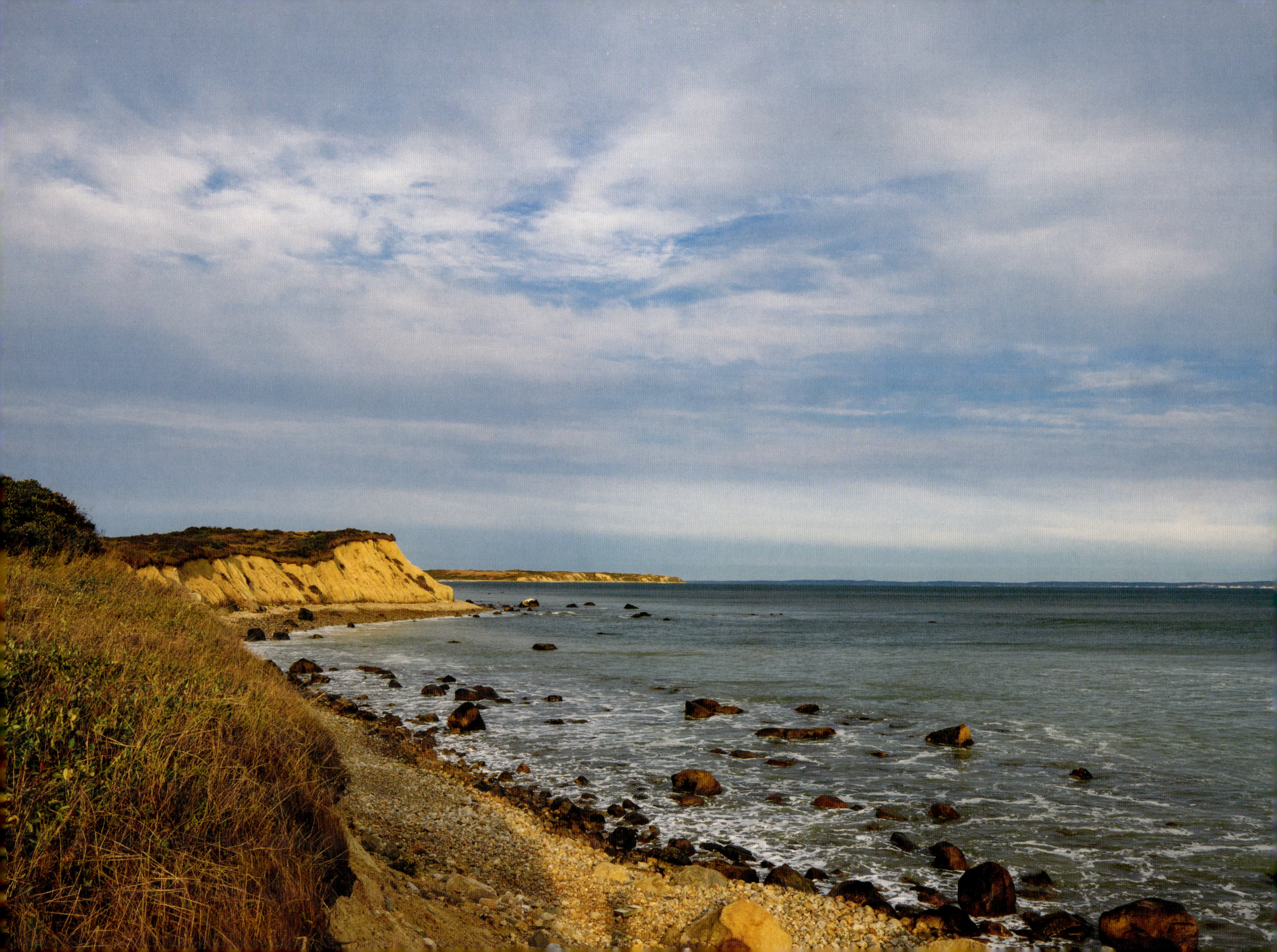

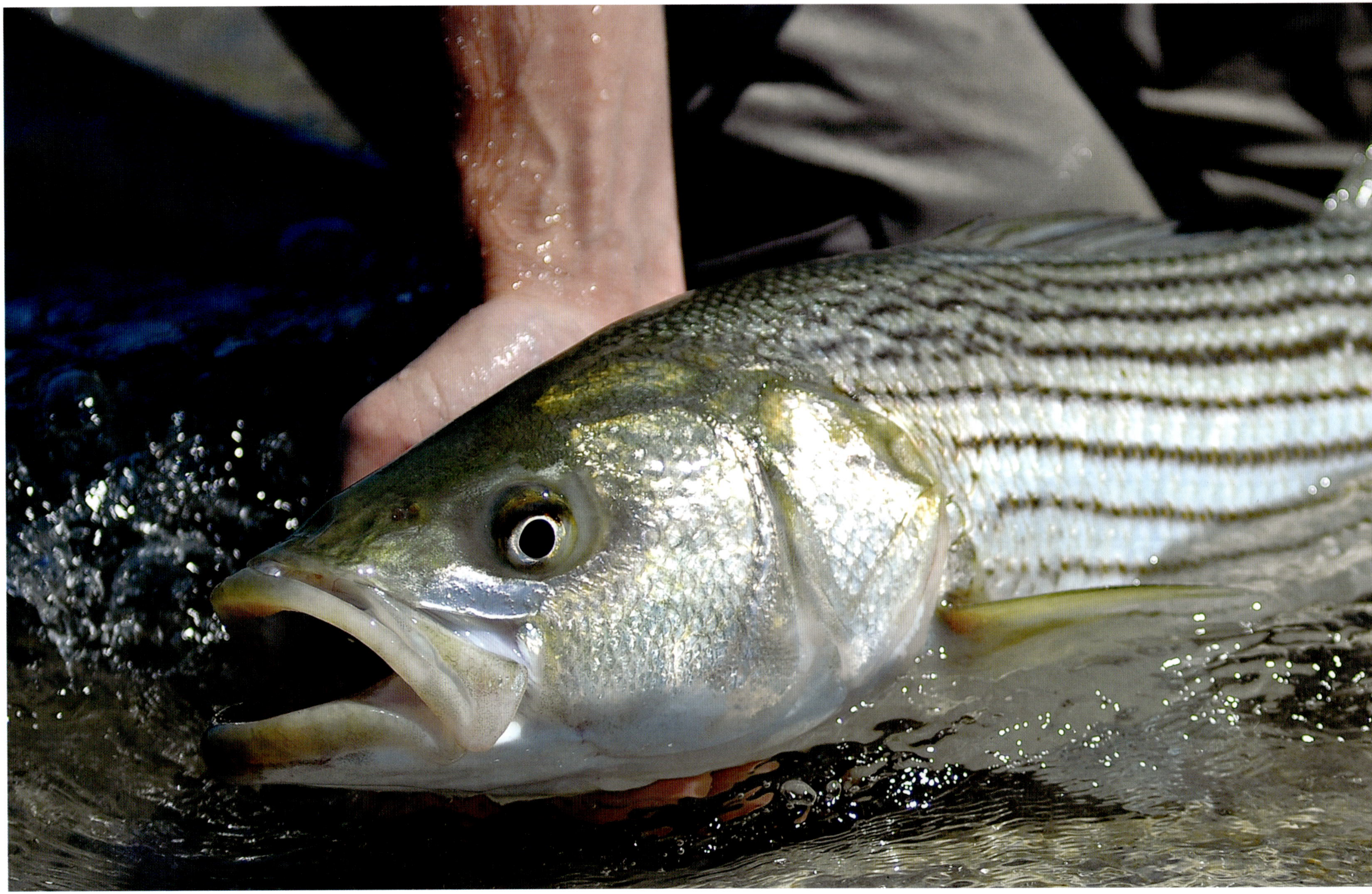

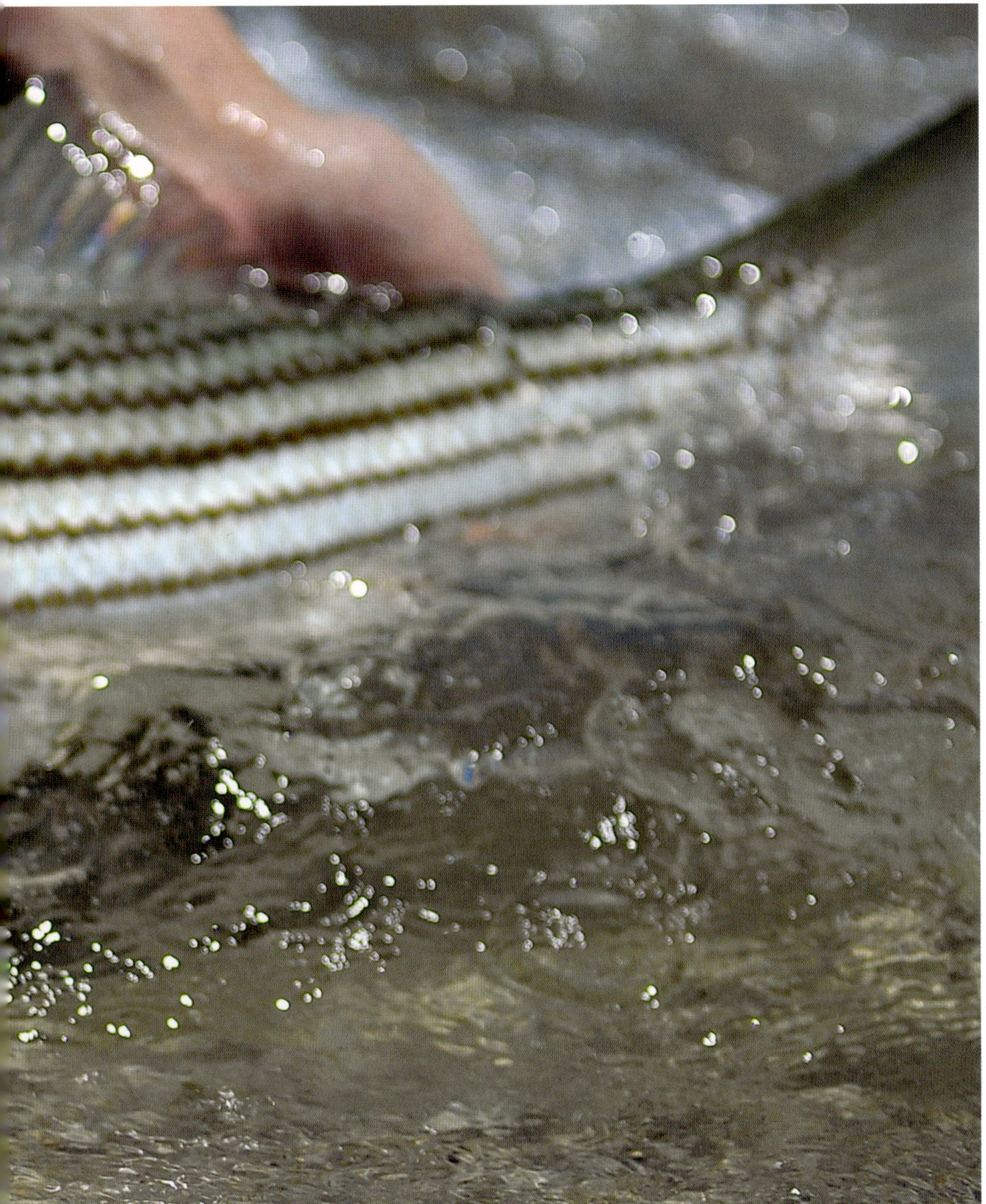

a bluff, the trees stunted and bent by the prevailing winds. They sculpt the fishermen, too, no matter how young and strong they are when they begin the chase or how hardheaded they once imagined themselves to be. In the island cemetery, the outline of a striped bass is chiseled onto the headstone of a longtime Cuttyhunk charter captain who had a good bark and chased the fish with intelligence and vigor. I visit the cemetery every trip, and it reminds me to fish like there is no tomorrow.

OVER THE YEARS I BECAME FRIENDS with some of the fishing characters on Cuttyhunk. Jimmy Nunes, Peter Lehner, Charlie Tilton, and Bruce Borges were four of the smartest old-school Yankee striper men I've known. Jimmy and Charlie have passed. Pete is 99 and no longer fishes. Bruce is still running charters, but he's not sure for how much longer.

"You looked at those guys and there was a depth to them," Pete once said of his friends. "The longer you fish, the more respect you have for the fish."

Pete chased bass for decades, starting in the 1950s. "Long enough to know something about them, and to know what I don't know," he said. He loved fly fishing and light tackle spin fishing from the 30-foot aluminum jet-powered boat that he helped design. The cockpit is open for casting, as is the small forward deck, corralled in a railing. Pete and I have hunted stripers 30 times or more from his boat.

The first question he'd ask when we'd run into each other on the island was, "Did you bring your fly rod?"

On one such early summer day, Sow and Pigs Reef is loaded with stripers. We head out to fish the ebb in the afternoon in a southwesterly wind.

A bright, handsome fish. Photo by David Skok.

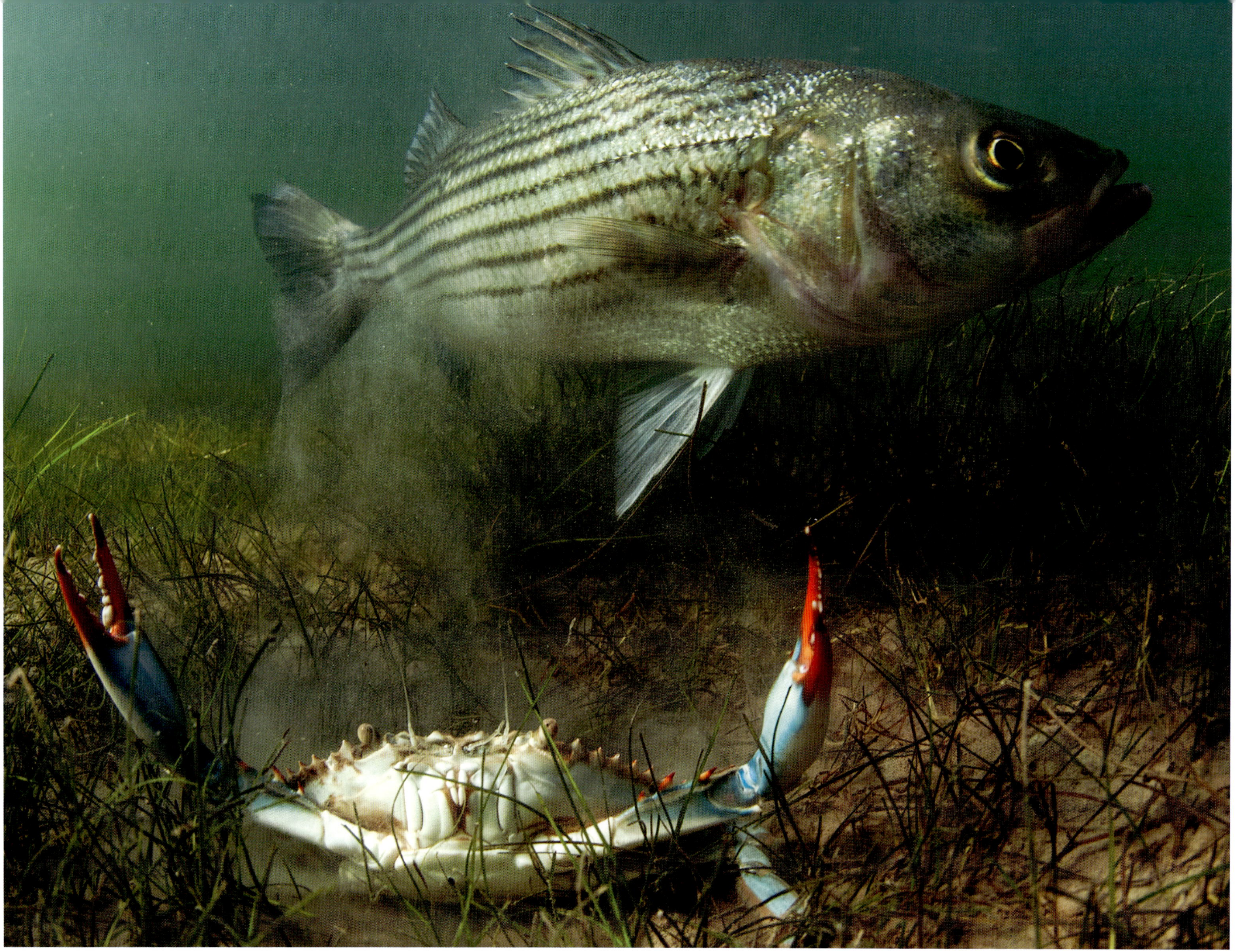

I am on the bow deck as Pete moves the boat inside a set of rocks that he calls his compass points. It feels as if I am looking into an aquarium filled with bass and bait. I spot dozens of stripers of various sizes, including some lovelies that appear to be four feet long.

The fish are feeding on top, and I quickly get them to eat a yellow Clouser on an 8-weight rod. I cast over several boulders into an open patch of water. "Let it sink. Let it sink a little longer," Pete said. "OK, now retrieve."

Three strips and I'm on. I work the fish to the boat, hand the rod to Pete, then scurry along the side deck to the cockpit where he hands the rod back to me and I boat the fish. That's the drill.

I take a half-dozen decent fish, including a 20-pounder. We are back on the water the next morning, but the early fog is slow to burn off and Pete needs to clearly see the rocks he must maneuver around. I have watched Pete in the past put the bow two feet from a submerged rock the size of a shed on this reef and hold it in a good current while I cast. "I don't want to bend a boat," he said on this morning.

Pete has had his share of boating adventures in the pursuit of stripers. "Sunk 'em three times," he told me once before. Injuries? "The boats, yes." One time the throttle linkage fell out and the boat turned broadside in a rip and filled with water. The two other times he was fishing close to the reef and the boat came down on a rock. "There's nothing quite like sliding down the face of a wave and seeing the rock you're going to hit," Pete said. "It's sort of like watching a noose."

ON ANOTHER VISIT TO THE ISLAND, I hear three girls who are playing in the island surf squeal as stripers glide through the clear waters. "It's a big striped bass!" shouts a tall, dark-haired adolescent, throwing her strong voice into the wind. "It's huge!"

Blue crab and Chesapeake school bass. Photo by Jay Fleming.

"Will it bite?" a companion wonders loudly.

Each summer, scores of sandy-colored fish that are feeding on small crabs and baitfish glide unseen past swimmers. I sometimes don a mask and snorkel and follow these nearshore fish. I hear indecipherable snippets of laughter and excitement from the oblivious swimmers as they frolic in the beach break. The emanations from my own species are as unintelligible through the mask and snorkel as the hunting songs of terns dropping on a school of bait just beyond them. The chatter and clamor mixing with the shore break is the song of summer.

AT THE END OF A WEEK FISHING CUTTYHUNK, I am cut, sore, bruised, sunburned, and limping. Two deep cuts on the bottom of my right foot refuse to heal. A tiny piece of gravel is lodged in the ball of my left foot, which I've had no success digging out. I have tiny razor cuts on my hands, feet, and legs from the white barnacles on the rocks. A charley horse in my right calf muscle has me biting the sheets around 3:00 a.m., an hour after I climb into bed. My fingers are cut, poked, and gouged from handling dozens of small, lively stripers that deliver the most annoying jabs as you unhook them—I don't like wearing gloves.

My hair stands in a *Mad Max* mohawk of salt and sweat. I haven't shaved in a week, and I've taken just one hot shower, preferring the cold outdoor showers in the afternoon. I am tired, but still pushing myself to fish another evening tide. Despite the aches, I never feel more alive than when I'm out here, fishing well and moving between tides and spots in a kind of flow state. I'm doing my best to follow Mary Oliver's advice: "Be good-natured and untidy in your exuberance."

Dressed in shortie wet suits, my 11-year-old son and I swim at high tide to my favorite rock. It's not far from shore. I boost him up and then climb aboard behind him. We share a rod.

No one else is fishing the shore, but to the west I make out a dory carrying two people. In this last bit of twilight, the silhouetted double-ender is a lovely, organic shape. It moves smoothly

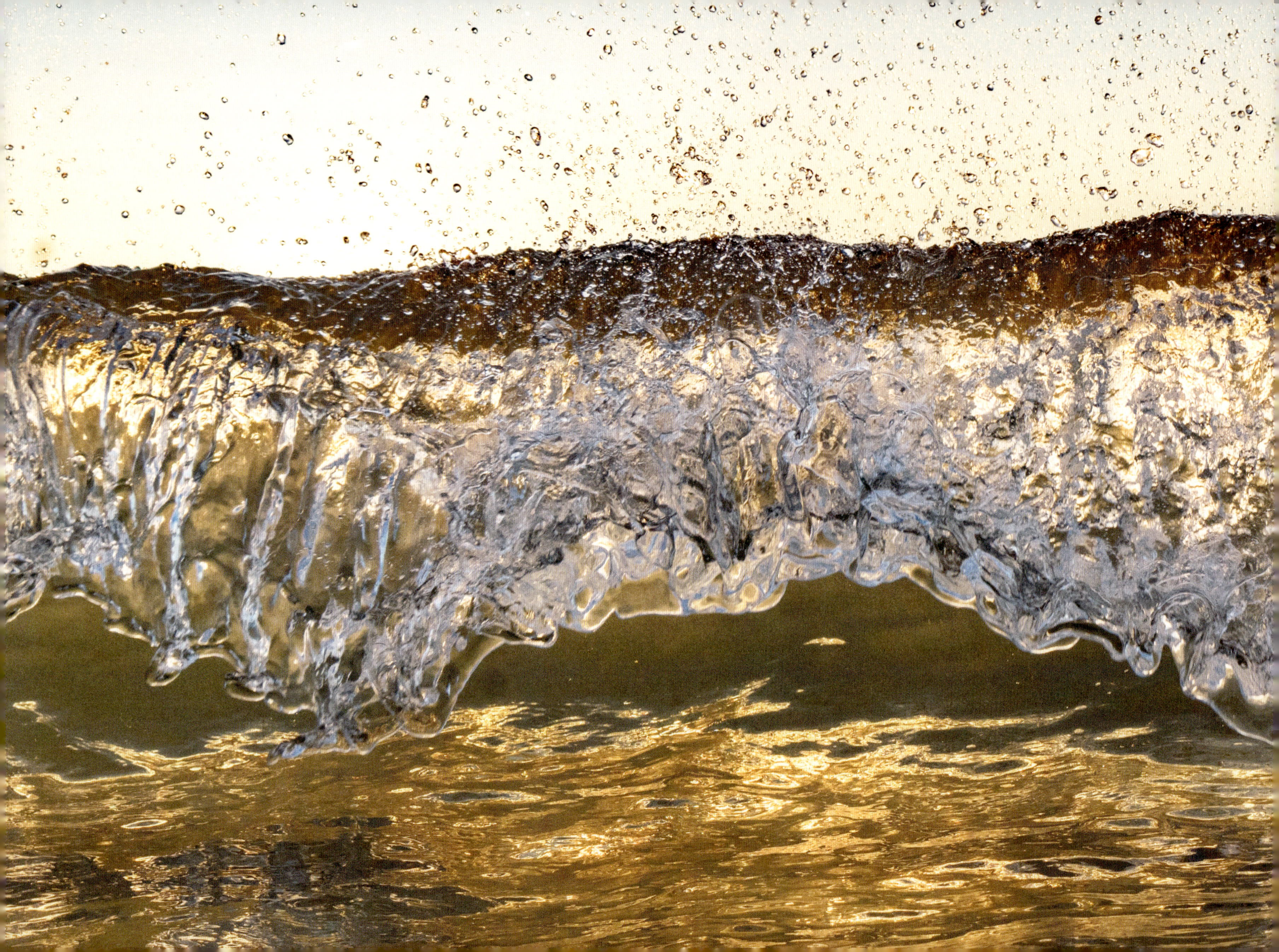

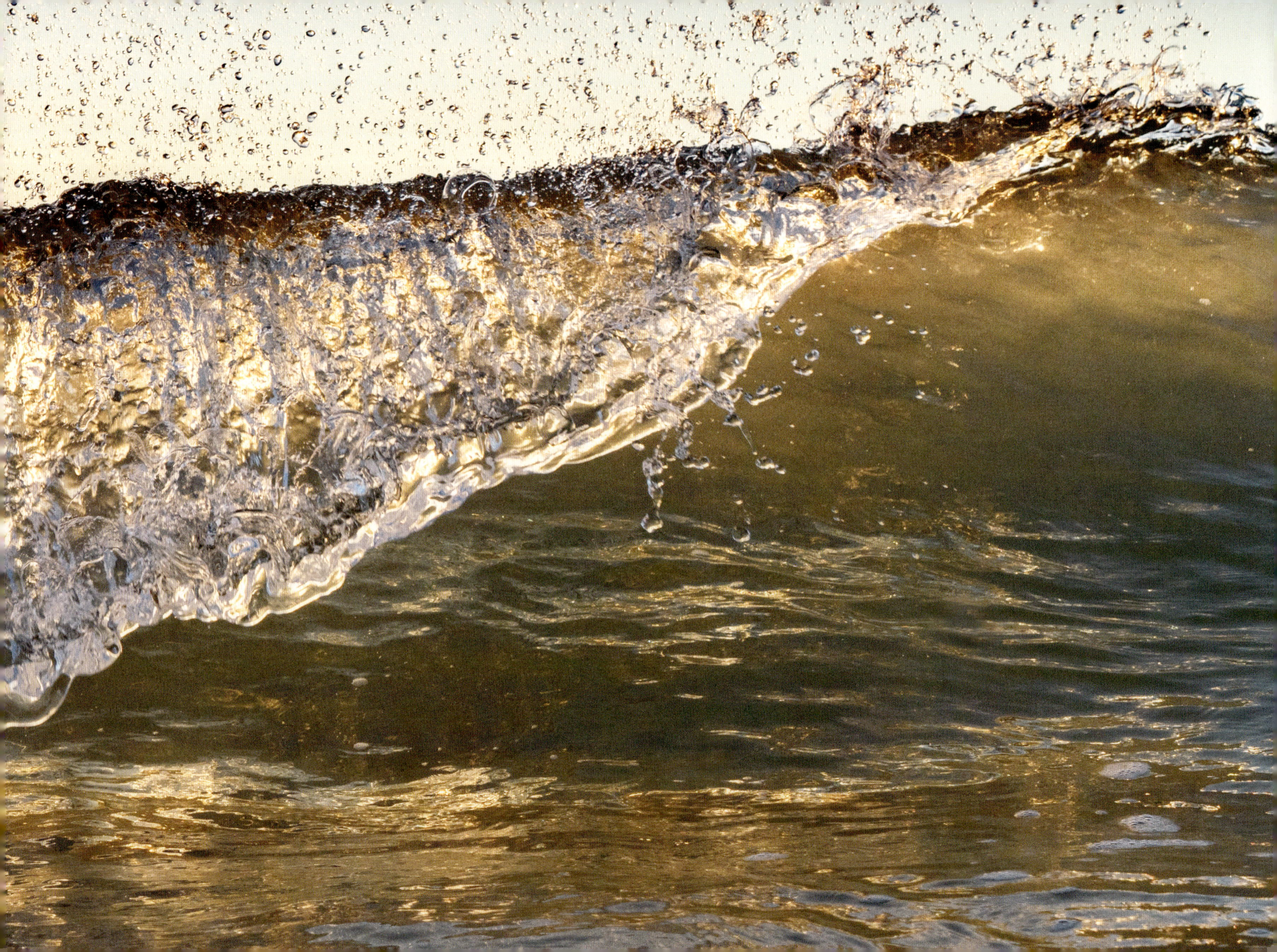

and quietly through the water. It could be a scene from the late 1800s when the Cuttyhunk Island Striped Bass Club was in full swing.

The men are fishing, the oarsman rowing carefully and quietly with his lights off. I watch as the man on the oars pulls off the point as his companion fights a good fish. A few minutes later, I hear the fish thumping in the boat. While it is still flopping, I hook a striper and hand the rod to my son. I've fished here four of the last five nights, with no shortage of decent fish into the high 20s. The drag is tight, and I grab the collar of Michael's wet suit to let him know he's not going to be pulled off the rock.

The striper weighs about 20 pounds and, given the high tide, we guide it behind our rock where I lip it easily, slide it onto our perch, and pop the hook out. The fish is fat, with its back and flanks beautifully colored in lavender and purple. We end the night early for me, just before midnight, with five fish and one tired boy.

I HAD STARTED MY SON BASS FISHING several summers earlier, trolling a series of shifting sandbars and drop-offs in a bay that serves as a summering ground for hordes of school bass. It's protected from the brunt of most winds, making it perfect for both the young and the old. The fish aren't large, but they're spirited, willing, and plenty lively on light tackle. I've been pulling them off the eelgrass meadows and deep spots here for two decades.

It is early July and a warm south breeze gusting into the 20s is blowing over the dunes. My son is six and has been asking to fish; I've been waiting for the right time to get him into his first striper, and this feels like a good place to start.

My plan is to troll a curved piece of aluminum called a "sparky," which is about six inches long, with a single hook onto which I thread a sandworm. The slower we move, the more enticing the wobble. It is a deadly combo. We are using a largemouth bait-casting rod with an Ambassadeur reel and 15-pound mono. All Michael has to do is hold on tightly.

We approach the drop-off moving west into the sun, which proves too bright even for polarized glasses. I lose the edge in the glare and wind up in the shallows in two feet of water; I trim up the outboard and swing back off the flat to deeper water. The detour produces Michael's first summer flounder, a serendipitous catch that delights him.

I tell him the story of my first striper, caught on a Niantic Bay Spinner and a sandworm, and how, when the rod bent and throbbed, I knew I'd hooked a fish and not the bottom.

I let out the line and hand him the rod. "Just don't drop the rod," I said. We move slowly along the edge, slipping in and out of gear.

"I think I have a hit," he said quickly.

"Nah, that's not a fish. You'll know it when you have one," I said.

He announces several more phantom strikes before I hear a change in his voice.

"Dad!" he said, with seriousness. "Dad!"

I look back. The rod is dancing, and he is wide-eyed. I shift into neutral, and the boy slowly and steadily reels in his first bass. It is a beautiful little fish, bright and shimmering in the early summer sun. He rubs his fingers along the scales. "This way is rough," he said. "This way is smooth." I hope his first striped bass proves to be as memorable and lasting as mine.

The fish are lying in a deep section where the current has cut into the flat. He asks me to tell the story of my first fish again, which I do as we troll into the current with the sun at my back. The rod tip soon starts throbbing again. "Got one," he said, oozing with the confidence of an instant expert into his second fish. The stripers are carbon copies of each other—perfectly shaped, handsome, and healthy. He lands four more on as many passes, and we call it quits.

Previous spread: Filigreed wave top. Photo by Tom Lynch.
Right: Bass and bikes at the Cape Cod Canal. Photo by John Doble.

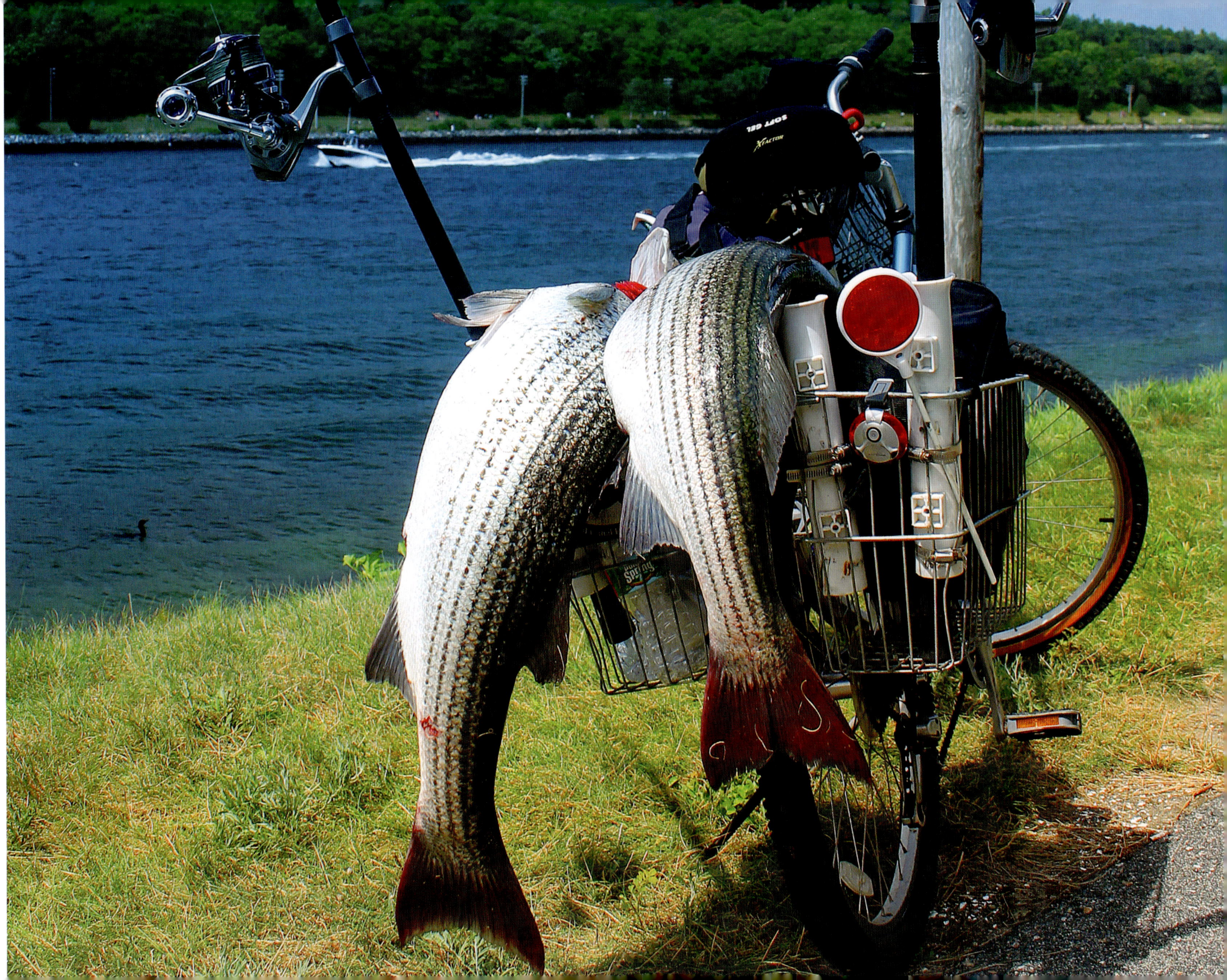

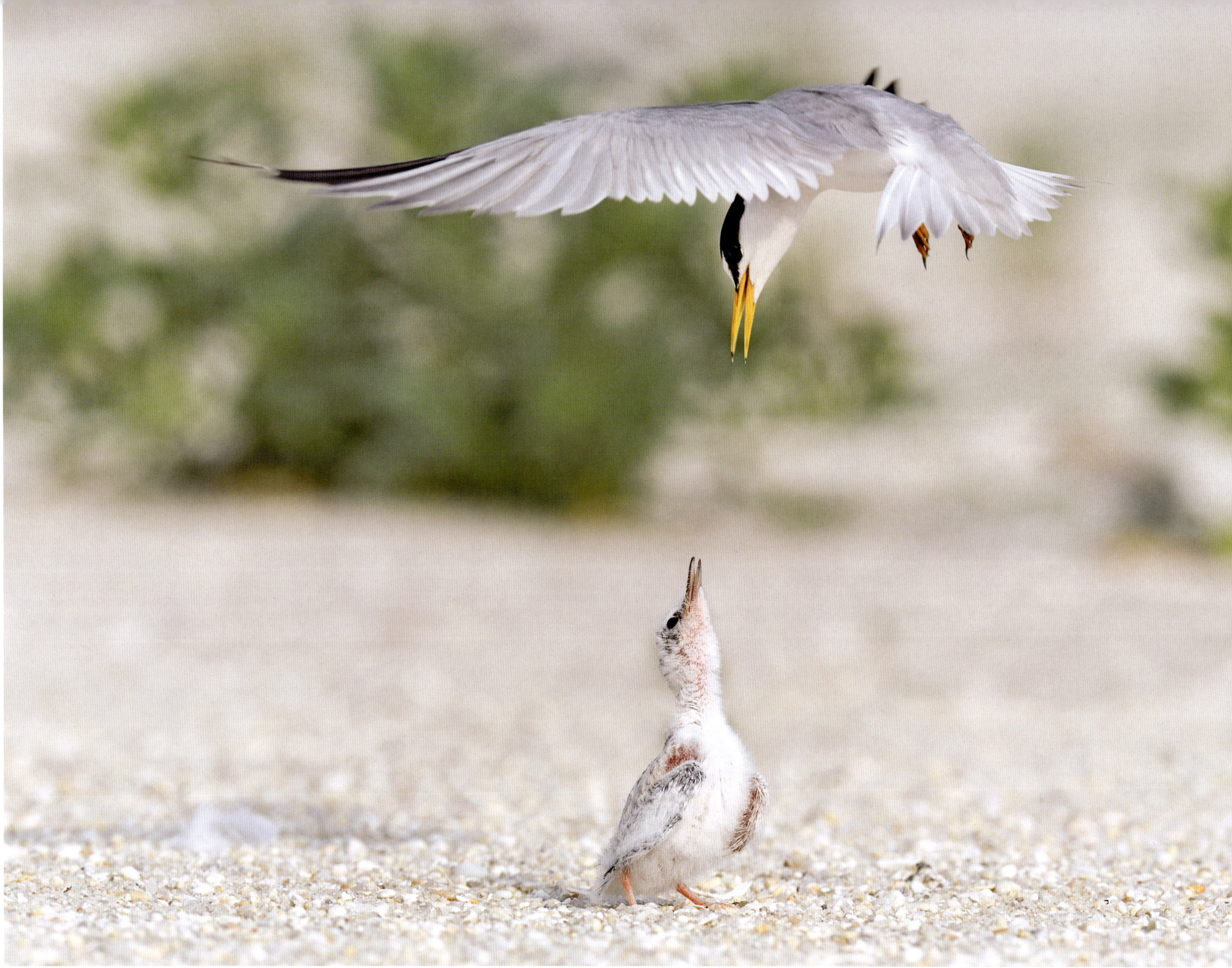

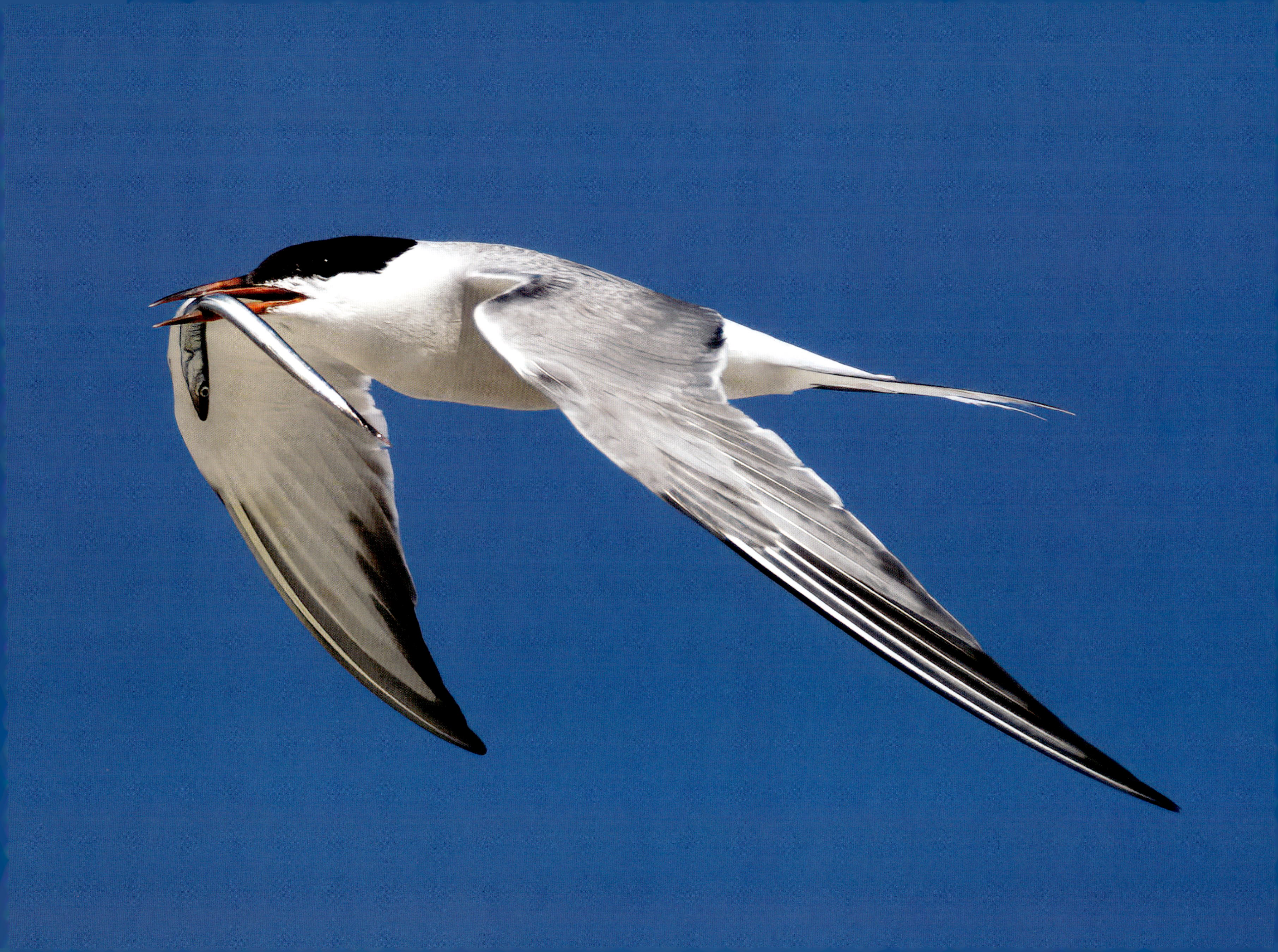

“The boat smells like fish,” he said on the way to the dock. Music to my ears on a perfect summer day.

MY FATHER IS 87 WHEN HE MAKES an unexpected announcement at breakfast. “I want to go fishing,” he says. It is as much a command as a wish. He hasn’t fished in almost 30 years. He used to take breaks from his general store and walk across the street to the town dock to spend an hour catching tinker mackerel or snapper blues.

A couple of days later, we are sitting side by side on the bench seat in my boat and heading down the bay. Same drill as with my son. I adjust the drag, feed the sparky and sandworm behind the boat, and hand Dad the rod. He remains seated. He hooks his first fish in less than five minutes, which he cranks to the boat as if racing a stopwatch. “Whoa, whoa. Slow down, Dad,” I say. “Let me get the leader.”

He asks if I ever fished with him off the town dock. The question stings. Those memories are among my earliest and sharpest, and I now realize he doesn’t remember me nestled between him and my older brother on the dock, each of us working a handline for cunners. He cranks in another fish, then another. He puts his head down on the side rail for a moment and I wonder, *What is he seeing? Or thinking?*

On this bright and breezy day in early July, we sit a couple of feet apart in a small boat, whirling separately through our internal universes and collective pasts, looking for common ground as the stripers do their best to jolt us into the here and now. As usual, he keeps score. He has tallied six schoolies when suddenly he announces, “OK, I’ve had enough. Let’s go.”

Despite the lovely weather and the plentitude of fish, I can’t tell whether he has really enjoyed himself. It’s not until later in the week, when I sit in a restaurant with his breakfast crowd,

Previous spread, left: Least tern and chick. Photo by Don Schroder.
Previous spread, right: Common tern with sand eel. Photo by Tom Lynch.
Right: A well-proportioned bass that Lynch took off the beach. Photo by Ted Tafaro.

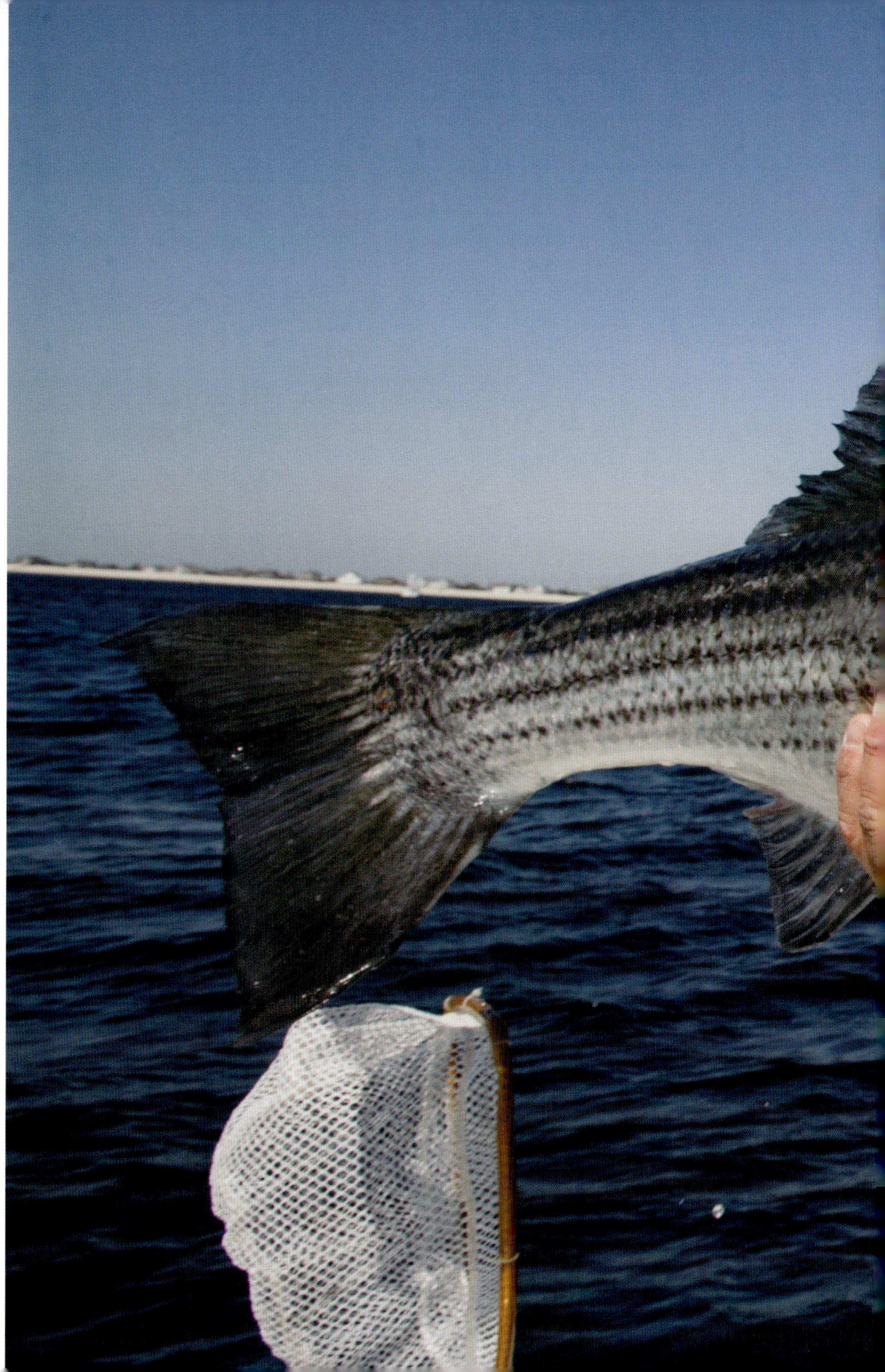

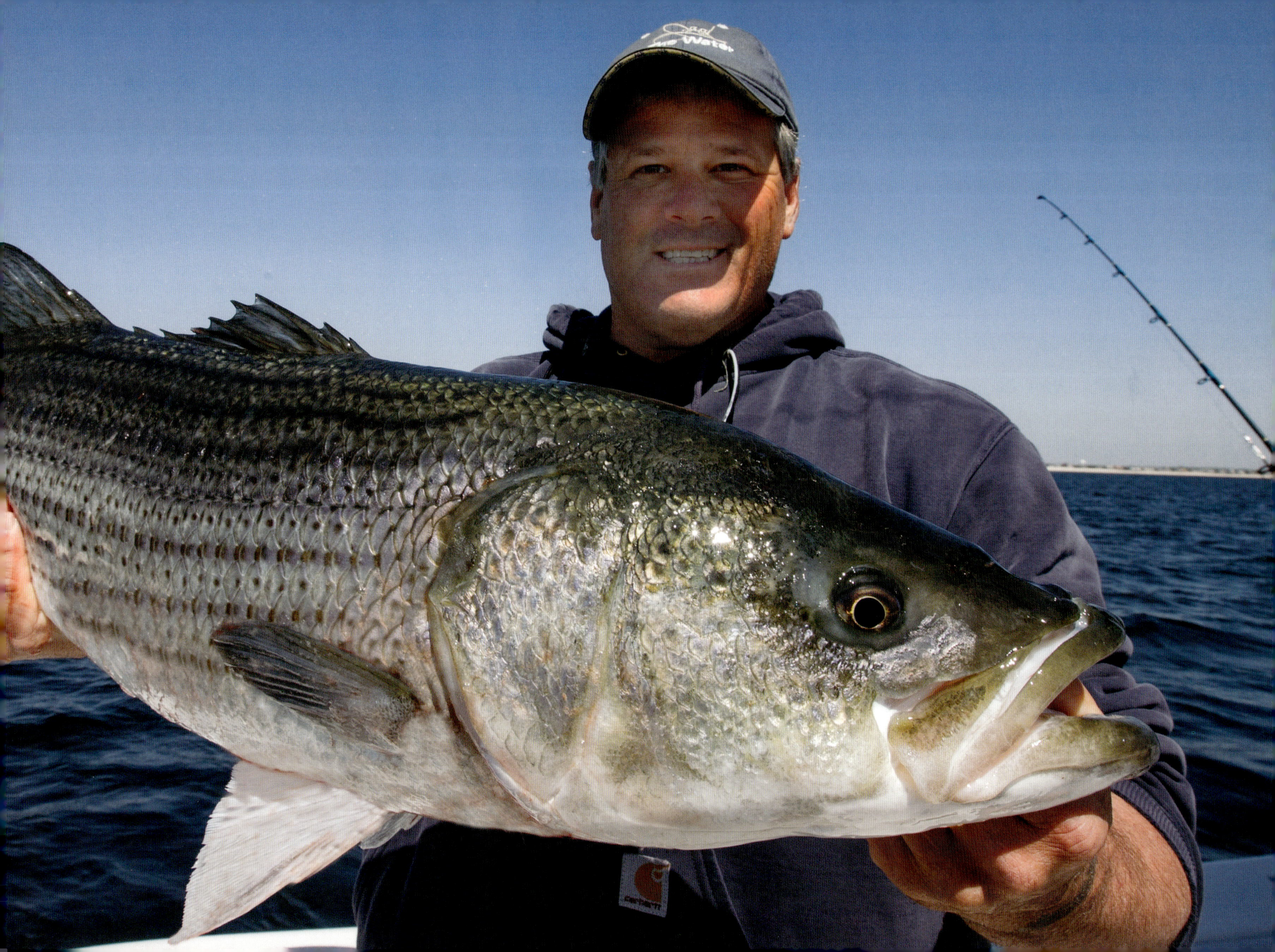

that they tell me how he won't stop bragging about all the fish he caught with his son. It's another reminder that, in fishing as in life, things aren't always as they appear on the surface.

IT IS MORNING ON CUTTYHUNK, and my youngest daughter, who is four and as observant as a fish hawk, chatters incessantly.

"Which is taller," she asks, "the house or the sky?"

"The sky," I answer.

"Which is bigger, the ocean or the sky?"

I think for a moment. "The oceans are larger than the land, but the sky is bigger than the oceans."

"Does the sky come down to meet the ocean?" she asks.

"Well, the sky comes down to meet the ocean and the ocean comes up to meet the sky," I say. "They meet together."

She seems satisfied.

"And then they turn blue," she notes.

The fish are always a part of the story, but they are not necessarily what you remember most.

IT IS A DAY PAST THE FULL MOON in August and far too pretty a night to sleep, even if fishing during the dog days can be tough. I am spending the weekend at my friends' beach cottage in Charlestown, Rhode Island. After dinner and a couple of beers, I begin to nod off. A phone call from my wife, who is in California, wakes me at 11:20 p.m. By the time we hang up, I am wide awake.

For the weekend, I've brought a fly rod, a nine-foot surf stick, and a light eight-foot spinning rod. I grab the spinning outfit and some plastic baits and head out for the beach, a 10-minute walk. I'm wearing the basic uniform for easy summer striper fishing: a bathing suit, T-shirt, and water sandals.

The moon suspended over Block Island Sound casts silver highlights on the water, rocks, and sand. I smell the beach fires before I see them. The summer constable must have the night off. I work the inner reaches of a reef that often holds fish, but tonight it feels deserted. A dozen casts go untouched. The swell has a surprising amount of snap—these waves did not result from this afternoon's prevailing southwesterlies, but instead were forged by something farther offshore. I take it as a good sign. I move about 100 yards to the west, where another set of rocks proves to be teeming with school bass. It's not a place where you typically find bass, but you never know until you make a few casts. I get whacked on my first one. I'm casting six-inch Slug-Gos, and small bass up to about 26 inches smack them as if it's the first meal they've had in days.

The beach fires blaze, the summer kids laugh, and I stand unnoticed between two large boulders, taking one fish after another. Enough clouds sail past to give the moon a dozen faces and to paint a mackerel sky. I stare dumbly at the heavens, moonstruck and content. The tide drains and drains, but the fish never stop as moonlight rains down. Summer perfection.

I leave at 2:20 a.m. with the fire still roaring and the kids dancing in a big circle. I strip in my friend's yard, hose the sand off everything, and sleep on a mattress on the floor beside a marmalade cat.

Tomorrow's dream. Photo by Todd Towle.

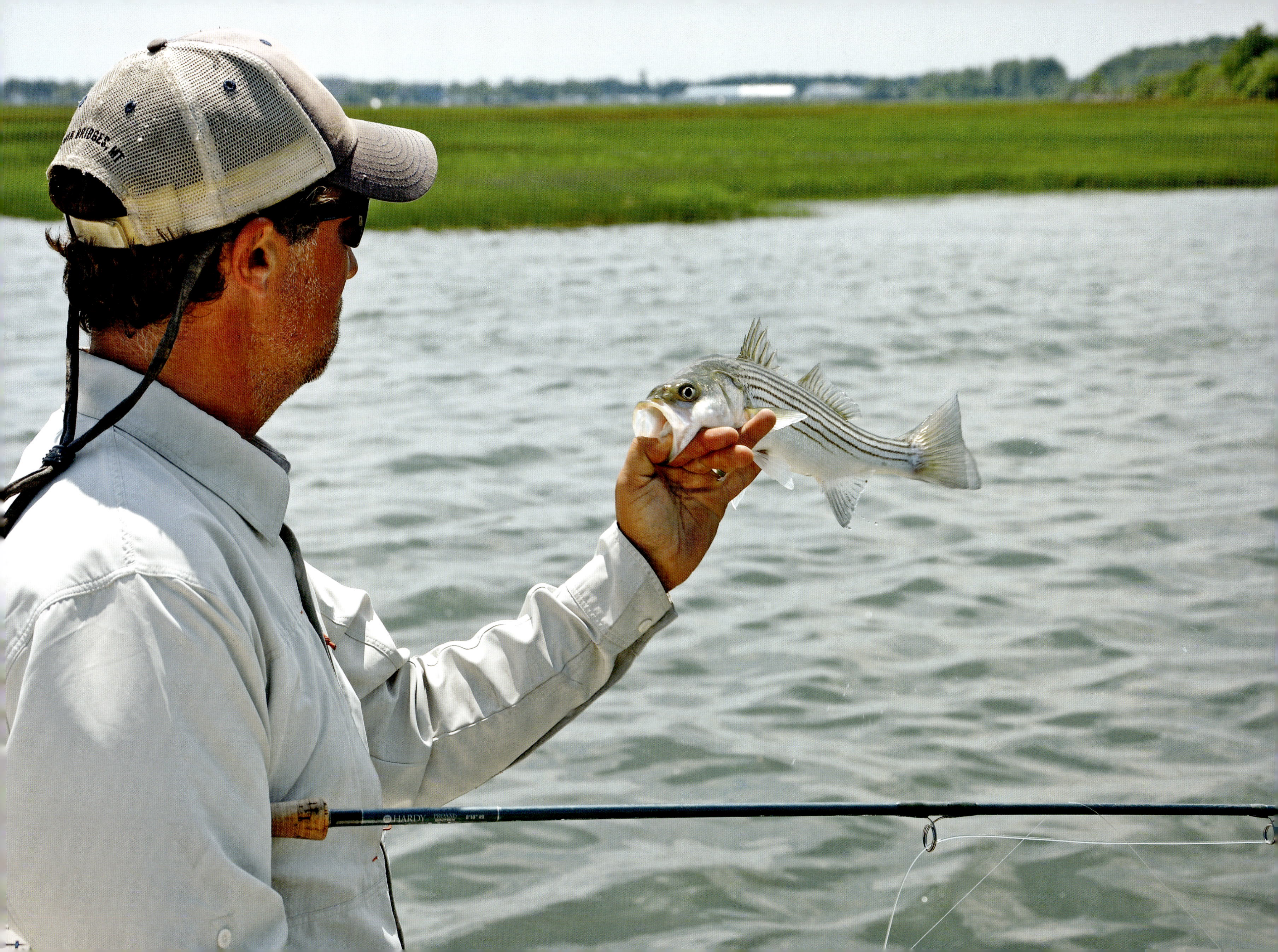
HARDY

Bass and Boats

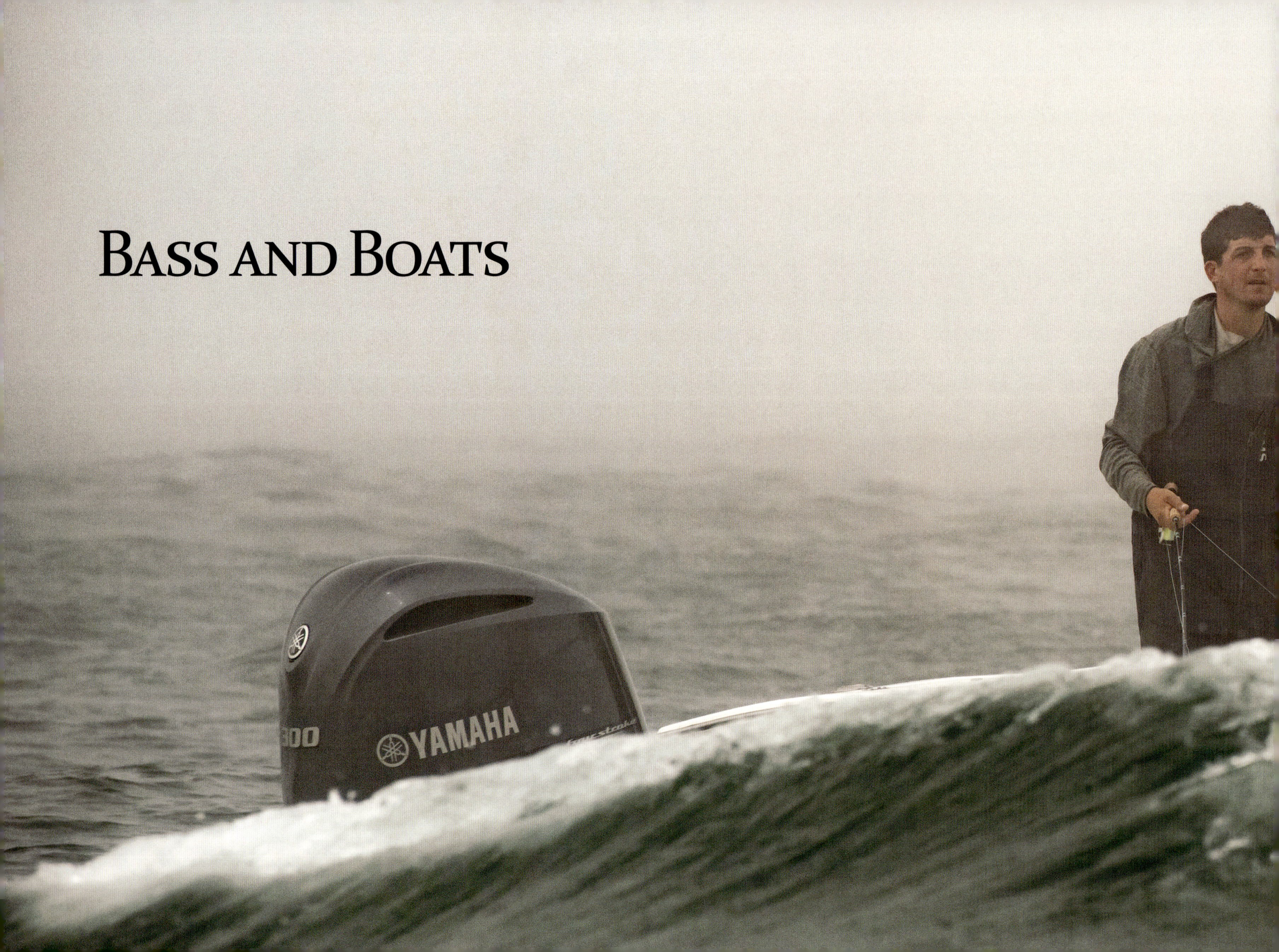

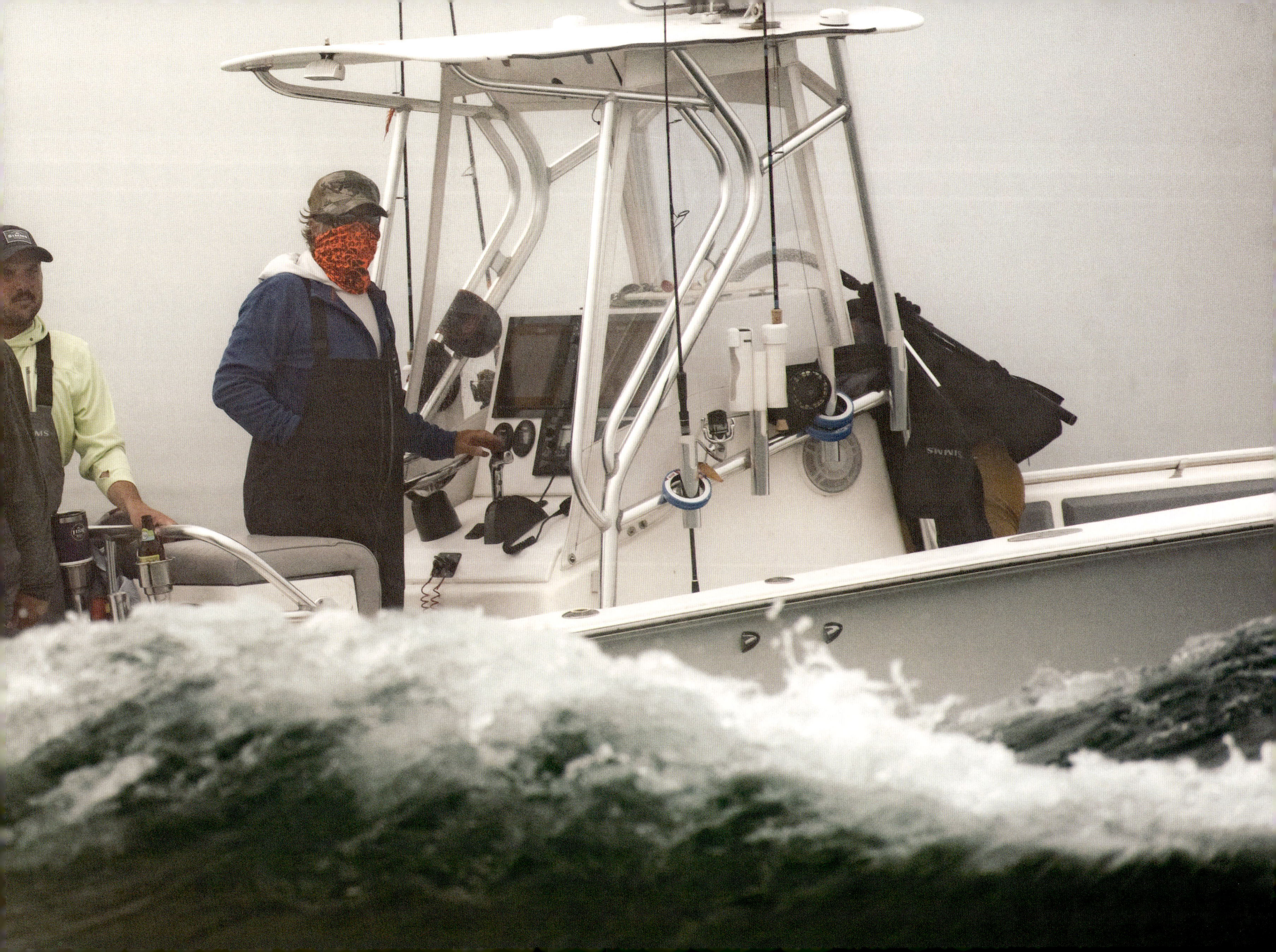
SIMMS

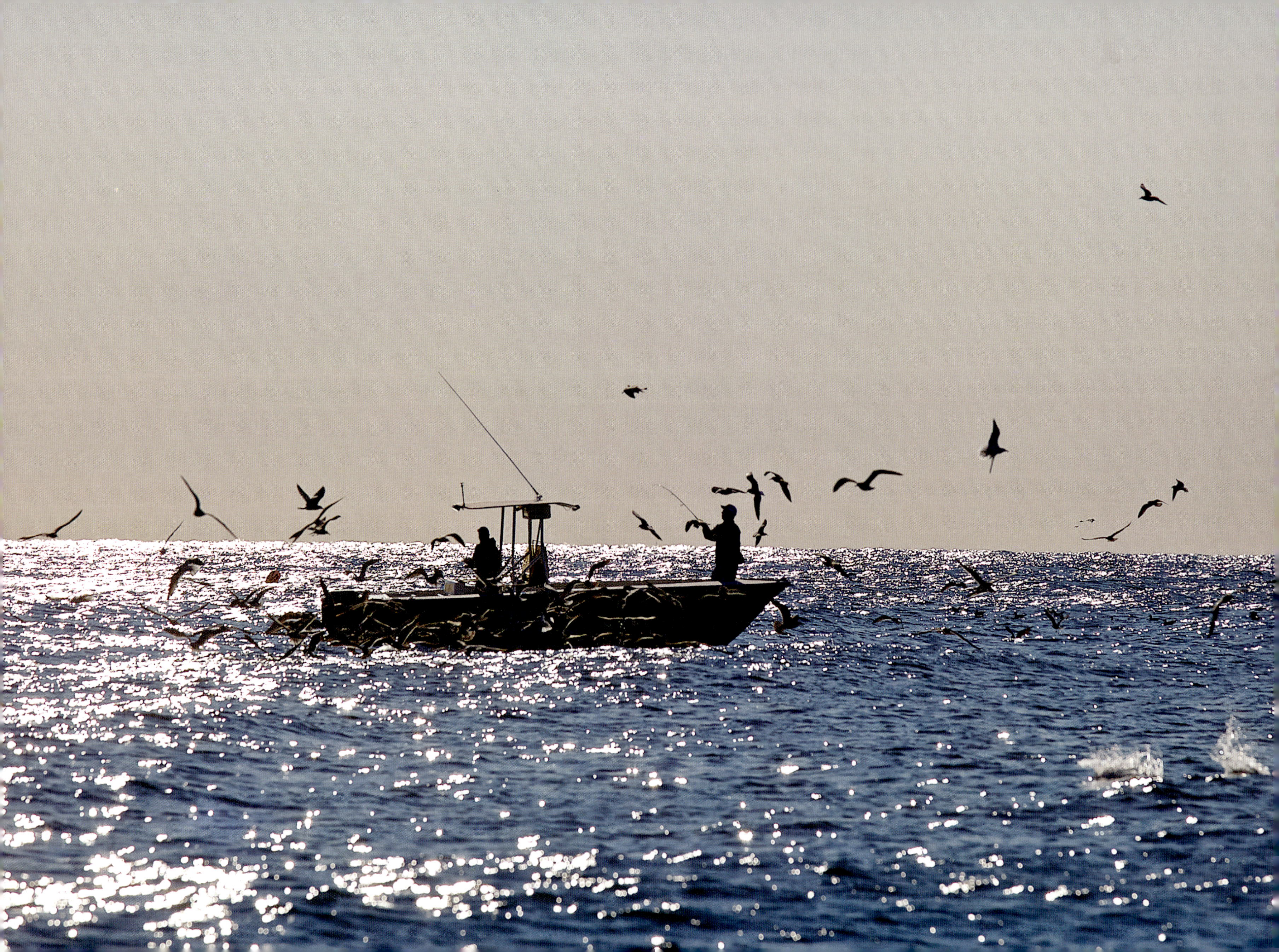

Fred the lobsterman is standing aft in his wooden skiff, one hand holding the extended tiller, the other on his hip. Dressed in torn khaki pants, a short-sleeve shirt, and knee-high rubber boots, he pulls the pipe from his teeth and points to a distant buoy. He is lean and tanned, and his arms are muscular from hand-hauling lobster traps on the shallow reefs off Watch Hill, Rhode Island.

"Hold on now," Fred said as we begin to swing east, moving over a reef. "Hold tight. It's going to get bouncy."

His 18-foot lobster skiff is rough, worn, and powered by a smoky old Evinrude of maybe 50 horsepower. I am sitting on the forward bench seat, just a kid. This is my first-ever run onto the series of reefs. The water seems alive with small, standing waves, which buffet the flat-bottom skiff, shoving it around. I'm startled but not frightened. I lift myself off the seat with my hands to soften the pounding on my tailbone as Fred steers toward one of his buoys.

Gazing shoreward at the Watch Hill Lighthouse, I easily pick out the rocks I stand on to cast seaward for stripers. For the first time, I am seeing the scene from the sea—the granite light tower, the white buildings with their red hip roofs, the carpets of white water draining off the rocks as the surf rolls over them. So mesmerizing is this turned-around perspective that even 50 years later it feels like last week.

The tide is almost slack as Fred approaches one of his buoys, snares the line with a boat hook, and begins hauling hand over hand. I sit there, all eyes, soaking it in.

Previous spread: Working a rip. Photo by Rex Messing.
Left: Busting bass and birds. Photo by Pat Ford.
Right: Revived and released. Photo by Rex Messing.

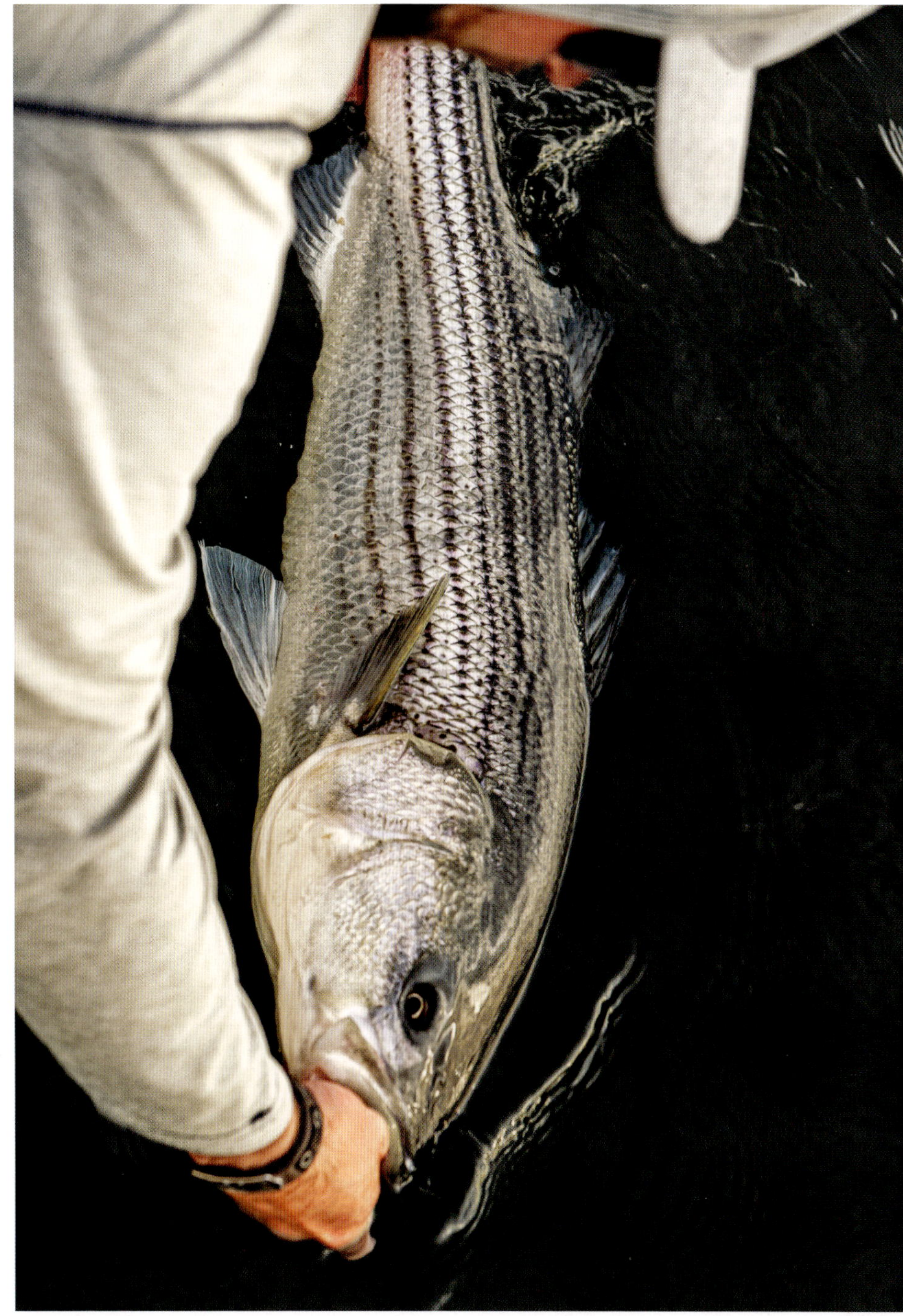

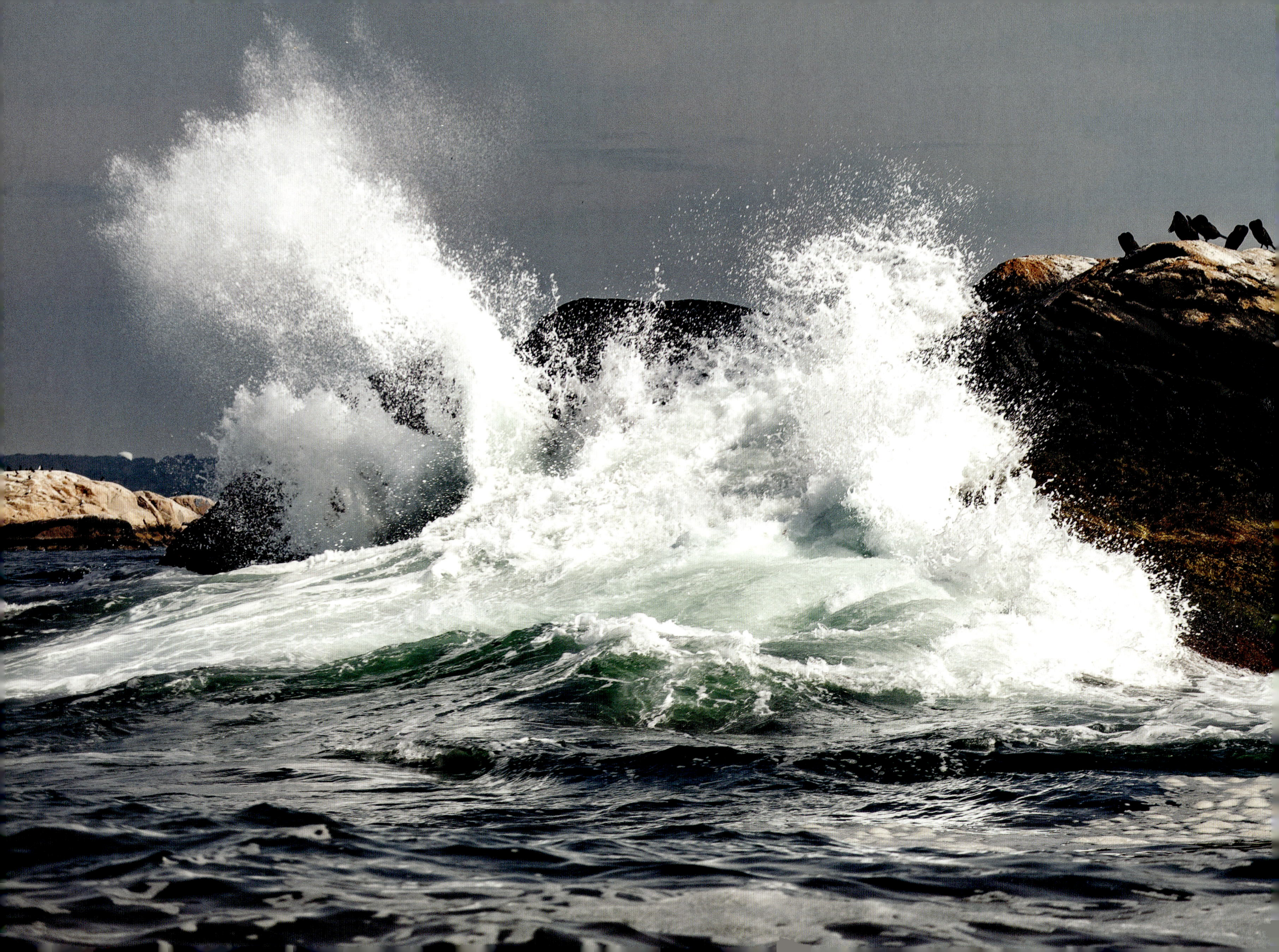

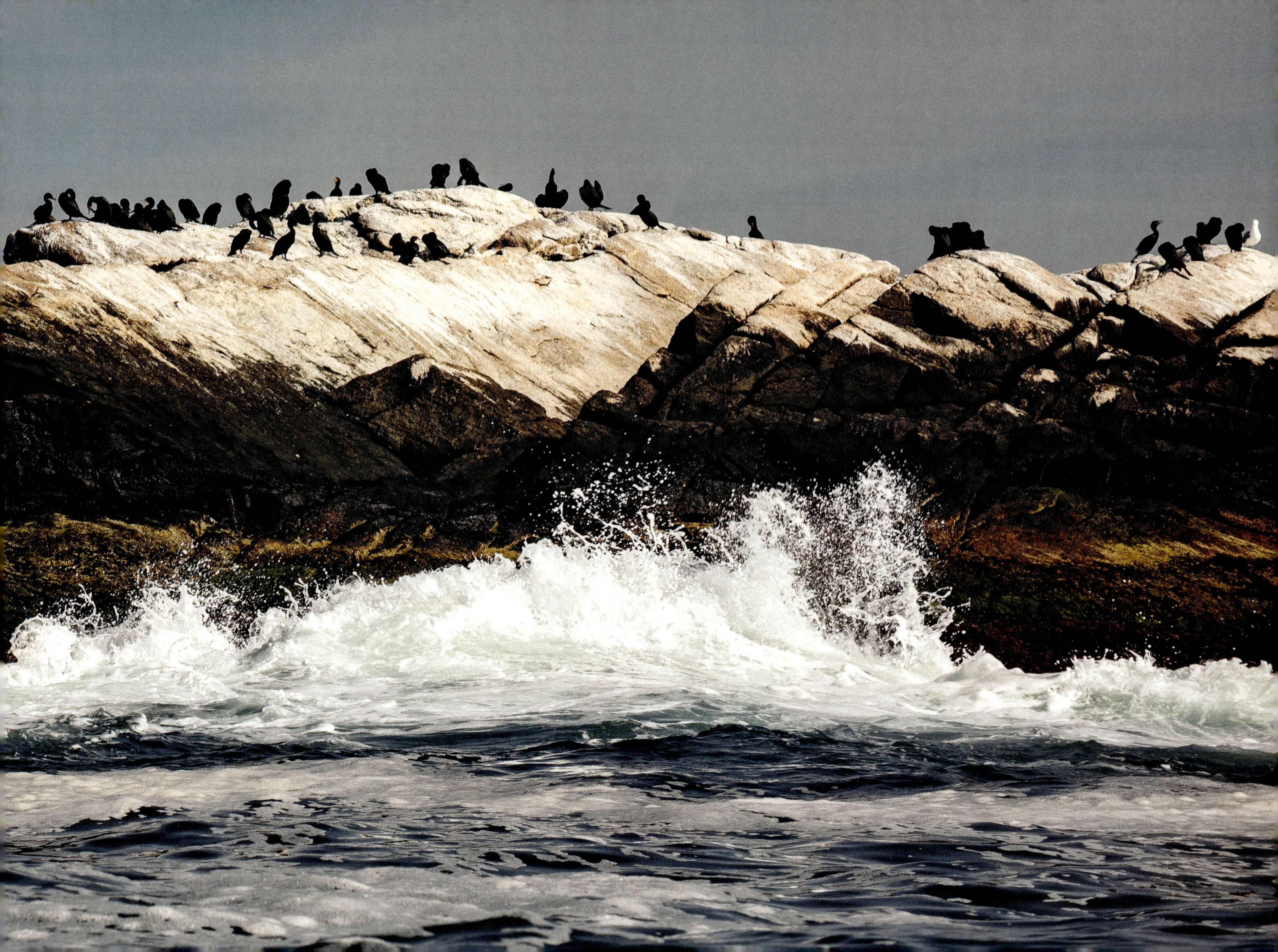

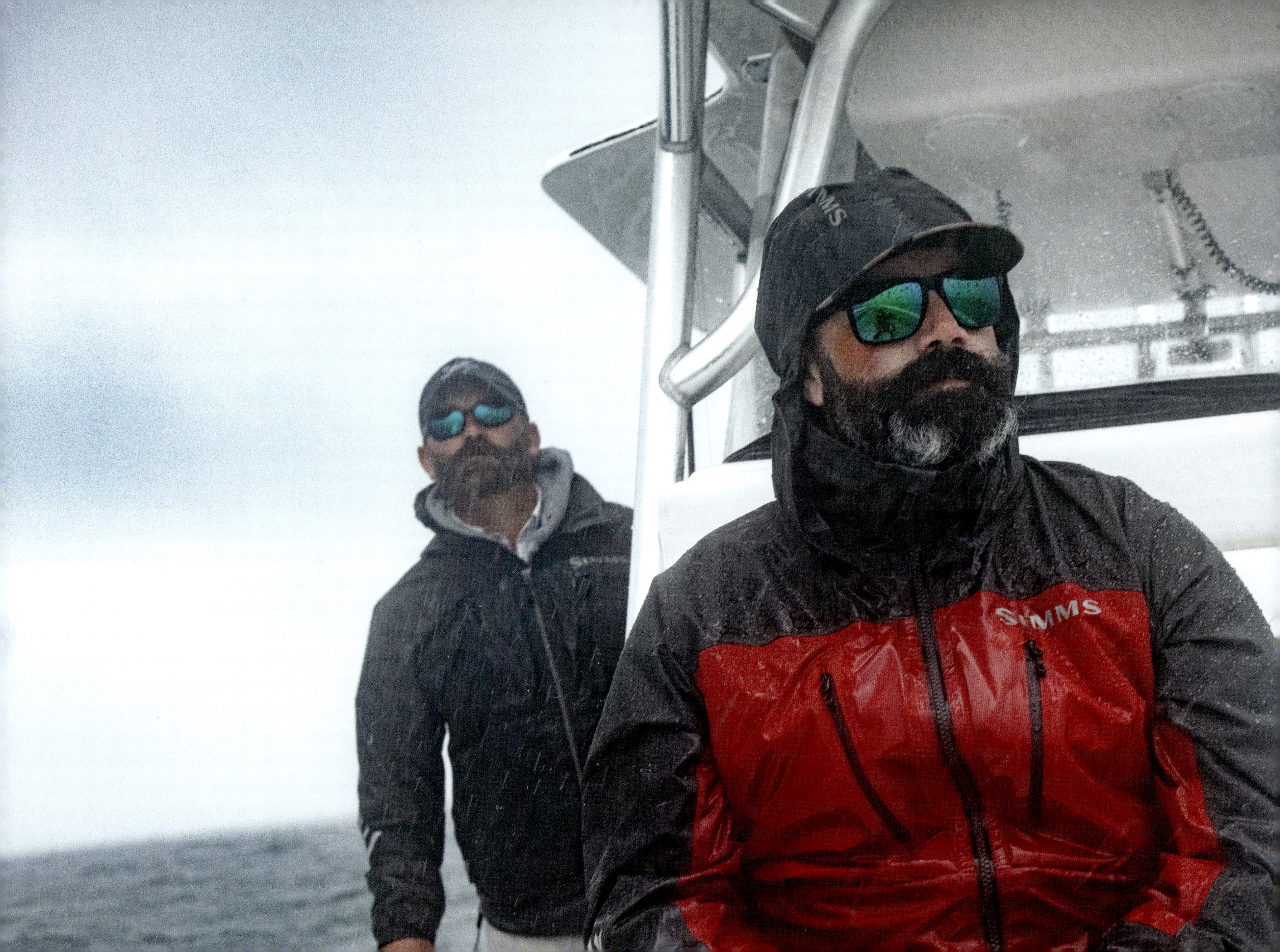
SIMMS

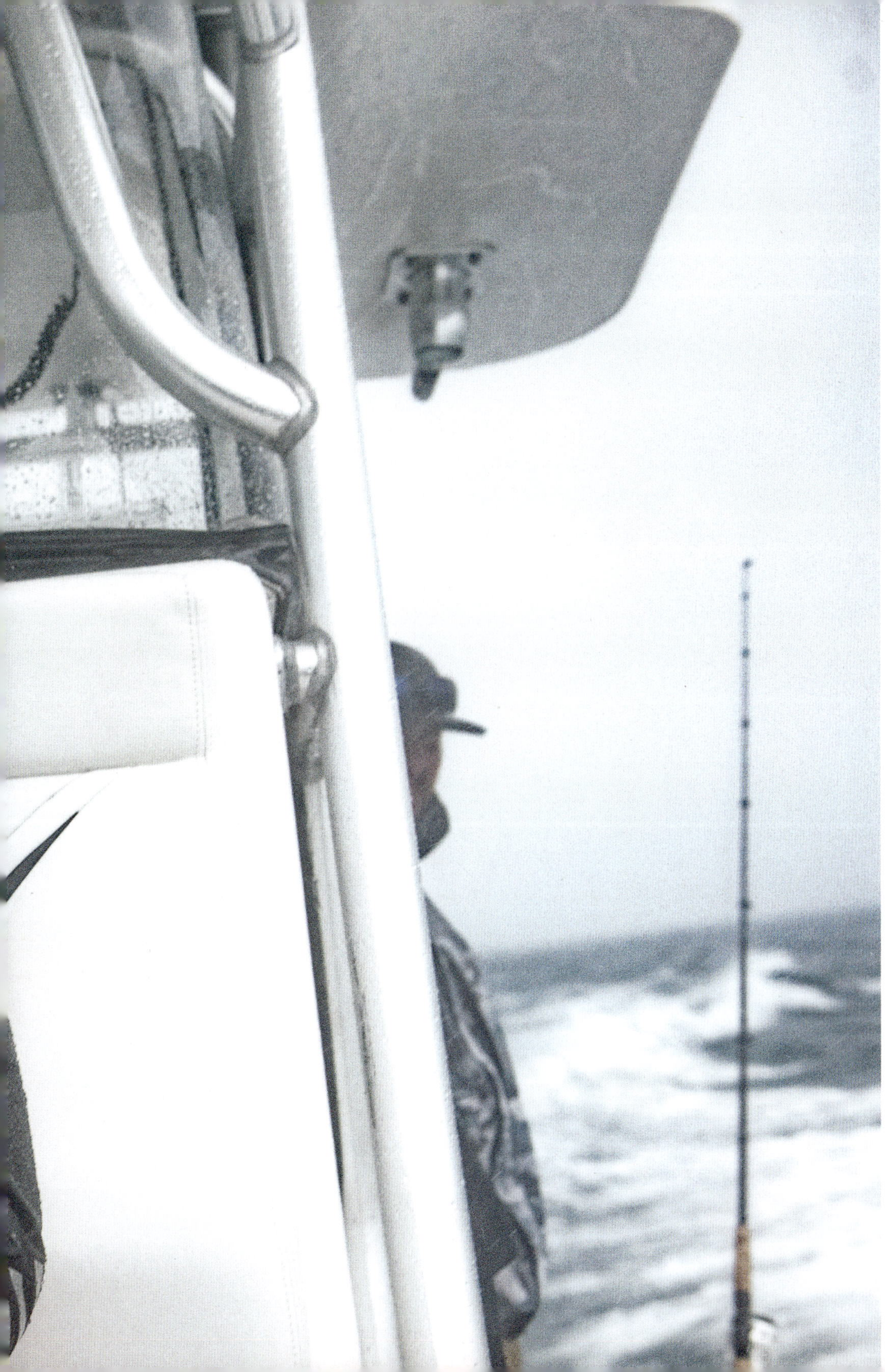

TO THIS ADOLESCENT, Fred Buckley was as large as the sun. He was as tough and tenacious as the herring gulls trailing his skiff. (His wife was my godmother, Aunt Loretta, and he was always Uncle Fred to me. My parents were such close friends with them that our two families for a time shared a house.) I was one of a small group of gangly, feral boys who spent hours at the Watch Hill Lighthouse, where Fred's father was once the assistant keeper. We fished, scoured the low-tide rocks for lost plugs, and terrified both fish and one another with our hand-sharpened spears. For several summers, I practically lived in the cove where Fred kept his skiff, and often watched him come and go from the reefs.

Those seasons forever shaped my perception of watermen, striped bass, and boats. They left me with a lifelong appreciation for the beauty, the utility, and, in the right hands, the seaworthiness of small craft, especially those derived from workboats. It was early exposure to form following function, and it served me well later in life when my growing obsession with stripers beckoned me into my own boats.

FOR STRIPED BASS FISHING, there is no single "right" boat. You can catch them from aluminum boats, kayaks, and skiffs; from both small outboard center consoles and large ones; from pulling boats or 55-foot convertibles. The type of boat is rarely the deciding factor in whether you catch fish or not. The boat gets you out and back, but it is on you to figure out the fish.

I like simple, open boats, especially those with workboat roots. Dependability and reliability rank high on my list of necessary traits. It's a practical perspective, again informed by my years of watching Fred and others like him. Watermen like Fred typically can't afford to be

Previous spread: A cormorant island. Photo by Rex Messing.
Left: Striper weather. Photo by Rex Messing.

sentimental about their boats; they treat them as tools. Indeed, boats are primarily transportation. But if you are fortunate, you fall in love, and they become part of the family.

On the water, functionality is its own form of luxury, more important than padded bolsters, dive doors, top-end speed, passenger capacity, and other specs. Boats, like people, are more than the sum of their parts. I try to view them holistically, understanding their strengths and weaknesses, and asking them only to do that for which they were designed and built. And sometimes just a bit more.

Fred taught me by example how important it is to run small boats with the wind, swells, and current. Not to fight the conditions or bash into them head-on, but rather to blend and bend. You work the angles so you don't hurt the boat or beat up the passengers. I am imprinted with the graceful movement of the eelgrass meadows waving in the current and swells just beyond Fred's boat ramp. The eelgrass modeled everything you need to know about bending to conditions.

I've fished thousands of hours over several decades from a fleet of small outboard boats. They've included center consoles, walkarounds, a power cat, and Down East skiffs, all less than 25 feet long. They were solid, dependable, well-maintained boats that have allowed my partners and me to fish hard season after season. We caught plenty of fish and always made it home, often after midnight.

My fishing partners and I leave an ever-shifting wake separating calculated risks from recklessness. Our ability to spot the line fades as the fish grow larger and the season grows older. We are wise enough to factor that fade into our decisions, but it's often not black and white. Is the risk worth the reward? Some nights we charge into the rips or make long, foolish runs in too much weather. Chastened, we later retreat and mutter about finding a bigger boat. We have to know how much our boats can handle. I have pushed myself into increasingly challenging conditions in daylight—more wind, bigger seas—just to see how well my boats perform. All boats have a little "something" you need to know about them, and this you learn only by logging many hours in varied conditions.

Years ago, someone revealed to me the formula for a long and happy boating life: buy the smallest boat that will get the job done, not the largest one you can afford. The right boat could be a 20-footer or a 60-footer, depending on where you fish, what you fish for, and how far you run. A corollary to this credo comes from a technical expert I know who works on the most complicated boat systems imaginable. He said the best way to ensure the most time on the water is to buy the simplest boat possible: "That's how you keep the sun on your back and the wind in your face."

Bruce Freeman, my fishing partner for a decade, and I fished with hunger and intensity. Neither of us had much money. We ran small, simple boats on lean budgets. I was a reporter raising kids and living paycheck to paycheck, and he was a boatwright who worked in a yard a stone's throw from my office. Forged of frugal Swamp Yankee stock, I was raised to see the virtue of moderation in all things, including boats. Modest power, modest cost, modest speed.

The two of us were often undergunned in our 17- and 18-footers, but we were both comfortable on the water—I grew up snorkeling and surfing, and Bruce led sea kayaking trips in Alaska in the 1970s. Good at reading the water and the weather, we also learned to recognize which spots to avoid on certain winds and tides, and we memorized or marked the locations of rocks, sandbars, unlit markers, and other obstructions to fishing at night.

MY FIRST BOAT WAS AN 18-FOOT Tashmoo lobster skiff built on Martha's Vineyard. She was simple and sea-kindly, with a strong sheer, low freeboard, ample flare, and a tumblehome

Author Bill Sisson fast to a December Chesapeake striper. Photo by Tom Lynch.

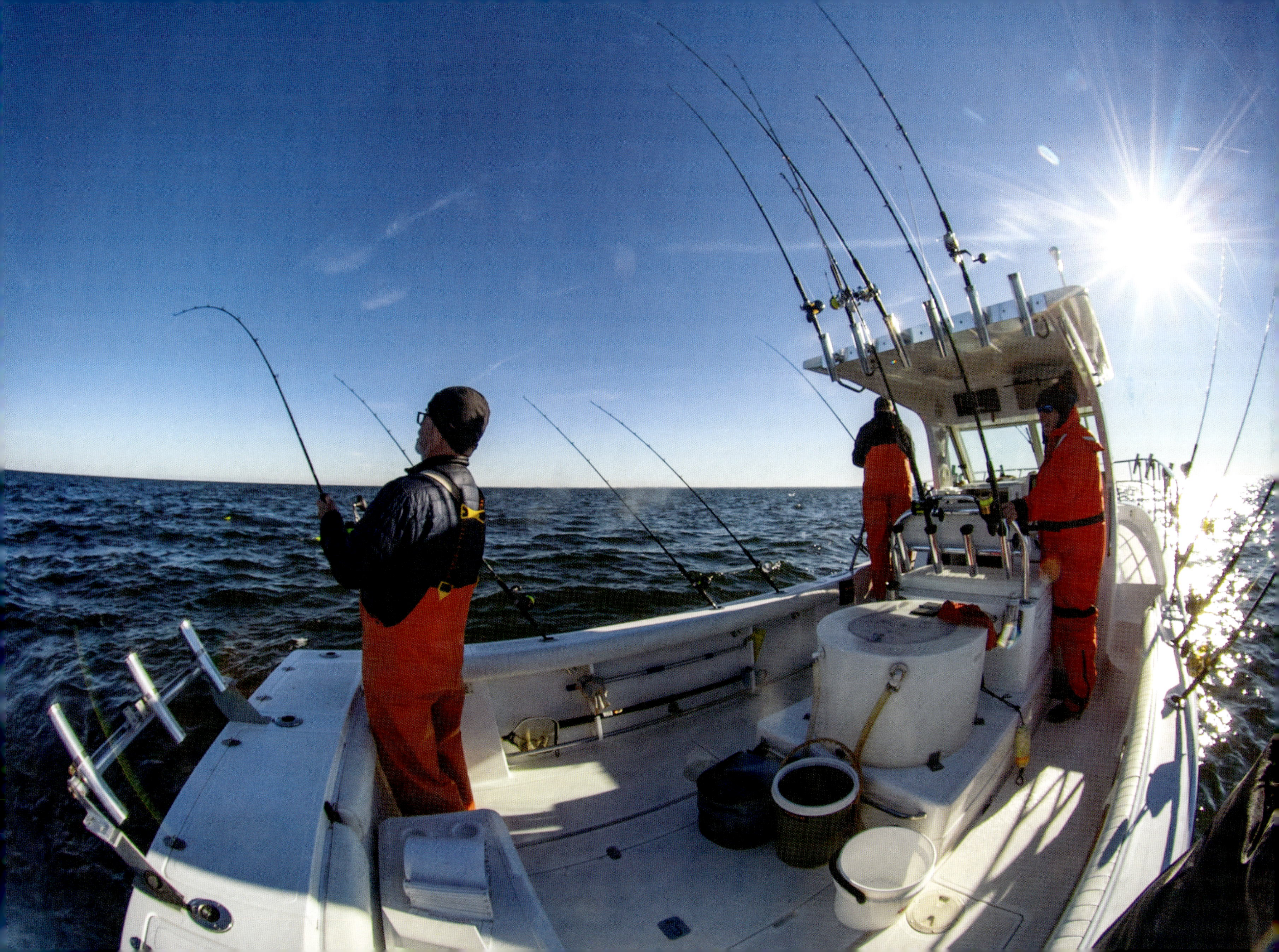

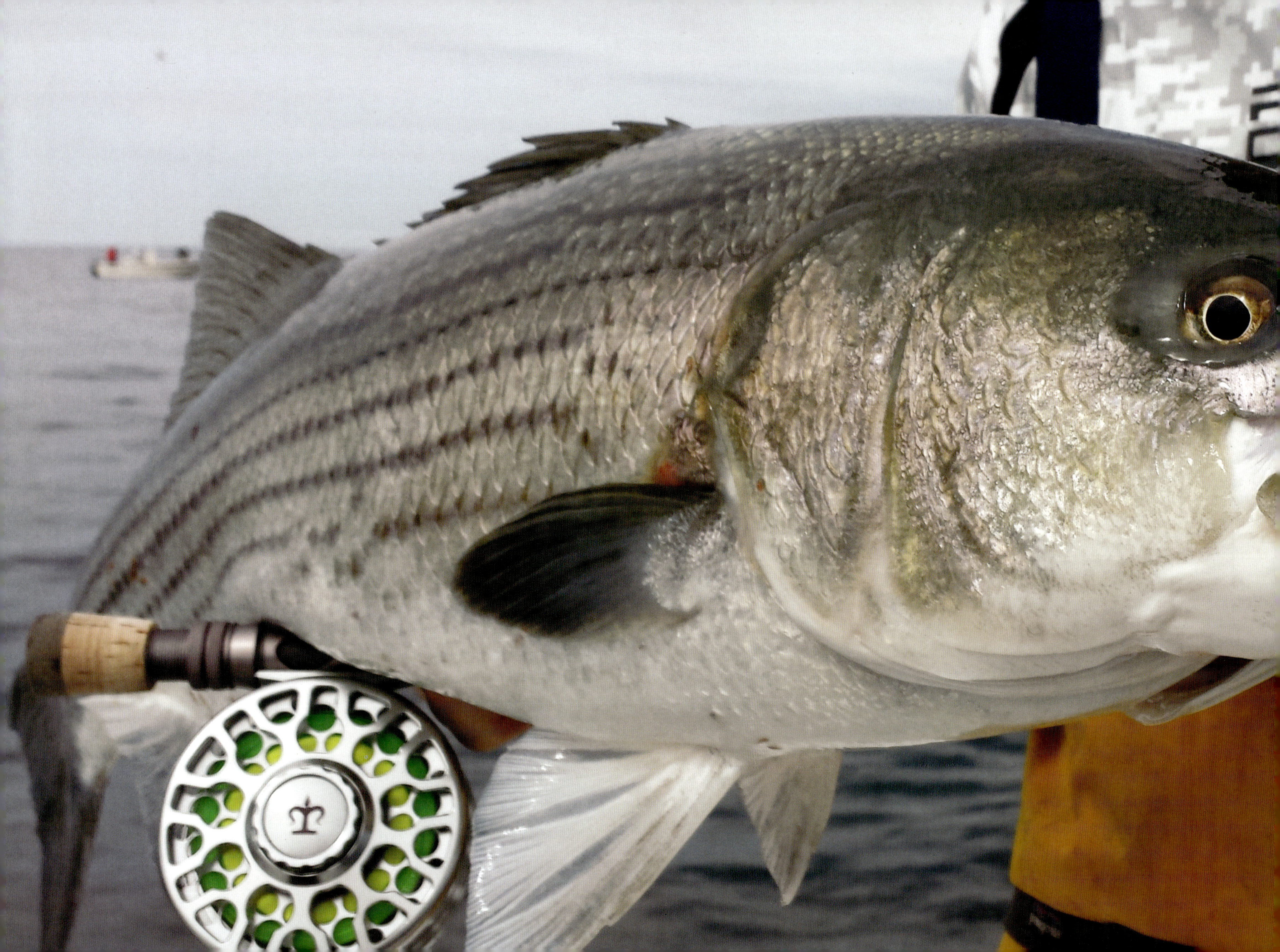

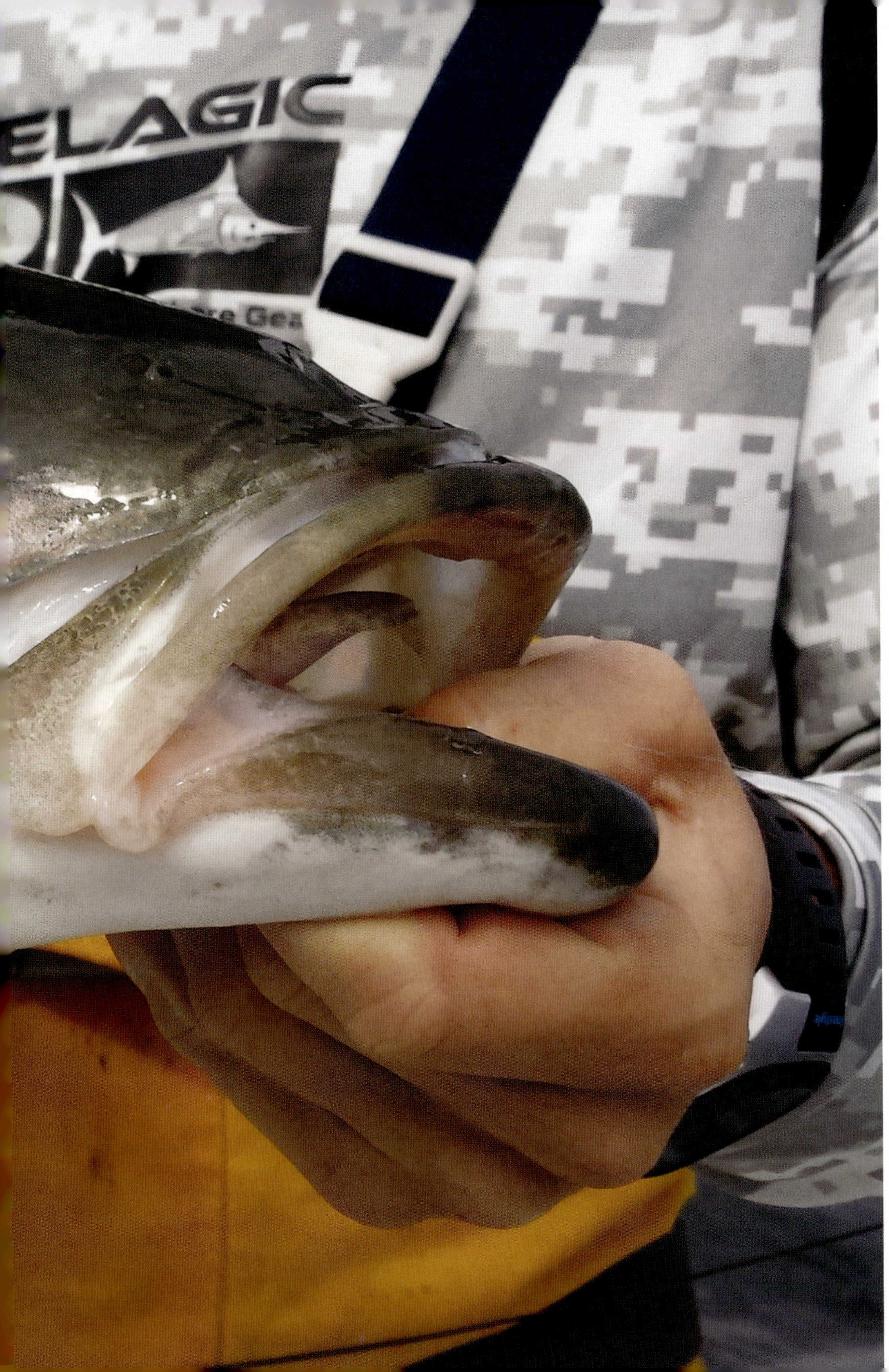

transom. Wet but sure-footed, she carried me through the fall rips when larger boats with more power retreated for quieter waters. The builder, Dan West, called her a "seagoing miniature." She was that and more, possessing that bit of magic you always seek in a boat.

The skiff and I had an agreement. I promised to maintain her properly and not push her too hard. She held up her end of the bargain by always getting me home. Her hull was graceful and well-proportioned—built for comfort, not speed. Pull back on the throttle, and she'd bring you back to the dock in dicey conditions.

The Tashmoo's lines were clean and graceful, a direct descendent of an old wooden lobster skiff that West had found deteriorating in a Menemsha salt marsh on Martha's Vineyard. He pulled a plug off the tired workboat and began producing Tashmoos in fiberglass, turning out faithful reproductions of the original skiffs that were built near Eastport, Maine, at least a half century earlier. She was specifically designed for working inshore waters, and West kept her original pedigree undiluted instead of trying to make her be too many things for too many people. The late Norwegian sailor Erling Tambs might have called her the "embodiment of usefulness."

My skiff was a sea swallow—small, light, well-balanced, nimble, and sturdy—a pure organic shape. She was out of step with the high-horsepower creations streaming in from points outside, but she was completely at home fishing nearshore waters and the small islands of birds, silversides, and bass. She cost $4,800 new, unrigged, which even a young reporter with a new child could afford with a small loan.

It took me several years to connect the dots and see the relationship between Fred's skiffs and my first boat; I'm certain the old lobsterman was smiling from on high. Both were purpose-built with a distinctive regional design.

A fly-caught Cape Cod linesider. Photo by John Jinishian.

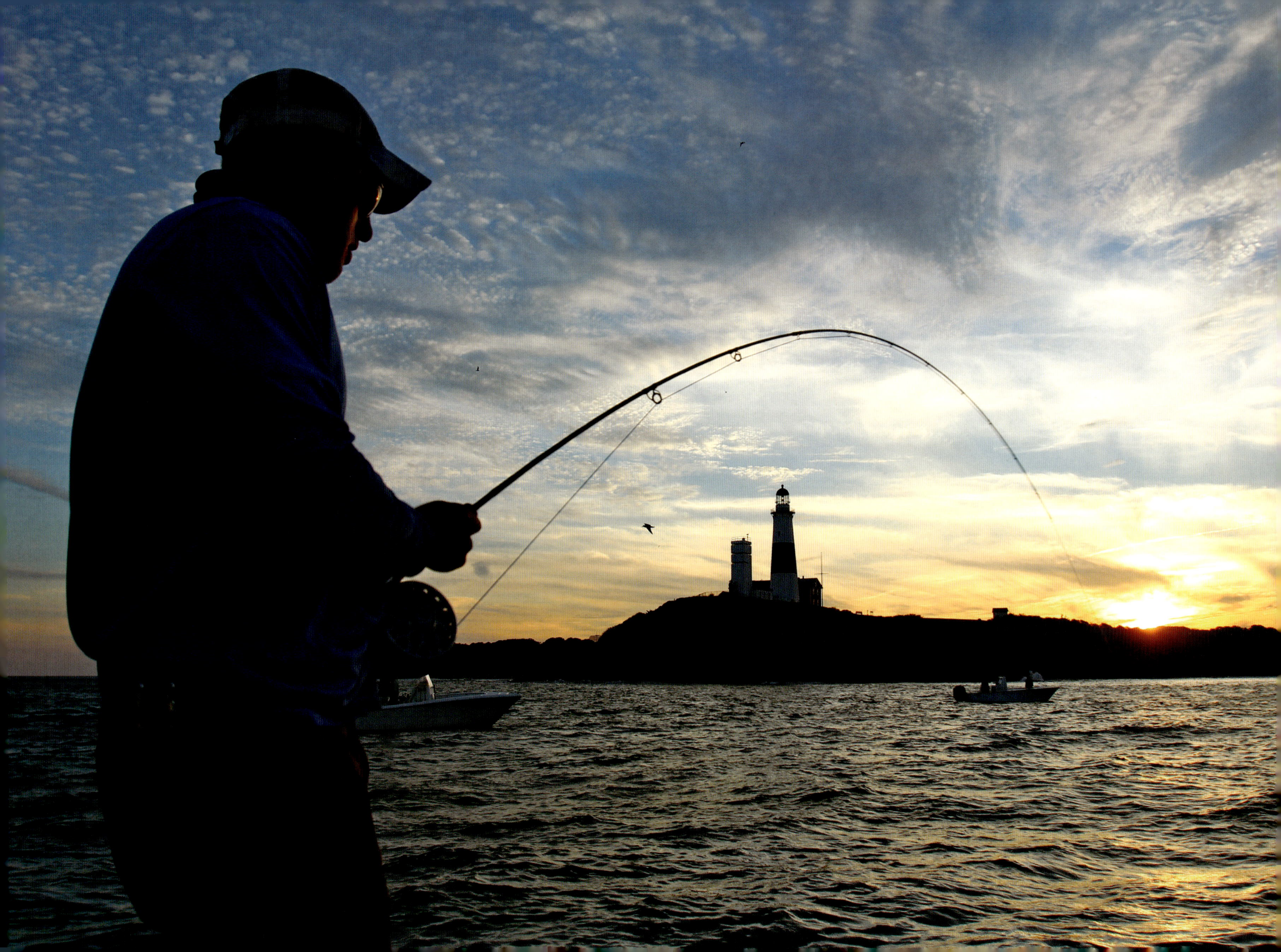

Antoine de Saint-Exupéry was a French writer, poet, and aviation pioneer. In his book *Wind, Sand and Stars,* he extolled the value of winnowing man-made contraptions down to their essences: "In anything at all, perfection is finally attained not when there is no longer anything to add, but when there is no longer anything to take away, when a body has been stripped down to its nakedness."

Saint-Exupéry, who also wrote *The Little Prince*, disappeared in 1944 during a flight over the Mediterranean while serving with a French air squadron. The author believed an aircraft built properly would be a "form flawless in its perfection, completely disengaged from its matrix, a sort of spontaneous whole, its parts mysteriously fused together and resembling in their unity a poem." I would argue that the same applies to a boat. Too many boats today lack this poetry.

Fish long and hard enough, and eventually you will be caught out in more wind and in larger seas than you'd planned for. That's an unassailable truth of striped bass fishing. What's also true is that a well-built small boat can absorb far more punishment than its skipper ever anticipated or feared. Of course, that's assuming the skipper knows the strengths and weaknesses of the craft and also makes smart decisions. Even the best small boat can be overwhelmed in steep, breaking seas or, worse, if caught inside breaking surf on a lee shore. At one time, I questioned if I was fishing hard enough simply because I hadn't sunk a boat. Silly, of course, but a reasonable concern given the way we were fishing.

FRED'S SKIFF WAS PERCHED at the top of a wooden ramp that descends about 60 feet from a seawall into a cove along the lighthouse point, which was protected from swells by a small jetty. His workboat reminded me of a scruffy herring gull—territorial and roughed up by life, but still

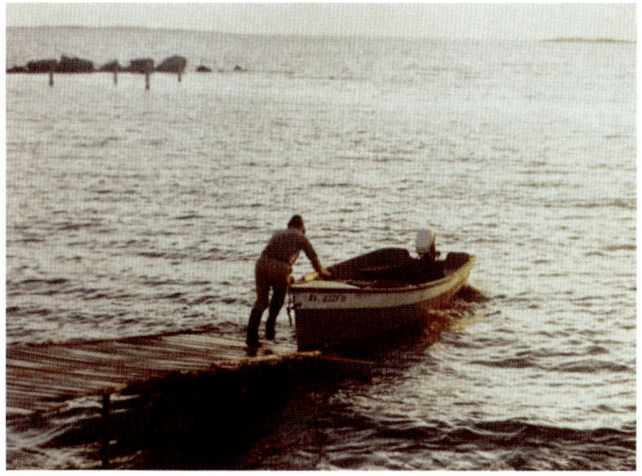

capable. Worn and low-sided, she carried totes, bait, a couple of six-gallon fuel tanks, oars, a gaff, and other tools of the inshore lobsterman's trade. These included a spinning rod and a peach basket from which Fred hung lures he plucked off his pot warps.

The lobsterman was opportunistic when it came to fishing for stripers. When they were busting all over the top, he'd stop hauling and catch them until they disappeared. It's just what you did. On Christmas and my birthday, I'd receive a neatly wrapped box from my godmother and Uncle Fred. Inside were a couple of nearly new plugs or jigs that Fred had harvested off his lines. To me, they were more valuable than anything bought from a tackle shop.

When it was time to launch the skiff, Fred would summon us kids from the water and our summer-long daydreams. We quickly assembled around the bow and along the gunwales, eager and usually dripping wet from spearfishing. After wetting the planks with buckets of seawater, we launched the nameless skiff using Norwegian steam—muscle power. On his command, we'd press all the lean, springy muscles of our backs and shoulders and legs into the task of sliding the skiff seaward.

"Come on boys," Fred would growl. "On three now." And once inertia was overcome, "Keep her moving. Keep her moving. Watch yourself."

We all knew who really made the boat move. Fred had powerful, ropey forearms and defined biceps. But we loved being part of it all: the boats, fish, lobsters, our expanding salty vernacular, and, perhaps most powerful, the sense that this was where we belonged. That we were locals, and most everyone else was an outsider. I found my people at an early age.

Left: A bent rod off Montauk. Photo by John Jinishian.
Right: Fred Buckley launches his skiff. Photo courtesy of Buckley family.

Into the Night

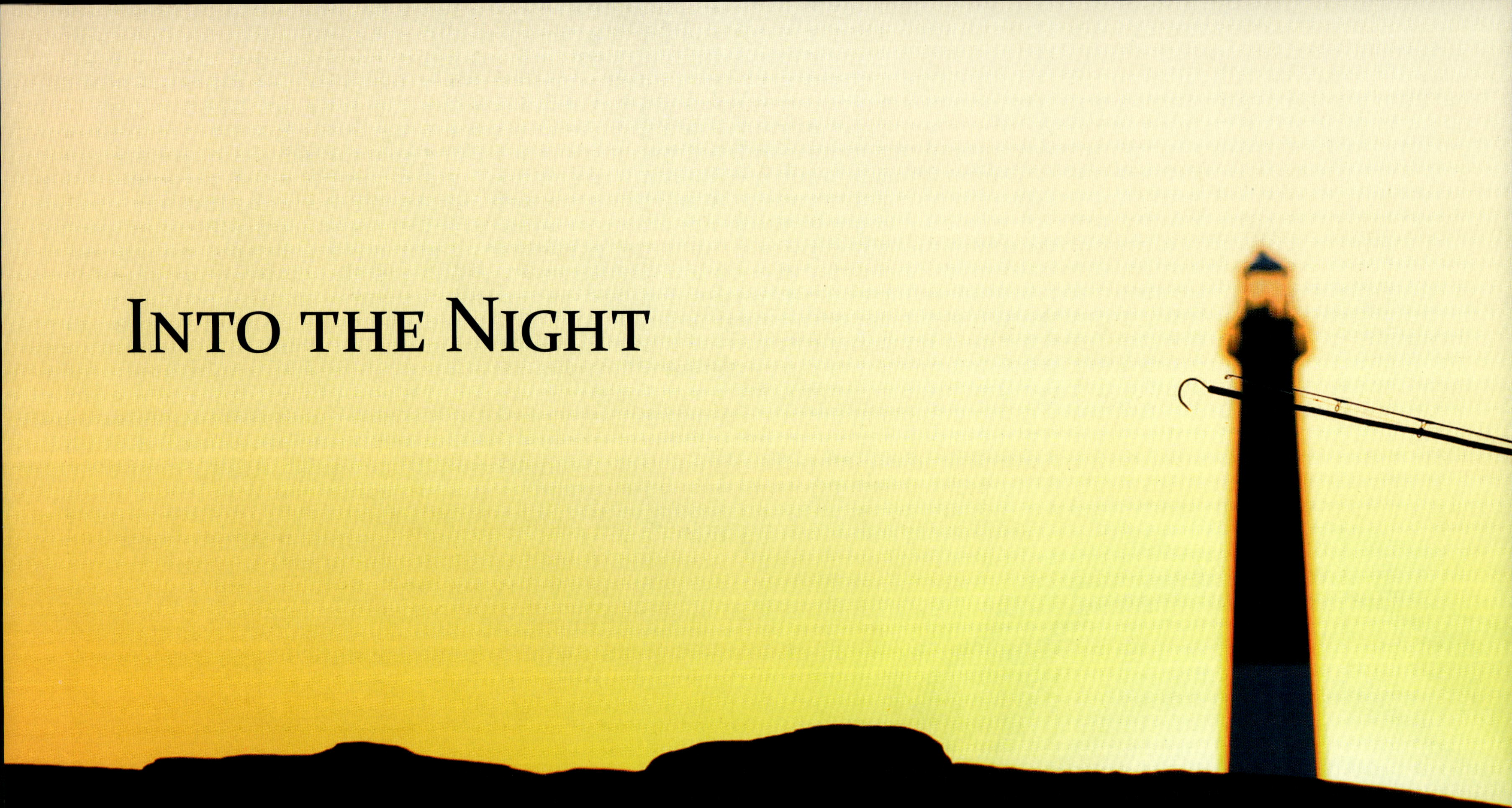

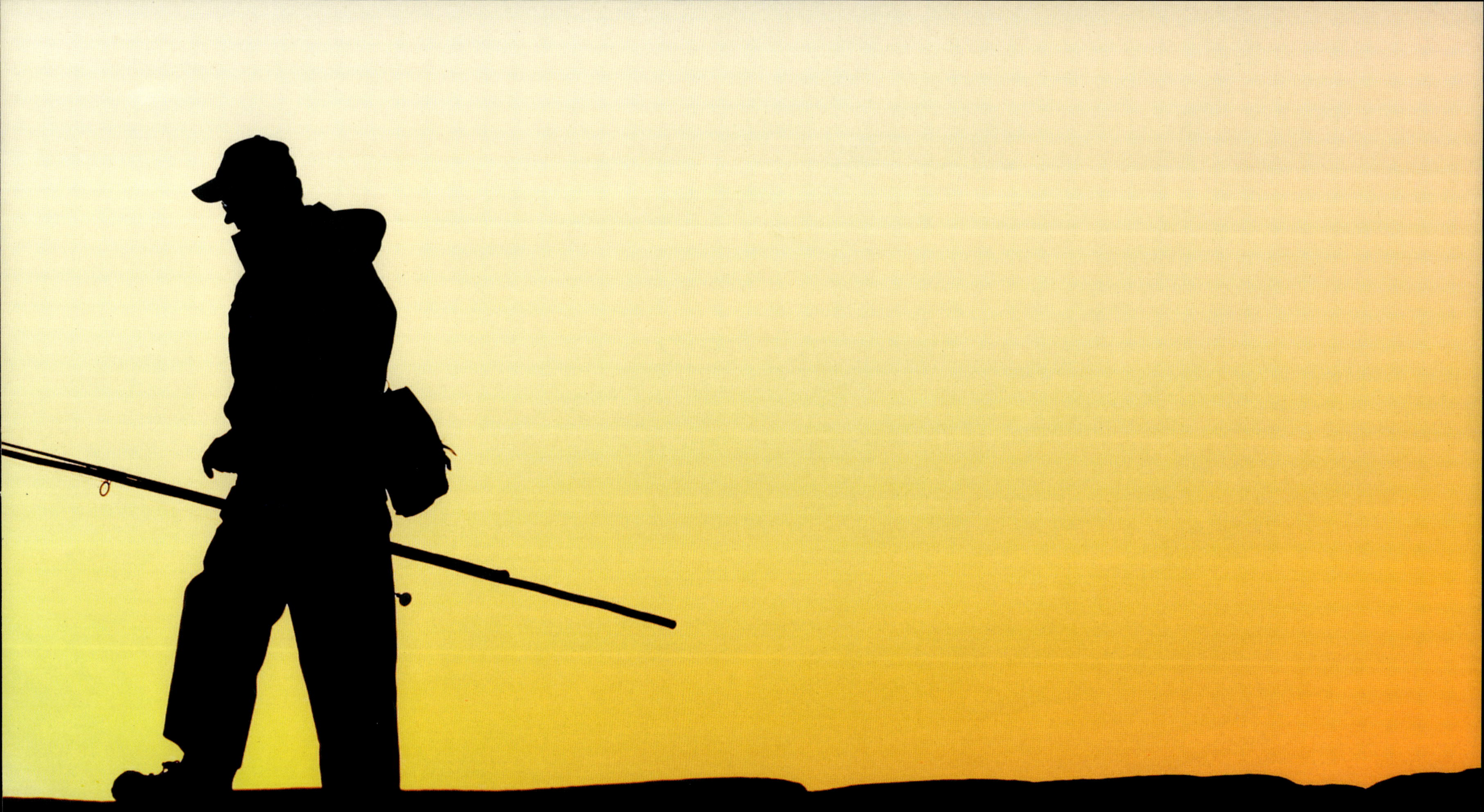

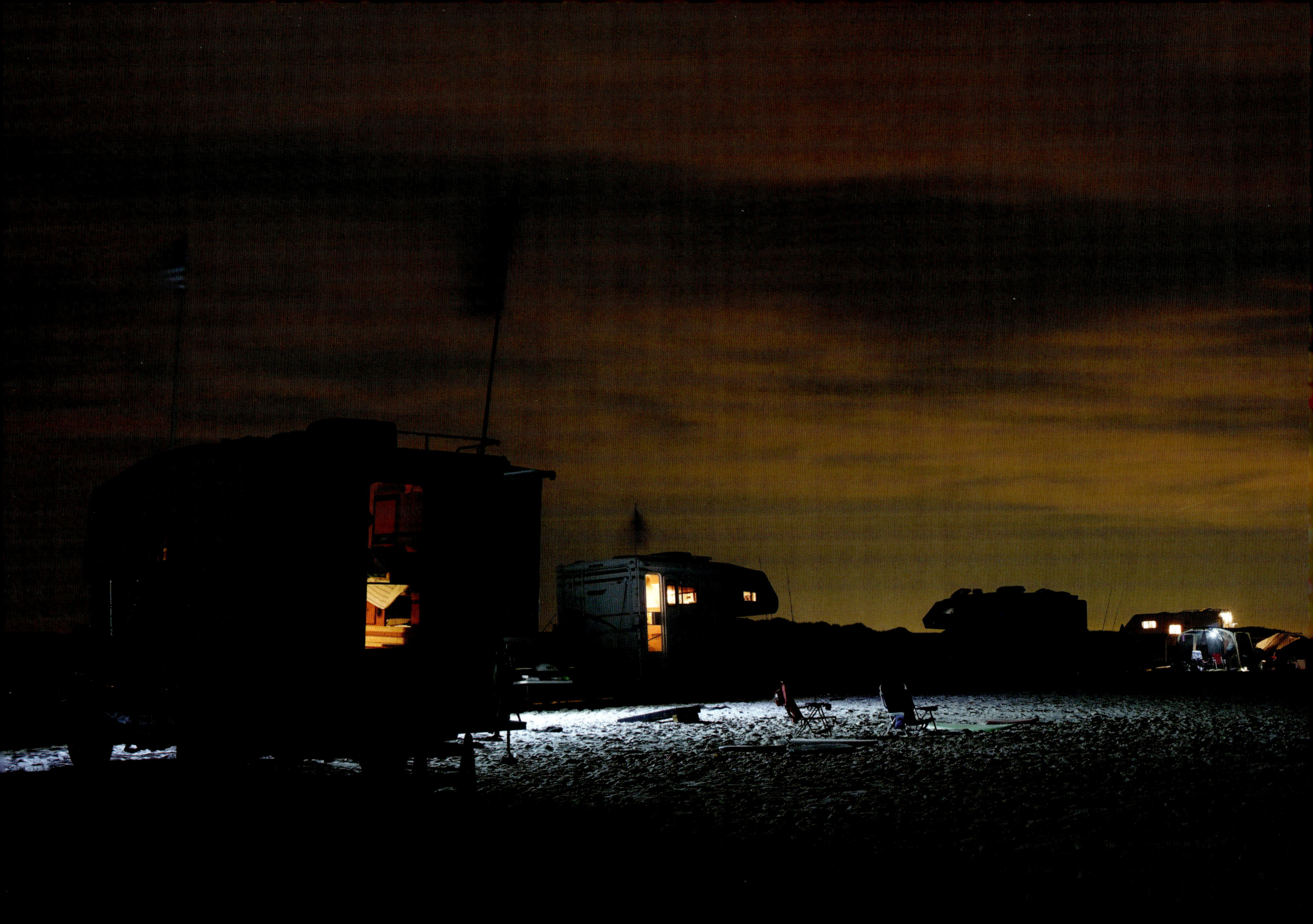

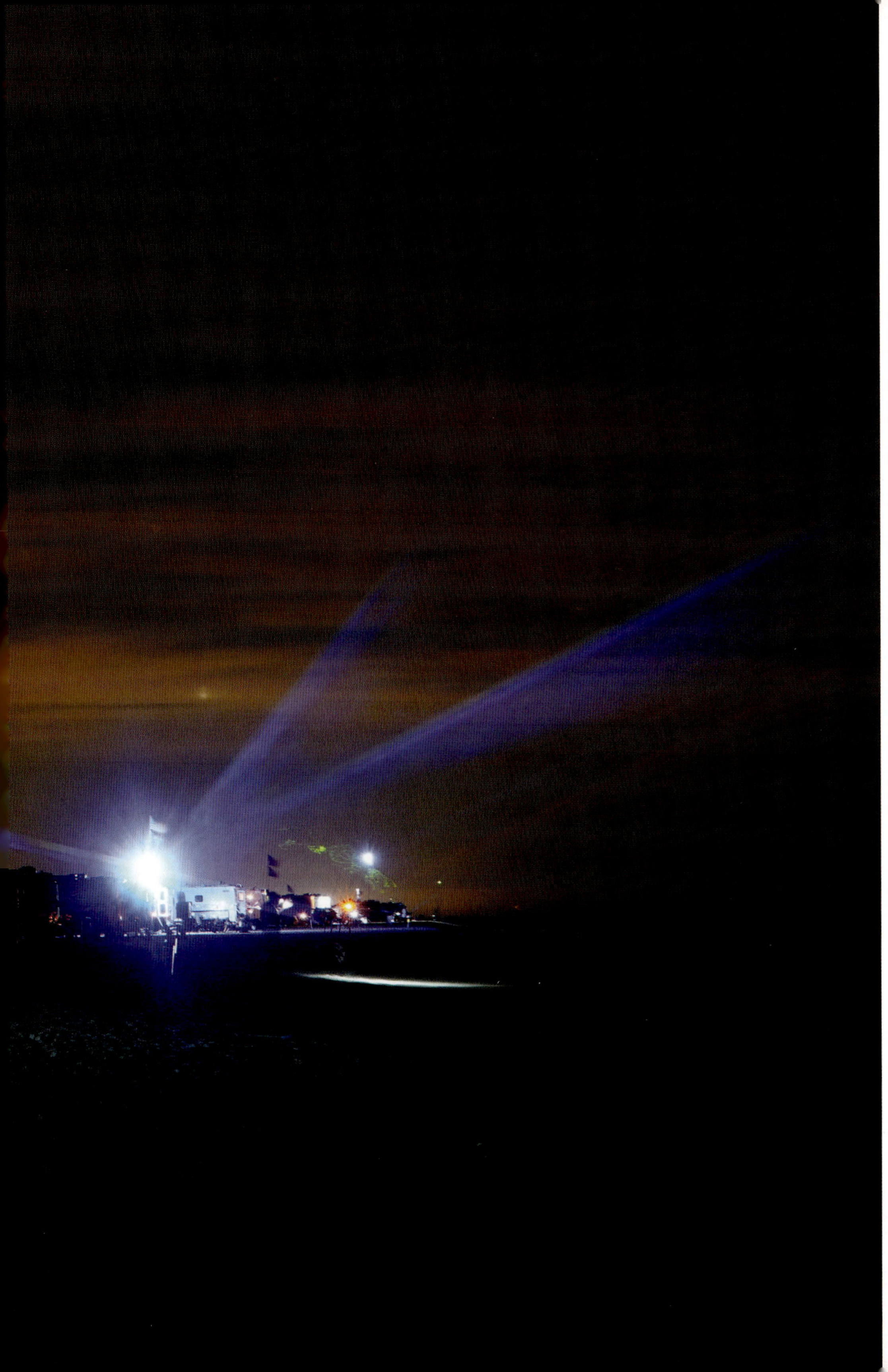

I've fished under supermoons, blood moons, new moons, lunar eclipses, and those lovely waxing or waning crescents with their horns facing left or right like an archer's bow. If you chase striped bass, you're likely familiar with all eight lunar phases and the many faces of night, including those evenings when it's blowing a gale and the rain is coming in sideways. Or the still nights in early summer when you'd give anything for a breeze to scatter the gnats and mosquitoes.

My merry band of night partners and I have fished in thunderstorms, under meteor showers, and beneath the bluffs from where summer residents in palatial island homes lit fireworks and partied like Gatsby. Meanwhile, we fished in darkened boats with our nav lights off, a clean rag covering the electronics—out of sight, out of mind, always.

NIGHT FISHING FOR STRIPED BASS is productive and beautiful. Fewer people fish after the sun sets, which means more room and fewer probing eyes, always a good thing. And a striper's proclivity for nocturnal feeding has allowed me and thousands of other like-minded souls to hold full-time jobs during the day and fish like striper bums under the cover of darkness. I've been doing it for more than 50 years.

We happily live Warren Zevon's mantra: "I'll sleep when I'm dead." I only fish regularly with people willing to go deep into the night without whining about how beat-up they are going to feel the next day. Whiners make abysmal striper partners. We burn the proverbial candle until it is a puddle of hard wax, knowing deep down that it won't last forever.

Previous spread: Heading out on the north jetty, Barnegat Inlet. Photo by Tom Lynch.
Left: The night crew. Photo by Tom Lynch.

I have a history with the night. When the fishing is good, I float through work on three to four hours of shut-eye, buoyed by the previous night's action and feeling like a lottery winner. It's one of my superpowers that I have never needed or cared for much sleep. During plenty of seasons, I log more hours fishing after the sun sets than when it is shining high in the sky.

I know my way around the boats I fish at night better than I do the darkened rooms in my house. I move fore and aft in pitching seas without falling. One hand for the boat and one hand for yourself. Dig your knees into the coaming. Watch the engine cutout. Don't trip over the eel cooler. If you cannot stand due to pitching or rolling, fight the fish on your knees. No one ever wants to go over the side, even in good conditions, but I recall a night or two when falling overboard could have been fatal.

IT WAS FROM THE SURF IN 1968 that I first fished for stripers after dark. I was 14, and Larry Maderia indoctrinated me into dunking fresh squid on the bottom on 8/0 J hooks and pyramid sinkers. Larry was five years my senior, had a car and a license, and was my first real fishing mentor. I used to accompany him on night trips to the reefs off Watch Hill, Rhode Island, where he'd anchor his 15½-foot aluminum skiff ahead of the rip. Then we'd drift big swimming plugs back in the current on lead line and let them work in the flood. When the action was slow, I'd fall asleep to the movement of the boat on the anchor line and the sound of the churning rip.

My mother had reason to worry, given the size of the boat—I wouldn't fish that reef today in a small aluminum skiff. But there is a modicum of truth to the old saying about the good Lord watching out for sailors and drunks, to which I would add striper anglers with moon tans.

Night regularly produces the biggest bass. Photo by Jerry Audet.

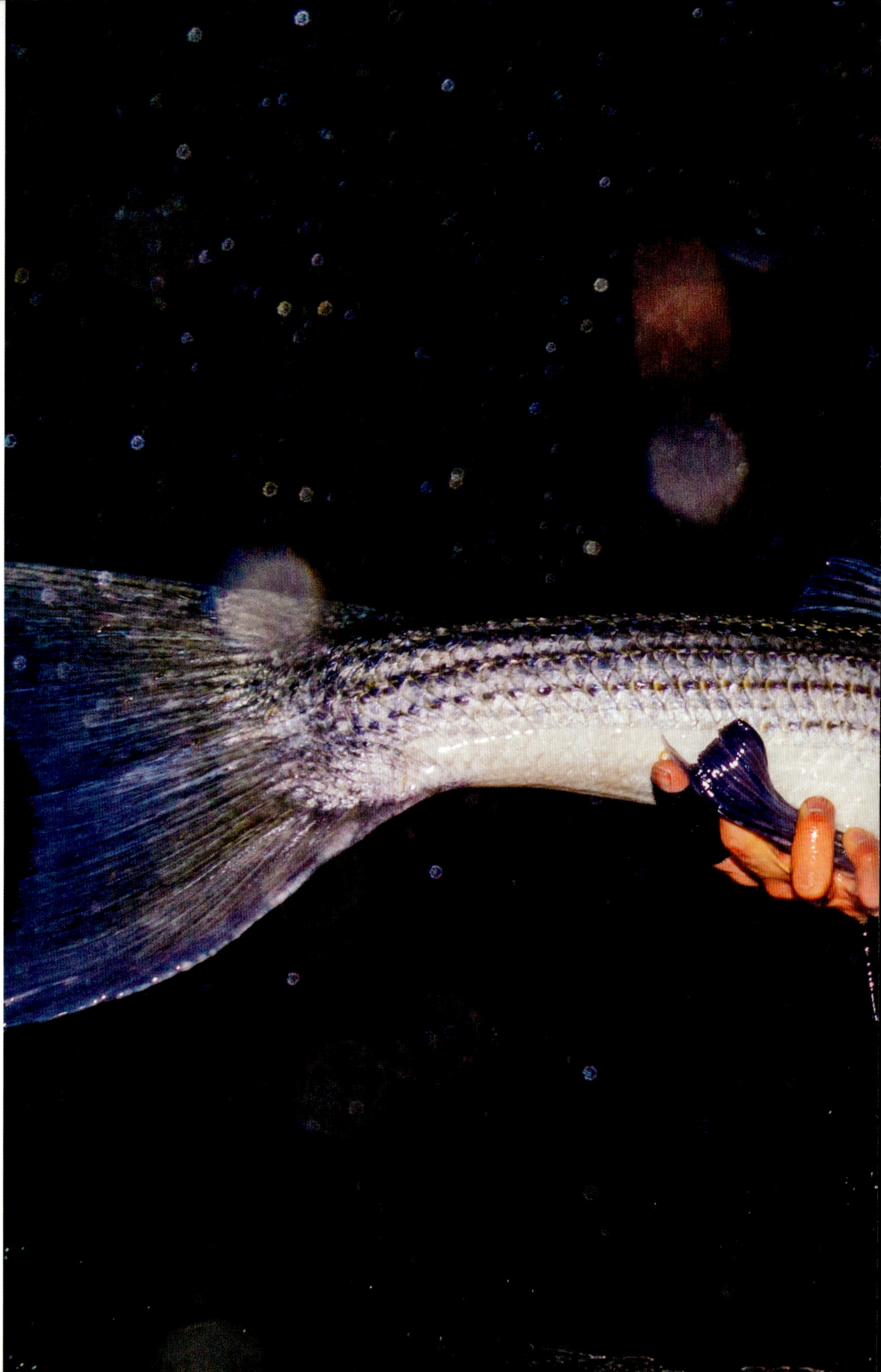

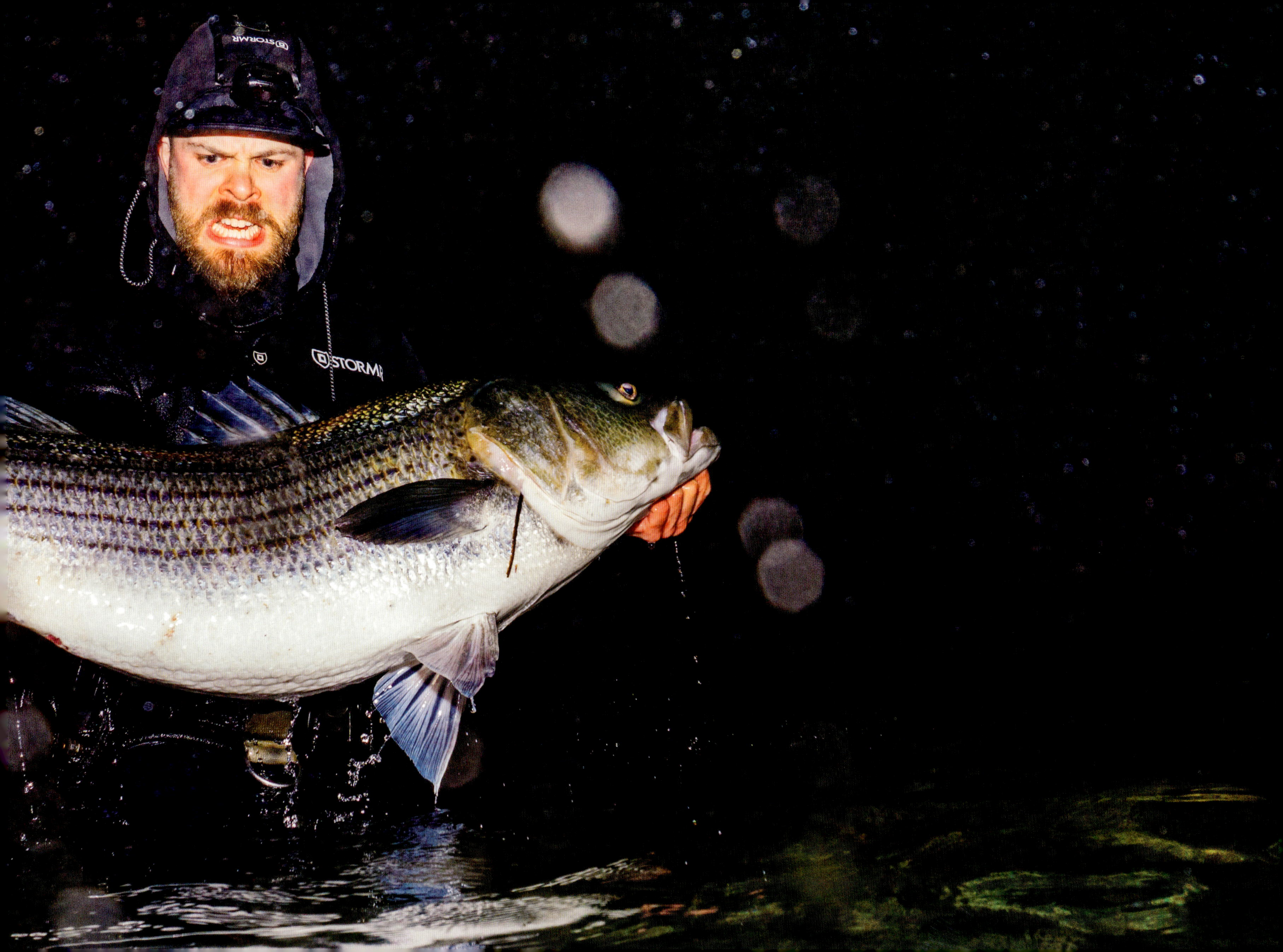
STORMR
STORMR

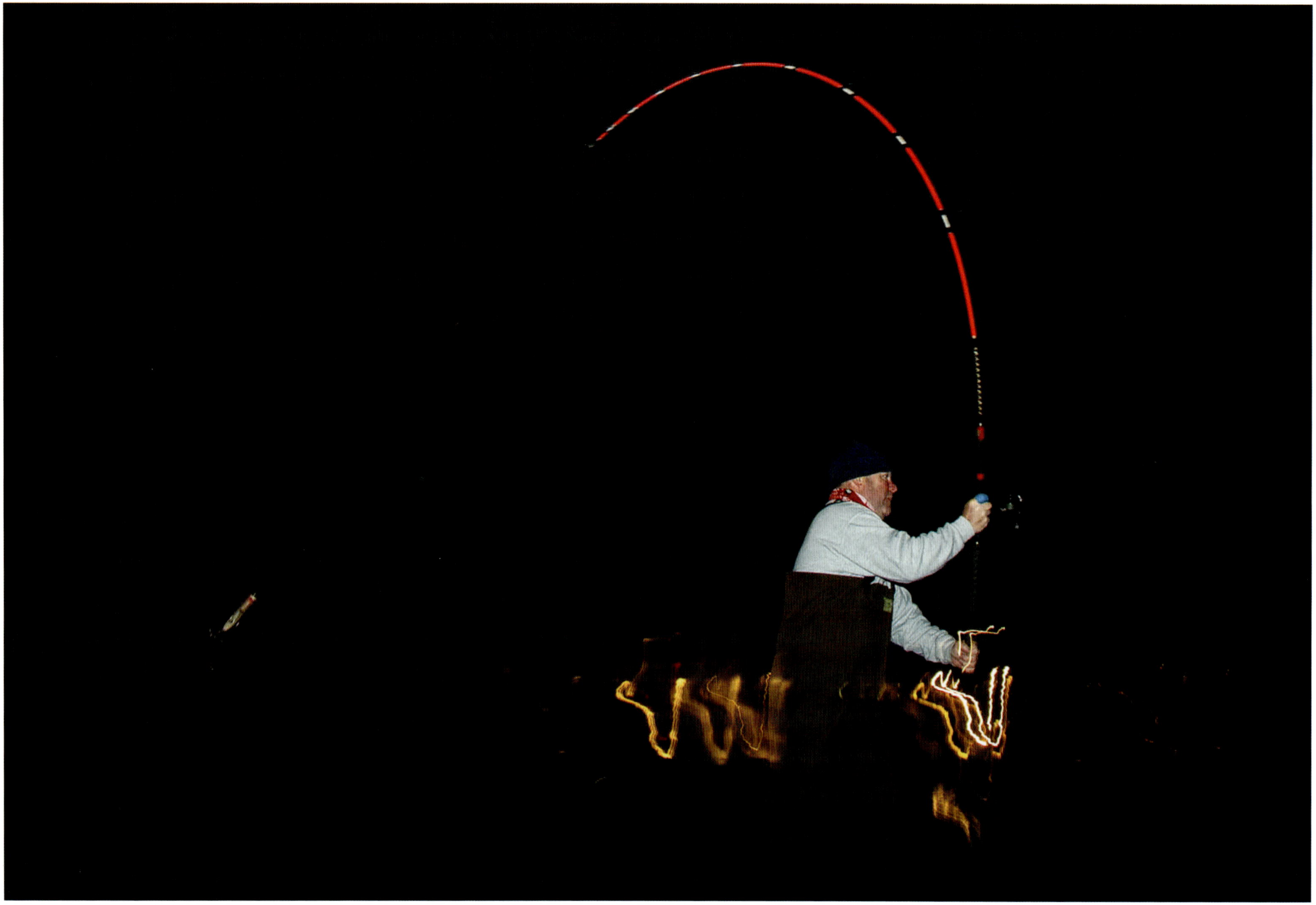

FISHING THE HARVEST MOONS OF September or October is magic. The flood pours in from the east and sweeps quietly out of the deep water until it runs into the small reef. There, it rears up white and noisy, recharging the shallows with food and cool water and triggering the bass strung out along the broken bottom to feed.

These are familiar stomping grounds. Back when the land was a patchwork of fields, orchards, and pastures, farmers would labor well into the night reaping crops ahead of a killing frost under harvest moons just as brilliant as the one that lifted off the sea horizon a couple hours earlier.

I have myself been harvesting this evening, plumbing the fast shallows with live eels on three-way rigs for the fleeting crop of striped bass starting its southbound migration. At the end of each drift, I fire up the outboard and run east, up-tide, carving big, graceful arcs over the broad fields of moonlight. I guide the skiff outside the red bell and up the channel to avoid spooking the fish lying along the top of the submerged ridge. In the half-light, you can see the smooth water quicken, stretch almost, as it nears the reef, "smells" the bottom, and rears up.

The fishing is easy and relaxed. No white knuckles. The wind is light, and small, standing waves collapse on themselves and slap the hull, but never threaten to leap the transom and join me in the cockpit. The stripers, too, are small—six to maybe 18 pounds. Without conviction, I grouse about how it would be nice if the fish were larger.

Truth is, I am at peace in this familiar little corner of the world illuminated so softly by the oyster-shell light streaming off the moon. Content with everything I have been given. No other boats, no other fishermen to watch over my shoulder. Moon, tide, plenty of fish, and a friend.

Night moves. Photo by Grant Monahan.

IT'S LATE AUGUST WHEN A FRIEND and I tie up our boat on a small island in the middle of a tide race. We fish for schoolies from shore until about 1:00 a.m. The fishing is relaxed and about what we expect. Plenty of bass, but none larger than 15 pounds. We hook a fish, drop one, miss three in a row, land two on successive casts, and so on.

The night is comfortably warm, and the pace pleasant and unhurried, like the languid rhythm of a midsummer ballgame at Fenway Park. When the tide finally peters out, we are in no hurry to hop back in the boat and make the 10-mile run to the dock.

We lean against an enormous log worn smooth by its pelagic wanderings and drink a couple of cold beers. We watch the tugs pulling east and west snuff out the lights on the mainland as they slide past. We ponder the night sky, read the little wind shifts, and talk as a new tide tries to make up. We take the time to listen to the night—to the young tide, the undertones of slumbering birds, the drone of a diesel a mile away.

We are living this evening off the clock. There is no place we must be. Work and deadlines can wait. The world is sleeping, and no one is expecting us. Just two friends on a tiny island surrounded by bass and cool, moving water beneath a brilliant Milky Way into which you can stare and imagine just about anything.

The nights in late fall are different. You sometimes feel the end of the season pouring down your collar and passing through your soul like a cold omen. The raw days and windy nights compound the sense of foreboding.

A FEW NIGHTS MADE ME THINK of something I'd read long ago in Bob Post's wonderful book about surf fishing on Martha's Vineyard, *Reading the Water*. I knew Bob and some of the characters in the book. In one chapter, the late Roberto Germani said, "Unless you're the type of person who needs a fishing buddy, you're going to spend many hours in dark, mysterious

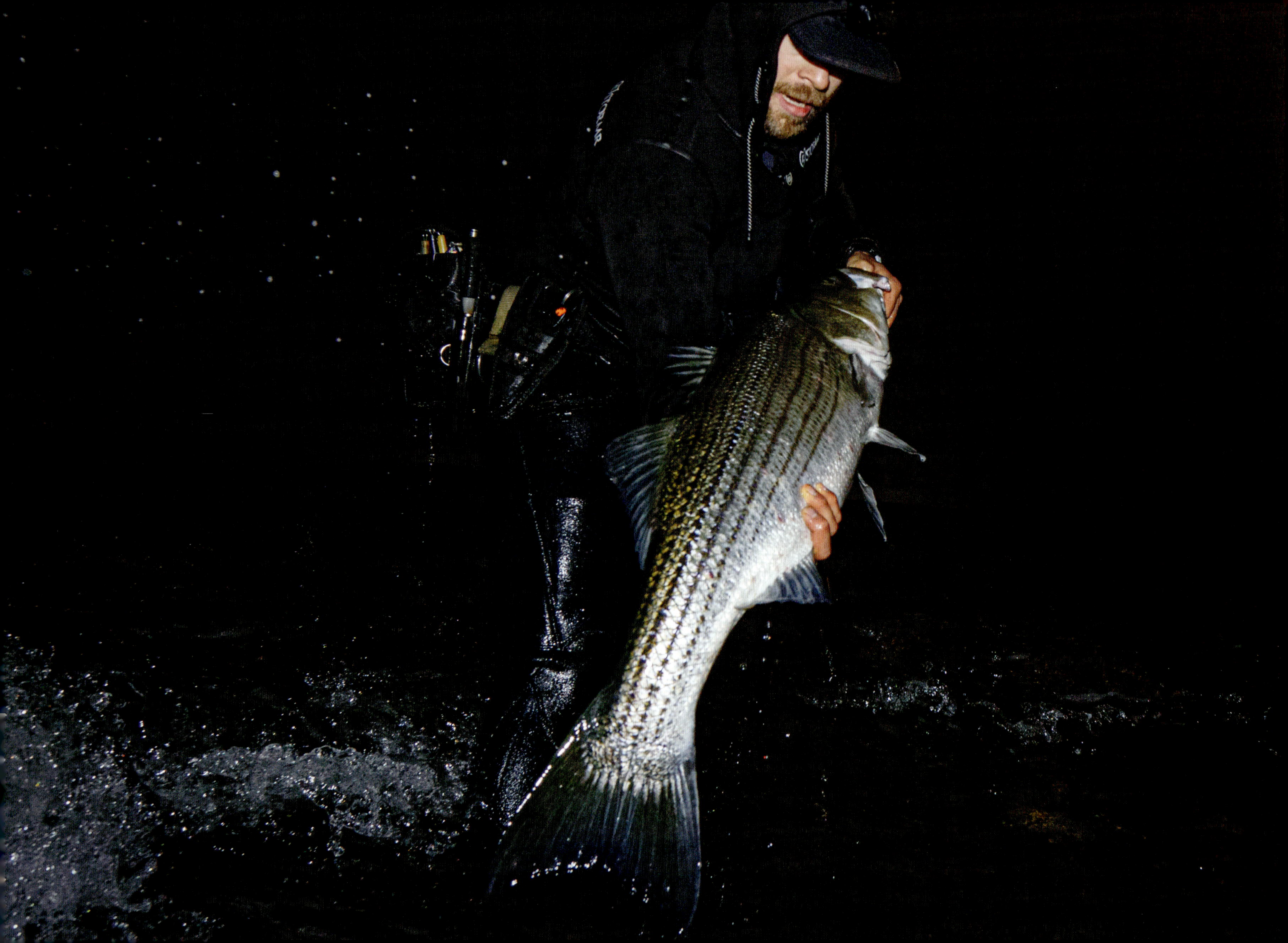

places where forces that have been long submerged and long forgotten come to the fore. You're going to get frightened for no apparent reason. You may see apparitions. You may feel insignificant." I love the dark, but I also listen to what my body tells me, especially when those fine hairs tingle. That's survival instinct, the stuff of fight-or-flight.

IT TAKES MORE THAN JUST A SET of chops to fish close and tight to rocky shores at night, especially with no moon, no starlight, and a good swell running. To fish effectively and safely also requires a collection of skills—to know exactly where you are in relation to the shore and rocks. To master your electronics. To ensure that your engine is reliable and purring. And to hone your senses: your smell, hearing, and night vision. One night, the smell of a salt marsh where there shouldn't have been one kept us off the bricks.

We didn't have radar on our small boats, so it was essential to keep a careful watch when running and to accurately interpret the running lights on each vessel we encountered. We did our best to avoid nights when conditions were right to form fog. We had waypoints and routes for each rocky shore we worked so we could stay just outside the rocks that were too shallow to drift across. I sometimes cast from the helm and kept my eye on the electronics.

At night, we got used to moving our heads as if on a swivel, scanning 360 degrees around the boat. We knew we couldn't spend too much time focused on any single thing, even if that single thing was unhooking a good fish lying on deck or retying a rig. Let your attention wander, and the wind and current can quickly and silently push you onto a rock or a lee shore. We gained the discipline to stop what we were doing and look up and around so we could move

Left: Soon to be released. Photo by Jerry Audet.
Right: Twilight on a salt pond. Photo by Barry Beck.

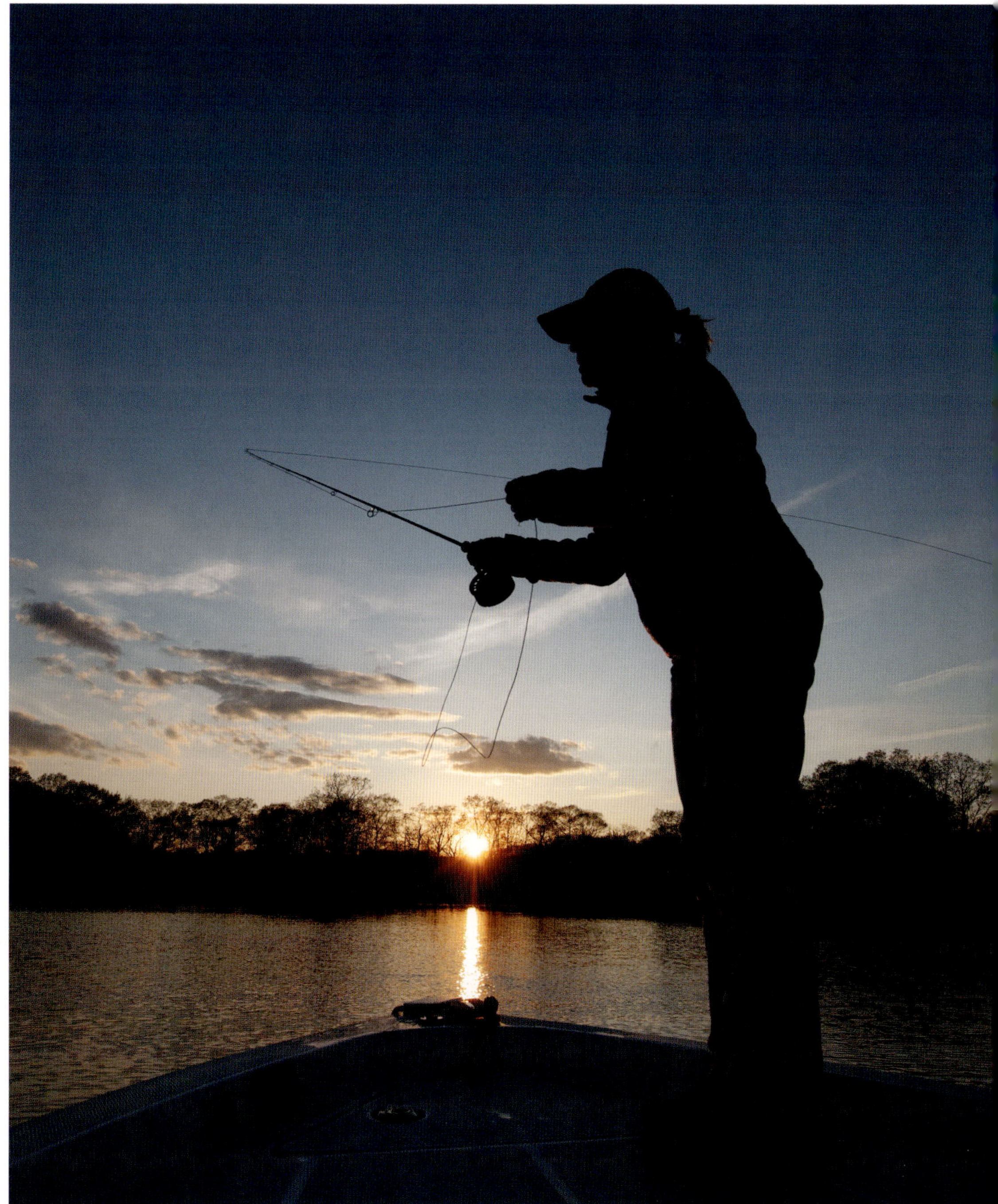

the boat when necessary. We made our way about the boat quietly, never shining a light on the water or into anyone's eyes.

We learned to scout by day the territory we intended to fish at night and to mark the rocks on the plotter that we wanted to approach but not hit. To take everything slowly. We made sure we knew the location of unlit markers. We recognized the strengths and weaknesses of our boats, knowing that the conditions we headed out in could change dramatically by the time we headed for the dock. That when fishing inshore, sometimes the safe way home was to alter course if sea conditions changed and to take the long way around to avoid pinch points, rips, and inlets.

We watched the weather closely and expected more wind than the forecast called for. The old joke is that if the National Weather Service calls for 15 to 20 out of the west, add them together. We knew that on some nights that was no joke but what you actually found.

Most important, we knew that whether you fish from shore or from a boat, once the sun is gone you move into a realm that exists parallel to the everyday world. On the water, night is many things. Rarely ever dull, it is instead beautiful and baffling, veiled and unfathomable, captivating, unsettling, and magical.

Outer Cape Cod. Photo by Jerry Audet.

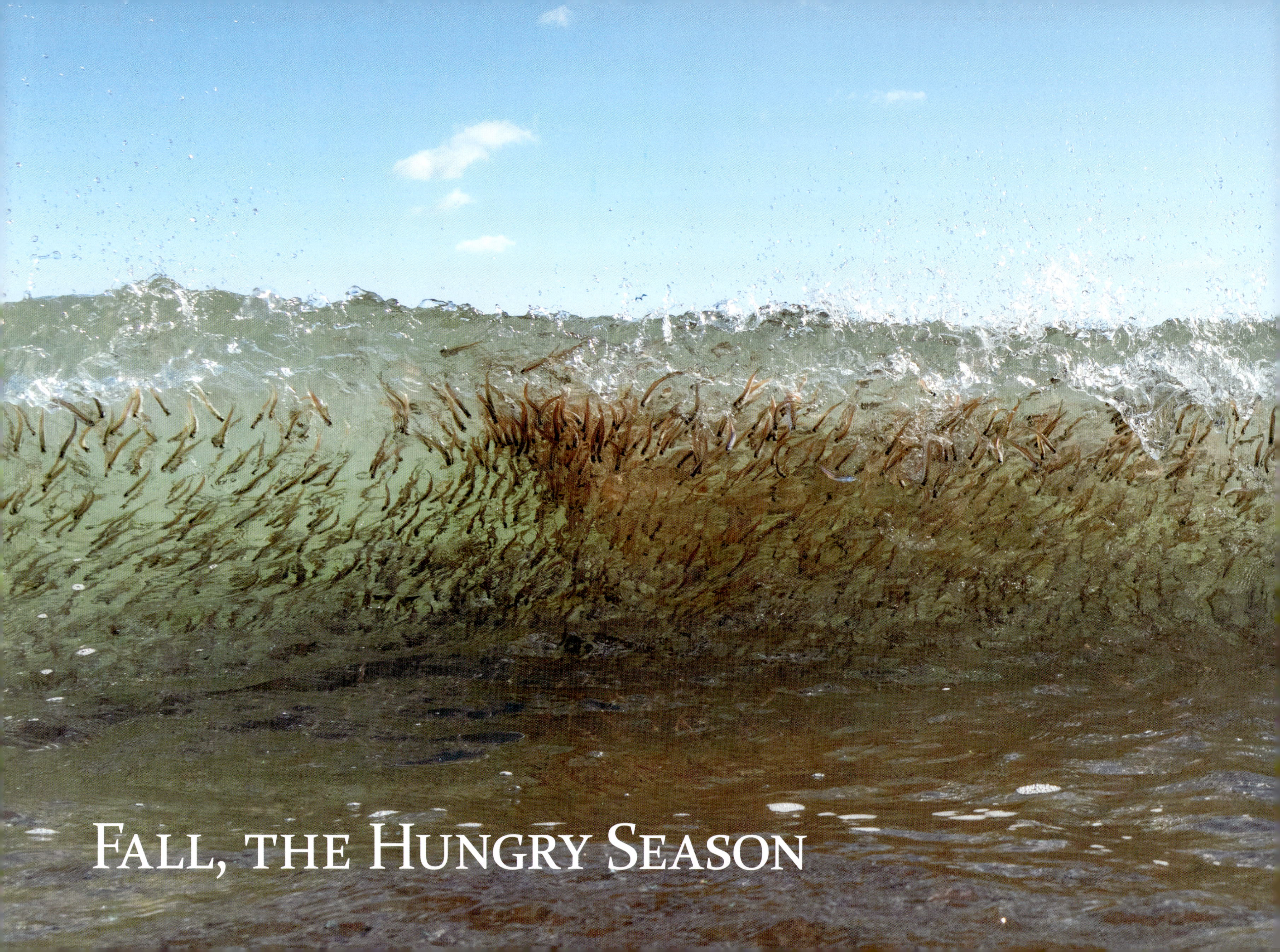

Fall, the Hungry Season

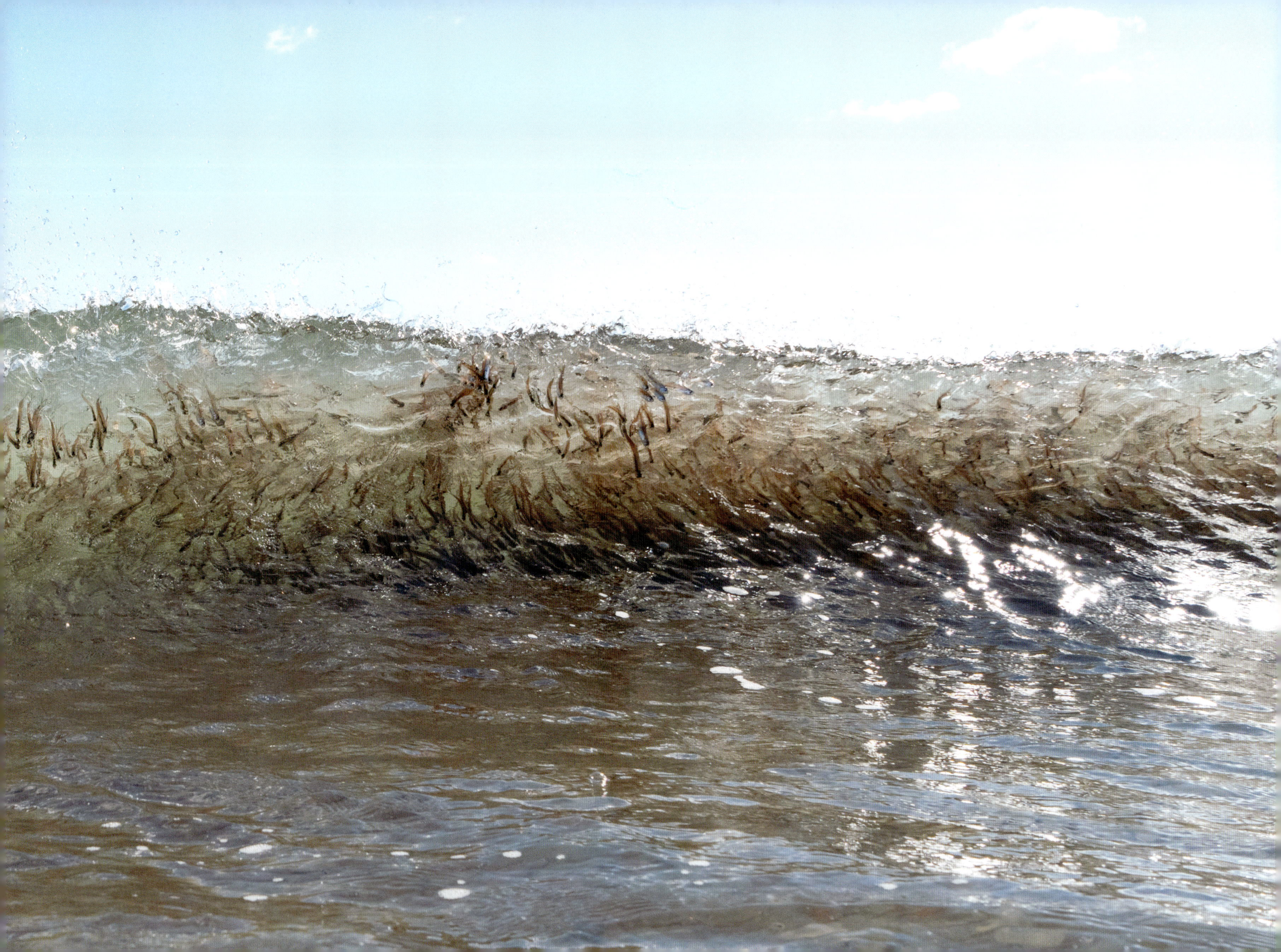

I am casting a popping plug at the horizon. With a north wind at my back and a lightweight 13-foot rod with a reel spooled with 30-pound braid in my hands, I am tossing the two-ounce lure as far as I can.

These long throws are not for sport, but of necessity. The fish are hitting at the end of the cast, out where a rocky bottom rises from a large, featureless stretch of sand. Pop, pop, pop (cue a cymbal crescendo and add a shower of spray), and a nice schoolie rises from its cool, green world and pounds the snot out of a plug. The action is so visual and the setting so perfect—barrier beach, ocean swell, swaying dune grass, blue skies, white clouds—that it feels like a dream.

Welcome to fall, the most spectacular season for the striper sect. Birds and bait and bass are on the move, along with boats and buggies and thousands of fired-up anglers who chase the moveable feast around the clock. Somewhere along the striper coast, tight-lipped loners and small groups of devotees are fishing every single tide. You can bet on it.

Time moves faster as the days grow shorter. The action is hot for several days, and then you shake your head one evening in late October and marvel at what you didn't see coming but knew would eventually occur—the shoal of fish you've been working for almost a week disappears between tides. Poof. Gone. Vanished until spring.

That's fall, too, with all its feelings of impermanence and the looming sense that you might miss a big slug of fish if you pick the wrong night to stay home. We fish like madmen, determined to not let a good tide slip past or, worse, the chance for a large fish. We race back and forth across a shifting line between what is enough and what is never enough, impelled by the thrum of old hungers and desires, old ways of keeping score.

Previous spread: Large silversides are a good sign. Photo by Tom Lynch.
Right: Surface plugs at Block Island. Photo by Jim Leedom.

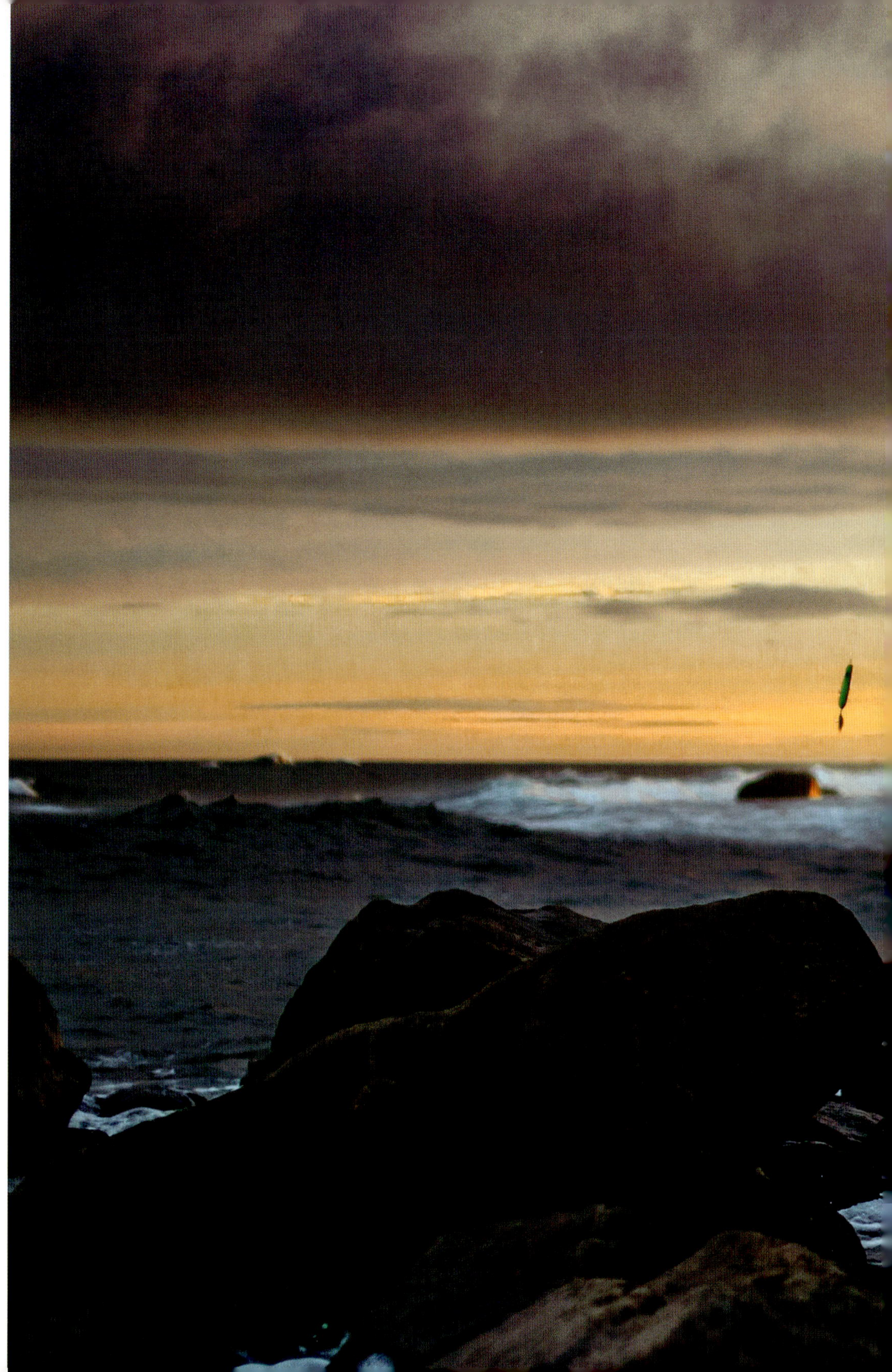

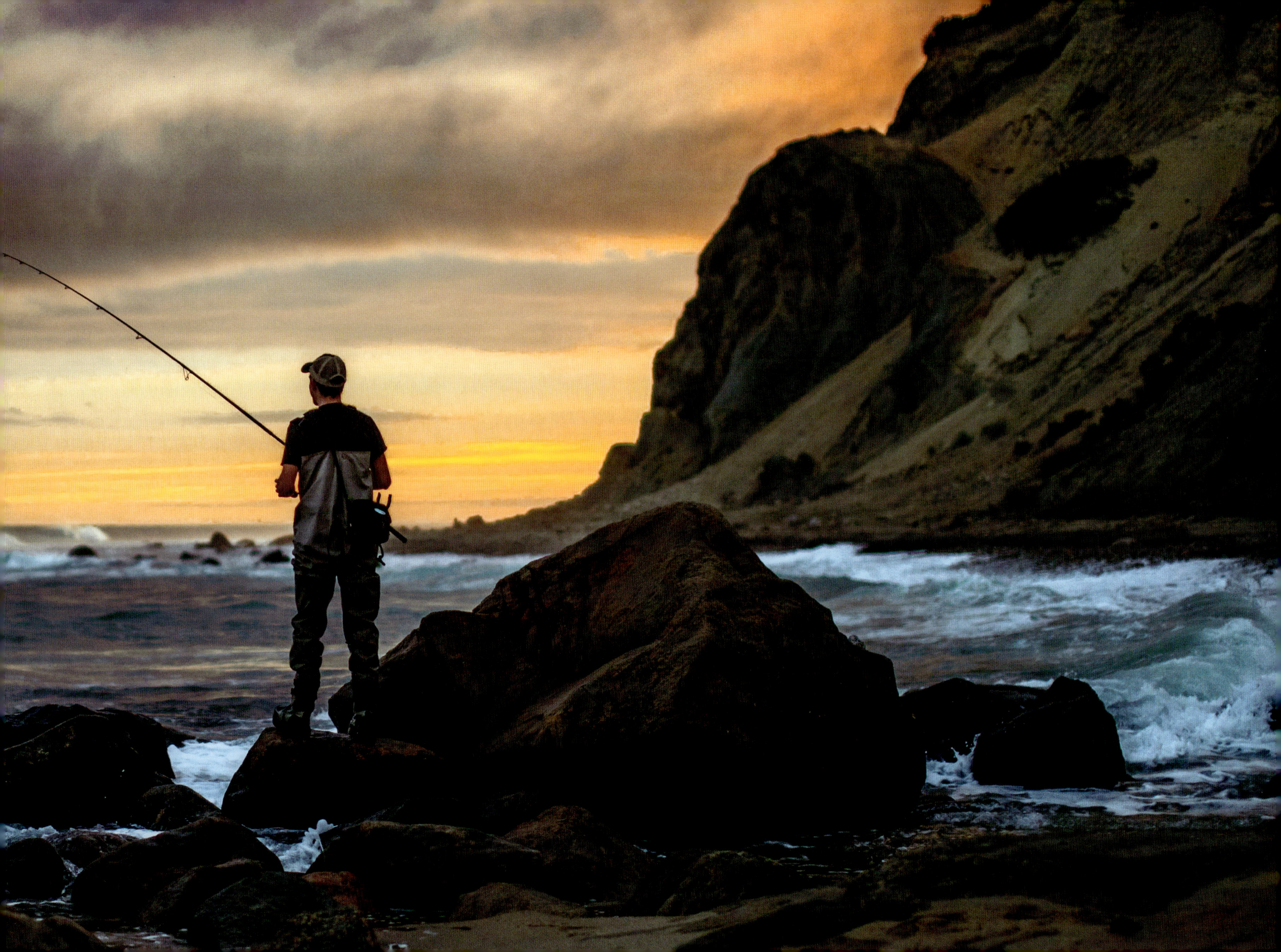

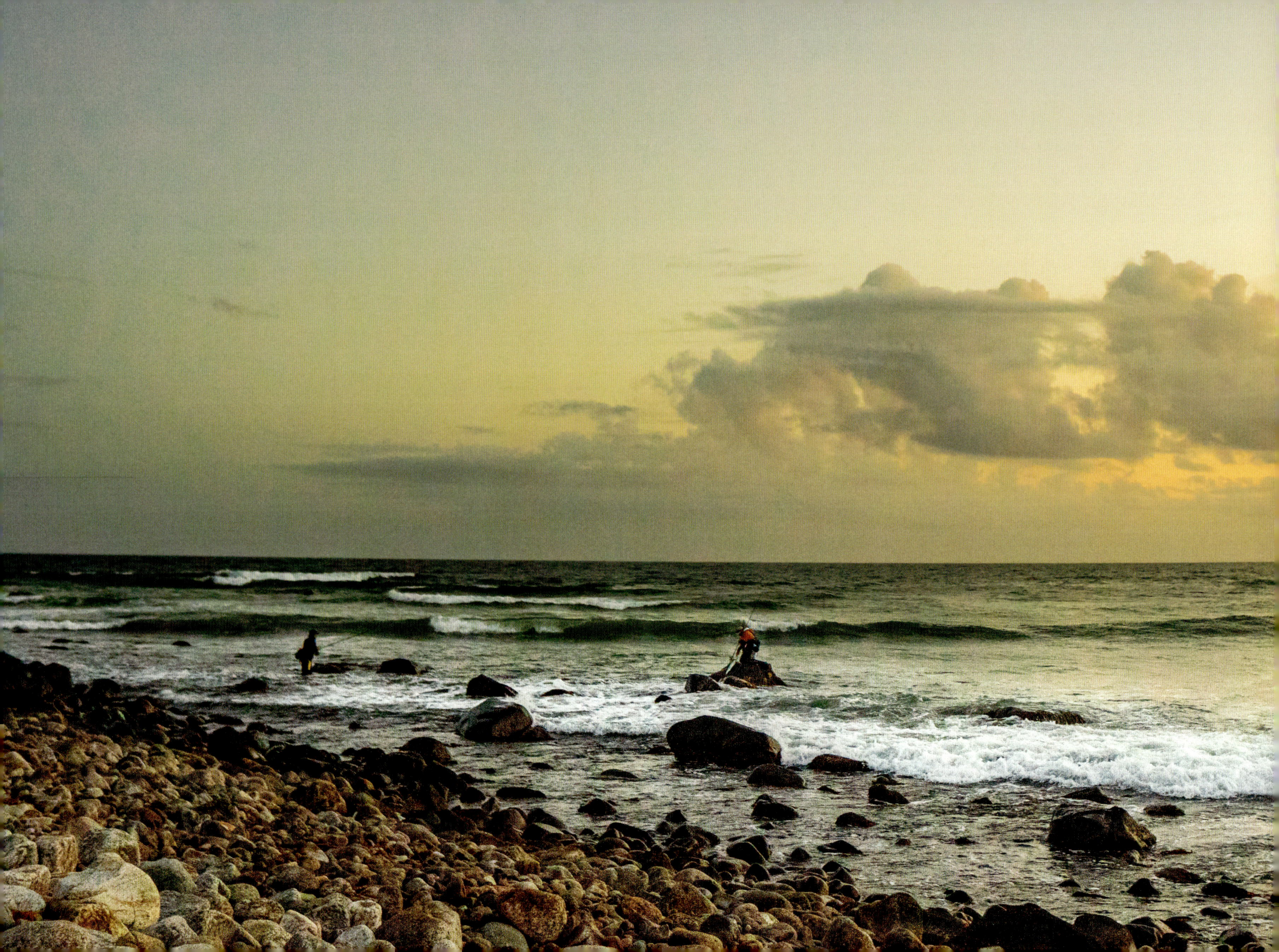

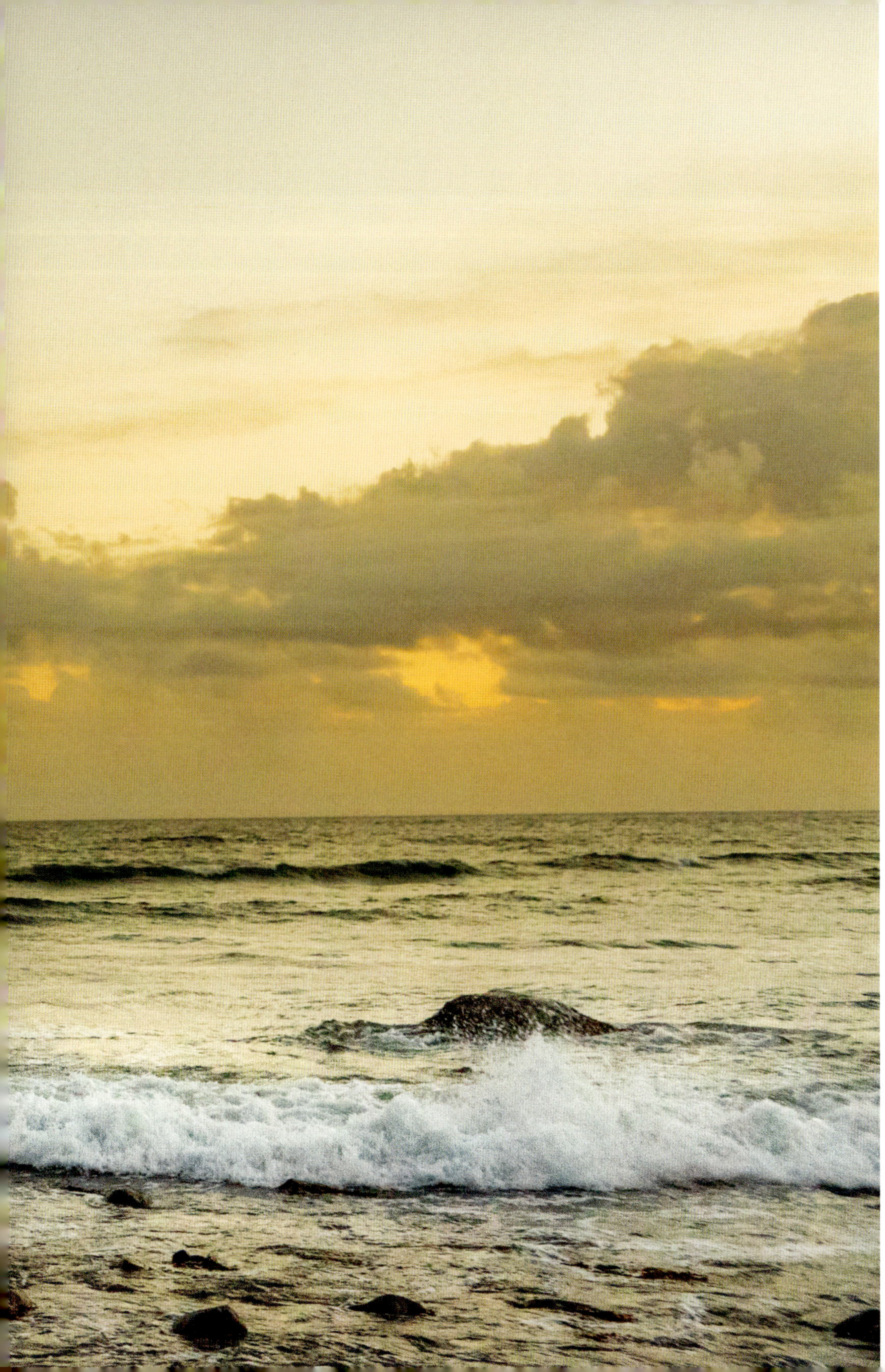

ON A LATE SEPTEMBER AFTERNOON, the full season is still ahead as I hike along the barrier beach. Nothing is showing. No rustling bait on the surface or diving birds to suggest any fish 70 yards offshore. You learn over time which spots hold stripers this time of year. I never walk past this one without making a few long casts to see if anyone is home. Today, the bass are indeed congregating here. Chunky schoolies strike every third or fourth cast, and the wind tosses plumes of spray with each detonation. My pulse races.

I focus on every movement, working to nail both the long casts and the speed and action of the retrieves. I'm half talking to myself, half praying to the fish gods as the popper splashes and gurgles and I wait for another fish to unload on the plug. "Come on," I say. "Come on. Hit it."

I live for this. The hold-your-breath anticipation as you wait for the surface explosion. It's what being alive feels like for me, as well as for the tall, lanky man fishing beside me. We meet on this beach each fall when fishy conditions hail us. We swap intel and catch up on fish action. We're similar in age and in our New England surf-guy vernacular. We see the striper world through similar eyes. He fishes hard and skillfully, and I enjoy sharing a stretch of beach or rocks with him. This afternoon it's just the two of us working these fish.

Catching chunky school bass between 12 and 25 pounds on surface plugs ranks high on my fall excitement meter. After fishing nights for so long, I still forget sometimes just how exciting the explosive daytime pyrotechnics are. They elevate the fish to another level.

This spot provokes unabashed strikes for reasons that remain a mystery. The fish don't simply swirl behind a plug or mealymouth a lure. They typically smack topwater lures hard—to stun, swallow, and destroy whatever it is they imagine good fortune has provided. Spray flies as

Bass from the rocks at Cuttyhunk. Photo by Jerry Audet.

you rear back and set the hook, feeling the weight of a decent fish as the line comes tight and the drag calls out. It's days like these you hope never end.

I hook another fish, and moments later a bass blows up my friend's popper. We're blessed to have this stretch of hard sand to ourselves, as monarch butterflies sail past and evening settles in. I'm fishing in a bathing suit, and the other guy is wearing waders. We are straddling summer and fall, and I'll wet-wade until water temperatures leave me shivering.

The last fish I hook is the best of the day. It runs well, then burrows its face into the sticky bottom, leveraging off the rear set of trebles on a plug I'd never fished before.

FALL IS ALL ABOUT LIVING THESE MOMENTS: the lovely late-afternoon flurry of fish, the sweet balm of a warm evening as the sun sets and the moon rises, a willing pod of fish, and a beach empty of all but a friend.

Some years, fall comes slowly. It starts in the summery water and light of early September and finishes in the cold winds of late November, when everything is shutting down and you're thankful to catch a few stragglers and call it a season. I love those last fish, small schoolies no larger than five or six pounds. Hooking one is like snatching a parachute seed out of the cool breeze with your hand.

But we have plenty of good fishing ahead. On this night, in the last days of September, I set my sights on a rocky point awash in strong currents. I'm optimistic, despite the report I receive from a surf fisherman I pass on my way out.

"It's dead," the guy tells me. "Three seals around. That's it."

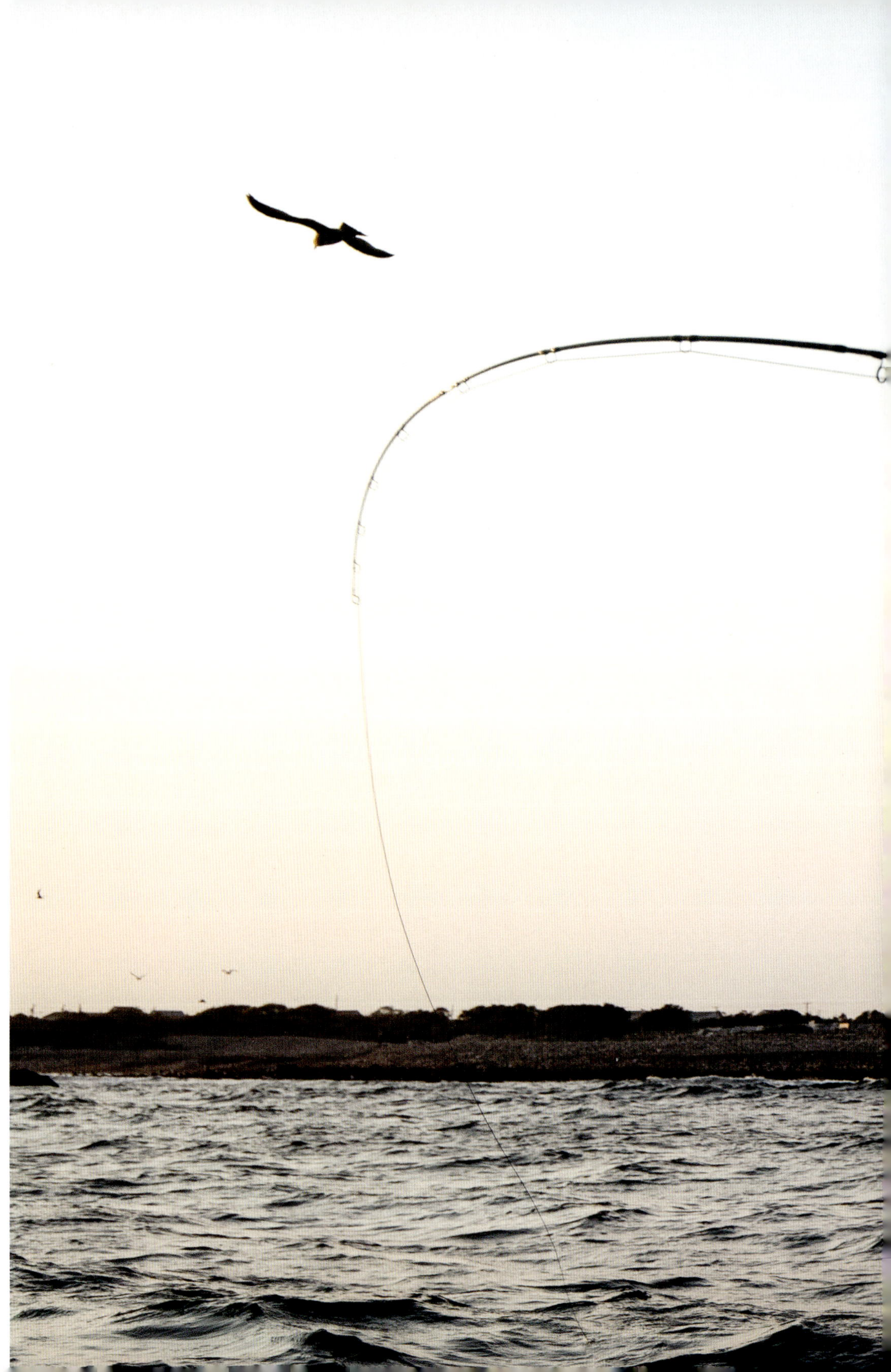

Early fall off Point Judith, Rhode Island. Photo by John Lee.

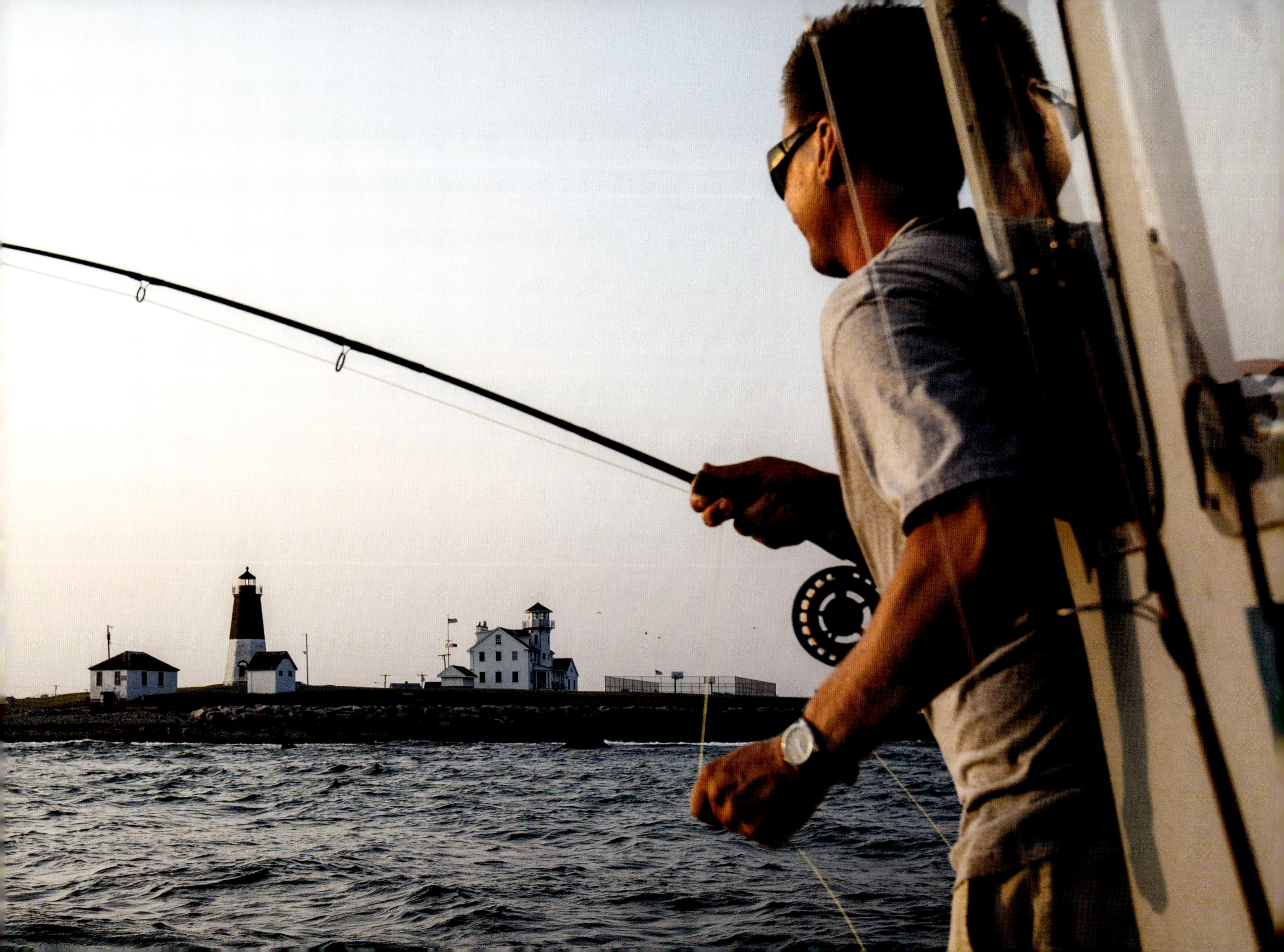

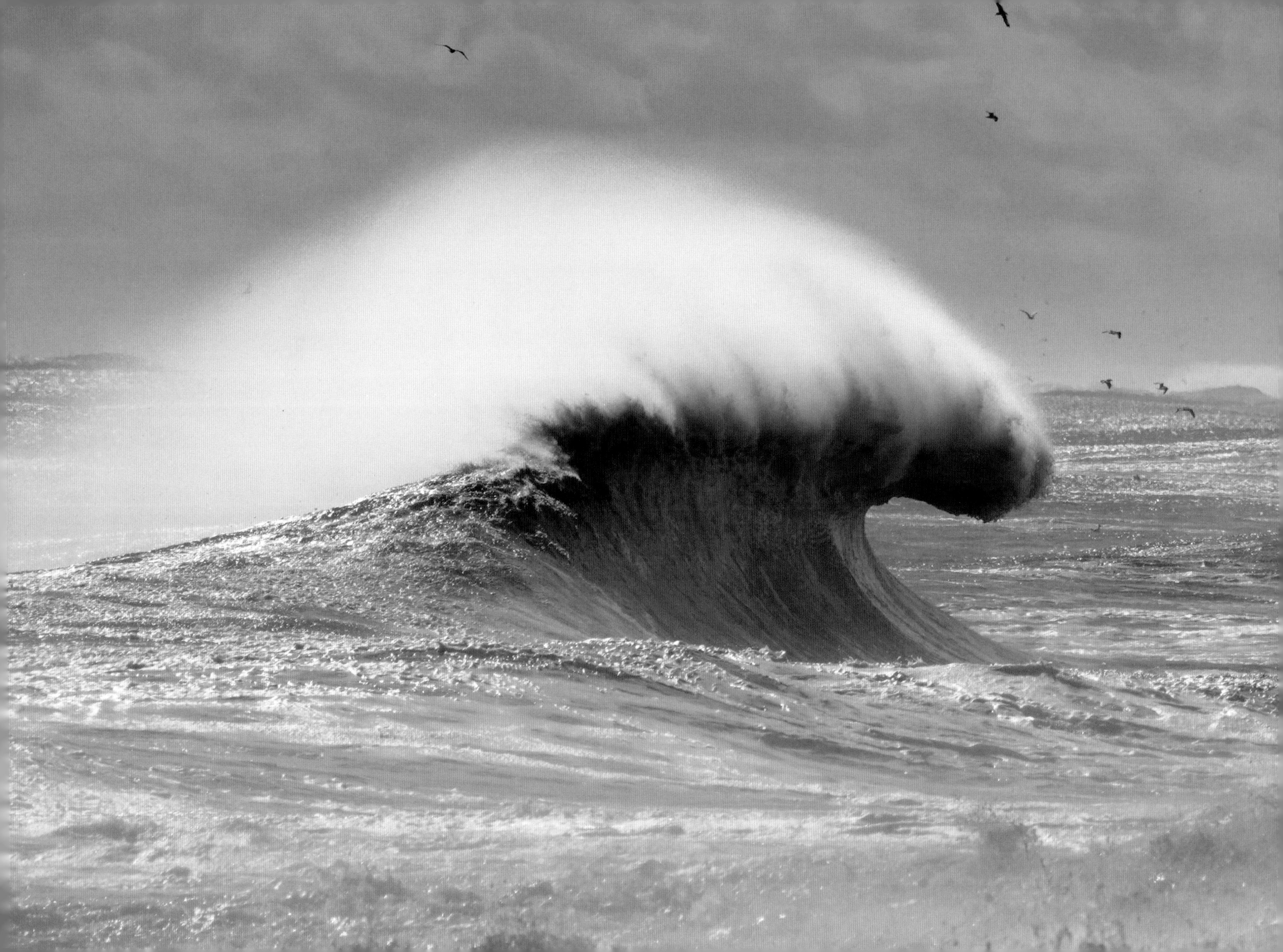

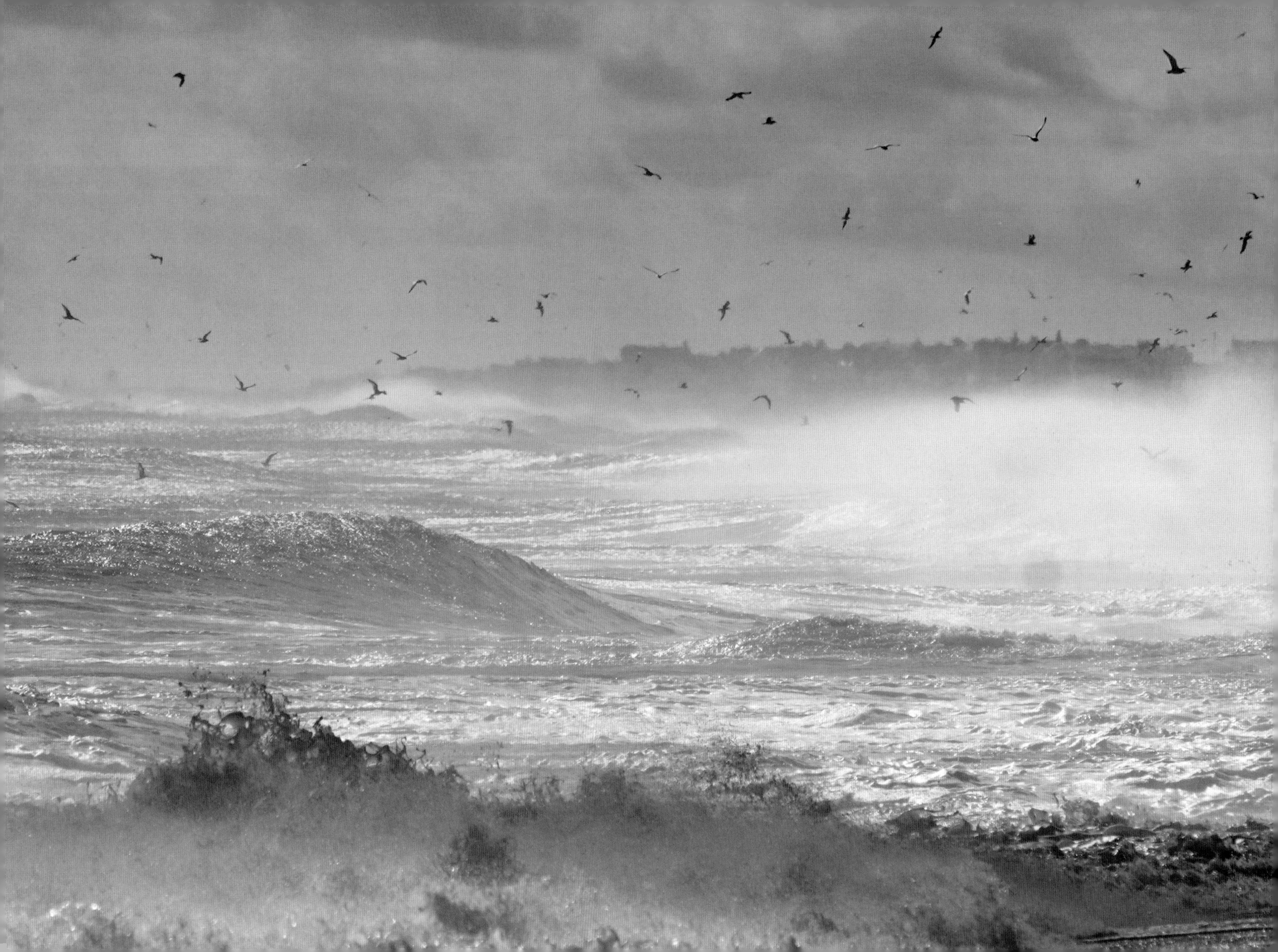

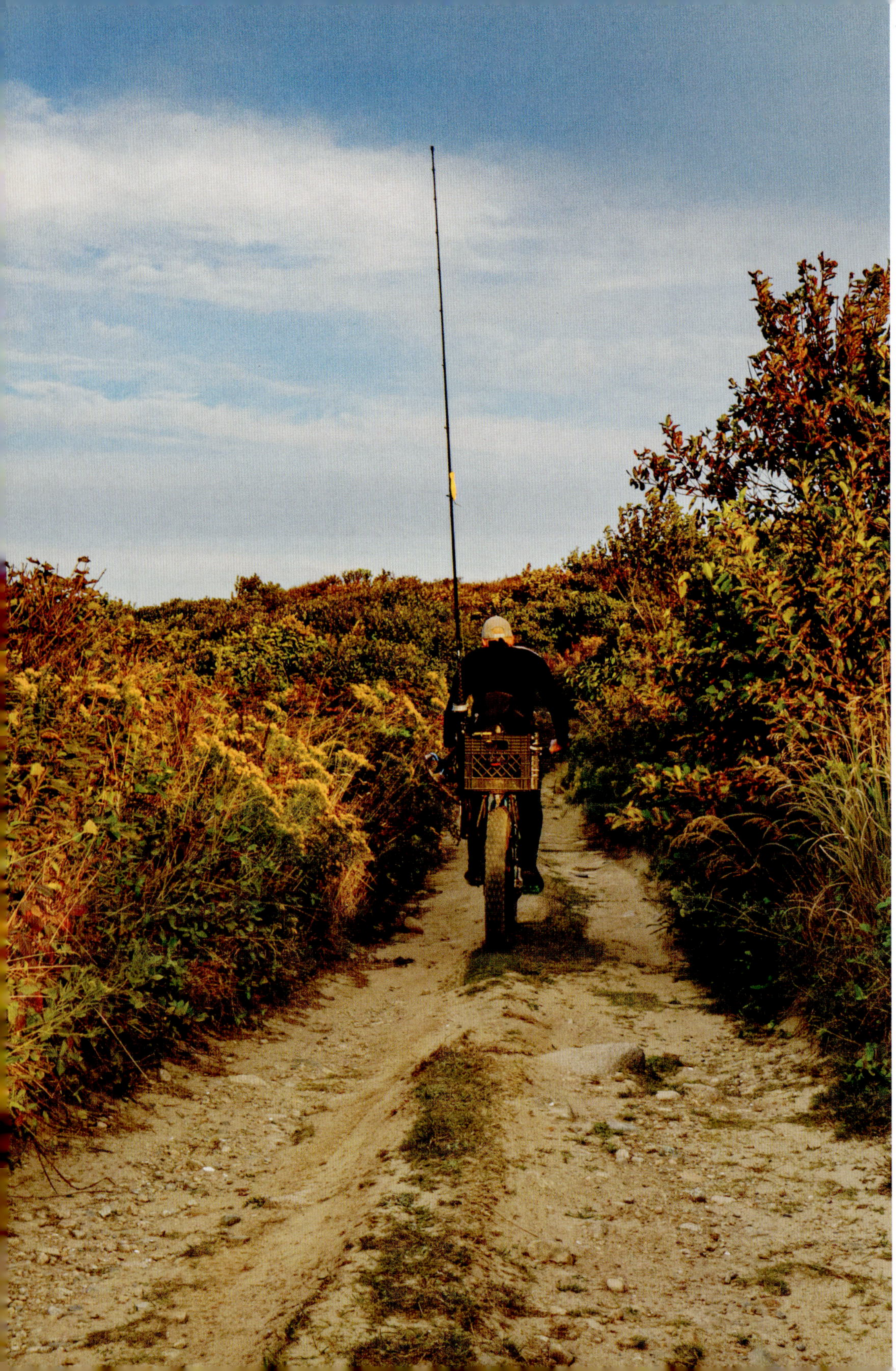

The north wind is light, the surf is small, and the tide is just starting to ebb. I slip a live eel onto a circle hook and climb aboard a familiar rock facing south. The place is empty, save for a lone fly fisherman standing 50 feet to my left. I'm surprised when a fish grabs the eel on the first cast, even more so when the 10-foot Lamiglas rod bows sharply and the fish rips off line with ease.

My first thought: *Hell yeah*. For a nanosecond, I think of the guy who gave me the pessimistic report. It's a good fish, and it runs and runs before finally tapping the brakes. I get a couple of wraps on the reel, and the fish bolts once more—then the line goes slack. It's gone. The piles of blue mussel shells crunching underfoot tell the story, as does the abraded line I strip off and cut away. Calmly and quickly, I tie on a new leader and hook, then rebait with another eel. During the next 20 minutes, I set the hook in two more good bass, and each one also scuffs me off. I curse each time I finger several more feet of frayed line.

The action slows, and I move to another rock, this one facing west, and keep casting. The night would have been memorable had it ended with the trio of lost fish. Not the happiest outing, but still one to remember. Some 15 minutes later, I gingerly lead to hand a beautifully proportioned, 46-inch bass with a big head and healthy girth. She, too, fights as if she'd swallowed the moon, and I don't realize how lucky I am to land her until I feel the line. The leader and several feet of 20-pound monofilament above the swivel are badly chafed. I pop it easily with a yank. I measure the bass and spend eight or nine minutes sitting in a knee-deep pool resuscitating the fish and replaying the evening in my mind.

Previous spread: November storm surf, Ocean County, New Jersey. Photo by Tom Lynch.
Left: Fat tires for a sandy island trail. Photo by Jerry Audet.
Right: Wind, surf, and fall light. Photo by Tom Lynch.

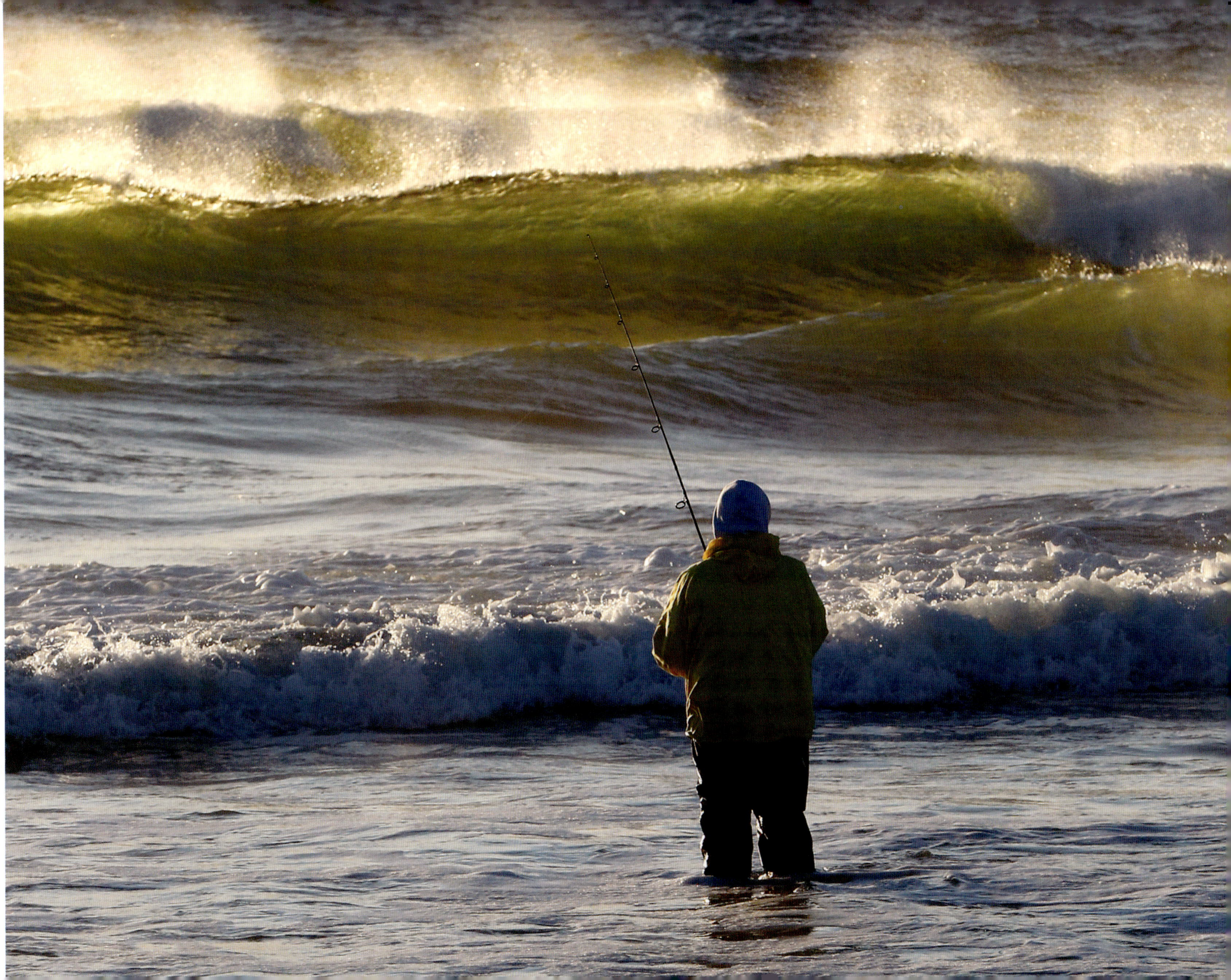

AS FALL ADVANCES, I CHASE FISH IN a dozen places between Martha's Vineyard, Massachusetts, and Montauk, New York, from boats, beaches, rocks, and breachways. This is the best time to be fishing those small, salty towns where striped bass still hold sway and where you won't get funny looks if you walk into a diner unshaven and wearing waders and a salt-stained hat. In places like these, it's the uniform of fall.

I watch a teenage boy in waders glide through Edgartown on his bike—in another time, another place, that was me. Rods stick out from beater station wagons, pickups, Mercedes SUVs, and utility trucks. The cops don't bother with cars and trucks driving beachfront roads at 3:00 a.m. with rods in roof racks or sticking out of tubes.

At a breakfast diner, my waitress tells another server that someone named Steve is taking her fishing tonight. "I don't care what he says," she declares. "He's taking me bass fishing. More coffee, hon?"

On a warm afternoon at Lucy Vincent Beach on the Vineyard, two women with a pair of small kids in tow lean their surf rods against a cut bank and spread out beach towels. After a few minutes, one of them peels off her clothes and runs to the water, her black Lab racing alongside. She dives in and lets out a cry. Fall is the season to whoop.

I stop at the Aquinnah Cliffs at the east end of the Vineyard, where migrating birds depart on their southbound journeys. I watch through binoculars as a peregrine falcon hanging in the updrafts suddenly drops at astonishing speed to pluck a westbound warbler out of the sky and eat it on the wing. You never see the one that gets you.

On a night in early October, I fish later than the action calls for because it's how my tribe is wired. The larger bass skedaddled with the last of the tide, nearly two hours ago. You stay because you are on the cusp of the season, and because the moon is pretty and it's unseasonably warm, and because there are still enough small fish to bat your plug around and keep you interested. You stay because there is no one to spoil it with noise or lights or sloppy fishing. You stay because you are on a flat rock, alone with your thoughts, and all sounds and lights are familiar friends. The cry from a startled shorebird, the fog signal from the sparkplug lighthouse off your right shoulder, the flash sequence from the granite light tower to the east that warns of reefs and woe. You stay because, as Thomas Merton said, "To really know a place, you have to experience all its moods." You stay because you are home.

ON A LATE AFTERNOON IN MID-OCTOBER, I cast along the jumble of rocks and boulders of a recessional moraine in Rhode Island. A school of juvenile bunker surfaces 100 yards beyond me. The action begins slowly, with nervous bait rippling the surface until it resembles a corrugated washboard. Within moments, the shimmering mass moves shoreward, driven by scores of bass. They cover the distance in two minutes, moving from 40 feet of water to flood the shallows.

Suddenly, bass and peanut bunker are just a few rod lengths away. Hundreds of silver bait take to the air like coins pouring wildly out of a slot machine. They flap helplessly on the wrack weed covering partially submerged rocks, the sun reflecting off their tiny scales. The contrast between these wriggling silver dollars and the dark shaggy boulders is striking.

We fall willing victims to the song of the season—the slurping, popping, and slapping of cartwheeling bass, and the whoosh of panicked bait taking to the air in sheets of futile togetherness. Bent rods are everywhere—in the armada of small boats squeezing in as tight as they dare to the rocky shore, in the hands of fellow rock hoppers standing to my left and right. I fish a white lead-head jig with a soft tail and hook fish after fish. The hardest part is working the jig beneath the carpet of bait.

Waiting for a striped traveler off Martha's Vineyard. Photo by Vineyard Colors.

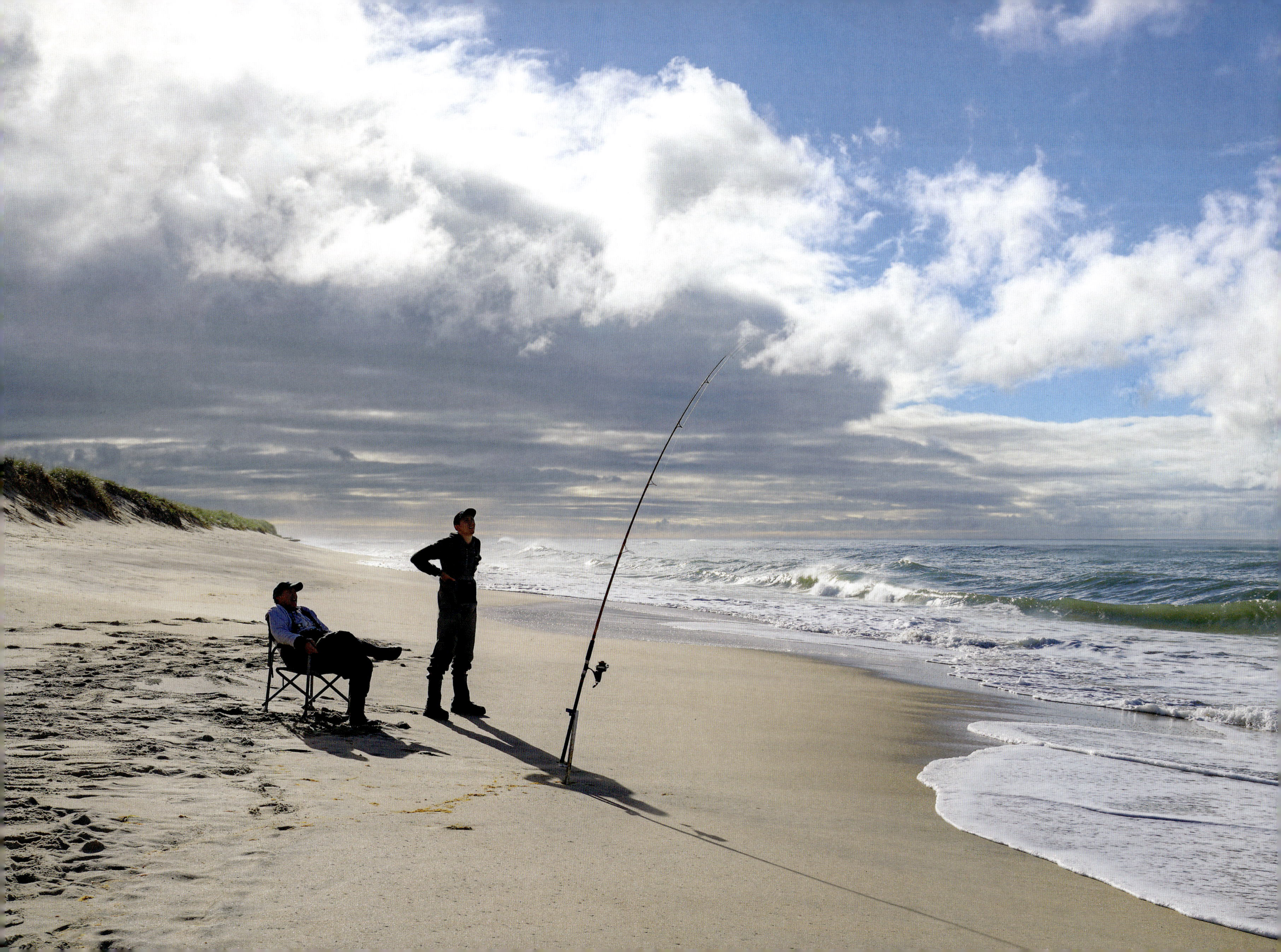

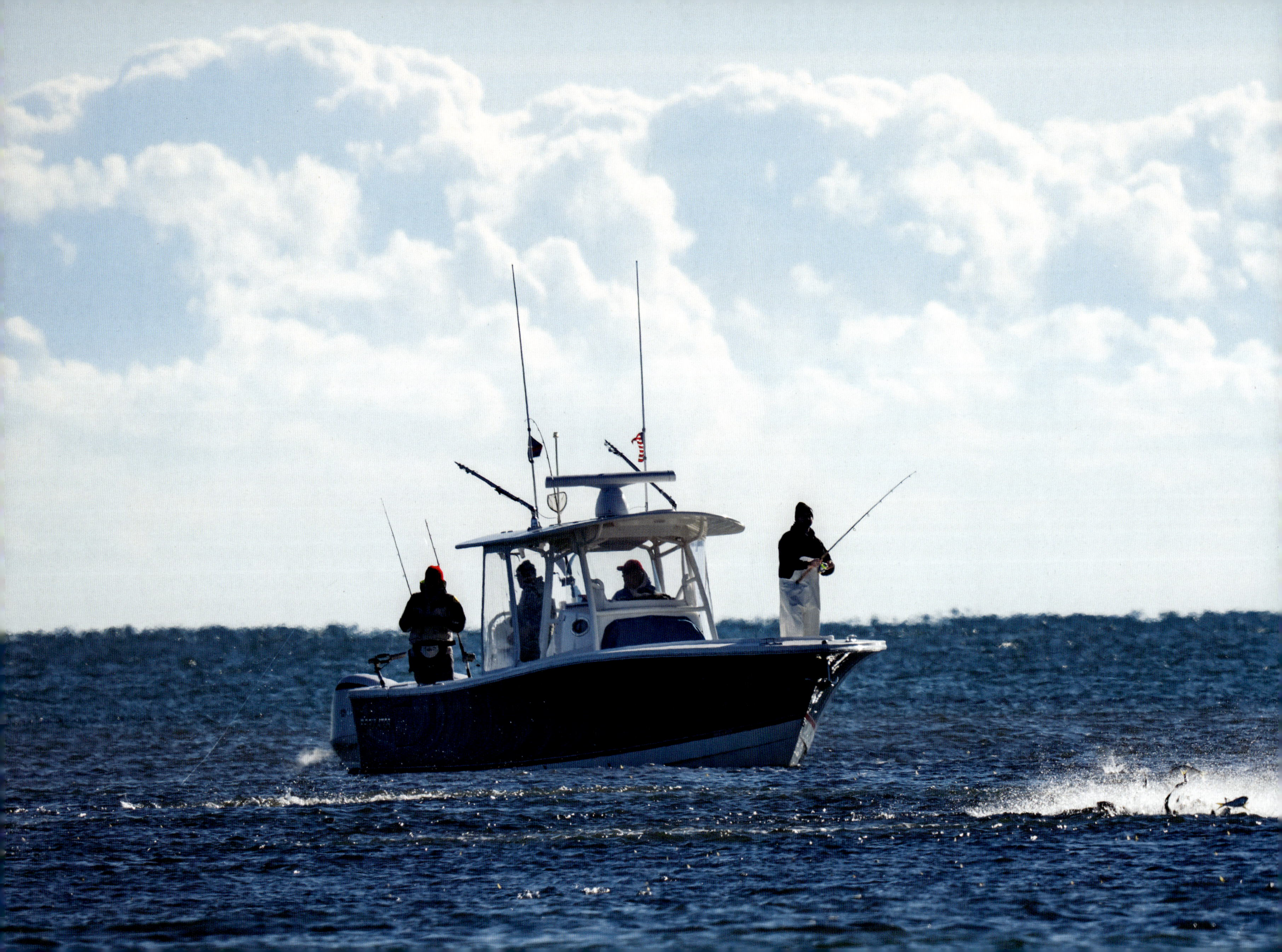

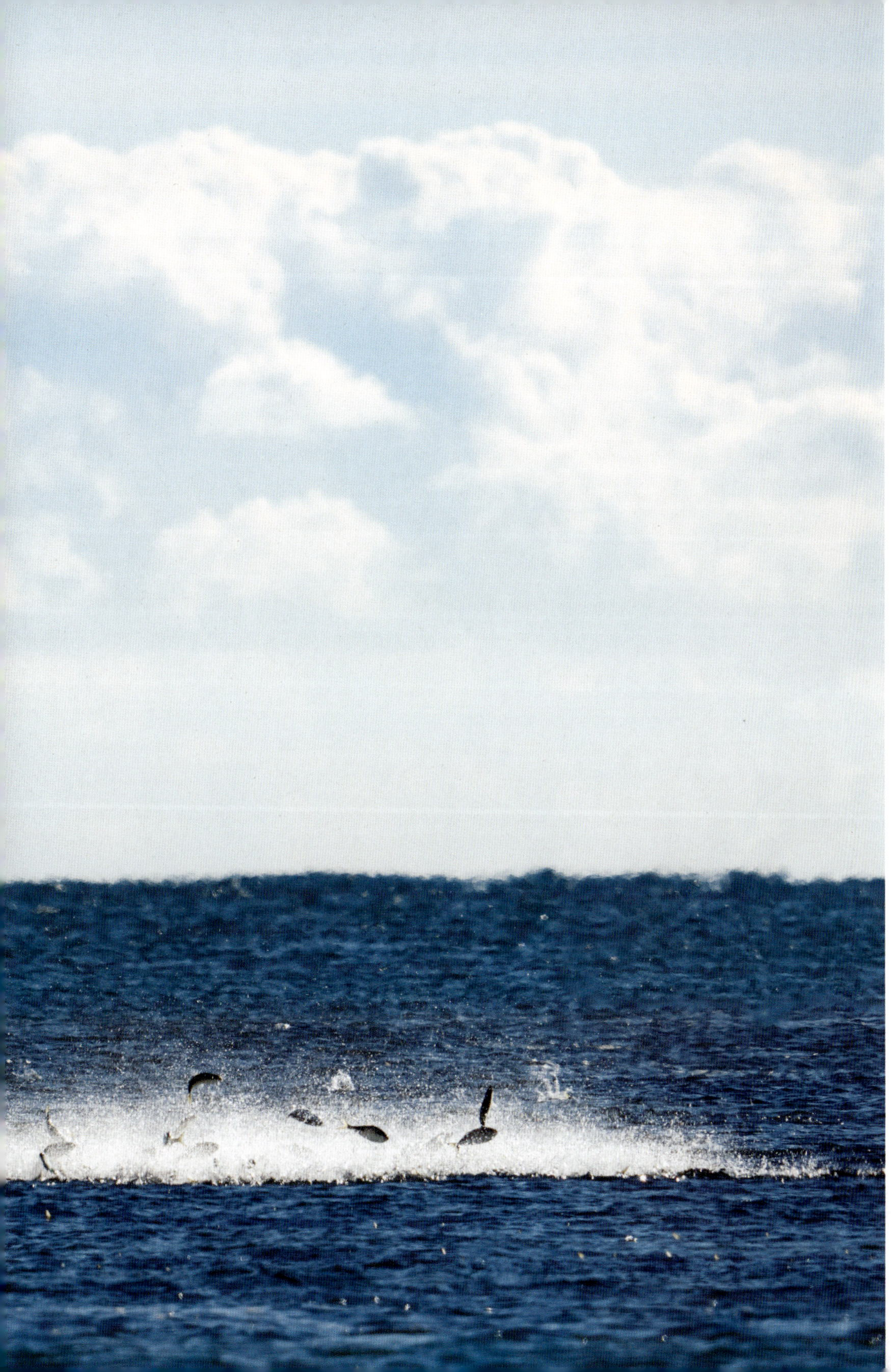

Your idea of surf fishing changes the first time you find yourself in one of these noisy fracases. I was in eighth or ninth grade when I first witnessed a school of stripers pushing thousands of panicked bait onto rocks, leaving them trapped and struggling in tide pools. The golden afternoon light, the busting bass, the jarring strike, the bent rod, and the 15-pound mono pouring off my reel were unforgettable. Experiencing it just once triggers a yearning for more. Those memories become imprinted, and they drag you back to the water's edge year after year, searching for a new episode, a fresh fix, another high.

Some evenings, when I am wet and chilled and the fish are nowhere to be found, I stay out anyway just for the fall light. I have an unwavering fondness for the low afternoon light of autumn, which is as clear and pure and defining as music, poetry, or laughter. It is a truth, a fleeting beauty that you search for each season in the open spaces where water meets the shore. The light carries a weight, texture, and presence unique to the season, and highlights details and textures you might ordinarily overlook.

The late-day sun fashions short-lived rainbows in the spray blowing off filigreed wave tops, transforms the wave faces into translucent green windows, and renders in pearly white the foam rushing up the beaches. A block-tin jig resting in my open palm resembles an old oil painting in this splendid light. The scratched silver body reflects the rich autumn glow and leaves the red thread and white bucktail glistening.

A dozen skittering gray-and-white sanderlings are gilded in reddish-gold, as are the blades of tawny dune grass. Hues of purple, bronze, and gold radiate along the shoulders and back of the bass you release into the afterglow of a lovely evening spent fishing. As October winds down, we sing a familiar lament—too much wind, too much sea, not enough boat. Gone are

Late-season surface action. Photo by Tom Lynch.

the calm nights when we'd slip behind the islands, traversing rips that were no more than knee- or waist-high. We too often run out in the dark, discover we've misjudged conditions, get our butts kicked, and race back to the dock with our tails between our legs.

In the surf, it's easier to shrug off bad weather. I move to another spot when necessary, find a bit of lee, or cast right into the teeth of the blow. Only when conditions everywhere are unfishable do I get in my truck and drive home.

I REACH OVER, SHUT OFF THE ALARM, and exhale quietly. A single word comes out: "Ugh." My wife recoils from my breath.

"Brush your teeth," she says. "Please."

I am a mess. My head hurts, one eye is glued shut with sleep, and dried eel slime and blood sticks to the back of my hands and forearms. I washed before slipping into bed, but some of this stuff has to be peeled off.

I have cuts on my hands, including a deep one on my right thumb that will take more than a week to heal. I'm dehydrated, and my feet ache. My stiff hair lays at wild angles like tufts of short cordgrass in a salt marsh. My left forearm is bruised from smashing down on the console after the boat landed hard off one of the short, steep waves on the sand shoals east of the river mouth. I look like hell and wobble like a drunk when I first swing my feet to the floor, but despite the dents and bruises in my chassis, I'm glowing inside. I am running on less than four hours of sleep, but I'll have a bounce in my step all day.

Last night, while the Eastern Seaboard slumbered, I stood in the cockpit of an outboard walkaround and cast eels at a rocky shore. We found the fish quickly, stacked into the eastern corner of a large, boulder-strewn cove named the Constellation. The challenge was the 15- to 20-knot onshore wind, which pushed small, whitecapped waves into the cove and wanted to do the same to us.

I repeatedly put the small boat in as tight to the outer rocks as I dared, spun the wheel to turn the bow into the wind, and slipped the outboard into gear as my partner and I stood side by side in the cockpit, firing long casts into the pocket. I nudged the throttle forward until the boat slowly moved into the wind as we took up the slack. Time and again, we were hit within eight seconds.

We didn't weigh or measure any fish that night. We landed two that might have nudged 30 pounds and released five or six that were larger than 20 pounds and several more in the teens. We hooked no monsters, but the stripers were aggressive travelers, full of October and the dark, gusty night. When I think back, I'm most surprised by how many bass were packed into one corner of the cove. It was a good night.

The endorphin rush lasted into the next week. I'll remember the wind, the surf, and the quick takes for as long as I am able to retrieve memories. How many of our fleeting days can you say that about?

I LIKE IT OUT HERE IN THE DARK, on a beach, in a boat, or among familiar rocks reflecting the last vestiges of fall. This is when I am living close to my bones. Hallowed and hollowed out. Cold pouring in from the north, and everything shutting down. Creatures winging southwest, fleeing for deeper water, burrowing into the mud. The Germans have a word for this seasonal restlessness: *Zugunruhe*. It's unmistakable in animals that are forcibly prevented from migrating, especially birds. Think of a raptor in a cage, longing for flight but going nowhere.

In late November, the beach is steep, windy, and lonesome. Dusk slopes into night, nothing slow or gentle about it. When I was younger, such emptiness unsettled me. With age and

Author Bill Sisson with a 50-plus-pounder that was tagged and released. Photo by Tom Lynch.

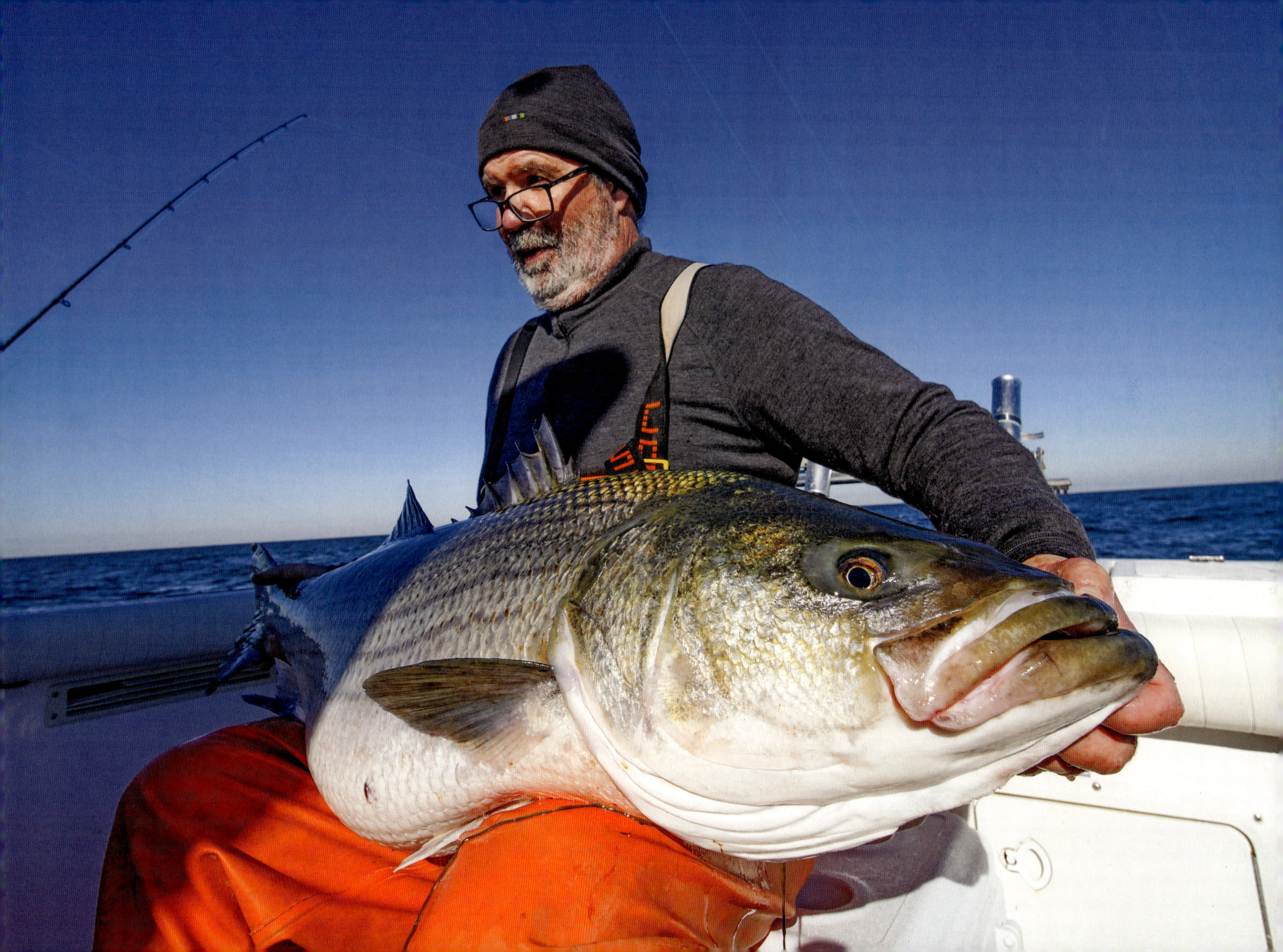

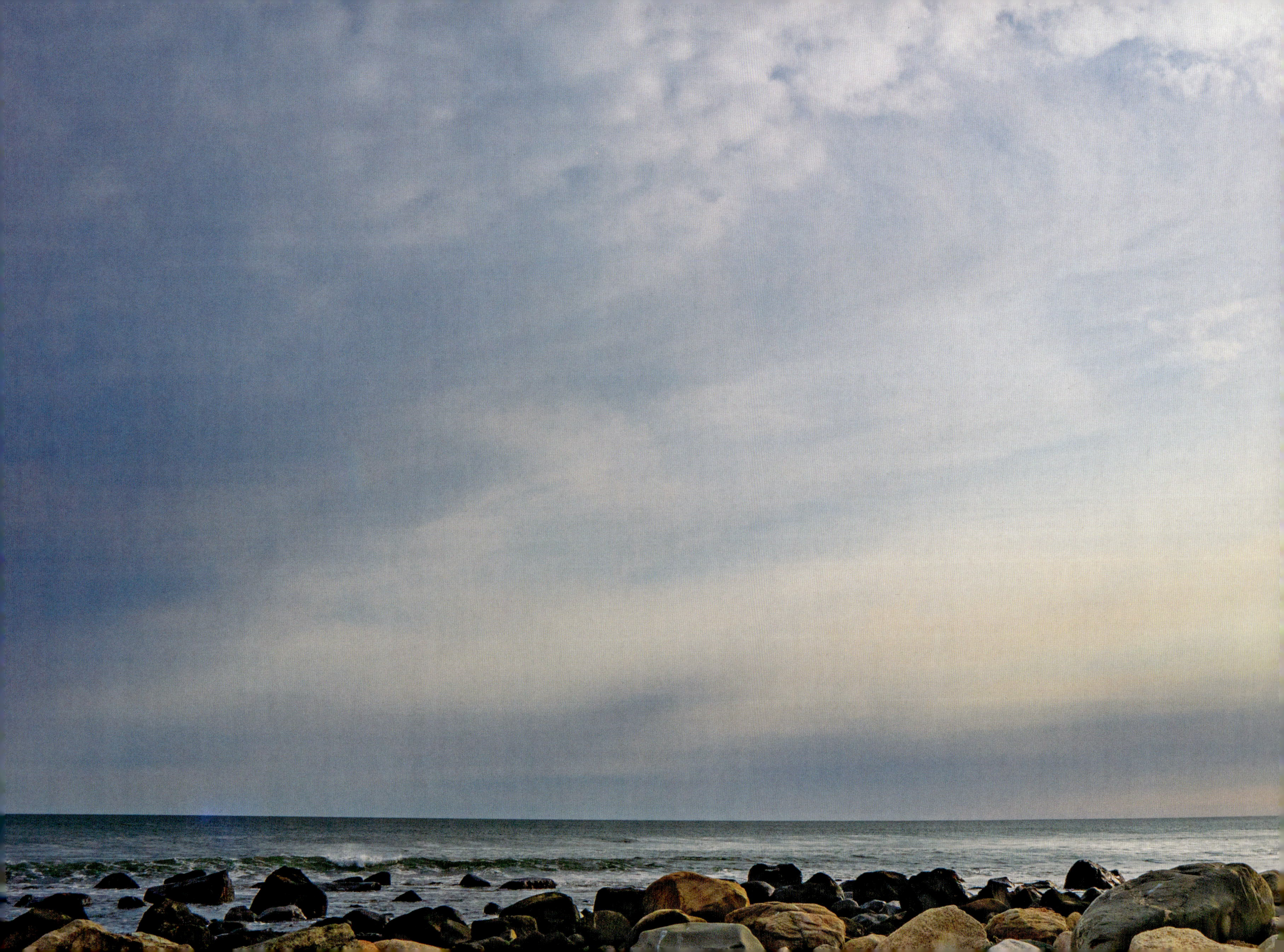

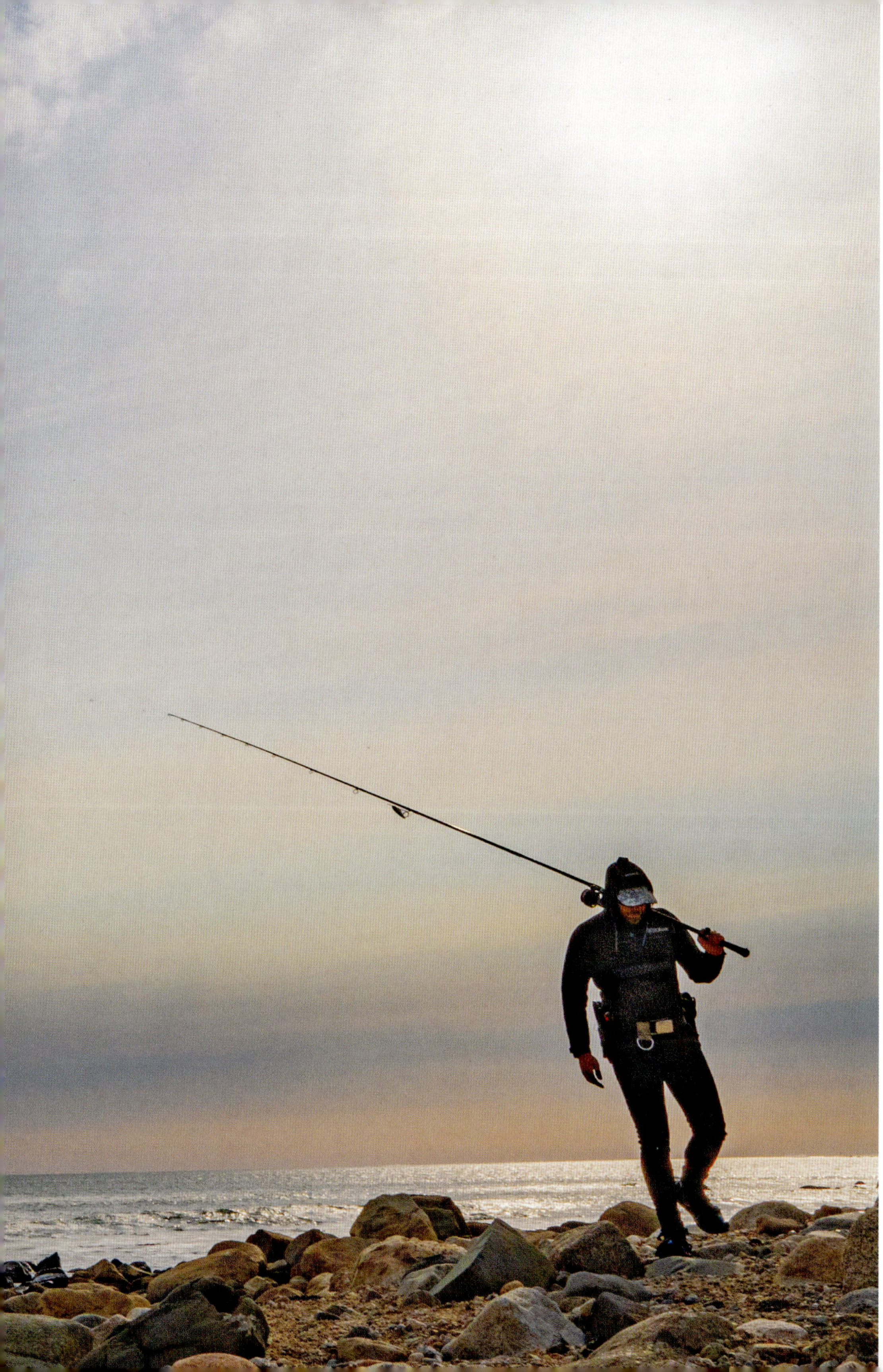

experience, I have come to relish the long shadows and the heavily textured sea, full of moguls and wind. In the words of Joyce Carol Oates, gone is the "ripe sun-warmed smell" of summer pears, replaced by the pungent odor of decay in salt marshes, tidal rivers, and the piles of seaweed pushed ashore by a storm. Fall is as hard and heavy as an anvil. It helps to have a bit of sand, a pinch of "downright cussedness" in your constitution, to quote my late Swamp Yankee nana.

Every boat in the harbor has been hauled, the mooring balls replaced by winter sticks. Frost coats my windshield and the eel cooler. Mine is the last car in the parking lot, the last house in the neighborhood where the leaves still lie unraked. The seaside town where I fish has hung holiday decorations from the light poles. Snow squalls beat down in the late afternoon. Big flakes fly horizontally like insects on the north wind. By the third day of gales, it's safe to say the season is just about kaput.

The end is marked by the smell of damp wool socks, the weird cacophony of yips and howls from a pack of coyotes calling up the moon from behind the marsh, the whistle from a night train across the bay. You are wet, cold, and alone. You pull your watch cap over your ears and sink into your coat. It is hard to feel anything but insignificant next to the dark water, sand, and boulders. One fish would change all that. You stay for the chance to catch just one last fish of fall.

Late-season solo. Photo by Jerry Audet.

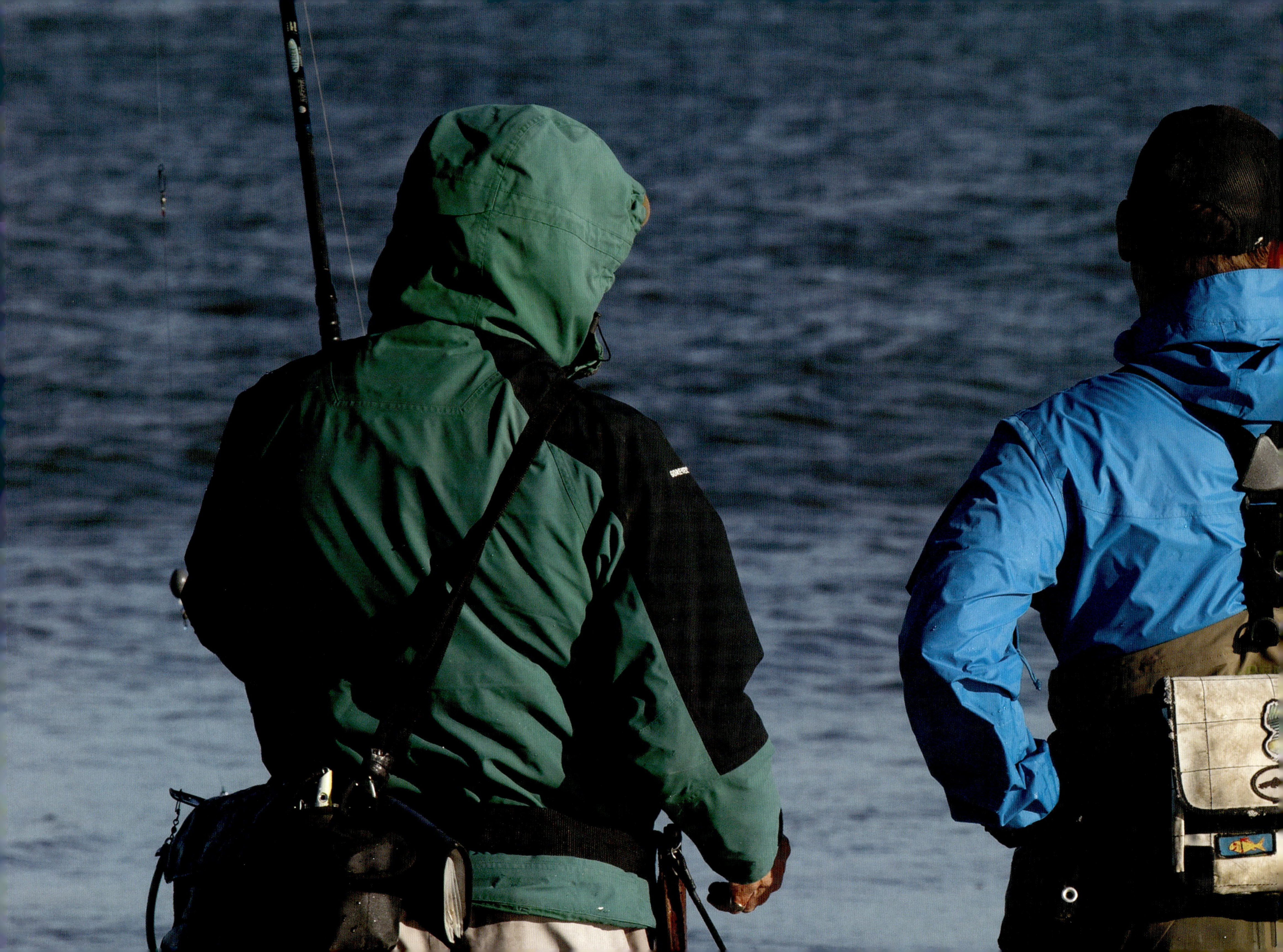

PARTNERS

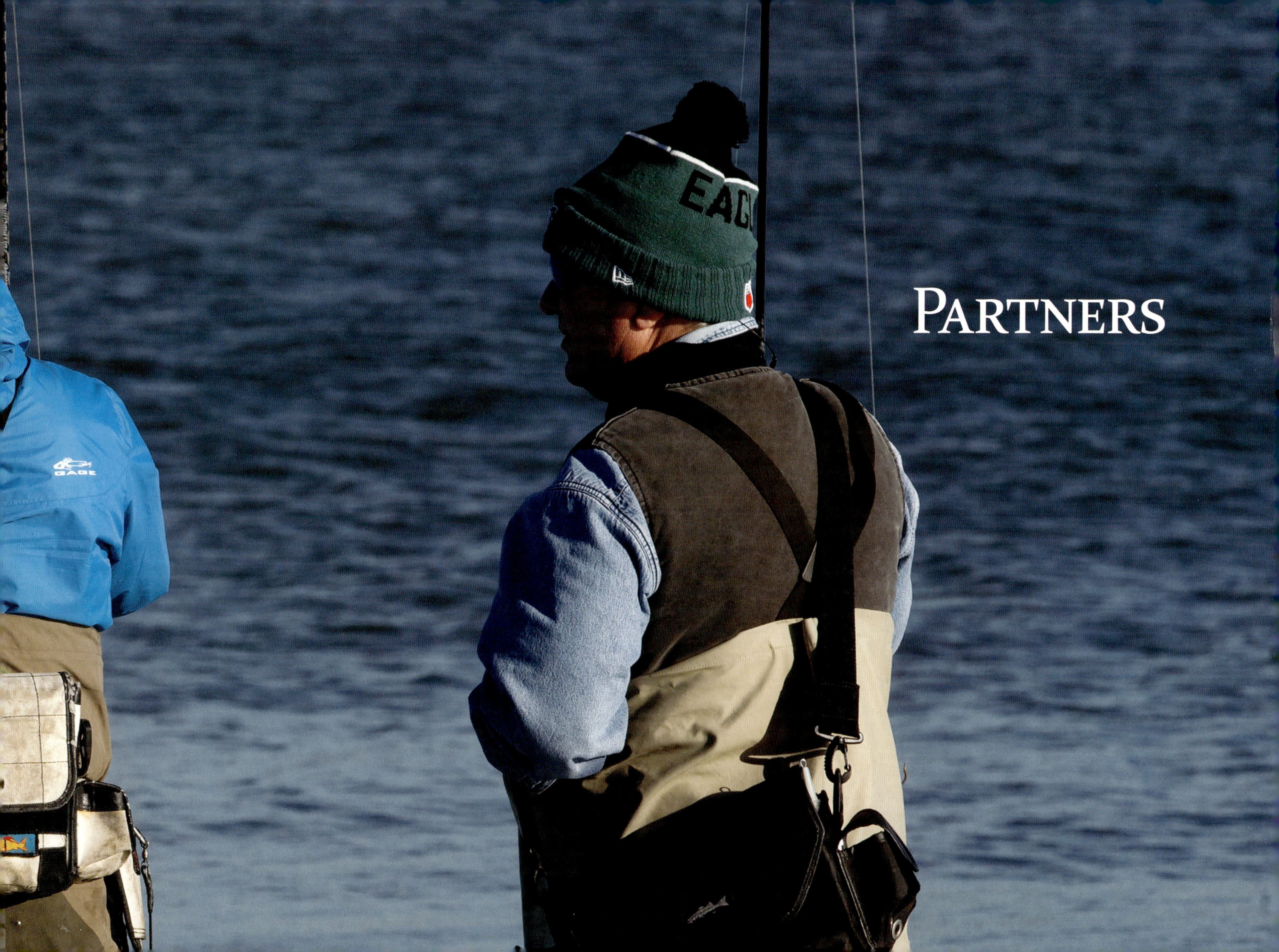

A special bond forms between people who spend hundreds of hours together pursuing linesiders from small boats or beaches in the middle of the night. I have relied on a partner's judgment while threading around rocky shores, setting up difficult drifts, or parsing the lights on commercial vessels. I suspect it is easier to find compatibility in love or business than it is in a fishing wingman. How many people are happy freezing their asses off in rocking boats at midnight in November? Or meeting at streams at 3:25 a.m., long before the first tweets of birdsong, to catch bait?

Unlike marriage, fishing unions are not meant to be lifelong affairs, though the friendships often outlast the fishing. The hours are tough, especially when you're working full time and have a family. On plenty of days, you spend more time with your fishing partner than with your life partner. The latter might resent the time you spend with the former, especially if left behind with small children.

"You know what the fish reminds me of?" asked Bob Popovics, the noted fly fisherman, fly tier, and striper fan. "The fish reminds me of my friends. I don't remember the fish as much as the friendships."

I'VE BEEN LUCKY. I'VE HAD FOUR FISHING PARTNERS in 50 years, and each has been wily, tough, and dependable. I remain friends with Larry, Wayne, Bruce, and Chris even after they've swallowed the anchor, moved away, or taken up other pursuits. Wayne Coddington is the second oldest at 72, and we still occasionally fish together. From surf or boat, we have all learned to step lightly, move quietly, keep a low profile, bend with the wind and tide like the eelgrass meadows, and disappear into the night and fog and troughs between waves. Author Isak Dinesen calls it "the art of moving gently."

There's more than a touch of frontier spirit in those who pursue striped bass hard over three seasons. Each man I have fished with has what author Wallace Stegner describes as the "mongrel smartness" of Huck Finn, the hard-won native intelligence gained not from books but from experience, from doing and seeing firsthand. And all of us were good at keeping secrets. We didn't brag outside our cadre of trusted mates, and we never drew unwanted attention. We didn't even paint a name on our boats so we would be that much harder to remember for anyone fishing nearby. We gave away nothing. We'd pull off a good, lightly fished spot if another boat appeared. If we had a fish on, we lowered the rod, loosened the drag, and thumbed the spool until they were gone. We pointed and feigned interest in some fiction happening hundreds of yards away to draw attention away from what we were doing.

I don't give away small spots that aren't already well-known. Effective striper hounds need to find their own "secret" spots, as we all have done. You'd be surprised by how many are still hiding in plain sight, just waiting to be figured out. With those whom we respect, we share information that is a few days old. They do the same with us. We all understand the loose rules of the game. You trust your partner and few others.

All of us were at home on the water. Three of my fishing friends have owned boats, and the fourth is a surf fisherman who, because he grew up with a surfboard as I did, is part seal. We have made each other better anglers and better boatmen. We have endlessly chased stripers to Timbuktu, forgoing sleep and enduring the wrath of those at home and work to indulge our passion, even after it bloomed into full-blown obsession.

Previous spread: Waiting, watching, talking. Photo by Tom Lynch.
Right: Longtime fishing friends discuss their next move. Photo by Grant Monahan.

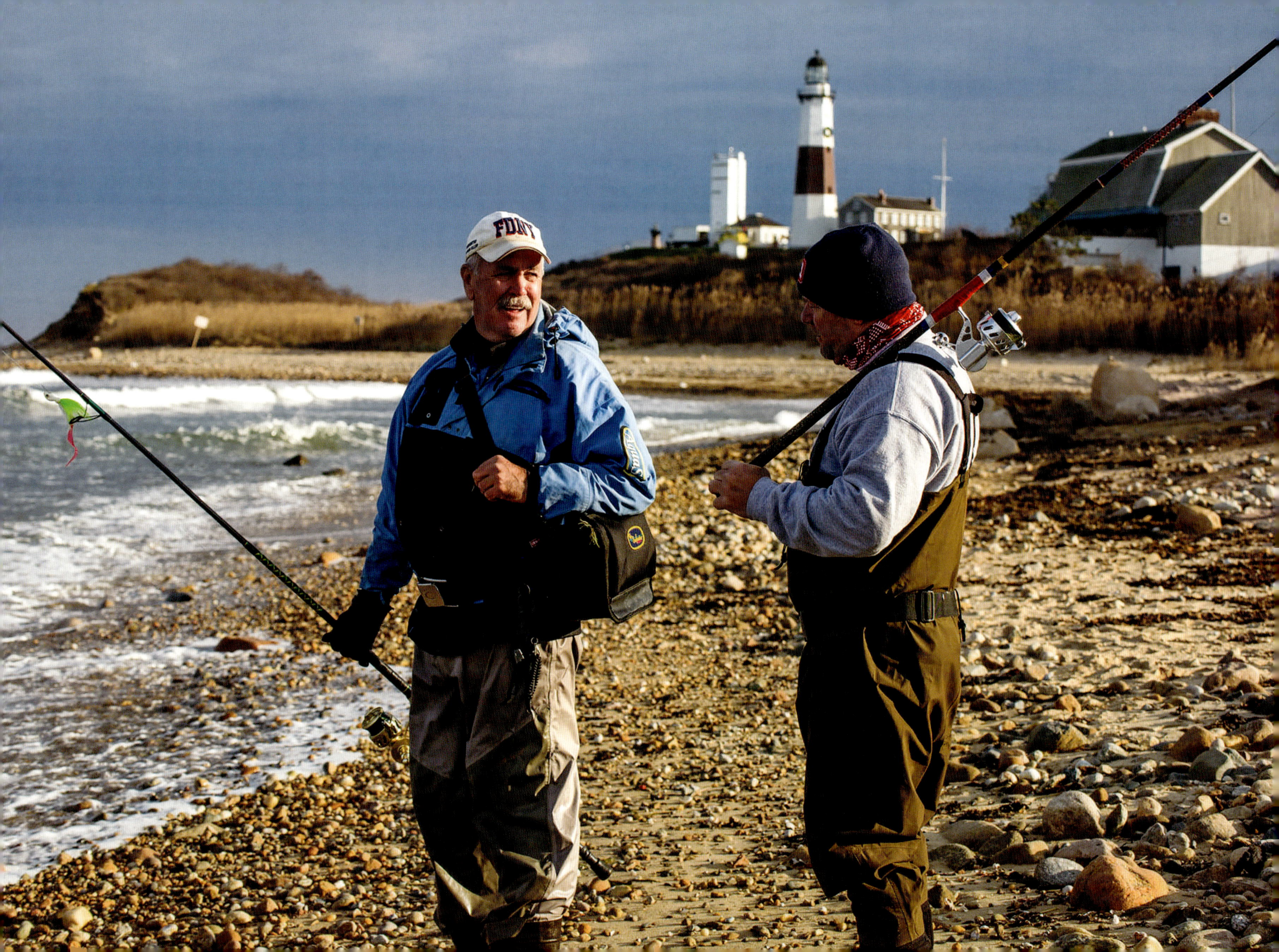
FDNY

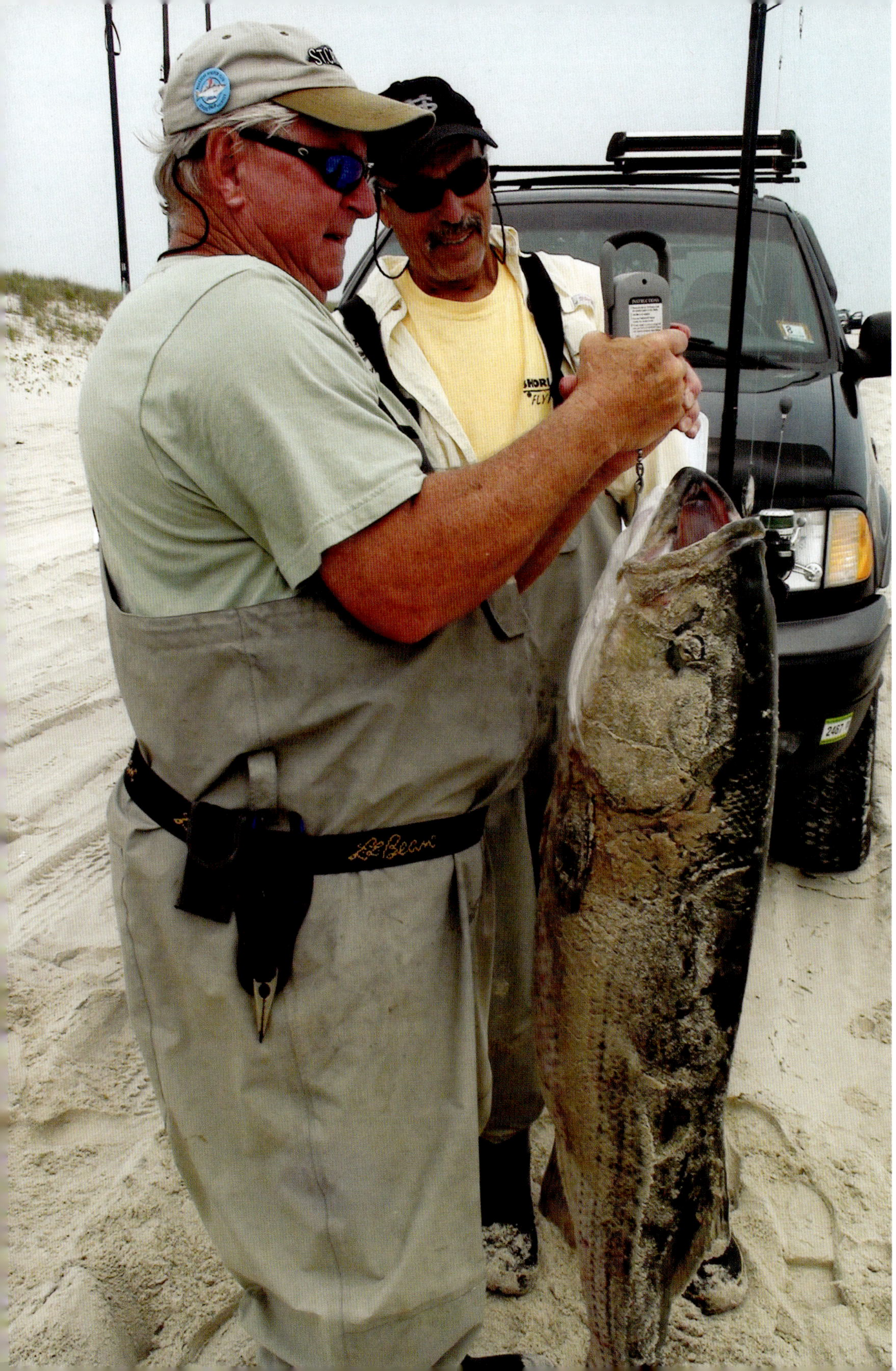

Most of us grew up around watermen: charter captains, closed-mouth sharpies, guys who fished commercially with rod and reel for stripers. We respected and learned from the stories told by the old-timers. I never tired of listening to Wayne talk about a neighbor, a Swamp Yankee who rowed live eels and eel skins behind a skiff at night along the rocky shore east of Quonochontaug Breachway.

"He was old school," Wayne recalled. His biggest fish under oars was a 61-pounder. If bass or blues were breaking along the beach, he was the kind of hard nut who would "shush" Wayne and his surf-casting friends as they jabbered excitedly over the fish.

"You'll scare 'em away," he'd claimed, as if the fish could hear voices on the shore.

WE VALUED STAMINA AND GRIT. When we were in our 30s, 40s, and 50s, we fished fanatically. For me, that continued until I hit my 60s. I remember watching Chris Landry battle a 37-pounder off Long Sand Shoal one night, alternating between cranking on the fish and throwing up over the side from a stomach bug.

On one long-ago evening in early September, Bruce Freeman and I worked several stretches of shore, casting eels until after 2:00 a.m. The night was lovely, even though the pick was slow and my head was throbbing. I drove myself to the emergency room at 6:30 a.m., where I was diagnosed with pneumonia.

Those are the sorts of stories that accumulate after many years of burning the candle to a nub. I've never had a partner who watched the clock too closely or worried aloud about how the late hour might affect his next day at work.

Left: A sandy weigh-in. Photo by Tom Lynch.
Right: The next generation. Photo by Tom Lynch.

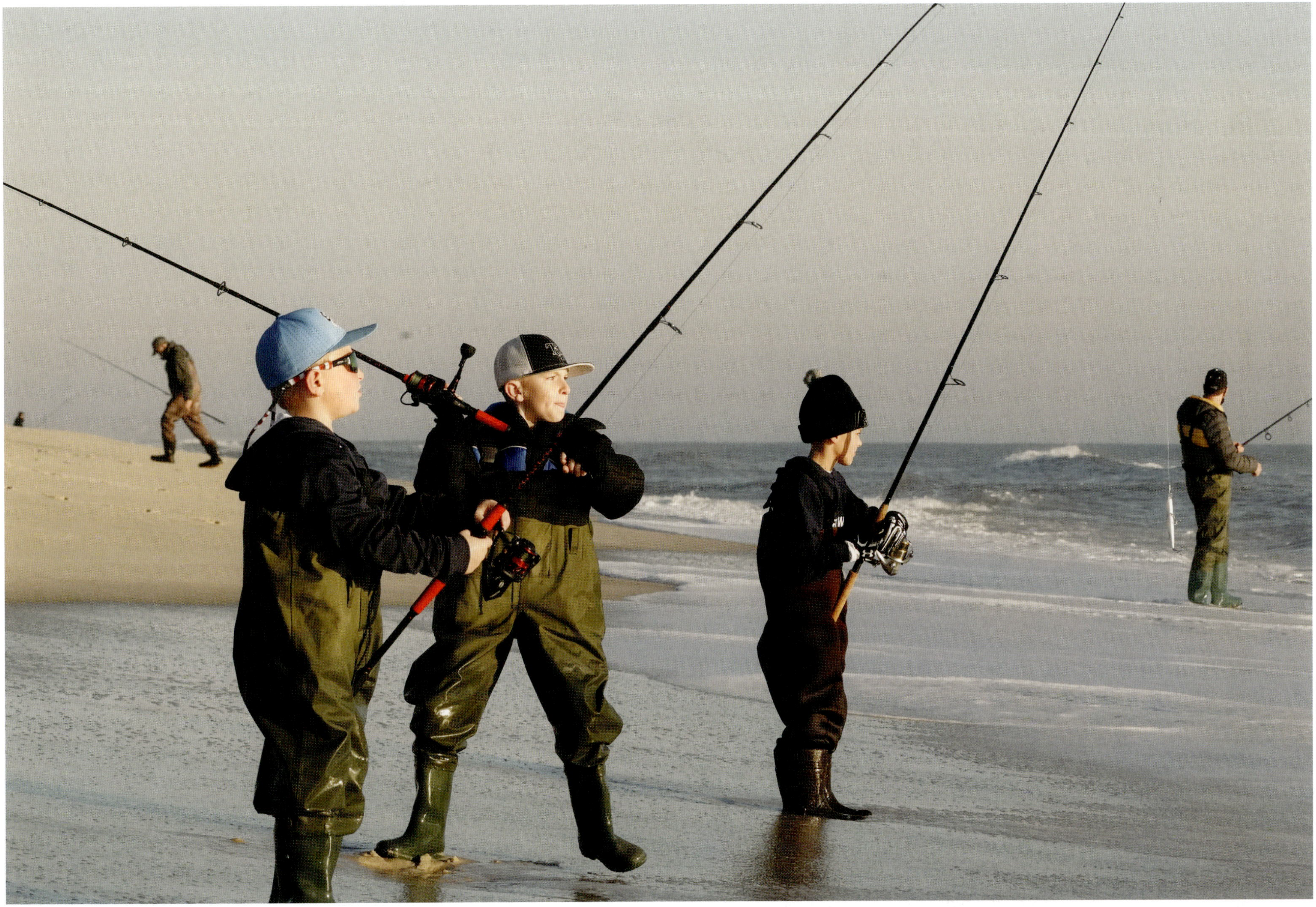

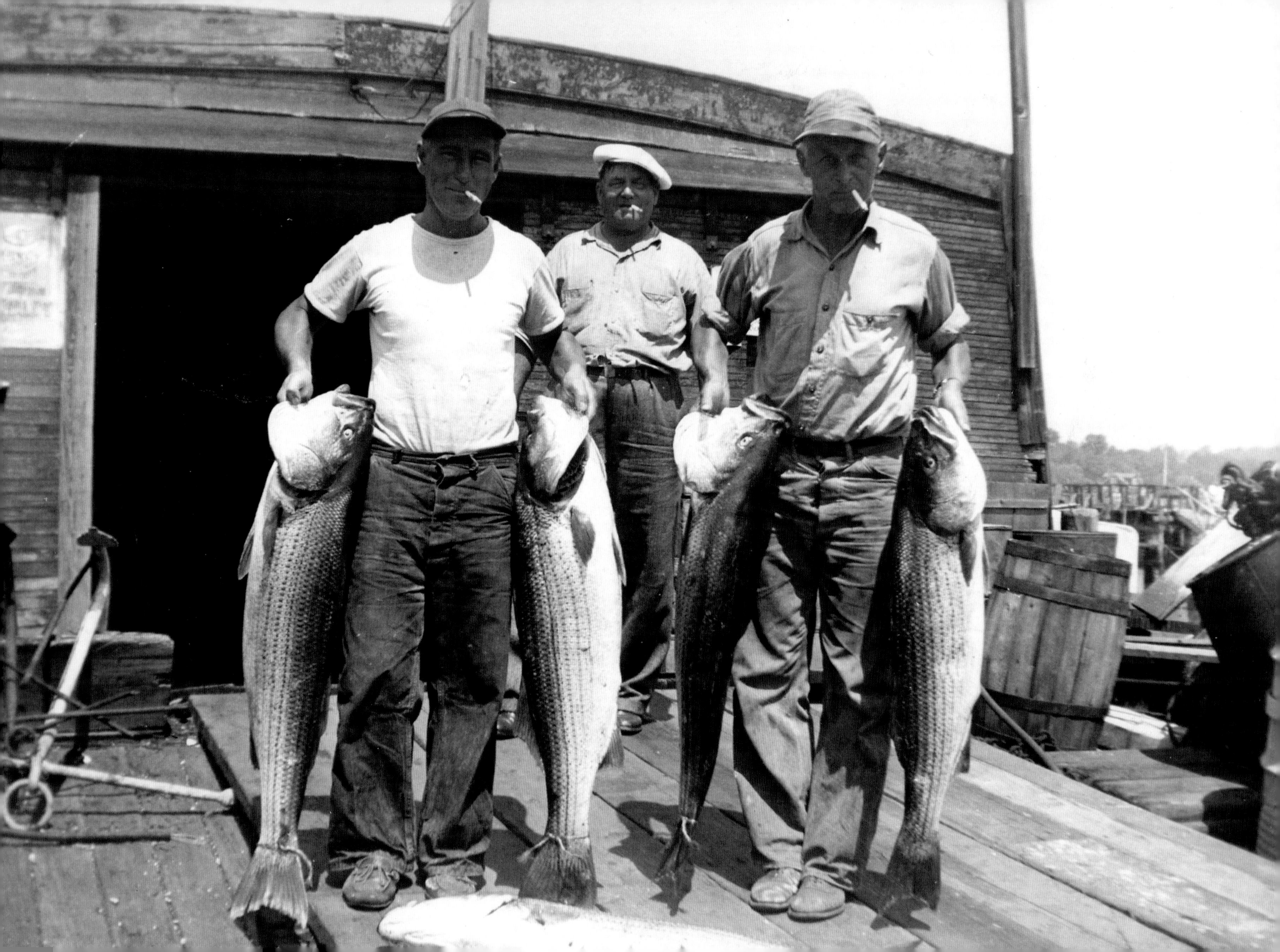

I WAS A BUDDING STRIPER FANATIC IN EIGHTH grade with far more enthusiasm than knowledge. Larry Maderia was a senior in high school. He came from a family of draggermen in Stonington, Connecticut, and he was fishy as hell. We lived a half mile from each other in the same river village, and I'd hear him on the school bus talking about striped bass. In those days, there was a hierarchy about who could sit where and with whom. The seniors sat in the back seats.

I bided my time, and when a spot on the seat next to Larry opened one afternoon, I swung in and started talking fish. He looked at the young interloper with surprise, but he knew my older brother, and fish talk is a language that bridges differences in age and experience, even in the quirky chasms of high school. I asked questions and listened intently to the fish stories he told.

I'm now certain that Larry, who was 18 and had lost his father that year, was happy to have a new fishing friend who was living in the moment and not asking questions about life and loss. I was just a kid who drew striped bass in the margins of my school notebooks, and I was a sponge for anything to do with tides, bait, lure color, retrieves, and knots. Larry, who is now 73, was dealing with a traumatic loss, while the biggest mysteries in my life were striped bass and girls. He played a pivotal role in baptizing me into the Tao of striped bass, bluefish, pollack, smelt, night fishing, and bottom fishing.

I MET WAYNE ON A LANDSCAPING CREW in 1972, and we began fishing the surf and rocks together that fall. Like Larry's dad, Wayne's father had died the previous year, at age 56. Wayne is as tight-lipped as anyone I know. I recall him burying a 31-pounder in the sand one night to keep his business private. He learned to fish the surf from his father, who mentored under Fred Benson, a Block Island legend, in the early 1950s. Wayne and his father patrolled the beaches of South County, Rhode Island, in a 1931 Model A Ford sedan, fishing with French-made Ru Mer reels.

He caught his first bass from the suds when he was nine or 10. Wayne's father taught him to fish the beach and rock piles with precision, especially the white water. He'd place one cast in the swath of broken water on the left side of a rock, the next cast in the pocket to the right. He'd work a stretch of shore methodically, always moving, picking up fish on days when others went fishless. "The guys who fished the white water got the fish," Wayne said, echoing an eternal chestnut of the fishery.

For years, his father's skin mount of a perfectly proportioned 26-pound striped bass hung on the living room wall of his beach cottage in Quonochontaug, Rhode Island. The totem announced the passion of father and son to anyone entering. Also decorating the walls was a collection of his father's fish art, including two prints from 1878 by Samuel A. Kilbourne: one of a striped bass and one of a bluefish. Several bamboo surf rods rounded out the decor.

The ghosts of surfmen long gone and their musty stories were never far away in Wayne's cottage, one reason I felt so at home there. On a recent visit, we hauled an old box of neglected saltwater plugs and tins from the 1920s and '30s out of the basement and onto his deck, examining them one by one. You couldn't help but sense the tingle of the magic with which they were once imbued.

MY PARTNER BRUCE AND I ARE KINDRED Swamp Yankees. We're comfortable with long silences, which is fortunate, given that we have spent hundreds of hours together and both prefer the sounds of night. Bruce, who is now 68, is the most competent boatman and innovative angler I've fished with. In our prime, we were both convinced we could have made a living catching and selling striped bass—or else would have killed ourselves trying. But our goal was always catching stripers, not killing them.

Captain Bud Kohn, right, and his mate in Great Kills Harbor, Staten Island, in the 1940s. Photo courtesy of Dick Kohn.

Bruce and I caught fish in dozens of ways across a hundred different spots for a decade. We experimented with tackle and techniques, and pushed each other to new levels. We fished together when we were at the peak of our fishing and physical powers. We had both come up through the hawsepipe of southern New England saltwater fishing. We'd chased stripers since boyhood. Both of us had fished nights since our early teens. Through trial and error, we'd learned the basics, everything from knots and working lures to fishing natural baits and fighting and landing fish.

Bruce worked as a boatwright in the same boatyard where my magazine had its office. We'd hide in a boat shed, away from the yard foreman with his fixation on billable hours, and scheme, plan, and dream. I felt like I was 16 again, except with better boats, better tackle, and more expertise.

Before I met him, Bruce ran guided kayak trips in Alaska and Baja California. He knew weather, navigation, seamanship, and survival, in addition to being mechanically gifted. He could cobble together just about anything and keep it running, an important skill given our strapped finances in those days.

We analyzed anything we thought might impact our ability to find and catch fish—from winds, tides, and weather to engine noise, eel size, and what corner of the mouth our circle hooks wound up embedded in. We built bait cars and live wells, swapped out electronics and busted tackle, hunted this river for live bunker, that stream for river herring, and that point for bass. We'd fish the ebb in Connecticut and trailer Bruce's boat to Rhode Island to fish a flood. We wore ourselves ragged, caught many fish, and made just as many memories. And we caught a handful of stripers exceeding 50 pounds, the sort that Atlantic salmon fanatic Topher Browne calls "nursing home fish"—the ones you think about once your fishing days are over.

Bruce was clever, careful, and didn't take foolish risks. I sometimes pushed him to fish tighter to a lee shore than was warranted, or to head out in more wind and larger seas than was sensible, knowing that he had a line he wouldn't cross. I counted on him to say "no" at the right time. We made a good team.

MY PARTNER CHRIS LANDRY lacked the striper experience of the others, but he brought something else to the table: he was fearless on the water. Strong, fit, and an able boatman, Chris was game to try anything and was eager to learn. With him, it was me who had to occasionally draw a line and say, "It's too rough," or "There's too much wind."

He is 54, more than a decade younger than me, and competes in marathons and triathlons. In the years we fished together, we routinely slammed our way to several islands in eastern Long Island Sound after nightfall, where for several seasons we were locked into large migrating fish in late September and early October. It was a 20-mile round trip in our small boats, often made through a short, steep chop. Chris never complained.

We cast live eels tight to shore on spinning gear. It was outstanding fishing. A big striper hooked in the shallows pounded the surface for a moment and then dove into the rocky, kelp-strewn bottom as the current dragged the boat along the shore. It reminded me of my battles with large fish from shore on Cuttyhunk Island. You literally had to winch them out of the heavy cover without chafing through leader or line.

All of it was magic while it lasted. Sadly, it never lasts. As predictably as the tides, life changes, and friends drift apart. I count myself fortunate in that I've always been able to pick back up with fishing pals as if nothing had changed. The older I get, the more I appreciate them. It's not about perfection. It's about the quirky traits, idiosyncrasies, and ingenuity that suit people like us in pursuing this worthy fish. Over time, most of the fish we caught have faded from memory, but my partners somehow remain ageless, as spry, eager, and hungry in my remembering as we were when first we began the chase.

Fishing friends relax under the stars at Block Island. Photo by Jim Leedom.

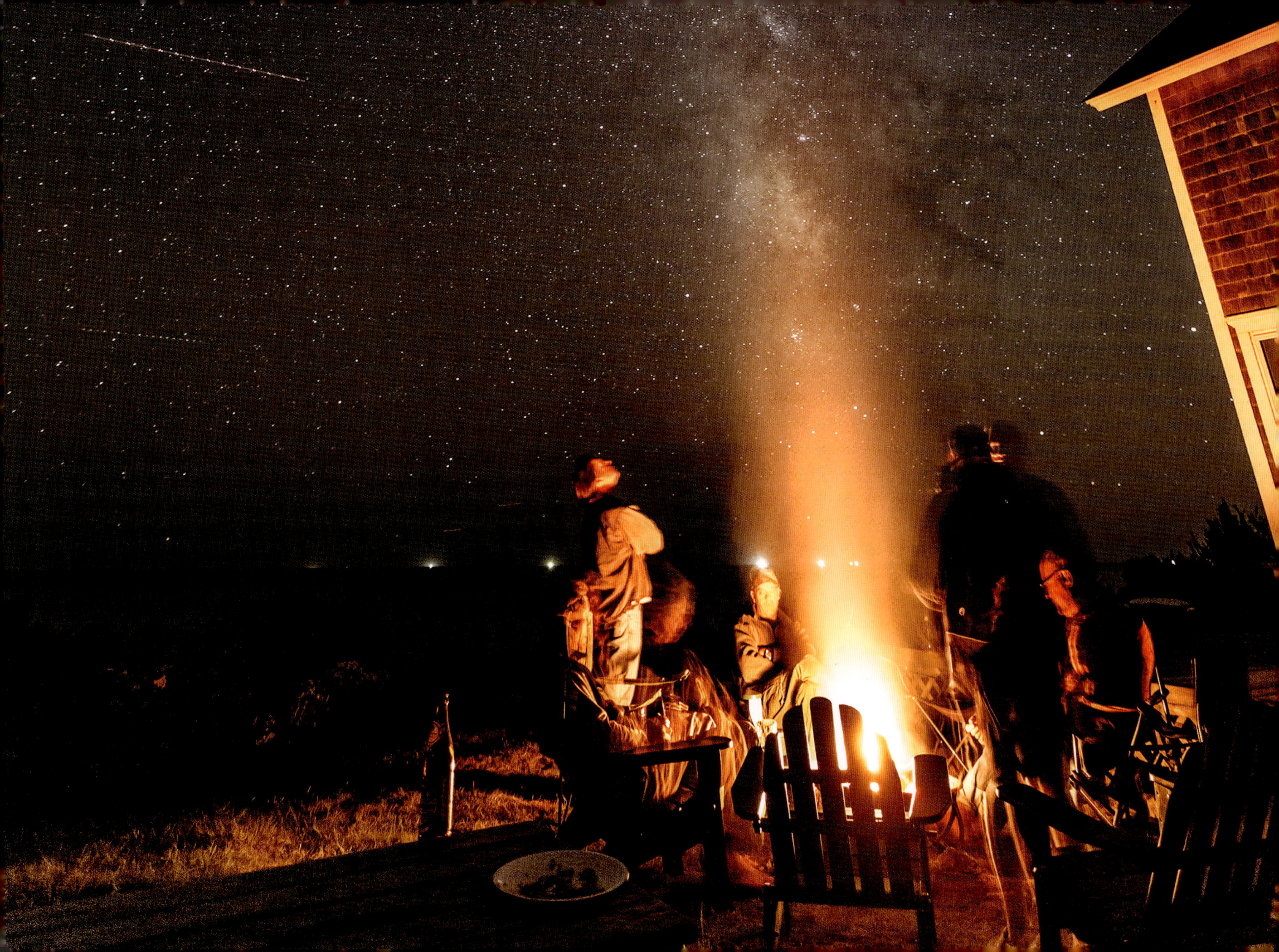

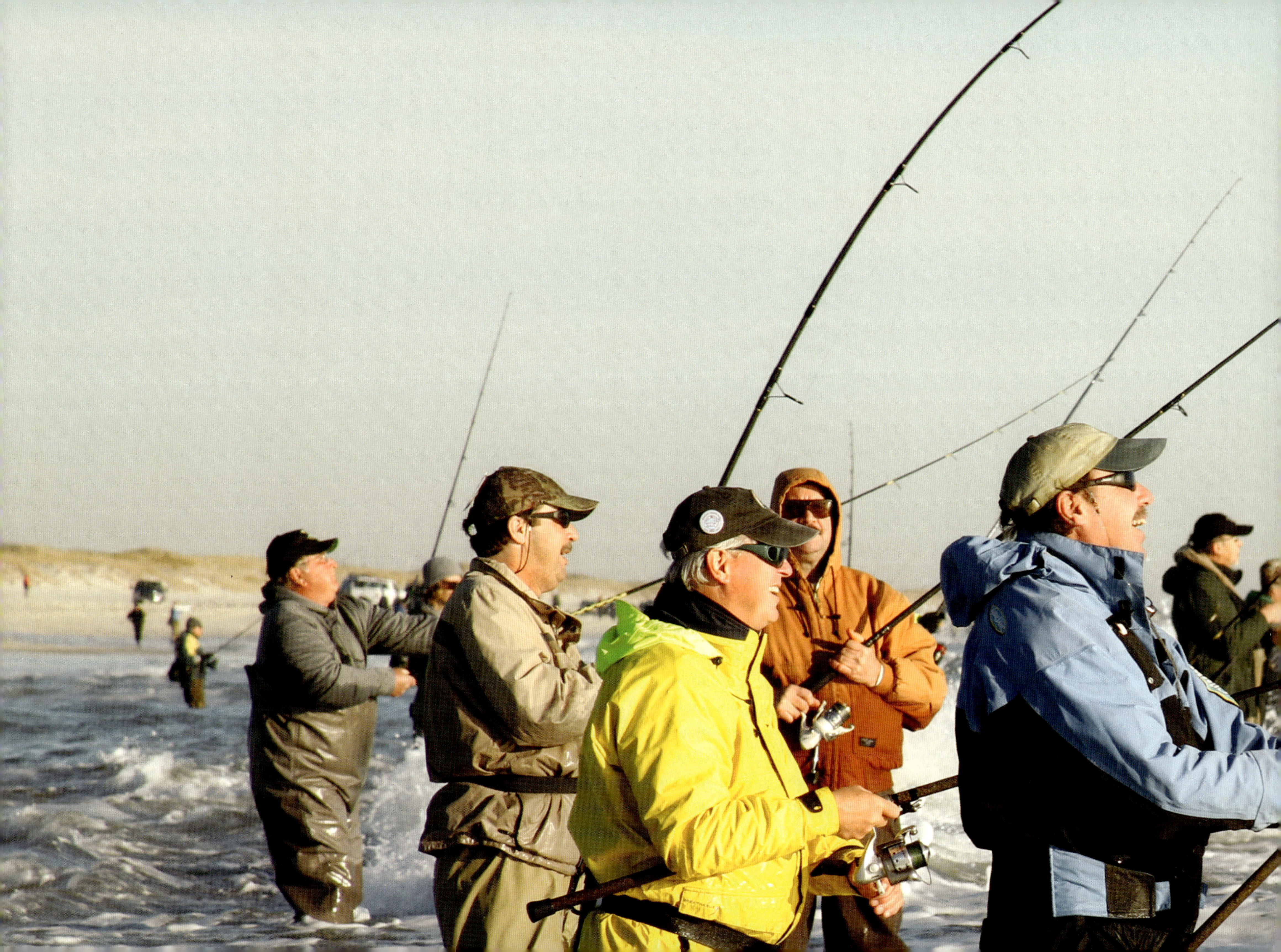

Epilogue

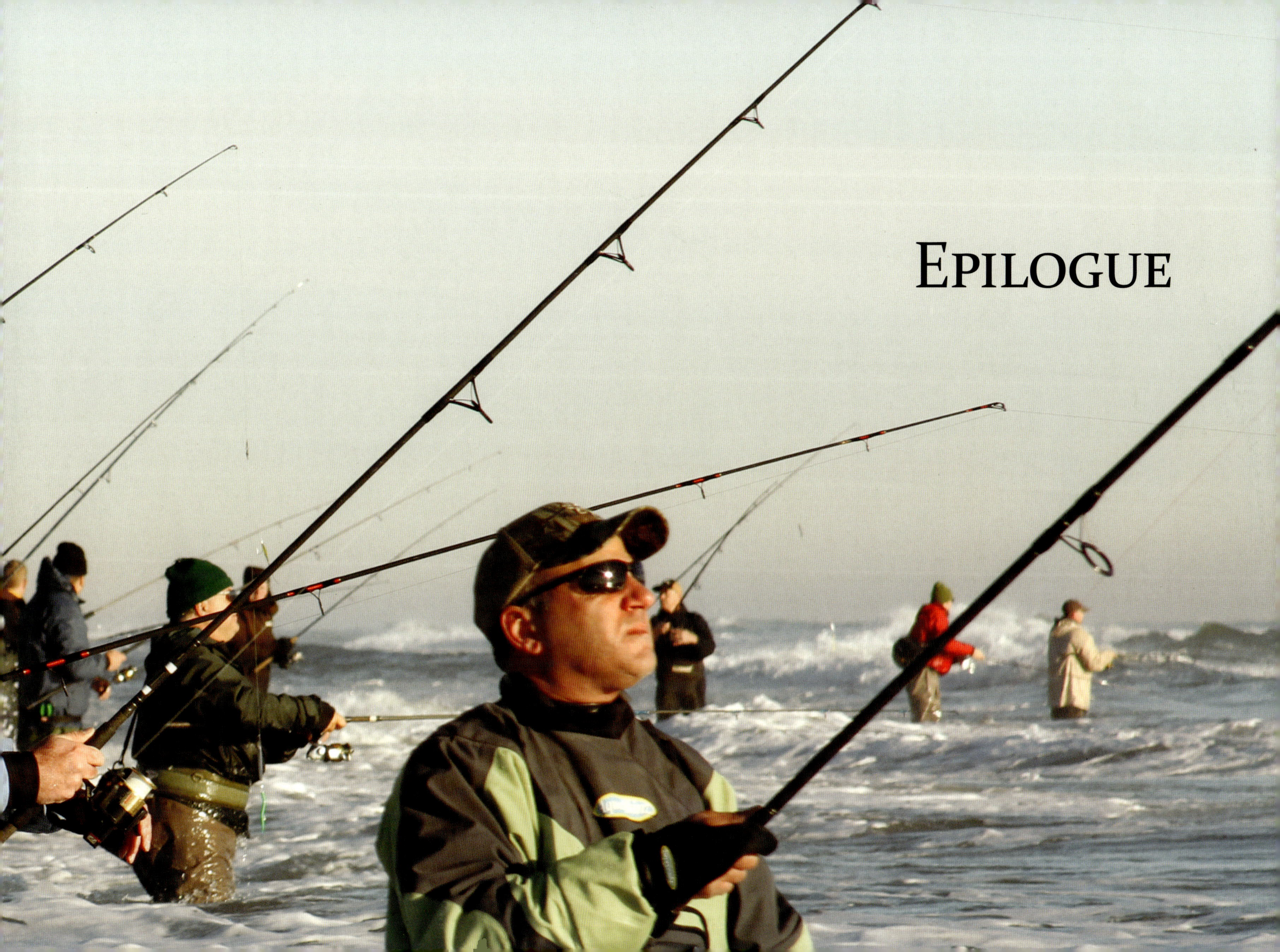

For all their magic and magnificence, striped bass could really use some help. The stock has been overfished since 2013, and the recruitment of young-of-the-year fish in Chesapeake Bay—the largest and most important spawning and nursery area for bass—was well below average in many of the seasons that followed.

The Atlantic States Marine Fisheries Commission (ASMFC), the interstate body that manages stripers, enacted new rules in 2020 to reduce the total coastwide catch by 18 percent. In addition to cutting the commercial harvest, the ASMFC established a slot limit for recreational anglers, allowing them to keep one fish a day between 28 and 35 inches. The slot is noteworthy because most stripers longer than 35 inches are females considered crucial to rebuilding stocks. These bigger females have greater fecundity than smaller fish. Stripers between 40 and 50 inches release between three and five million eggs each, and not only are these eggs more viable, the fry they produce are also generally more robust than those hatched from the eggs of smaller bass. It was the first time the ASMFC imposed a slot limit on the coastal fishery of stripers.

"I really like this. I've been a proponent of the slot long before we moved to it," said John A. Tiedemann, assistant dean of the School of Science at Monmouth University in West Long Branch, New Jersey, and a longtime advocate for stripers. "From a long-term sustainability perspective, we're allowing a fish to mature and to spawn at least once or twice before it's taken. And then we're protecting the big spawners." Tiedemann, who also is the director of the Marine and Environmental Biology and Policy program at the university, has long advanced the idea that anglers should release what are sometimes called BOFFFFs—Big Old Fat Fecund Female Fish—based on their contribution to the spawning stock.

John Waldman, an aquatic conservation biologist and a professor at Queens College in New York, was also hopeful that the management moves would strengthen stocks. "The slot limit will have the dual effect of reducing that evolutionary pressure toward catching faster-growing fish preferentially over slower-growing fish as they surpass a traditional size limit," said Waldman, who has studied stripers for decades and has written numerous scientific papers on the fish. And, he noted, it will preserve the large spawners.

Overfishing in the 1970s and early '80s brought the Chesapeake stock to the brink of collapse and led to a five-year moratorium starting in 1985. The moratorium was lifted in 1990, and the ASMFC declared the stock fully recovered in 1995. The recovery was hailed as a major fish-management success, and there was no shortage of pronouncements about how we'd never again let the fishery decline.

"It's easy to beat your chest and say we're not going to let this happen again, but meanwhile it's happening again," Waldman said. "Scarcity is what steels us to take the right actions, but it's sad that that's the case."

Tiedemann said he teaches his students something referred to as the "double-edged sword" of recovery. "That's where we rebuild the stocks and then relax the regulations and start hammering them again," he said. "The striper is a good example of that. And 20 years later, we're right back where we were. Now it's overfished again. It's a shame."

Chesapeake Bay historically has produced between 70 and 90 percent of the striped bass along the East Coast. Rebuilding the stock once again hinges on getting as many female fish on the spawning grounds of the Chesapeake as possible. After that, Mother Nature must cooperate and produce favorable environmental conditions for spawning and survival, which is a roll of the dice.

"The way that the Chesapeake stock was brought back from its dramatic decline in the early '80s was by preserving the one-year class [1982] that was moderate and essentially turning

Previous spread: Shoulder to shoulder in the New Jersey surf. Photo by Tom Lynch.
Right: David Glassberg tagged and released this fish in the high 40s off Sandy Hook, New Jersey, in December while fishing with Chuck Many. Photo by Tom Lynch.

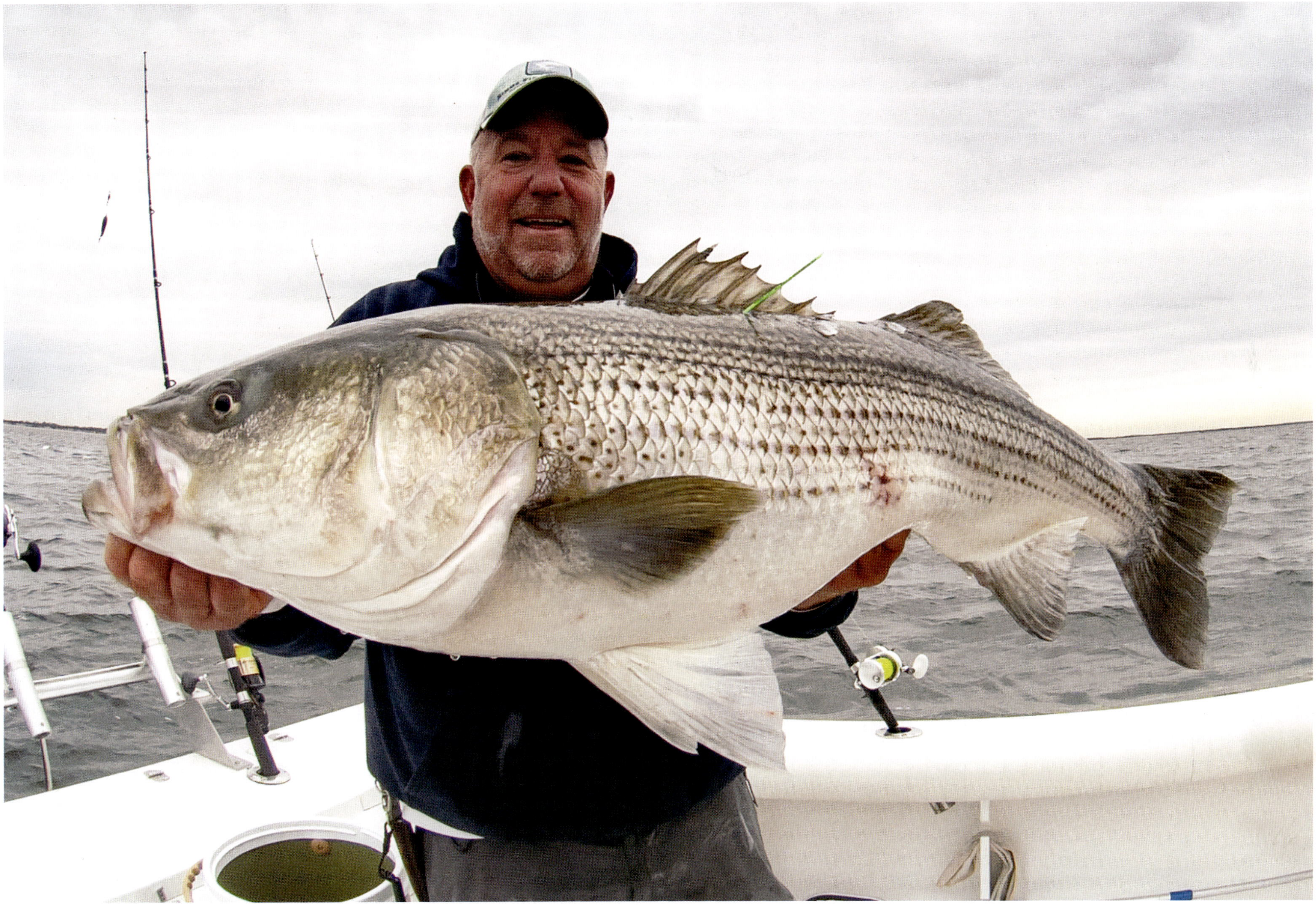

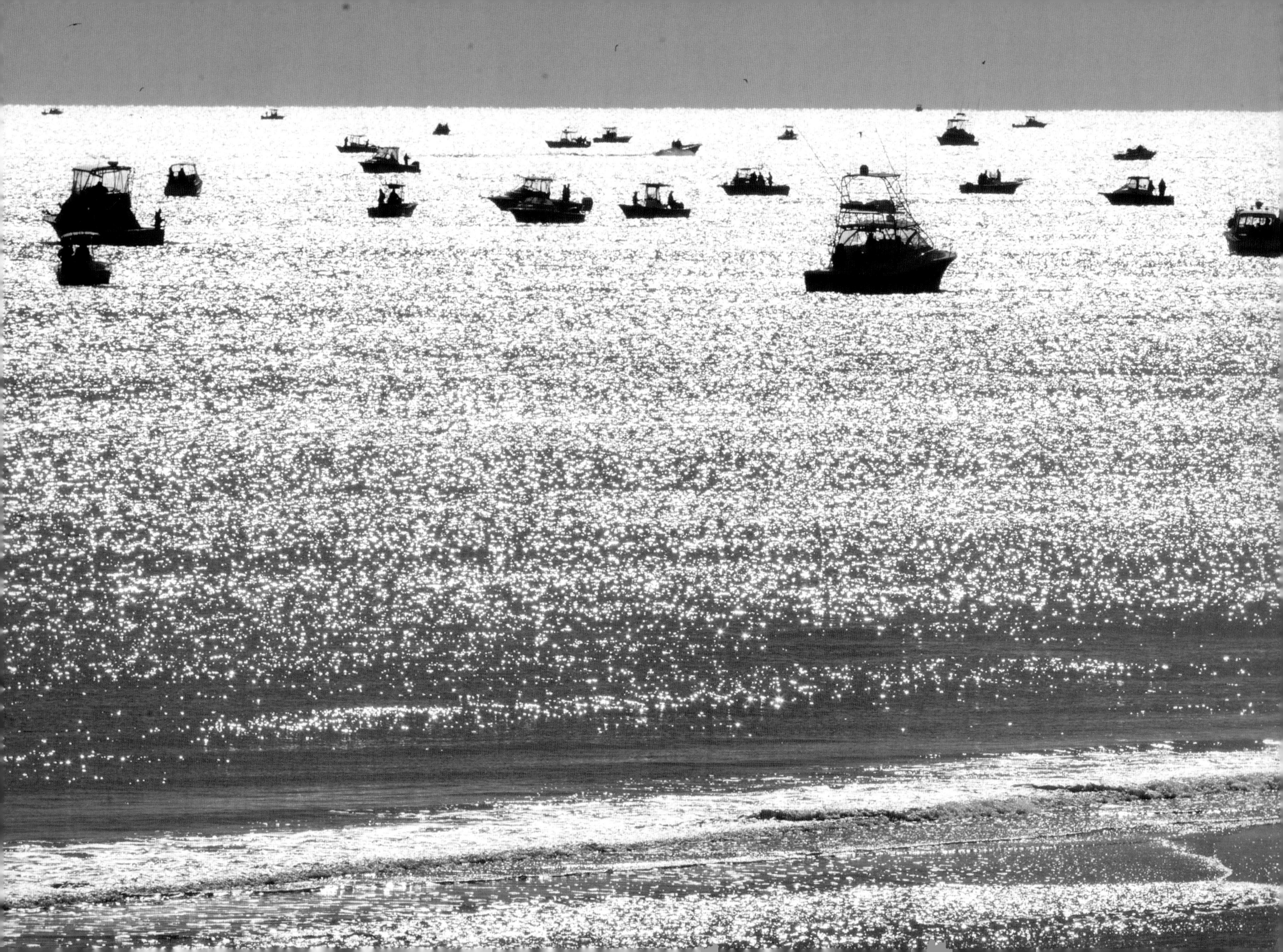

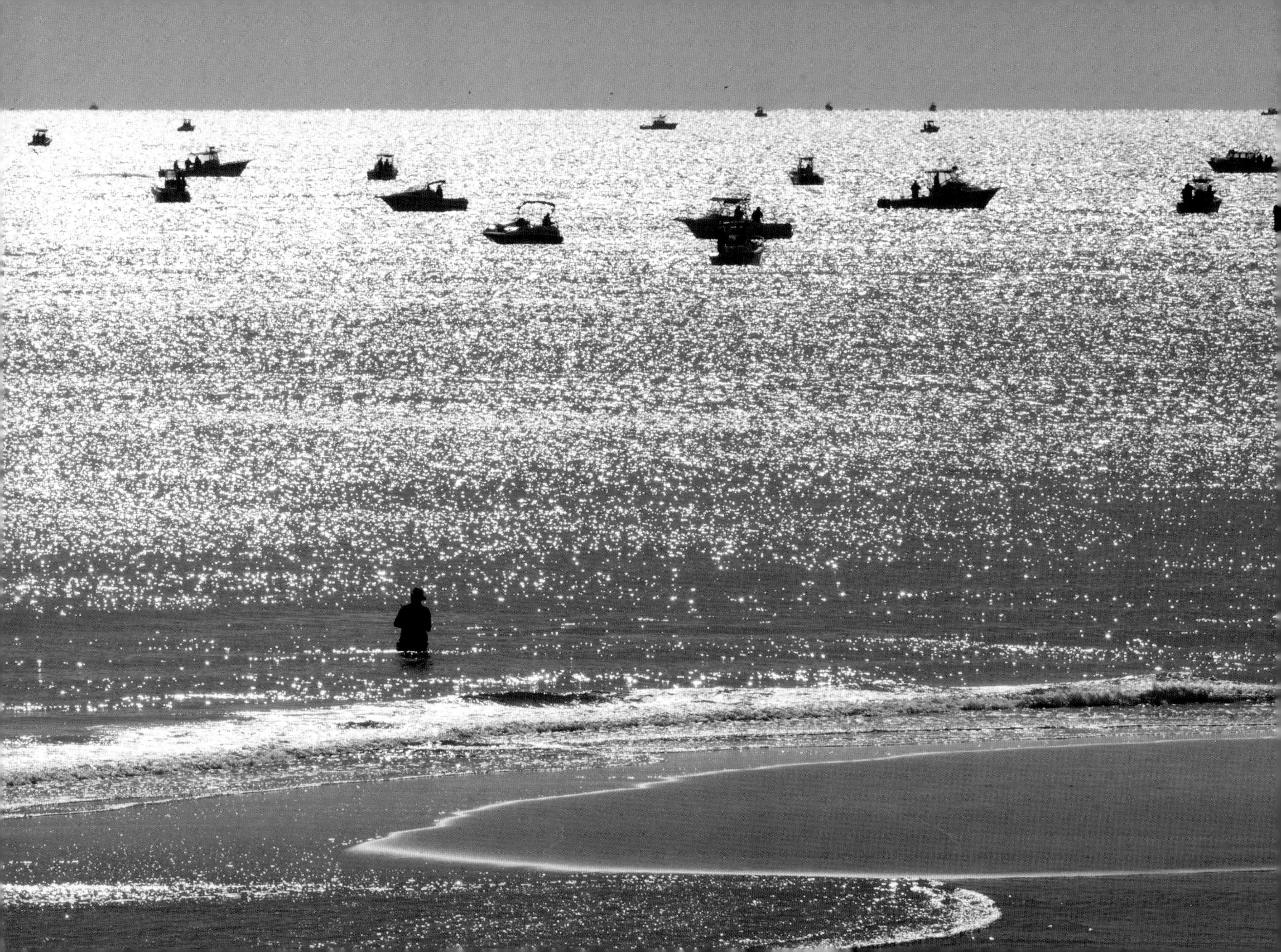

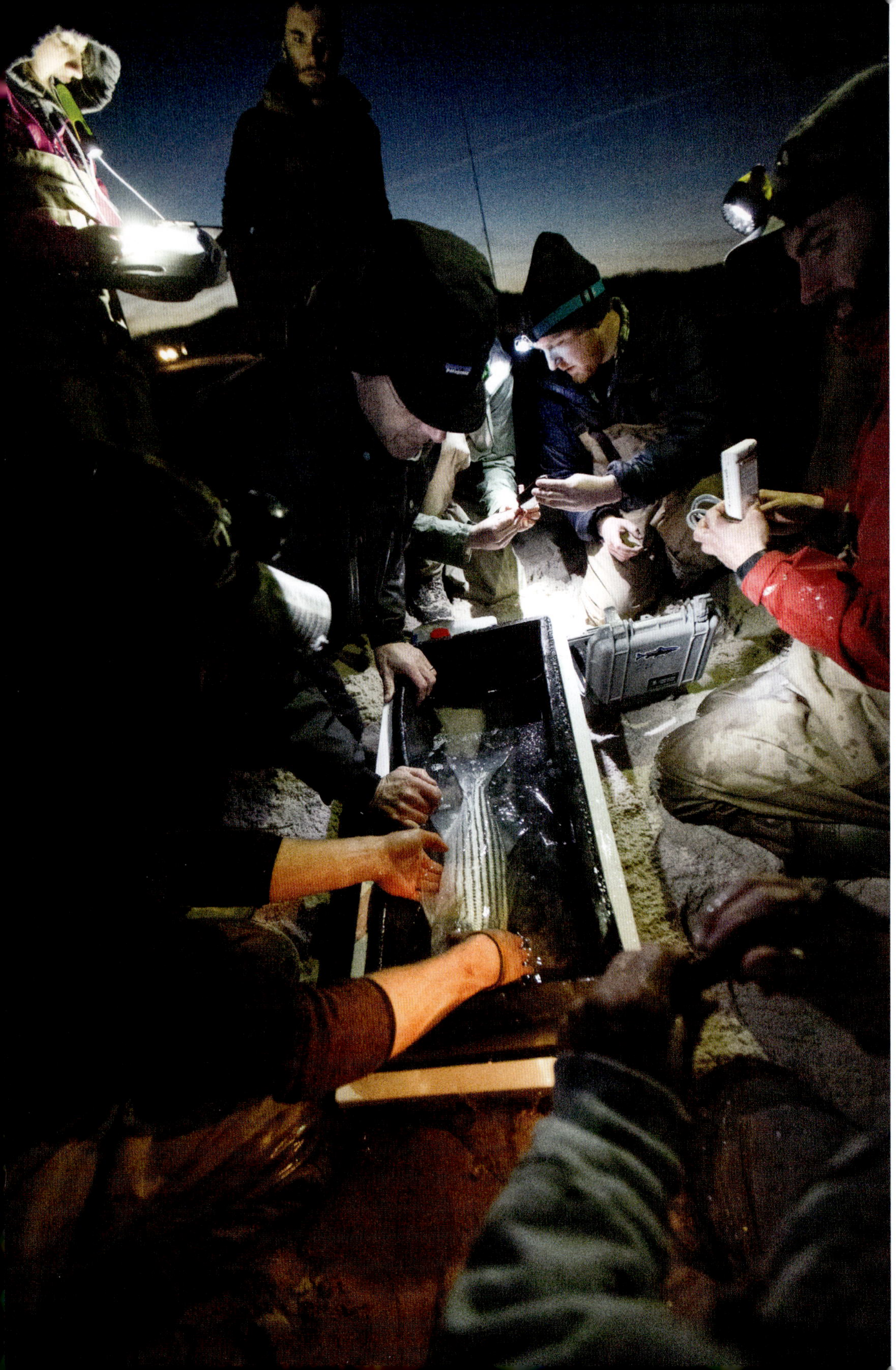

it into a dominant year class by removing as much of the fishing mortality as we possibly could," said Waldman, who is also an avid surf fisherman. "The problem was the population was becoming essentially egg-starved because there weren't enough females out there to produce the eggs to then produce a dominant year class. By having the blanket protections [of the moratorium], they were able to essentially goose up a typical year class into a dominant year class."

Can we get lucky twice?

"It could be that the current regime will work," Waldman said. "We just don't know. We need to give it a chance."

The mid-Atlantic stock, which stretches from North Carolina through New England to the Bay of Fundy, is made up of four populations, but only the Chesapeake has the potential to produce enormous year classes and support the entire coastal fishery, according to Waldman.

"The Hudson, the Delaware, and the Roanoke play important supporting roles, but you could have good years with those smaller stocks, and they don't make up for a series of bad years in the Chesapeake," said Waldman, who has been involved in several studies of the relative contributions of each of those stocks to the overall fishery. "But when the Chesapeake is on, it is producing 90 percent or more of the total fish. And when it's off, you get a combination of the others making up some of the difference, but it's not going to be good fishing."

Tiedemann was hopeful the new rules would halt the decline and restore stocks. "I think it's definitely a positive step," he said. "Time will tell." The longtime striper advocate and angler is also realistic. "It's so complicated," he added, citing just some of the many issues facing Chesapeake Bay. "We have the habitat-related factors. We have pollution issues. We still have the industrial bunker fishery that has an impact."

Chesapeake Bay conservationists cite several challenges facing newly hatched and young stripers in the bay: chemical contaminants and acidity in some spawning areas; reduced availability of forage, especially young menhaden; low dissolved oxygen in deeper bay waters, which eliminates much of the fish's summer habitat; and poor water quality from runoff and sewage-treatment practices. "We're finally getting managers to think about ecosystems-based management," said Tiedemann. "Hopefully, some of the habitat and forage issues get dealt with in the next few years."

The ASMFC has also mandated the use of circle hooks when anglers are fishing with bait to reduce the number of bass that die after being released. Fishery managers estimate that about nine percent of the fish die after they're released. Rank-and-file anglers can help make a difference by handling stripers more carefully. Since 1990, about 90 percent of the total annual striped bass catch is released alive, either due to angler preference or regulations, according to the ASMFC.

Even though the nine percent mortality rate for released fish is considered a "low rate," the ASMFC says catch-and-release fishing results in a significant source of mortality, given the popularity of striped bass. In 2019, the total recreational catch of striped bass was around 30.9 million fish, of which 28.8 million were released. More fish are estimated to have died in 2019 from catch-and-release fishing (2.59 million) than were kept by recreational anglers (2.2 million), according to the ASMFC.

"My whole focus for the last 10 years has been to try and help anglers understand more about the resource and what they as individuals can do to promote the healthiest fish possible when they release it," Tiedemann said. "We haven't been preaching catch-and-release only. It's fine to keep a fish consistent with the regulations. What I tell anglers is that everybody is going to be a catch-and-release angler because you are either going to be over your bag limit or, now with the slot, under or over the size limit.

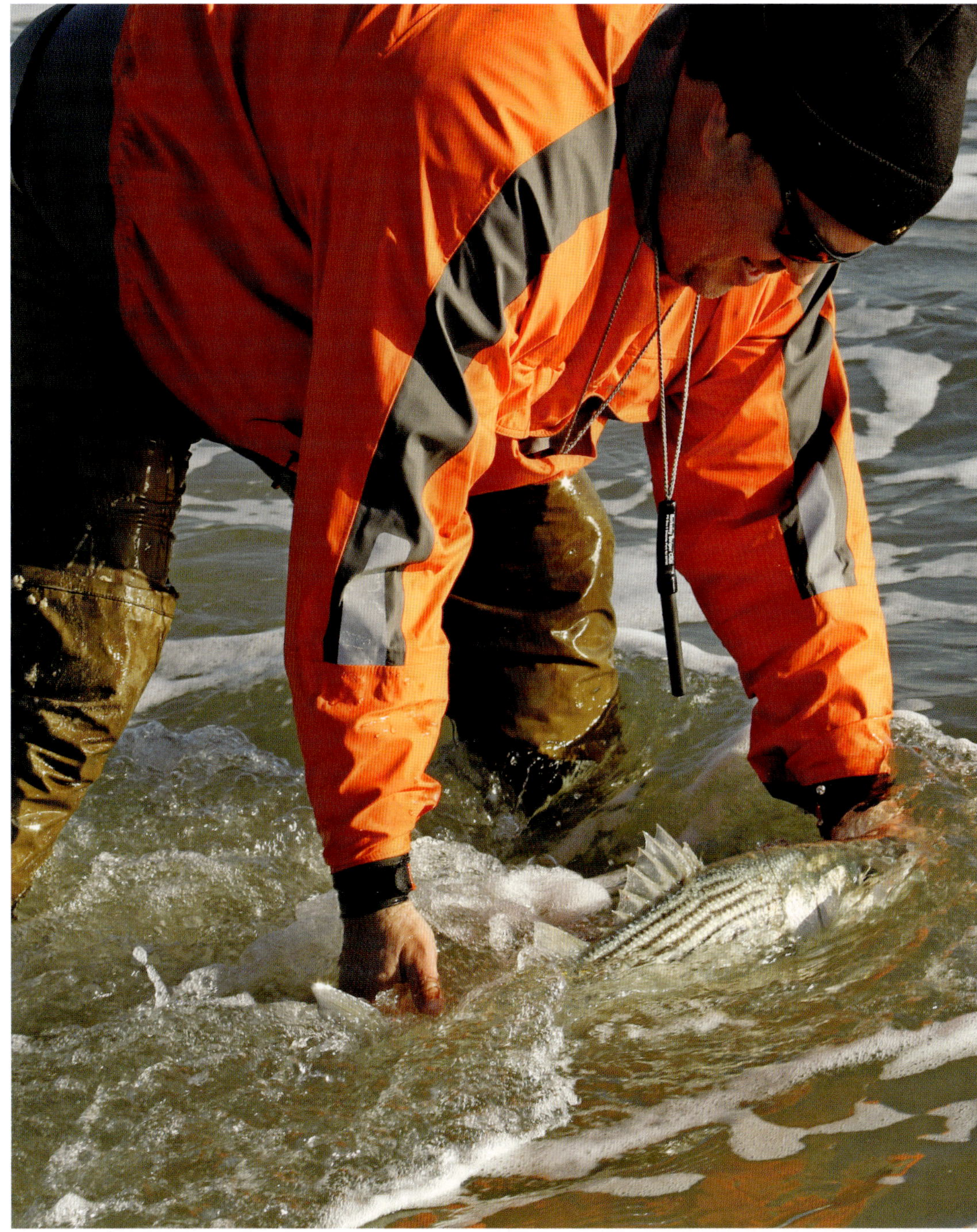

Previous spread: The fall fleet out in force. Photo by Tom Lynch.
Left: Beachside science and conservation at work. Photo by Tom Lynch.
Right: The correct way to release a fish. Photo by Tom Lynch.

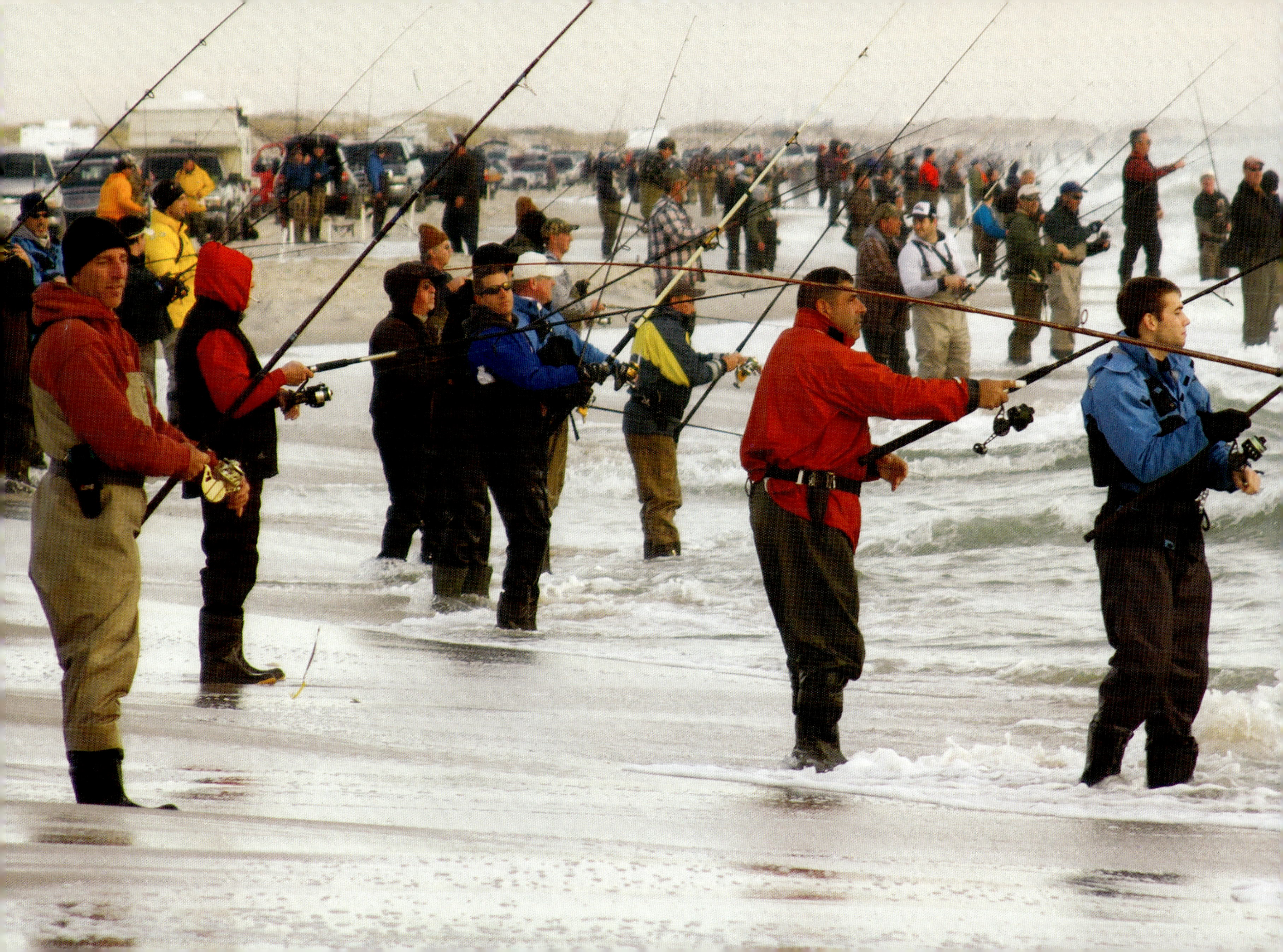

Any illusion that recreational fishermen don't have the horsepower to fish the stocks to the brink should have been put to rest long ago. "Technology has been the single worst enemy of fish stocks the world over," said Captain Barry Gibson, 71, who has been chartering out of Boothbay, Maine, for 51 years and has been active in New England groundfish management for decades. "Technology has allowed people to become more efficient than ever in finding and catching striped bass."

We pursue the fish in larger, faster, and more capable boats. GPS and fish-finders are ubiquitous, and radar is appearing on ever-smaller boats. Significant improvements have been made in tackle, apparel, and gear. We now fish longer, harder, and farther afield in more comfort and safety than ever. And easy access to information on where and how to catch bass is widely available online, through social networks, and in books, magazines, and seminars.

"If you unleashed all that technology on striped bass—if there were no regulations—I don't think there would be any striped bass left," said Gibson, a former editor of *Salt Water Sportsman*. "They'd all be gone."

After striped bass stocks recovered in 1985, a Chesapeake Bay scientist told me his biggest concern was whether there existed the foresight, wisdom, and will to properly "manage abundance." While his fears proved well founded, I'm ever hopeful the stocks will recover. When they do, we owe it to the fish, future generations, and ourselves to provide proper protection to these wondrous fish and the waters they call home.

Left: Recreational fishing pressure is significant. Photo by Tom Lynch.
Following page: Photo by Steven Salgado.

Here are some suggestions to help boost the survival rates of striped bass, courtesy of John Tiedemann.

DO:

1. Unhook and release fish without taking them out of the water.
2. Handle fish with wet hands or gloves.
3. Cradle fish with one hand under the belly and one under the shoulder.
4. Resuscitate bass by pulling them forward or in a figure eight through the water by the lower lip. Never move fish backward.
5. Get fish back in the water quickly. Try to limit air exposure to 10 to 15 seconds.
6. Use barbless hooks for quick release.
7. Use circle hooks when bait fishing.
8. Leave deep hooks in the fish by cutting the leader off close to the hook.
9. Match the rod and reel to the size of the fish you are targeting.

DON'T:

1. Lift bass by the mouth, gill cover, or tail. This can cause serious internal injury.
2. Handle fish with dry hands.
3. Drag fish across dry sand or excessively handle them in a manner that removes their protective mucous coating.
4. Kick or step on fish. This will damage internal organs.
5. Touch the red gill rakers or gill area. They are the equivalent of human lungs.
6. Gaff a fish you intend to release.
7. Fight fish to exhaustion or release them without first resuscitating.

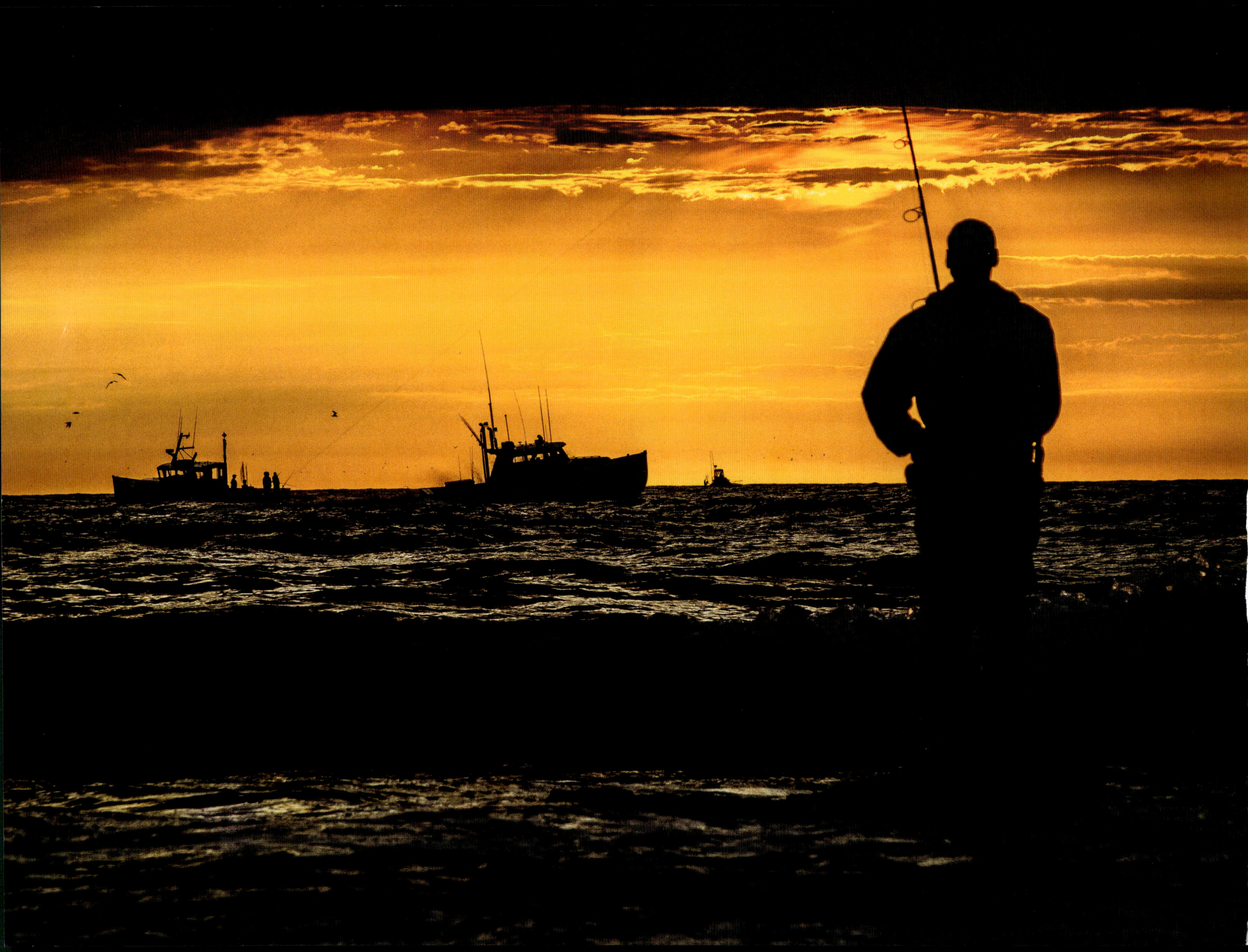